College Accounting 1–15

College Accounting 1–15

Judith M. Peters, C.P.A.
Professor of Accounting
College of DuPage

Robert M. Peters, Ph.D., C.P.A.
Touche Ross Distinguished Professor
DePaul University

1989

**BPI
IRWIN**

Homewood, IL 60430
Boston, MA 02116

Cover photo: Geoffrey Grove/The Image Bank

Executive editor: John R. Black
Project editor: Margaret Haywood
Production manager: Bette Ittersagen
Designer: Lucy Lesiak
Compositor: Arcata Graphics/Kingsport
Typeface: 11/13 ITC Garamond Book
Printer: Von Hoffman Press

Library of Congress Cataloging-in-Publication Data

Peters, Judith M.
  College accounting 1–15.

  Includes index.
    1. Accounting.   I. Peters, Robert M.   II. Title.
III. Title: College accounting, one to fifteen.
HF5635.P489 1989   657'.044   88–7384
    ISBN 0-256-06927-1

Printed in the United States of America
1 2 3 4 5 6 7 8 9 0 VH 6 5 4 3 2 1 0 9

To our parents

Preface

In writing *College Accounting,* our intention was to develop a textbook and teaching package that would accomplish two goals. First, we wanted to assist students in introductory accounting courses to develop a clear understanding of accounting that would help them as they pursued their future career and personal goals. Second, we wanted the instructor's teaching experience to be a positive one.

To meet these goals, we strived to develop a textbook of superior readability, clarity, and consistency. To ensure consistency, we wrote the components of the learning package ourselves. This includes the Comprehensive Problems, the Instructor's Solutions Manual, Working Papers, Student Study Guide, Test Banks, Instructor's Resource Guide, and five of the practice sets and their solutions.

College Accounting is intended for students taking introductory accounting courses at two- and four-year colleges, proprietary schools, and in the business environment. The textbook can accommodate the single course model, traditional semester terms, and two-quarter sequences. We assume that students have limited or no previous experience in accounting.

▮▮▮▮ FEATURES OF COLLEGE ACCOUNTING

READABILITY AND CLARITY

To achieve superior readability and clarity, we wrote and rewrote the manuscript, then submitted it to meticulous editing. We present material in a logical sequence and link key concepts with short transitions. New concepts are defined when introduced and demonstrated with examples that are simple but effective. We chose words carefully to achieve conciseness and, most important, clarity. The tone of this book is businesslike but friendly because we want to invite participation in the learning process.

CONSISTENCY

Readers will find our word choice, phrasing, formats, and procedures consistent throughout the textbook. The account titles, transactions, phrasing, arithmetic requirements, and level of computational difficulty in the end-of-chapter assignments mirror those in the chapter. We avoid loose rephrasing and synonyms that might confuse or frustrate students.

To enhance consistency, an extended example, The Kitchen Taylor, spans Chapters 2 through 15. As new concepts and procedures are introduced, The Kitchen Taylor is utilized to demonstrate the appropriate accounting. Furthermore, the Instructor's Solutions Manual, Test Banks, Instructor's Resource Guide, Working Papers, and Student Study Guide are consistent with the text.

INTEGRATION OF THEORY AND PRACTICE

As teachers, we understand the need for a clear and orderly presentation of procedures balanced with accounting theory appropriate for the beginning student. We provide a simple theoretical frame of reference to enhance the student's understanding of accounting procedures. This frame of reference lays the groundwork for the development of accounting logic and will reduce the need for painful memorization. The skillful integration of theory and procedure ensures that the student leaves the accounting course able to bridge the gap between the classroom and the contemporary world.

LEARNING OBJECTIVES

Learning objectives function as the skeletal structure of each chapter. Learning objectives link the chapter material to the end-of-chapter assignments, the Instructor's Solutions Manual, the Instructor's Resource Guide, and the Student Study Guide.

▮▮▮▮ ORGANIZATION OF THE TEXT

The text is organized into three parts that gradually build the student's skill and understanding of beginning accounting.

Part I   The Basic Accounting Cycle (Chapters 1–6)

Chapters 1 through 6 introduce accounting and the development of the basic accounting cycle. Concepts are illustrated with an ongoing example, The Kitchen Taylor, a sole proprietorship, in a service business.

Chapter 1 is nontechnical and easily covered without prior student preparation. This facilitates full use of the first class session.

Comprehensive Review Problem 1 reviews and reinforces concepts from Chapters 1 through 6 through the completion of a two-month accounting cycle for Morgan Cleaning Services.

Part II   Accounting for a Professional Service Business, Cash, and Payroll (Chapters 7–10)

Chapters 7 through 10 include accounting for a professional service business, various cash-related topics, and two payroll chapters.

Part III   Accounting for a Merchandising Business (Chapters 11–15)

Chapters 11 through 15 introduce a merchandising business and cover special journals and subsidiary ledgers.

Comprehensive Review Problem 2 reviews and reinforces topics covered in Chapters 9–15. Students complete a one-month accounting cycle for a merchandising business, Dawson Products.

MASTER GLOSSARY

End-of-chapter glossaries are compiled into an end-of-text glossary to facilitate the quick and efficient review of terminology. The chapter where the term is defined is indicated by the number in parentheses following the definition.

▐▐▐▐ CHAPTER PEDAGOGY

LEARNING OBJECTIVES

For students, the learning objectives that open each chapter represent short-term goals, a brief preview of the chapter, and a way to assess the mastery of the chapter material. For instructors, the learning objectives represent the essentials of the chapter and the linkage between the text, end-of-chapter materials, and other supplementary materials. The text highlights objectives in the margin to indicate where they are discussed. Exercises and problems are keyed to chapter learning objectives to ensure mastery of specific objectives.

EXAMPLES

Each new concept, term, or procedure is introduced with a readable definition and a clear example. Examples are used extensively to demonstrate, reinforce, and integrate important concepts.

EXTENDED EXAMPLE

In Chapter 2, we introduce The Kitchen Taylor, a service business owned and operated by Dennis Taylor that refinishes kitchen cabinets. As the discussion of the accounting cycle evolves, The Kitchen Taylor is used to demonstrate the new material. In Chapter 11, The Kitchen Taylor becomes a merchandising business that sells new kitchen cabinets. Using The Kitchen Taylor from Chapter 2 to Chapter 15 gives students a sense of continuity and confidence as they progress into more complex material.

COMMENTS

The comments, located at strategic points in the presentation, are designed to clarify and expand finer points. As teachers, we believe that timely clarification will ensure success with a difficult concept, method, or procedure.

MATH TIPS

Math tips are positioned in various chapters to assist students in making accounting-related computations. Arithmetic skills are reviewed by briefly discussing and illustrating relevant techniques. As teachers, we believe the math tips will enhance the student's accounting progress.

FLOW CHARTS

Flow charts provide visual summaries of procedures and relationships. The flow charts are deliberately simple to ensure clarity.

CHAPTER SUMMARY

Each chapter includes a chapter summary that utilizes the word choice and phrasing from the chapter as much as possible. This repetition provides the reinforcement and consistency that is important to the beginning student.

CHAPTER GLOSSARY

New terms in each chapter appear in an end-of-chapter glossary to reinforce learning and provide convenient reference.

QUESTIONS FOR DISCUSSION

Each chapter includes eight questions for discussion. Using a format of describe, define, or discuss, these questions review the major topics covered in the chapter. The questions cover topics in the order in which they occur in the text. Phrasing of questions is consistent with that in the chapters.

EXERCISES

Each chapter has eight exercises. These exercises, labeled as to content and keyed to the chapter learning objectives, are simple applications of chapter material. Each exercise focuses on only one new concept. The exercises are carefully designed to closely parallel examples used in the chapter.

PROBLEMS

The problems are more complex applications of chapter material than the exercises. The problems help students integrate new concepts, procedures, and methods into the overall accounting cycle. The problems generally follow the sequence of chapter discussion, progress in increasing difficulty, and are keyed to chapter objectives. Every chapter has an A and a B set of problems. Each set is similar in focus, design, and difficulty.

COMPREHENSIVE REVIEW PROBLEMS

The text contains two comprehensive review problems. Comprehensive Review Problem 1 reviews and reinforces the material from Chapters 1 through 6 through the completion of a two-month accounting cycle at Morgan Cleaning Services. Comprehensive Review Problem 2 reviews Chapters 9–15 topics by completing a one-month accounting cycle for Dawson Products, a merchandising business.

MINI-CASES

The mini-cases are an opportunity to bridge the gap between the classroom and the contemporary world. The mini-cases facilitate the application of accounting logic to business and personal situations, promote class participation, and develop written and oral communication skills.

▊▊▊▊ SUPPLEMENTARY MATERIALS FOR STUDENTS

STUDENT STUDY GUIDE

Elements for each chapter are the learning objectives, helpful hints, chapter outline, demonstration problem, true/false and multiple choice (questions that are different from the test banks), matching using the chapter glossary, completion, three exercises keyed to learning objectives, and solutions to the above.

CHECK LIST OF KEY FIGURES

Key figures have been carefully checked for accuracy and conformity with the Instructor's Solutions Manual. Key figures for sets A and B problems are available in bulk to adopters.

WORKING PAPERS

Working papers have been carefully reviewed to ensure coordination with the text. Account titles, forms, schedules, and notation conform with the text, the Instructor's Solutions Manual, the Instructor's Resource Guide, and transparencies.

PRACTICE SETS

NAME	TYPE	TYPE OF BUSINESS	CHAPTER FOCUS
Eagle Express	Manual/ Computer-assisted	Service business, express delivery, sole proprietorship	Chapters 1–6
Holiday Health Club	Manual/ Computer-assisted	Service business, health club, with payroll, sole proprietorship	Chapters 1–10
John Webster, Attorney-at-Law	Manual	Legal practice, sole proprietorship, combination journal	Chapters 1–10
Kenneth Parker, MD	Manual	Medical practice, sole proprietorship, combination journal	Chapters 1–10
The Frame Up	Manual	Payroll, sole proprietorship	Chapters 9–10

| Wheeler Dealer | Manual/ Computer- assisted | Merchandising business, motorbikes, sole proprietorship | Chapters 1–15 |

SOFTWARE

VISIBLE ACCOUNTING CYCLE   This program, developed by John Wanlass of DeAnza College, allows students to convert a manual accounting system to a computerized system for a service business.

COMPUTER ASSISTED TUTORIAL   Developed by JEM Software, Inc., this tutorial enables the student to review the chapter and self-test, using a PC. A master copy will be made available free to adopters.

▌▌▌▌ SUPPLEMENTARY MATERIALS FOR INSTRUCTORS

INSTRUCTOR'S SOLUTIONS MANUAL

Answers to the questions for discussion, exercises, problems (sets A and B), mini-cases, and comprehensive review problems are provided for each chapter. Learning objectives are keyed to the exercises and problems for each chapter. Computations are extensive. Quality design and typography facilitate efficient use. Although prepared by the authors, the solutions were independently rechecked three times.

INSTRUCTOR'S RESOURCE GUIDE

The Instructor's Resource Guide, separate from the Instructor's Solutions Manual, is designed to assist busy professionals in developing lectures and selecting homework assignments. Each chapter contains the chapter learning objectives keyed to suggested homework assignments, a chapter outline, the chapter summary from the text, and a demonstration problem accompanied by a solution.

TRANSPARENCIES

Acetate transparencies of solutions to all exercises, problems (sets A and B), and comprehensive problems are available to adoptors. Large type and quality manufacturing ensure high resolution projection.

TEACHING TRANSPARENCIES

A set of teaching transparencies reinforces the lecture by highlighting selected material from the text.

EXAMINATION MATERIALS

Testing material is available in four formats:

Test Bank: The test bank, a booklet of machine-gradeable items, consists of approximately 700 objective questions in a true/false and multiple choice format. Each chapter has a separate and independent set of questions to ensure instructor flexibility. The test bank design and typography facilitate easy duplication.

CompuTest II: CompuTest is a computerized version of the test banks. CompuTest allows the instructor to select, alter, and/or add test items. CompuTest is capable of generating different versions of the same test. CompuTest, menu-driven and including a well-documented instructor's manual, is available for use on IBM and Apple computers.

Teletest: Teletest is a Richard D. Irwin service that prepares examinations when adopters phone in requests. Within 72 working hours of providing the required information to Teletest, the instructor will receive an examination and answer key by mail.

Achievement Tests: Two series (A and B) of preprinted achievement tests are available. Every test in each series covers only one chapter, allowing instructor flexibility. The test format is true/false, multiple choice, and other machine-gradeable items.

▊▊▊▊ ACKNOWLEDGMENTS

We are indebted to many individuals, faculty members, professional colleagues, and students who have contributed to the development of this text. Particular acknowledgment should be given to the following:

Linda Bruenjes   William Carriato
Bay State Junior College of Business   Arthur Young & Co.

Janet Cassagio
Nassau Community College

Yolande Croteau
Springfield Technical Community
College

Irving Denton
Northern Virginia Community
College

Patrick Farenga
DePaul University

Donald Foster
Diablo Valley College

Sheila Frye
Columbus State Community College

Jon Gartman
Texas State Technical Institute

Joseph Goodro
Metropolitan Technical Community
College

Julie Harrison
Columbus State Community College

Thomas Hilgeman
St. Louis Community College,
Meramac

Ephraim Iwe
Webster Career College

Leonard Kreitz
Rio Hondo College

Ann Montminy
Sullivan Junior College of Business

Cecily Raiborn
Loyola University—New Orleans

Russell Vermillion
Prince George's Community College

David Yankee
Arthur Andersen & Co.

Sherry Young
North Harris County College

Thaddeus L. Zielinski
Milwaukee Area Technical College

Special thanks to Michael Hojnacki of DePaul University for his helpful suggestions and thorough review of the text and all the supplementary materials. Thanks are also due to Frank Korman of Mountain View College for his painstaking review of the entire manuscript on a very tight schedule.

We are particularly indebted to our editor, John Black, for the expert attention given to this book and its many supplements. We wish to thank Deborah Jackson-Jones for all her assistance on the numerous and varied supplements. For her help in coordinating a variety of editorial and developmental projects, our thanks to Cydney Capell. Special thanks to Jennie Cole for developmental support and constructive criticism.

We would be remiss not to acknowledge the production staff. Of particular importance are Loretta Scholten and Margaret Haywood, without whom it would have been impossible to complete this project.

Judith M. Peters
Robert M. Peters

Contents

|||||||||||||||||||||
P A R T 2 ACCOUNTING FOR A PROFESSIONAL SERVICE BUSINESS, CASH, AND PAYROLL   216

Practice Sets: Holiday Health Club
            John Webster, Attorney-at-Law
            Kenneth Parker, MD
            The Frame Up

13 MERCHANDISING BUSINESS: ACCOUNTING FOR CASH   441

14 MERCHANDISING BUSINESS: THE WORK SHEET   486

College Accounting 1–15

The Basic Accounting Cycle

||||||||||||||||
CHAPTER

PART 1

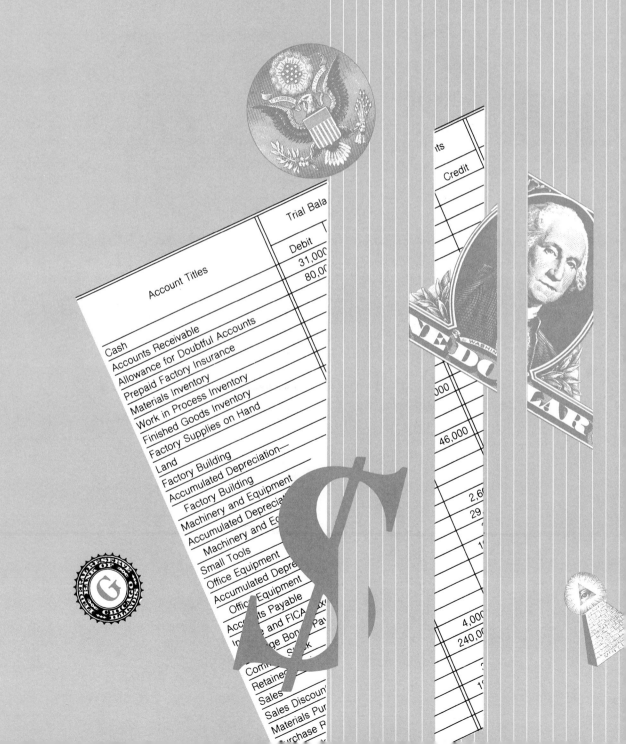

The Accounting Environment

AFTER STUDYING THIS CHAPTER, YOU SHOULD BE ABLE TO:

1 Define the accounting process.

2 Discuss the similarities and differences between manual and computerized accounting systems.

3 Describe the role of accountants.

4 Describe the three major accounting career paths.

5 Explain the business entity concept, matching principle, and historical cost principle.

6 Discuss accrual-basis versus cash-basis accounting.

7 Describe three ownership structures.

8 Classify businesses by their type of business activity.

9 Describe the users of accounting information.

Everyone who makes economic decisions uses accounting. Accounting is so essential to decision making that many refer to accounting and its terminology as the language of business. Accounting terms such as net income, accounts receivable, gross profit, and depreciation are frequently used by lawyers, engineers, doctors, investors, and creditors as well as management.

Even if you do not choose a business-related profession, you should be comfortable with the language of business. You will be making economic decisions throughout your life. For example: Is the company offering you a job with financial security? Is the interest on your bank loan computed correctly? Should you take your stockbroker's advice? How is your business doing? Are you able to prepare the financial information needed for your automobile loan? These and other questions emphasize how a knowledge of accounting will increase the quality of your personal economic decisions and sharpen your understanding of the business environment.

This textbook begins with a brief study of the accounting environment. First, we define the accounting process and then explain the role of accountants. Next, because accounting has become a popular career choice, we describe the three major career paths available to accountants. You will also take a look at three important accounting principles and a comparison of accrual-basis versus cash-basis accounting. This is followed by a discussion of ownership structures and business activities. The chapter concludes with a brief discussion of the users of accounting information.

▐▐▐▐ ACCOUNTING AND ACCOUNTANTS

OBJECTIVE 1
DEFINE THE
ACCOUNTING PROCESS

Broadly defined, **accounting** is a process of analyzing, classifying, recording, summarizing, and interpreting economic events. In accounting, these economic events are called transactions. A **business transaction** is an economic event that can be measured in dollars and affects the financial condition of a business. Common business transactions include selling goods or services, buying land, renting equipment, and making insurance payments. Although the resignation of a key executive may be a disruptive event for a company, it is not a business transaction since this event cannot be accurately measured in dollars. Persons known as bookkeepers often record the most common daily transactions.

OBJECTIVE 2
DISCUSS THE
SIMILARITIES AND
DIFFERENCES BETWEEN
MANUAL AND
COMPUTERIZED
ACCOUNTING SYSTEMS

The process of accounting for business transactions is similar for all businesses. However, the speed with which the process is accomplished depends on whether a business uses a manual accounting system or a computerized accounting system. Both systems are based on the same accounting principles and procedures, but they differ in who will perform the procedures—a person or a machine. Some accounting procedures require thought and analysis; these procedures must be performed by a person. Other procedures are mechanical and may be performed manually or by a computer.

For students, employees, or business owners, a basic knowledge of the accounting process is essential regardless of whether the accounting system

is manual or computerized. In this textbook, we will assume the use of a manual accounting system which will provide you with a set of basic skills that can easily be adapted to a computerized system.

OBJECTIVE 3
DESCRIBE THE ROLE OF ACCOUNTANTS

Both manual and computerized accounting systems are set up, monitored, and operated by accountants. The primary role of accountants is to provide accounting information in a usable form to interested parties on a timely basis. Accountants are no longer stereotyped as small men with green eye shades bending over long pages of figures. During the last half century, accounting has gained the same professional status as the medical and legal professions with equal opportunities for both women and men. The next section discusses the career opportunities for accountants.

▮▮▮▮ ACCOUNTING CAREERS

OBJECTIVE 4
DESCRIBE THE THREE MAJOR ACCOUNTING CAREER PATHS

The need for accountants has existed since trading and commerce blossomed in the 15th and 16th centuries. In 1494, Luca Pacioli, a Franciscan monk, wrote a book describing the double-entry accounting process. The ideas expressed in Pacioli's manuscript still form the backbone of modern accounting. You will learn this double-entry process in the chapters that follow.

The Industrial Revolution of the 18th and 19th centuries brought an even greater need and opportunity for accountants as the factory system emerged and small companies became large manufacturing enterprises. Accountants became involved in solving management problems and providing all types of information to help company managers make decisions.

Today, aided by the electronic computer, accountants provide accurate decision-making data for almost every spectrum of our economic society. As a result, at least three major career paths are available to accountants: public accounting, management accounting, and government/not-for-profit accounting.

PUBLIC ACCOUNTING *serving the public*

To the average person, accountants in the field of public accounting are probably best known for the income tax service they provide individuals. In addition, public accountants provide auditing, tax, and consulting services to many different businesses and organizations for a fee.

Public accountants who pass an examination prepared and graded by the American Institute of Certified Public Accountants (AICPA) and also fulfill other educational and work experience requirements are licensed as certified public accountants (CPAs). CPAs provide an objective opinion on management reports to people not directly involved in managing the business. For example, stockholders, creditors, board members, trustees, and others rely on the opinions of CPAs.

MANAGEMENT ACCOUNTING

Accountants working in the field of management accounting are employed by one company and provide services only for that company. They perform general accounting, tax, budget, and cost accounting services for a single employer.

The role of management accountants is to provide business managers with accounting information that will help them make decisions. The accountants who provide this decision-making information gain a more professional status when they pass a rigorous examination that gives them the title of certified management accountant (CMA).

GOVERNMENT/NOT-FOR-PROFIT ACCOUNTING   *Public Service*

Government/not-for-profit accounting careers involve employment with the federal, state, or local government in such positions as auditors, revenue agents, or contract supervisors. Not-for-profit organizations such as churches, schools, clubs, and charities also employ accountants for various accounting duties ranging from general accounting to specialized accounting services.

Accountants employed in the three accounting fields—public, management, and government/not-for-profit—frequently specialize in certain aspects of their particular accounting field. Some accountants work in two or three accounting fields during their careers. Also, accountants often move into other professions. Many of today's executives and senior managers began their careers as accountants in public, management, and government/not-for-profit accounting.

Now that you have a general idea about the career opportunities for accountants as well as the nature of accounting and accountants, you are ready for an introduction to three accounting principles that guide many of the accounting procedures presented in this textbook.

▌▌▌ ACCOUNTING PRINCIPLES

OBJECTIVE 5
EXPLAIN THE BUSINESS
ENTITY CONCEPT,
MATCHING PRINCIPLE,
AND HISTORICAL COST
PRINCIPLE

In the United States, accountants follow generally accepted accounting principles (GAAP)—the official concepts, rules, procedures, and guidelines of accounting. GAAP are essentially developed by the Financial Accounting Standards Board (FASB), which was organized in 1973 and consists of seven, independent, full-time members. These principles provide a common frame of reference so that similar accounting treatment is given to similar situations. We introduce GAAP in Chapter 1 so that you become aware of them at the beginning of your study of accounting. Understanding these principles also gives you a starting point in making decisions when you later use accounting in actual business situations that may be different from those presented in this textbook.

Accountants use many generally accepted accounting principles. This textbook—your introduction to accounting—concentrates on the business entity concept, matching principle, and historical cost principle. In the chapters that follow, you will find yourself frequently referring back to these three principles.

Building Blocks

very important

BUSINESS ENTITY CONCEPT

In accounting, a business entity is an economic unit that is separate from its owner(s) and from other businesses. The business entity concept requires the separation of the owner's personal and business transactions. If an owner owns two or more businesses, each business is treated as a separate entity.

To separate the personal transactions of the owner from those of the business, probably the first thing the owner of a new business does is to open a checking account in the name of the business. Only business-related money is deposited in this account, and only business-related checks are written against this account. The personal affairs of the owner are transacted through the owner's personal account. Should the owner own two or more businesses, each business would have its own checking account.

MATCHING PRINCIPLE

All profit-seeking businesses expect to earn revenues. Revenue is the amount that a business charges a customer for a service performed or a product provided. Businesses also expect to have expenses, which are the costs incurred in the process of earning revenues.

The matching principle requires that these revenues and expenses be recorded in the time period that they occur. When a business wants to determine its income or loss for a specific period of time, it compares, or matches, the revenues and expenses recorded during that period of time. An excess of revenues over expenses results in net income. An excess of expenses over revenues results in a net loss. Thus, through a proper matching of revenues and expenses, a business is able to compute its income or loss for a specified period of time. In Chapter 2, the matching principle is illustrated with more specific examples of revenues and expenses.

HISTORICAL COST PRINCIPLE

1985 - bought a house for $100,000

1989 - still on books $100,000

The historical cost principle requires that accountants record items, such as equipment and land, at their original cost. This acquisition cost, known as historical cost, is not changed as the current value of the item changes. For example, a business would not adjust its records upward if land purchased several years ago at a cost of $10,000 had increased in current market value to $14,000.

In addition to the business entity concept, matching principle, and historical cost principle, you should be introduced to the accrual basis of accounting before beginning your study of the accounting process in Chapter 2. As you will see in the next section, GAAP require the use of the accrual basis of accounting.

▐▐▐▐ ACCRUAL-BASIS VERSUS CASH-BASIS ACCOUNTING

OBJECTIVE 6
DISCUSS ACCRUAL-
BASIS VERSUS CASH-
BASIS ACCOUNTING

There are two bases of accounting: the accrual basis and the cash basis. Under **accrual-basis accounting,** revenues must be recorded when they are earned, regardless of whether the cash has been received. When the product or service has been provided to the customer, the revenue has been earned and must be recorded. Expenses also must be recorded in the period in which they are incurred, regardless of whether the cash is paid out at that time or later. When we have accepted a product or service from someone else, the expense has been incurred and must be recorded. Under **cash-basis accounting,** revenues are recorded when the cash is received and expenses are recorded when the cash is paid out.

Let's look at a comparison of how the same business transaction is handled under each basis.

Transaction	Accrual Basis	Cash Basis
Sold product to customer on credit.	Since product was provided to customer, revenue is recorded.	Since cash was not received, revenue is not recorded.
Had office painted but have not yet paid the bill.	Since service was accepted from someone else, expense is recorded.	Since cash was not paid out, expense is not recorded.

Cash-basis accounting works well for individuals and small service-oriented businesses, but most companies use the accrual basis. It is generally agreed that accrual-basis accounting results in a more timely measurement of income. In fact, GAAP require the use of accrual-basis accounting. The matching principle, as you will recall, requires that revenues and expenses be recorded in the time period they occurred. Unless otherwise instructed, you can assume the use of the accrual basis throughout this textbook.

So far our environment of accounting has included the accounting process, accountants and their career opportunities, three accounting principles, and accrual-basis versus cash-basis accounting. Now, we shift gears and direct our attention to ownership structures and business activities.

OWNERSHIP STRUCTURES

OBJECTIVE 7
DESCRIBE THREE
OWNERSHIP
STRUCTURES

A business may be organized as a sole proprietorship, partnership, or corporation. The accounting process is similar under each of these ownership structures.

SOLE PROPRIETORSHIP

(family (one group))

A sole proprietorship is a business owned by one person and usually managed by the same person. It is the most common type of business organization. A sole proprietorship is easy to organize and gives the owner the opportunity to be his or her own boss. Under this structure, the owner receives all the income but must also assume all the risk—a risk that can go beyond the owner's investment in the business. Should the business be unable to pay its bills, the bill collectors can collect from the owner's personal assets such as a personal savings account, a car, or even the owner's home.

PARTNERSHIP

(sole proprietorship = a bunch of heads)

A business owned by two or more persons is a partnership. It is a multiple proprietorship where income, risk, and responsibility are shared by the partners. These individuals must agree on such things as the amount of money each is to invest in the partnership, how the work of the partnership is to be divided, and how partnership income or loss is to be divided.

Although a partnership can be organized with a verbal agreement, a written partnership agreement is preferred. This agreement is dissolved when a current partner leaves or a new partner wants to join. For the business to continue, a new partnership must be formed. Although a partnership has limited life, the partners have unlimited personal liability. If the partnership has financial difficulty, the personal assets of the partners may be used to pay the debts of the business.

CORPORATIONS

A corporation is a business owned by many individuals whose participation in the business is often limited. Unlike a sole proprietorship or partnership, a corporation issues shares of stock which allow for the division of ownership into many parts. Owners (stockholders) may transfer their ownership by transferring their shares of stock. If the corporation has financial difficulty, stockholders usually cannot lose more than their original investment.

The unique stock ownership structure of corporations makes them a popular form of investment for individuals. The distribution of income, risk, and responsibility depends on the number of shares owned. Since stockholders are not generally involved in the day-to-day activities of the corporation, the responsibility for daily operations is usually given to professional managers. The stockholders' interests are monitored by a board of directors and reviewed annually by public accountants hired by the stockholders.

▐▐▐▐ BUSINESS ACTIVITIES

OBJECTIVE 8
CLASSIFY BUSINESSES BY
THEIR TYPE OF BUSINESS
ACTIVITY

Accountants also classify businesses by their type of business activity. Most businesses sell either a service or a product. This leads to the following classification:

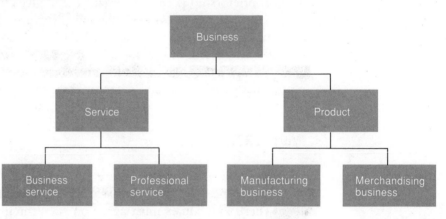

A **service business** sells a skill or technique that has no physical existence. As shown above, service businesses sell either a business service or a professional service. Examples of business services would include the services of dry cleaners, stockbrokers, realtors, and insurance agents. Professional services are provided by physicians, attorneys, public accountants, and educators.

A business that sells a product either makes the product or buys the product ready-made from a supplier. A **manufacturing business** buys various components, such as cloth, thread, and buttons, and makes a product, such as coats. A **merchandising business,** such as your local discount store, buys ready-made products from suppliers and resells them to its own customers.

Some businesses sell both products and services. For example, an automobile repair shop is primarily a service business, but the shop also sells automotive parts.

We have almost completed our discussion of the accounting environment except for a quick look at the users of accounting information.

▐▐▐▐ USERS OF ACCOUNTING INFORMATION

OBJECTIVE 9
DESCRIBE THE USERS OF
ACCOUNTING
INFORMATION

Accounting is used by many individuals and groups with diverse needs. These many users of accounting information can be divided into two general groups: internal users and external users.

INTERNAL USERS

Those who manage the business, collectively known as management, are the internal users of accounting information. Managers are decision makers who are constantly faced with such questions as:

What products or services are the most profitable?

Will the business have enough cash to pay its debts as they come due?

Should the company borrow money to expand its facilities?

Are sales greater this month than last?

Are customers paying their bills on time?

To answer these questions, managers depend on a steady flow of reliable accounting information.

EXTERNAL USERS

External users are individuals or groups outside the business who have either a direct or indirect financial interest in the business. Examples of those with a direct interest would include present or potential investors, bankers, and suppliers. Those with an indirect interest would include taxing authorities, regulatory agencies, labor unions, financial advisors, and customers.

To satisfy the needs of many external users, accountants prepare general-purpose financial statements that summarize the past activities of the business. The information contained in these statements is used to evaluate the company's past performance as well as to predict its future performance. You will become familiar with these financial statements as you study the chapters in this textbook.

Chapter Summary

We began our study of the accounting environment by broadly defining accounting as a process of analyzing, classifying, recording, summarizing, and interpreting economic events. Business transactions are economic events that can be measured in dollars and affect the financial condition of a business.

The speed with which the accounting process is accomplished depends on whether a business uses a manual or computerized accounting system. Both systems are based on the same accounting principles and procedures and are set up, monitored, and operated by accountants. The primary role of accountants is to provide accounting information in a usable form to interested parties on a timely basis.

Almost every spectrum of our economic society requires accounting information. As a result, three major career paths are open to accountants: public accounting, management accounting, and government/not-for-profit accounting.

This chapter introduced three important accounting principles—the business entity concept, matching principle, and historical cost principle. You also received your first glimpse of accrual-basis accounting. This was followed by a brief introduction to ownership structures and business activities. The chapter ended with a discussion of the internal and external users of accounting information.

In Chapter 2, you will be introduced to Dennis Taylor and his business, The Kitchen Taylor. As you follow the progress of The Kitchen Taylor, your knowledge of accounting will grow—knowledge you can relate to everyday business experiences.

Glossary

ACCOUNTING
The process of analyzing, classifying, recording, summarizing, and interpreting economic events.

ACCRUAL-BASIS ACCOUNTING
A system of recording financial information that requires revenues to be recorded when they are earned (product sold or service provided) and expenses to be recorded when they are incurred (product or service accepted), regardless of whether cash has been received or paid.

BUSINESS ENTITY CONCEPT
An accounting rule requiring that a business entity be treated as an economic unit that is separate from its owner(s) and other businesses; it requires a separation of personal and business transactions.

BUSINESS TRANSACTION
An economic event that can be measured in dollars and affects the financial condition of a business.

CASH-BASIS ACCOUNTING
A system of recording financial information that requires revenues to be recorded only when cash is received and expenses to be recorded only when cash is paid out.

CERTIFIED MANAGEMENT ACCOUNTANTS (CMAs)
A title given to management accountants who pass a rigorous examination.

CERTIFIED PUBLIC ACCOUNTANTS (CPAs)
A title given to public accountants who pass an examination prepared and graded by the American Institute of Certified Public Accountants (AICPA) and also fulfill other educational and work experience requirements.

CORPORATION
A business owned by many individuals whose participation in the business is often limited; ownership is evidenced by shares of stock.

EXPENSE
A cost incurred in the process of earning revenue.

EXTERNAL USERS
External users of accounting information are individuals and groups outside the business who have either a direct or indirect financial interest in the business. *DIRECT - investors, bankers & suppliers; INDIRECT - taxing authorities, regulatory agencies, labor unions, financial advisors, and customers.*

FINANCIAL ACCOUNTING STANDARDS BOARD (FASB)

A group consisting of seven, independent, full-time members that is influential in the development of GAAP.

GENERALLY ACCEPTED ACCOUNTING PRINCIPLES (GAAP)

The official concepts, rules, procedures, and guidelines followed by accountants.

HISTORICAL COST PRINCIPLE

A principle of accounting that requires accountants to record items at their original cost. The cost figure is not changed as the current value of the item changes.

INTERNAL USERS

The internal users of accounting information are business managers who need a steady flow of reliable accounting information in order to function as decision makers.

MANAGEMENT ACCOUNTING

A field of accounting that provides general accounting, tax, budget, and cost accounting services for a single employer.

MANUFACTURING BUSINESS

A business that buys various components and makes a product that it sells.

MATCHING PRINCIPLE

A principle that requires revenues and expenses to be recorded in the same time period they occur.

MERCHANDISING BUSINESS

A business that buys ready-made products from suppliers and resells them to its own customers.

PARTNERSHIP

A business owned by two or more persons; it is a multiple proprietorship.

PUBLIC ACCOUNTING

A field of accounting that provides auditing, tax, and consulting services to many different individuals, businesses, and organizations for a fee.

REVENUE

The amount that a business charges a customer for a service performed or a product provided.

SERVICE BUSINESS

dry cleaners, stockbrokers, realtors, insurance agents

A business that sells a skill or technique that has no physical existence.

SOLE PROPRIETORSHIP

A business owned by one person and usually managed by the same person.

professional services are provided by physicians, attorneys, public accountants, & educators.

Questions for Discussion

1. Define accounting.

2. Discuss the basic similarities and differences between a manual and computerized accounting system.

3. Describe the role of accountants.

4. Describe the three major career paths open to accountants.

5. *a.* GAAP is an abbreviation for what phrase?
   b. FASB is an abbreviation for what organization?

6. What is the purpose of GAAP?

7. *a.* Explain the business entity concept.
   b. Explain the matching principle.
   c. Explain the historical cost principle.

8. Discuss the concept of accrual-basis accounting.

9. Describe three types of ownership structures.

10. Discuss the differences among a service business, a manufacturing business, and a merchandising business.

11. Describe the users of accounting information.

CHAPTER 2

Analyzing Transactions:
The Accounting Equation

||||||||||||||||||||
L E A R N I N G
O B J E C T I V E S

AFTER STUDYING THIS CHAPTER, YOU SHOULD BE ABLE TO:

1 Explain the concept of the accounting equation.

2 Use the accounting equation to analyze basic transactions in terms of increases and decreases.

3 Describe the content and purpose of the three basic financial statements.

4 Explain how the three basic financial statements are related.

5 Prepare financial statements.

You will recall from Chapter 1 that accounting was defined as a process of analyzing, classifying, recording, summarizing, and interpreting economic events called business transactions. The entire accounting process operates within the framework of one equation—the accounting equation. This chapter begins with an explanation of the accounting equation. Next you will learn to analyze, classify, and record business transactions within the framework of the accounting equation. Then you will learn to prepare financial statements which summarize transactions that have occurred over a specified period of time.

▮▮▮▮ THE ACCOUNTING EQUATION

OBJECTIVE 1
EXPLAIN THE CONCEPT OF THE ACCOUNTING EQUATION

As defined in Chapter 1, a business transaction is an economic event that can be measured in dollars and affects the financial condition of a business. Typical business transactions include making sales, purchasing supplies, and paying salaries. The basic accounting equation is the framework in which all business transactions are analyzed. This basic equation is:

$$\text{Assets} = \text{Liabilities} + \text{Owner's Equity}$$

Let's begin our study of the accounting equation by defining its components.

Assets are all things of value owned by a business, whether paid for or not. Assets include such things as cash, supplies, land, buildings, and equipment. A separate record, known as an account, is kept for each individual asset. We do not have an account titled assets. The term asset refers to a classification or type of account.

Liabilities are amounts owed (debts) to people outside the business known as creditors. Liabilities, like assets, are a classification or type of account. Liability accounts include Accounts Payable, Notes Payable, and Mortgage Payable. Most liability accounts have the word *payable* in their title. This reminds us that these are amounts we have agreed to pay in the future.

Owner's equity represents the net worth of a business: the difference between all a business owns (assets) and all it owes (liabilities). We might also think of owner's equity in terms of rights to assets. The left side of the accounting equation contains all the things of value (assets) owned by a business. Who has rights to those assets? The right side of the equation answers this question. The liability component expresses the rights or equity of creditors in those assets. Remember, we must pay liabilities out of assets, so our creditors have certain rights to our assets. The remaining rights or equity in assets is expressed in the owner's equity component of the equation. Owner's equity describes the rights of the owner to business assets. The term *capital* means the same thing as owner's equity. These two terms are often used interchangeably by accountants.

Owner's equity is a classification or type of account. An example of a specific owner's equity account would be Mary Jones, Capital. In a sole proprietorship, the title of the owner's equity account is always the owner's name followed by a comma and the word Capital.

The accounting equation (A = L + OE) must always be in balance. The total of everything to the left of the equal sign must always equal the total of everything to the right of the equal sign. In other words, the total of all assets must always equal the total of all rights to assets (creditors' plus owner's).

ANALYZING TRANSACTIONS

OBJECTIVE 2
USE THE ACCOUNTING EQUATION TO ANALYZE BASIC TRANSACTIONS IN TERMS OF INCREASES AND DECREASES

As we have noted, all business transactions must be analyzed within the framework of the accounting equation. The analysis process involves three steps. Let's study this three-step process before considering any specific transactions.

Step 1:   Read and think.
The analysis process always begins with a thorough understanding of the event that has taken place. Before picking up a pencil:

- Read the given data carefully.
- Think about the data using good, old-fashioned common sense.

This step is crucial. You cannot analyze what you don't understand and you cannot understand what you haven't read and thought about carefully. So remember, read and think before you write!

Step 2:   Identify accounts, classifications, and effect.

- **Accounts.** Name the specific accounts involved in each transaction (Cash, Supplies, Equipment, etc.). *INVENTORY*
- **Classifications.** Classify each account (asset, liability, or owner's equity).
- **Effect (+ or −).** Determine the effect (increase or decrease) on each account.

Step 3:   KEY Check the accounting equation (A = L + OE) for balance.
The accounting equation is in balance if the total of everything on the left side of the equation is equal to the total of everything on the right side of the equation. A lack of balance indicates an error in Step 1 and/or Step 2.

Let's practice our analytical skills by considering the case of Dennis Taylor. Dennis decided to convert his hobby, refinishing wooden surfaces, into a profit-making business specializing in refinishing old kitchen cabinets. Dennis named his new business The Kitchen Taylor and organized it as a sole proprietorship. The Kitchen Taylor is a service business because it sells a service (refinishing) rather than a product. Let's analyze some basic transactions that occurred during the first month of operations.

▌ TRANSACTION *(a)*

Step 1:　Dennis invested $10,000 cash in his new business in a checking account in the name of The Kitchen Taylor.

|||||||||||||||||||||
C O M M E N T

Always start your analysis with the easiest part of the transaction saving the most difficult for last. Most students easily understand the flow of cash, so it's usually the best place to begin. Is **cash** (including checks) involved in a transaction? That is, is cash changing hands (being received or paid out) in the current transaction? Be aware that a dollar sign does not necessarily indicate that cash is changing hands.

Step 2:　Account?　　　　Cash
　　　　　　　Classification?　Asset
　　　　　　　Effect?　　　　+ $10,000

　　　　　　　Account?　　　　Dennis Taylor, Capital
　　　　　　　Classification?　Owner's Equity
　　　　　　　Effect?　　　　+ $10,000

|||||||||||||||||||||
C O M M E N T

Remember the business entity concept. The accounting equation represents the status of The Kitchen Taylor, not Dennis Taylor.

Step 3:

	Assets	**= Liabilities +**	**Owner's Equity**
	Cash =		Dennis Taylor, Capital
Before	–0–	–0–	–0–
Trans. *(a)*	+ 10,000		+ 10,000
After	10,000 =	–0–	10,000

▌ TRANSACTION *(b)*

Step 1:　The Kitchen Taylor purchased a truck for which $6,000 in cash was paid.

|||||||||||||||||||||
C O M M E N T

The word **paid** indicates that cash is involved.

Step 2:

Account?	Cash
Classification?	Asset
Effect?	− $6,000

Account?	Truck
Classification?	Asset
Effect?	+ $6,000

||||||||||||||||||||||||
C O M M E N T

Notice that all the activity in this transaction is occurring in the assets section of the equation. The pool of assets is being rearranged, but total assets remain the same. Notice also that owner's equity is not affected by this transaction. The Kitchen Taylor's net worth is unchanged.

Step 3:

	Assets		=	**Liabilities**	+	**Owner's Equity**
	Cash +	Truck =			+	Dennis Taylor, Capital
Before	10,000			—0—		10,000
Trans. (b)	−6,000	+6,000				
After	4,000 +	6,000 =		—0—	+	10,000

$$\underbrace{\qquad\qquad}_{10,000} \qquad\qquad \underbrace{\qquad\qquad}_{10,000}$$

▮ **TRANSACTION** *(c)*

Step 1: The Kitchen Taylor purchased $125 worth of sandpaper, steel wool, chemicals, and various other supplies, promising to pay in the near future.

||||||||||||||||||||||||
C O M M E N T

There is no cash involved in this transaction. The Kitchen Taylor is buying supplies with a promise to pay in the future. This promise represents a liability. More specifically, the promise is recorded as an increase in a liability account known as Accounts Payable. This type of transaction is frequently described as a **purchase on account.**

Step 2:

Account?	Accounts Payable
Classification?	Liability
Effect?	+ $125

Account?	Supplies
Classification?	Asset
Effect?	+ $125

Step 3:

	Assets			=	Liabilities	+	Owner's Equity
	Cash	+ Truck	+ Supplies	=	Accounts Payable	+	Dennis Taylor, Capital
Before	4,000	+ 6,000		=	–0–		10,000
Trans. *(c)*			+125		+125		
After	4,000	+ 6,000	+ 125	=	125	+	10,000
		10,125				10,125	

▌ **TRANSACTION** *(d)*

Step 1:   The Kitchen Taylor refinished several cabinets for a customer who paid $500 in cash.

||||||||||||||||||||||
C O M M E N T

Revenue is the amount that a business charges a customer for the service performed or the product provided. The $500 in this transaction represents revenue earned by The Kitchen Taylor. Revenue is a classification or type of account. Revenue accounts have various titles such as Sales, Fares Earned, or Fees Earned. Dennis has chosen Fees Earned as the title for The Kitchen Taylor's revenue account.

Step 2:

Account?	Cash
Classification?	Asset
Effect?	+ $500
Account?	Fees Earned ~ SALES
Classification?	Revenue (Owner's Equity) CAPITAL
Effect?	+ $500 (+ $500)

||||||||||||||||||||||
C O M M E N T

It should be noted that revenue has a special relationship to owner's equity. The basic relationship between revenue and owner's equity is that revenue increases owner's equity.

$$A = L + OE$$
$$\uparrow$$
$$+R$$

Day to day, as transactions occur, revenue is not recorded directly in the owner's capital account but is recorded in a separate revenue account (like Fees Earned). However, as we will learn in Chapter 6, through a procedure performed at year-end, all revenue eventually will be moved to the owner's capital account. In view of this special relationship, whenever revenue is earned, the balance in a specific revenue account increases. That, in turn, means that owner's equity also increases.

Step 3:

	Assets			=	Liabilities	+	Owner's Equity		
	Cash	+ Truck	+ Supplies	=	Accounts Payable	+	Dennis Taylor, Capital	+	Fees Earned
Before	4,000	+ 6,000	+ 125	=	125	+	10,000		
Trans. *(d)*	+500								+500
After	4,500	+ 6,000	+ 125	=	125	+	10,000	+	500
	10,625						10,625		

■ TRANSACTION *(e)*

Step 1:   The Kitchen Taylor paid $125 to a creditor on account.

Step 2:

Account?	Cash
Classification?	Asset
Effect?	− $125

Account?	Accounts Payable
Classification?	Liability
Effect?	− $125

||||||||||||||||||||
C O M M E N T

In Transaction *(c)*, The Kitchen Taylor made a purchase on account. That promise to pay in the future was recorded as a liability. The Kitchen Taylor is now paying that liability. This is frequently described as making a **payment on account.**

Step 3:

	Assets			=	Liabilities	+	Owner's Equity		
	Cash	+ Truck	+ Supplies	=	Accounts Payable	+	Dennis Taylor, Capital	+	Fees Earned
Before	4,500	+ 6,000	+ 125	=	125	+	10,000	+	500
Trans. *(e)*	− 125				− 125				
After	4,375	+ 6,000	+ 125	=	−0−	+	10,000	+	500
	10,500						10,500		

▌ TRANSACTION *(f)*

Step 1:   The Kitchen Taylor refinished several cabinets, charging the customer $400 for the completed work. The customer promised to pay The Kitchen Taylor in the near future.

|||||||||||||||||||||||
C O M M E N T

In place of cash, The Kitchen Taylor has received a promise to pay from the customer. This promise has value and is, therefore, considered to be an asset. More specifically, it is recorded as an increase in an asset account known as Accounts Receivable. This type of transaction is frequently referred to as a **sale on account.**

Step 2:

Account?	**Fees Earned**	
Classification?	Revenue	(Owner's Equity)
Effect?	+ $400	(+ $400)
Account?	**Accounts Receivable**	
Classification?	Asset	
Effect?	+ $400	

|||||||||||||||||||||||
C O M M E N T

Notice that revenue has been recorded even though The Kitchen Taylor has not yet been paid. Why? The Kitchen Taylor is on the accrual basis of accounting as described in Chapter 1. This means that revenue must be recorded when it is earned, regardless of whether the cash has been received. We consider the revenue to be earned when the product or service has been provided to the customer.

Step 3:

	Assets				=	**Liabilities**	+	**Owner's Equity**	
				Accts.		Accts.		Dennis Taylor,	Fees
	Cash	+ Truck +	Supplies +	Rec.	=	Pay.	+	Capital +	Earned
Before	4,375	+ 6,000 +	125		=	–0–		10,000	500
Trans. *(f)*				+ 400					+400
After	4,375	+ 6,000 +	125 +	400	=	–0–	+	10,000 +	900

10,900   10,900

▌ TRANSACTION *(g)*

Step 1:   The Kitchen Taylor paid $300 monthly rent for a small office and storage space.

|||||||||||||||||||
C O M M E N T

Expenses are costs incurred in the process of earning revenue. Expenses represent a classification or type of account. Examples of specific expense accounts would include Rent Expense, Salary Expense, and Utilities Expense.

Step 2:	Account?	Cash	
	Classification?	Asset	
	Effect?	− $300	
	Account?	Rent Expense	
	Classification?	Expense	(Owner's Equity)
	Effect?	+ $300	(− $300)

|||||||||||||||||||
C O M M E N T

It should be noted that expenses, like revenue, have a special relationship to owner's equity. Expenses decrease owner's equity.

$$A = L + OE$$
$$+R \quad -E$$

Day to day, as transactions occur, expenses are not recorded directly in the owner's capital account. Instead, expenses are recorded in individual expense accounts (such as Rent Expense). However, through a year-end procedure we will study in Chapter 6, all expenses ultimately will be moved to the owner's capital account. Let's review this special relationship. Whenever an expense is incurred, the balance in a specific expense account increases. However, as the expense account balance increases, it will, in turn, cause owner's equity to decrease.

Step 3:

	Assets				=	**Liabilities**	+	**Owner's Equity**		
				Accts.		Accts.		Dennis Taylor,	Fees	Rent
	Cash	+ Truck +	Supplies +	Rec.	=	Pay.	+	Capital +	Earned −	Exp.
Before	4,375 +	6,000 +	125 +	400	=	–0–	+	10,000 +	900	
Trans. (g)	− 300									+ 300
After	4,075 +	6,000 +	125 +	400	=	–0–	+	10,000 +	900 −	300

10,600   10,600

▌ **TRANSACTION (h)**

Step 1:   The Kitchen Taylor received a $100 payment on account from a charge customer.

|||||||||||||||||||||
C O M M E N T In Transaction *(f)*, The Kitchen Taylor made a sale on account and received a promise to pay from the customer. At that time, the customer's promise was recorded as an account receivable. In Transaction *(h)*, the customer is making good on that promise. This means that, in addition to recording the receipt of cash, we must return to the Accounts Receivable account and record a decrease. Observe that no revenue is recorded in this transaction because the related revenue has already been recorded in Transaction *(f)*.

Step 2:	Account?	Cash
	Classification?	Asset
	Effect?	+ $100
	Account?	Accounts Receivable
	Classification?	Asset
	Effect?	− $100

Step 3:

	Assets				=	**Liabilities**	+	**Owner's Equity**		
	Cash	+ Truck	+ Supplies	+ Accts. Rec.	=	Accts. Pay.	+	Dennis Taylor, Capital	+ Fees Earned	− Rent Exp.
Before	4,075	+ 6,000	+ 125	+ 400	=	–0–	+	10,000	+ 900	− 300
Trans. *(h)*	+ 100			− 100						
After	4,175	+ 6,000	+ 125	+ 300	=	–0–	+	10,000	+ 900	− 300
	10,600							10,600		

▌ TRANSACTION *(i)*

Step 1:   A small repair, costing $25, had to be made on the truck. The Kitchen Taylor promised to pay for this in the near future.

||||||||||||||||||||||
C O M M E N T Routine maintenance and repairs to assets are considered expenses of doing business.   *REVENUE — INCREASES OE,*
EXPENSE — DECREASES

Step 2:	Account?	Repair Expense	
	Classification?	Expense	(Owner's Equity)
	Effect?	+ $25	(− $25)
	Account?	Accounts Payable	
	Classification?	Liability	
	Effect?	+ $25	

|||||||||||||||||||||
C O M M E N T

Observe that The Kitchen Taylor has recorded this expense even though the bill has not been paid. Why? **Accrual-basis accounting** requires that expenses be recorded when they are incurred, regardless of whether the cash is paid out now or later. An expense has been incurred when a product or service is accepted from someone else.

Step 3:

		Assets			=	**Liabilities**	+		**Owner's Equity**		
				Accts.		Accts.		Dennis Taylor,	Fees	Rent	Repair
	Cash	+ Truck +	Supplies +	Rec.	=	Pay.	+	Capital +	Earned −	Exp. −	Exp.
Before	4,175	+ 6,000 +	125 +	300	=	–0–	+	10,000 +	900 −	300	
Trans. (*i*)						+25					+25
After	4,175	+ 6,000 +	125 +	300	=	25	+	10,000 +	900 −	300 −	25

10,600   10,600

▮ **TRANSACTION** *(j)*

Step 1: Dennis withdrew $200 in cash from the business for personal use.

|||||||||||||||||||||
C O M M E N T

Dennis is the owner of The Kitchen Taylor. He is not an employee. Only amounts paid to employees are recorded as salary expense. Since the owner is not an employee, amounts withdrawn by the owner cannot be recorded as salary expense. In fact, amounts withdrawn by the owner for personal use cannot be recorded as any type of expense. Remember, expenses, by definition, are incurred in order to earn revenue. Withdrawals by the owner for personal use are recorded in a separate account known as a *drawing account*. The drawing account title contains the owner's name followed by a comma and the word Drawing (Dennis Taylor, Drawing).

Step 2:　Account?　　　Cash
　　　　　　　Classification?　Asset
　　　　　　　Effect?　　　　− $200

　　　　　　　Account?　　　Dennis Taylor, Drawing
　　　　　　　Classification?　Drawing　　(Owner's Equity)
　　　　　　　Effect?　　　　+ $200　　　(− $200)

|||||||||||||||||||||
C O M M E N T

Just as revenue and expense accounts have special relationships to owner's equity, so does the drawing account. The basic relationship between drawing and owner's equity is that withdrawals by the owner decrease owner's equity.

$$A = L + OE$$
$$+R \ -E \ -D$$

Day to day, as transactions occur, withdrawals for personal use are not recorded directly in the owner's capital account (Dennis Taylor, Capital). Instead, these withdrawals are recorded in the owner's drawing account (Dennis Taylor, Drawing). However, through the year-end procedure mentioned earlier, all withdrawals ultimately will be moved to the owner's capital account. Let's review this special relationship between drawing and owner's equity. Whenever the owner makes a withdrawal for personal use, the balance in the drawing account will be increased. However, as the balance in the drawing account increases, it will, in turn, cause the owner's equity to decrease.

Step 3:

	Assets				=	Liab. +		Owner's Equity				
	Cash +	Truck +	Supplies +	Accts. Rec.	=	Accts. Pay. +	Dennis Taylor, Capital −	Dennis Taylor, Drawing +	Fees Earned −	Rent Exp. −	Repair Exp.
Before	4,175 +	6,000 +	125 +	300	=	25 +	10,000		+ 900	− 300	− 25
Trans. *(j)*	− 200							+ 200			
After	3,975 +	6,000 +	125 +	300	=	25 +	10,000 −	200 +	900	− 300	− 25

10,400   10,400

▌ TRANSACTION *(k)*

Step 1: The Kitchen Taylor determined that $75 worth of supplies had been used during the month.

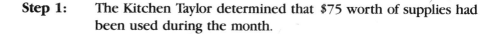

||||||||||||||||||||||
C O M M E N T

Supplies are an asset as long as they are unused. However, as soon as a supply has been used, it is considered an expense. The financial records must be periodically adjusted to reflect this change from an asset to an expense.

Step 2:

Account?	Supplies
Classification?	Asset
Effect?	− $75

Account?	Supplies Expense	
Classification?	Expense	(Owner's Equity)
Effect?	+ $75	(− $75)

Step 3:

				Accts.	Accts.	Dennis Taylor,	Dennis Taylor,	Fees	Rent	Repair	Supplies
	Cash	+ Truck	+ Supplies	+ Rec. =	Pay.	+ Capital	− Drawing	+ Earned	− Exp.	− Exp.	− Exp.
Before	3,975	+ 6,000	+ 125	+ 300 =	25	+ 10,000	− 200	+ 900	− 300	− 25	
Trans. *(k)*			−75								+75
After	3,975	+ 6,000	+ 50	+ 300 =	25	+ 10,000	− 200	+ 900	− 300	− 25	− 75

10,325   10,325

▌▌ SUMMARY OF TRANSACTIONS (a) THROUGH (k)

Figure 2-1 summarizes our analysis of Transactions *(a)* through *(k)* and their effect on the accounting equation. Use this summary to review each transaction by briefly describing the event being recorded in each transaction. When necessary, return to the explanation given earlier in the chapter to refresh your memory.

▌▌ FINANCIAL STATEMENTS

OBJECTIVE 3
DESCRIBE THE CONTENT
AND PURPOSE OF THE
THREE BASIC FINANCIAL
STATEMENTS

One of the basic functions of accounting is to summarize financial data. Day to day, we analyze, classify, and record transactions as they occur. Periodically (usually monthly or yearly), that data must be summarized in a format that is more helpful to users of financial data such as owners, creditors, or government agencies. Financial statements provide that format.

Accountants prepare three basic financial statements:

● Income statement

● Statement of owner's equity

● Balance sheet

As a group, these statements present a financial picture of the business (Figure 2-2). It is important to understand that no single statement gives the whole picture. Each statement presents only a part of the total picture.

INCOME STATEMENT

The purpose of the income statement is to compute net income or loss for a specified period of time. Only revenue and expense accounts are displayed on the income statement. To compute net income, total expenses are

FIGURE 2-1

	Assets				=	Liabilities	+	Owner's Equity					
	Cash +	Truck +	Supplies +	Accts. Rec.	=	Accts. Pay.	+	Dennis Taylor, Capital –	Dennis Taylor, Drawing +	Fees Earned –	Rent Exp. –	Repair Exp. –	Supplies Exp.
Balance	-0-				=	-0-	+	-0-					
(a)	+10,000							+10,000					
Balance	10,000				=	-0-	+	10,000					
(b)	-6,000	+6,000											
Balance	4,000 +	6,000			=	-0-	+	10,000					
(c)			+125			+125							
Balance	4,000 +	6,000 +	125		=	125	+	10,000					
(d)	+500									+500			
Balance	4,500 +	6,000 +	125		=	125	+	10,000	+	500			
(e)	-125					-125							
Balance	4,375 +	6,000 +	125		=	-0-	+	10,000	+	500			
(f)				+400						+400			
Balance	4,375 +	6,000 +	125 +	400	=	-0-	+	10,000	+	900			
(g)	-300										+300		
Balance	4,075 +	6,000 +	125 +	400	=	-0-	+	10,000	+	900	–	300		
(h)	+100			-100									
Balance	4,175 +	6,000 +	125 +	300	=	-0-	+	10,000	+	900	–	300		
(i)						+25						+25	
Balance	4,175 +	6,000 +	125 +	300	=	25	+	10,000	+	900	–	300	–	25	
(j)	-200								+200				
Balance	3,975 +	6,000 +	125 +	300	=	25	+	10,000	–	200	+	900	–	300	–	25	
(k)			-75										+75
Balance	3,975 +	6,000 +	50 +	300	=	25	+	10,000	–	200	+	900	–	300	–	25	–	75

Cash	$ 3,975
Truck	6,000
Supplies	50
Accounts receivable . . .	300
Total assets	$10,325

Accounts payable	$ 25
Dennis Taylor, capital	10,000
Dennis Taylor, drawing	-200
Fees earned	900
Rent expense	-300
Repair expense	-25
Supplies expense	-75
Total liabilities and owner's equity	$10,325

subtracted from total revenues. An excess of expenses over revenues would result in a net loss.

Observe that the date line on the income statement reflects a period of time, usually a month or year. Since net income is a summary figure representing a combination of revenue earned and expenses incurred over a period of time, it is important that the date line reflect the period of time covered by the statement. It would be impossible, for example, to draw any valid conclusions about net income being "good" or "bad" without knowing whether the income statement reflected results for a month or a year.

STATEMENT OF OWNER'S EQUITY

The statement of owner's equity updates the owner's capital account. This statement always begins with the capital account balance on the first day of the specified period of time. This statement always ends with the capital account balance on the last day of the specified period of time. Between the beginning and ending capital account balances, the items that created the change are displayed:

+ Net income

+ Investments by the owner

− Net loss

− Withdrawals by the owner for personal use

Observe that the date line on the statement of owner's equity also reflects a period of time.

BALANCE SHEET

As its name implies, the balance sheet proves that the accounting equation is in balance as of a specified date. Observe that the date line on the balance sheet indicates a specific day, not a period of time. Only asset accounts, liability accounts, and the owner's capital account are shown on this statement. The balance sheet displays the balances in these accounts on the day specified in the date line.

Figure 2-2 shows The Kitchen Taylor's financial statements for its first month of operations. Remember, these statements summarize the data recorded in Transactions *(a)* through *(k)*. The summary of Transactions *(a)* through *(k)*, shown in Figure 2-1, provides the information necessary to prepare The Kitchen Taylor's financial statements. Observe the relationship between the column totals shown in Figure 2-1 and the account balances shown on the financial statements in Figure 2-2.

FIGURE 2 - 2

THE KITCHEN TAYLOR
Income Statement
For the Month Ended January 31, 19X1

Revenue:				
Fees earned			$	900 00
Expenses:				
Rent expense	$ 300 00			
Supplies expense	75 00			
Repair expense	25 00			
Total expenses			400 00	
Net income			$ 500 00	

for a period of time

THE KITCHEN TAYLOR
Statement of Owner's Equity
For the Month Ended January 31, 19X1

Dennis Taylor, capital, January 1, 19X1			$ —0—
Add: Investment by Dennis Taylor	$ 10,000 00		
Net income for January	500 00	10,500 00	
Subtotal		$ 10,500 00	
Deduct: Withdrawals by Dennis Taylor		200 00	
Dennis Taylor, capital, January 31, 19X1		$ 10,300 00	

for a period of Time

THE KITCHEN TAYLOR
Balance Sheet
January 31, 19X1

Assets			
Cash		$ 3,975 00	
Accounts receivable		300 00	
Supplies		50 00	
Truck		6,000 00	
Total assets		$ 10,325 00	
Liabilities			
Accounts payable		$ 25 00	
Owner's Equity			
Dennis Taylor, capital		10,300 00	
Total liabilities and owner's equity		10,325 00	

Observe that the financial statements are separate but related. We pick up the net income figure from the income statement ($500) and use it in the statement of owner's equity. Then we pick up the up-to-date capital account balance from the statement of owner's equity ($10,300) and use it in the owner's equity section of the balance sheet.

It is important to remember that no single statement tells the whole story. For example, the income statement indicates how much revenue a business has earned during a specified period of time. It says nothing about how much of that amount has or has not been received in cash. For information about cash and accounts receivable, we have to look at the balance sheet.

OBJECTIVE 5
PREPARE FINANCIAL
STATEMENTS

PREPARATION GUIDELINES

1. Financial statements follow a standard format. In doing homework, follow the chapter examples carefully in reference to placement, spacing, and indentions.

2. Statements are formal in tone. Therefore, no abbreviations may be used, account titles must be complete, and correct spelling and neatness are absolutely essential.

3. Every statement has a three-line heading containing the company name, title of the statement, and the date.

4. Dollar signs are used only at the top of a column and with totals and subtotals.

5. Single rules (lines) extend across the entire column and indicate that the figures above the rules are to be added or subtracted.

6. Double rules extend across the entire column and are drawn below a figure to indicate that figure is a total.

7. On the income statement, expenses are listed in descending order (highest to lowest) by amount with miscellaneous expense always shown last. There is really no binding rule regarding the order of expenses. The order suggested in this book is a commonly accepted convention.

8. On the balance sheet, assets are listed in liquidity order. By liquidity, we mean closeness to cash. For example, accounts receivable are more liquid than land because they can be converted to cash more quickly.

9. On the balance sheet, liabilities are listed by due date. Those due first are listed first.

Chapter Summary

The basic accounting equation is the framework in which all business transactions are analyzed.

$$\text{Assets} = \text{Liabilities} + \text{Owner's Equity}$$

This equation must always be kept in balance. The total of everything on the left side of the equation must always equal the total of everything on the right side of the equation.

In analyzing each transaction, we should:

Step 1:   Read and think carefully before writing.

Step 2:   Identify

- Accounts?
- Classifications?
- Effect? (+ or −)

Step 3:   Check the accounting equation for balance.

Day to day, we analyze, classify, and record transactions as they occur. Periodically, this accumulated data is summarized in the form of financial statements: income statement, statement of owner's equity, and balance sheet. The purpose of each statement may be summarized as follows:

Statement	Purpose
Income statement	Computation of net income (Revenue − Expense = Net income or loss)
Statement of owner's equity	Updates the owner's capital account (Beginning capital + Investments + Net income − Net loss − Withdrawals = Ending capital)
Balance sheet	Proves the accounting equation is in balance (Assets = Liabilities + Owner's equity)

As a group, financial statements present a financial picture of the business. Individual statements present only a part of the total picture.

The following chart illustrates the flow of data through the accounting process:

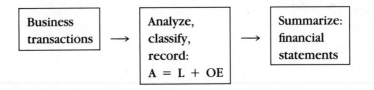

In Chapter 3, you will learn to use debits and credits to record increases and decreases in the accounts.

Glossary

ACCOUNT

A record used to record increases and decreases within each component of the accounting equation.

ACCOUNTING EQUATION

$$\text{Assets} = \text{Liabilities} + \text{Owner's Equity}$$

The framework in which all business transactions are analyzed.

ACCRUAL-BASIS ACCOUNTING

A system of recording financial information that requires revenues to be recorded when they are earned (product or service provided) and expenses to be recorded when they are incurred (product or service accepted), regardless of whether cash has been received or paid.

ASSETS

Things of value owned by a business.

BUSINESS TRANSACTION

An economic event that can be measured in dollars and affects the financial condition of a business.

CASH

An asset; includes coin, currency, and checks.

CREDITOR

A person or company to whom a debt is owed.

EXPENSES

Costs incurred in the process of earning revenue. *Decreases O.E.*

LIABILITIES

Amounts owed to creditors; debts.

LIQUIDITY

Closeness to cash. For example, accounts receivable are more liquid than land because they can be converted to cash more quickly.

NET INCOME

The excess of revenues over expenses.

NET LOSS

The excess of expenses over revenues.

OWNER'S EQUITY

The net worth of a business (assets minus liabilities); defines the owner's rights to business assets.

PAID

Indicates an outflow of cash.

PAYMENT ON ACCOUNT

accts payable

Paying for something previously purchased with a promise to pay in the future.

PURCHASE ON ACCOUNT

Buying something with a promise to pay in the future.

REVENUE

The amount that a business charges a customer for a service performed or a product provided.

SALE ON ACCOUNT

accts receivable

Providing a customer with a product or service in exchange for the customer's promise to pay in the future.

Questions for Discussion

1. Define each of the five types of accounts: asset, liability, owner's equity, revenue, and expense.

2. Explain how the right side of the accounting equation expresses who has rights to the assets of a business.

3. What three questions must be answered when analyzing a business transaction within the framework of the accounting equation?

4. *a.* Which liability account is used to record a purchase on account?
   b. Which asset account is used to record a sale on account?

5. Why are withdrawals by the owner of a business not recorded as salary expense?

6. What three types of accounts have a special relationship to owner's equity?

7. Name the three basic financial statements and the purpose of each.

8. How are the three basic financial statements related to one another?

Exercises

EXERCISE 2-1
COMPLETE
ACCOUNTING
EQUATION
(L.O.1)

Use the accounting equation to solve the following:

a. Company 1: A = $85,000   L = $33,000   OE = ?

b. Company 2: A = 23,000   L = ?   OE = $15,000

c. Company 3: A = ?   L = 34,000   OE = 63,000

EXERCISE 2-2
PROVIDE MISSING
NUMBER
(L.O.1)

Solve the following:

a. Company A owns assets totaling $72,000 and owes $34,000 to creditors. What is its owner's equity?

b. Company B has owner's equity of $53,000 and assets totaling $90,000. How much do liabilities total?

c. During the month, Company C's assets increased by $28,000 while liabilities decreased by $2,000. What is the change in owner's equity?

EXERCISE 2-3
CALCULATE YEAR-END
LIABILITIES
(L.O.1)

Garcia Company begins 19X1 with assets totaling $140,000 and liabilities totaling $85,000. During 19X1, assets decreased by $20,000 while owner's equity decreased by $15,000. What is the amount of Garcia's total liabilities at the end of 19X1?

EXERCISE 2-4
CLASSIFYING
ACCOUNTS
(L.O.2)

Classify the following 10 accounts. Use the letter codes given.

A = Asset   O = Owner's equity   E = Expense

L = Liability   R = Revenue

1. Equipment.   **6.** K. Macek, Capital.

2. Accounts Payable.   **7.** Fees Earned.

3. Rent Expense.   **8.** Supplies Expense.

4. Supplies.   **9.** Truck.

5. Cash.   **10.** Accounts Receivable.

EXERCISE 2-5
INCOME STATEMENT OR
BALANCE SHEET
ACCOUNTS
(L.O.3)

Indicate whether the following accounts appear on the income statement or the balance sheet. Use the letter codes given.

I = Income statement

B = Balance sheet

1. Repair Expense.
2. Accounts Receivable.
3. Carol Morgan, Capital.
4. Fees Earned.
5. Supplies.

6. Cash.
7. Truck.
8. Utilities Expense.
9. Building.
10. Accounts Payable.

EXERCISE 2-6
TRANSACTION ANALYSIS
(L.O.2)

Following are weekly business transactions for Chan's Photo Shop:

1   Received cash for photo services performed.

2   Purchased supplies on account.

3   Performed photo services for customers on account.

4   Paid for minor repair to photo equipment.

5   Made a payment on account to a creditor.

6   Received a payment on account from a charge customer.

7   Susan Chan, the owner, withdrew cash from the business for personal use.

8   Used supplies purchased in Transaction 2.

Indicate the effect of each transaction on the accounting equation by selecting A, B, C, D, or E as follows:

A. Increases assets, increases liabilities.

B. Increases assets, increases owner's equity.

C. Increases one asset, decreases another asset.

D. Decreases assets, decreases liabilities.

E. Decreases assets, decreases owner's equity.

EXERCISE 2-7

TRANSACTION ANALYSIS
(L.O.2)

Indicate the effect of each of the following transactions on total assets, total liabilities, and owner's equity using the chart format given. The transactions will increase (+), decrease (−), or have no effect (NE) on each of the account classifications.

Transaction		Total Assets	Total Liabilities	Owner's Equity
1	Paid employees' salaries.			
2	Purchased supplies on account.			
3	Owner withdrew cash for personal use.			
4	Performed services on account.			
5	Paid creditor on account.			
6	Purchased equipment for cash.			
7	Received payment on account.			
8	Recorded supplies used during the month.			

Problems—Set A

On January 1, 19X1, Mary Flanigan started a data processing business known as Quick Data Services. Transactions for the first month of operations were as follows:

Transaction
Number

1   Mary invested $25,000 cash in the business.

2   Paid $15,000 for equipment.

3   Purchased $1,000 worth of supplies on account.

4   Performed data processing services for a customer who paid $400 in cash.

5   Paid $500 to a creditor on account.

6   Performed $650 worth of data-processing services for a customer who promised to pay in the near future.

7   Paid $700 monthly rent for office space.

8   Received a $325 payment on account from a charge customer.

9   Paid for a small repair to equipment, $75.

10   Mary withdrew $250 in cash from the business for personal use.

11   It was determined that $145 worth of supplies had been used during the month.

INSTRUCTIONS

Analyze the preceding transactions by identifying the following for each transaction:

a. Accounts. Name the specific accounts involved in each transaction.

b. Classifications. Classify each account (asset, liability, owner's equity, revenue, expense, or drawing).

c. Effect. Determine the effect (+ or −) on each account.

PROBLEM 2-2A
ACCOUNTING
EQUATION;
TRANSACTION ANALYSIS
(L.O.1, 2)

INSTRUCTIONS
Referring to Problem 2-1A, record Transactions 1 through 11 in columnar form using the following format. To verify that the accounting equation is in balance after each transaction, be sure to subtotal each column after every transaction.

	Assets			= Liab. +		Owner's Equity					
Trans.		Accts.			Accts.	M. Flanigan,	M. Flanigan,	Fees	Rent	Repair	Supp.
No.	Cash +	Rec. + Supplies +	Equip. =	Pay. +		Capital	− Drawing	+ Earned	− Exp.	− Exp.	− Exp.

PROBLEM 2-3A
FINANCIAL STATEMENTS
(L.O.3–5)

The following accounts and balances appear on the books of the Bellomo Insurance Agency on December 31, 19X1:

Accounts Payable	$ 5,000
Office Furniture	4,000
Commissions Earned	26,000
Salary Expense	8,000
Cash	9,000
Rent Expense	3,000
Accounts Receivable	8,500
Office Supplies	500
Utilities Expense	1,000
Equipment	6,000
Frank Bellomo, Drawing	10,000

The balance in Frank Bellomo, Capital on January 1, 19X1, was $19,000.

INSTRUCTIONS
Prepare the following financial statements for the year ending December 31, 19X1:

  a. Income statement.

  b. Statement of owner's equity.

  c. Balance sheet.

PROBLEM 2-4A
TRANSACTION ANALYSIS;
FINANCIAL STATEMENTS
(L.O.1–5)

Joe Kowalski opened Imperial Dry Cleaners, a sole proprietorship, on May 1, 19X1. Business transactions for the first month of operations were as follows:

Transaction
Number

1   Joe transferred $20,000 from his personal savings account to the company checking account.

2   Purchased equipment on account, $7,000.

3   Purchased supplies for cash, $1,000.

4   Performed cleaning services for customers on account, $2,400.

5   Paid for a small repair to cleaning equipment, $125.

6   Paid $10,000 in cash for a delivery truck.

7   Paid monthly rent, $1,000.

8   Received payment on account from a charge customer, $750.

9   Paid employees' salaries, $500.

10 Performed cleaning services for cash, $400.

11 Determined that $600 worth of supplies were used during May.

12 Joe withdrew $300 in cash from the business for personal use.

INSTRUCTIONS

1. Record Transactions 1 through 12 in columnar form using the following format:

Assets					=	Liab. +		Owner's Equity						
Trans.		Accts.				Accts.	J. Kowal-ski,	J. Kowal-ski,	Fees	Rent	Repair	Supp.	Salary
No. Cash +	Rec. +	Supplies +	Truck +	Equip.	=	Pay. +	Capital −	Drawing +	Earned −	Exp. −	Exp. −	Exp. −	Exp.

2. Prepare the following monthly statements:

a. Income statement.

b. Statement of owner's equity.

c. Balance sheet.

Problems—Set B

PROBLEM 2-1B
TRANSACTION ANALYSIS
(L.O.1, 2)

On January 1, 19X1, Jill Sullivan started an interior decorating business known as Beau Decor. Transactions for the first month of operations were as follows:

Transaction
Number

1   Jill invested $10,000 cash in the business.

2   Paid $4,000 for equipment.

3   Purchased $800 worth of supplies on account.

4   Performed decorating services for a customer who paid $200 in cash.

5   Paid $250 to a creditor on account.

6   Performed $300 worth of decorating services for a customer. The customer promised to pay in the near future.

7   Paid $400 monthly rent for office space.

8   Received a $150 payment on account from a charge customer.

9   Paid for a small repair to equipment, $65.

10   Jill withdrew $225 in cash from the business for personal use.

11   It was determined that $115 worth of supplies had been used during the month.

INSTRUCTIONS
Analyze the preceding transactions by identifying the following for each transaction:

a. Accounts. Name the specific accounts involved in each transaction.

b. Classifications. Classify each account (asset, liability, owner's equity, revenue, expense, or drawing).

c. Effect. Determine the effect (+ or −) on each account.

PROBLEM 2-2B
ACCOUNTING
EQUATION;
TRANSACTION ANALYSIS
(L.O.1, 2)

INSTRUCTIONS

Referring to Problem 2-1B, record Transactions 1 through 11 in columnar form using the column headings that follow. To verify that the accounting equation is in balance after each transaction, be sure to subtotal each column after every transaction.

	Assets				= Liab. +		Owner's Equity					
Trans. No.	Cash +	Accts. Rec. +	Supplies +	Equip. =	Accts. Pay. +	Jill Sullivan, Capital −	Jill Sullivan, Drawing +	Fees Earned −	Rent Exp. −	Repair Exp. −	Supp. Exp.	

PROBLEM 2-3B
FINANCIAL STATEMENTS
(L.O.3–5)

The following accounts and balances appear on the books of LaCosta Associates on December 31, 19X1:

Accounts Payable	$ 8,200
Office Furniture	3,500
Commissions Earned	21,000
Salary Expense	6,000
Cash	8,000
Rent Expense	4,000
Accounts Receivable	7,500
Office Supplies	400
Utilities Expense	800
Office Equipment	5,000
Tony LaCosta, Drawing	9,000

The balance in Tony LaCosta, Capital on January 1, 19X1, was $15,000.

INSTRUCTIONS

Prepare the following financial statements for the year ending December 31, 19X1:

a. Income statement.

b. Statement of owner's equity.

c. Balance sheet.

PROBLEM 2-4B
TRANSACTION ANALYSIS;
FINANCIAL STATEMENTS
(L.O.1–5)

Stan Kozak opened Stan's TV Repairs, a sole proprietorship, on May 1, 19X1. Business transactions for the first month of operations were as follows:

Transaction
Number

1   Stan transferred $10,000 from his personal savings account to the company checking account.

2   Purchased equipment on account, $3,500.

3   Purchased supplies for cash, $500.

4   Performed repair services for customers on account, $750.

5   Paid for a small repair to equipment, $70.

6   Paid $5,000 in cash for a truck.

7   Paid monthly rent, $500.

8   Received payment on account from charge customer, $200.

9   Paid employees' salaries, $250.

10   Performed repair services for cash, $150.

11   Determined that $300 worth of supplies were used during May.

12   Stan withdrew $650 in cash from the business for personal use.

INSTRUCTIONS

1. Record Transactions 1 through 12 in columnar form using the following format:

Assets					= Liab. +	Owner's Equity						
Trans. No.	Cash +	Accts. Rec. +	Supplies +	Truck +	Equip. =	Accts. Pay. +	Stan Kozak, Capital −	Stan Kozak, Drawing +	Fees Earned −	Rent Exp. −	Repair Exp. −	Supp. Exp. −	Salary Exp.

2. Prepare the following monthly statements:

   a. Income statement.

   b. Statement of owner's equity.

   c. Balance sheet.

Mini-Cases

CASE 2-1

Hampton Painting and Decorating has earned more revenue this year than last. However, this year's net income is lower than last year's. Mark Hampton, the owner, does not understand how this could be possible. How would you explain this situation to Mark?

CASE 2-2

Each month Hilda Wasser, owner of Hilda's Hair Boutique, withdraws $1,000 for personal use. Hilda records these withdrawals as salary expense. As Hilda's new accountant, how would you respond to this situation?

CASE 2-3

You are the accountant for Lamb Real Estate. Gary Lamb, the owner, observes that you have recorded some unpaid bills as expenses for this year. He questions recording these items as expenses since no cash has been paid out. Explain this situation to Gary.

Analyzing Transactions: Debits and Credits

AFTER STUDYING THIS CHAPTER, YOU SHOULD BE ABLE TO:

1 Use T-accounts in analyzing transactions.

2 Use debits and credits to record increases and decreases in accounts.

3 Analyze transactions using debits and credits.

In the last chapter, you learned to analyze transactions within the framework of the accounting equation. In Chapter 3, you will study debits and credits, which are a simple extension of that process of analysis. First, you will be introduced to T-accounts. Next, you will learn to use debits and credits to record increases and decreases in the accounts. Then, returning to The Kitchen Taylor, you will learn to analyze transactions using both T-accounts and debits and credits.

▌▌▌▌ THE T-ACCOUNT

OBJECTIVE 1
USE T-ACCOUNTS IN ANALYZING TRANSACTIONS

In Chapter 2, a columnar format was used to record increases and decreases in specific accounts. In practice, accountants often use T-accounts to analyze transactions. A **T-account** is a more convenient format for recording increases and decreases in the accounts. An example of a T-account is shown below. In view of its "T" shape, its name seems appropriate.

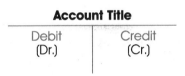

Account Title

| Debit (Dr.) | Credit (Cr.) |

Observe that the left side of the T-account is always the **debit** side and the right side is always the **credit** side. This never changes regardless of the type of account. Although arbitrary, this is a rule observed by all accountants, just like the rule of stopping for red and advancing on green lights is observed by all drivers.

The balance in a T-account is computed as follows:

Step 1:   Total the debit amounts.

Step 2:   Total the credit amounts.

Step 3:   Subtract the smaller total from the larger total. The difference is called the **balance.**

Step 4:   The balance is written on the side of the account with the larger total.

For practice, let's compute the balance in the following T-account:

Account Title

	Debit		Credit	
		500	350	
		1,200	500	
		125	850	(Step 2)
(Step 1)		1,825		
(Steps 3 and 4)	Bal.	975		

In this example, the credit total ($850) is smaller and is subtracted from the debit total ($1,825) resulting in a debit balance of $975. Totals are written in small pencil figures known as **footings**.

▌▌▌▌ DEBITS AND CREDITS

OBJECTIVE 2
USE DEBITS AND
CREDITS TO RECORD
INCREASES AND
DECREASES IN
ACCOUNTS

In the previous chapter, you analyzed transactions by identifying accounts, classifying those accounts, and deciding the effect in terms of increases and decreases. Debits and credits are simply the tools accountants use to record those increases and decreases in the accounts.

Debits may be used both to increase and decrease account balances. Credits may also be used both to increase and decrease account balances. So how do you know which to use when? Usage is determined by account classifications and the accounting equation.

To demonstrate, let's set up a T-account for each account classification. Each T-account will represent how all the individual accounts within each classification will function.

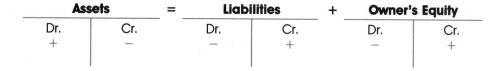

Observe that assets appear on the *left* side of the equation. Assets are increased with debits, which are always recorded on the *left* side of a T-account. To decrease asset accounts, we credit—the only remaining possibility.

Observe that liabilities and owner's equity both appear on the *right* side of the equation. Both are increased with credits, which are always recorded on the *right* side of a T-account. To decrease liability and owner's equity accounts, we debit—the only remaining possibility.

You learned in Chapter 2 that revenue, expense, and drawing accounts have special relationships to owner's equity. Let's review those relationships.

- Revenue increases owner's equity.
- Expenses decrease owner's equity.
- Withdrawals for personal use decrease owner's equity.

Day to day, revenue, expense, and withdrawal transactions are recorded in separate accounts—not directly in the owner's capital account. However, at the end of every year, the amounts accumulated in those accounts throughout the year will be transferred to the owner's capital account. Let's continue our discussion of debits and credits with these relationships in mind.

Revenue accounts are increased with credits and decreased with debits based on the relationship of revenue to owner's equity.

1. Revenue increases owner's equity.

2. Credits increase owner's equity.

3. Therefore, as the balance on the credit side of a revenue account increases, this credit indirectly increases owner's equity.

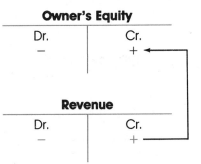

Expense accounts are increased with debits and decreased with credits based on the relationship of expenses to owner's equity.

1. Expenses decrease owner's equity.

2. Debits decrease owner's equity.

3. Therefore, as the balance on the debit side of an expense account increases, this debit indirectly decreases owner's equity.

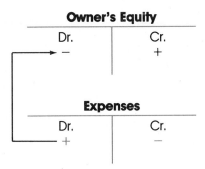

Drawing accounts are increased with debits and decreased with credits based on the relationship of drawing to owner's equity.

1. Withdrawals by the owner for personal use decrease owner's equity.

2. Debits decrease owner's equity.

3. Therefore, as the balance on the debit side of the drawing account increases, this debit indirectly decreases owner's equity.

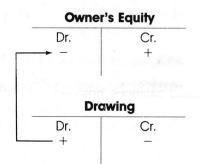

DEBIT AND CREDIT REVIEW

The rules of debit and credit are summarized in the following chart. Use it to review the debit and credit relationships described earlier in this chapter.

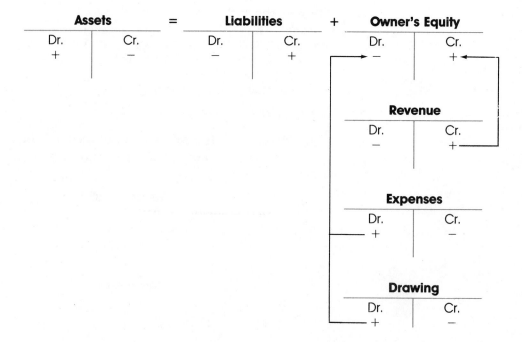

▋▋▋▋ NORMAL BALANCES

Accountants frequently use the term *normal balance.* The normal balance side of an account is simply the side on which increases are recorded.

Classification	Normal Balance
Asset	Debit
Liability	Credit
Owner's equity	Credit
Revenue	Credit
Expense	Debit
Drawing	Debit

It is possible for an account to have a balance on its decrease side. Such abnormal balances, however, are relatively infrequent and usually of short duration.

▋▋▋▋ ANALYZING TRANSACTIONS USING DEBITS AND CREDITS

OBJECTIVE 3
ANALYZE
TRANSACTIONS USING
DEBITS AND CREDITS

Let's practice our expanded analytical skills by returning to The Kitchen Taylor and again considering Transactions *(a)* through *(k)* from Chapter 2. We will continue to use the three-step process studied in the previous chapter. However, at the end of Step 2, we will determine how to record the increases and decreases using debits and credits. In Step 3, we will record the debits and credits in T-accounts rather than in the columnar format shown in Chapter 2. We will check the accounting equation for balance by checking for the equality of debits and credits. For the accounting equation to be in balance, the debits recorded in the accounts must equal the credits recorded in the accounts.

▋ TRANSACTION *(a)*

Step 1:   Dennis invested $10,000 cash in his new business in a checking account in the name of The Kitchen Taylor.

Step 2:

Account?	Cash
Classification?	Asset
Effect?	+ $10,000
How?	Debit
Account?	Dennis Taylor, Capital
Classification?	Owner's Equity
Effect?	+ $10,000
How?	Credit

||||||||||||||||||||||| The word *debit* is frequently abbreviated by dr. which is derived from the Latin
C O M M E N T word *debere*. Credit is frequently abbreviated cr. from the Latin word *credere*.

Step 3:

Cash			Dennis Taylor, Capital		
Dr.		Cr.	Dr.		Cr.
(a) 10,000					*(a)* 10,000

||||||||||||||||||||||| Remember, in order for the accounting equation to be in balance, total debits
C O M M E N T must always equal total credits.

■ TRANSACTION *(b)*

Step 1:   The Kitchen Taylor paid $6,000 for a truck.

Step 2:   Account?   Cash
                 Classification?   Asset
                 Effect?   − $6,000
                 How?   Credit

                 Account?   Truck
                 Classification?   Asset
                 Effect?   + $6,000
                 How?   Debit

Step 3:

Cash			Truck		
Dr.		Cr.	Dr.		Cr.
		(b) 6,000	*(b)* 6,000		

■ TRANSACTION *(c)*

Step 1:   The Kitchen Taylor purchased $125 worth of sandpaper, steel
                wool, chemicals, and various other supplies, promising to pay
                in the near future.

Step 2:   Account?   Accounts Payable
             Classification?   Liability
             Effect?   + $125
             How?   Credit

             Account?   Supplies
             Classification?   Asset
             Effect?   + $125
             How?   Debit

Step 3:

Supplies			Accounts Payable		
Dr.		Cr.	Dr.		Cr.
(c)	125			(c)	125

▌ TRANSACTION *(d)*

Step 1:   The Kitchen Taylor refinished several cabinets for a customer who paid $500 in cash.

Step 2:   Account?   Cash
             Classification?   Asset
             Effect?   + $500
             How?   Debit

             Account?   Fees Earned
             Classification?   Revenue
             Effect?   + $500
             How?   Credit

Step 3:

Cash			Fees Earned		
Dr.		Cr.	Dr.		Cr.
(d)	500			(d)	500

▌ TRANSACTION *(e)*

Step 1:   The Kitchen Taylor paid $125 to a creditor on account.

Step 2:   Account?   Cash
               Classification?   Asset
               Effect?   − $125
               How?   Credit

               Account?   Accounts Payable
               Classification?   Liability
               Effect?   − $125
               How?   Debit

Step 3:

Cash			Accounts Payable		
Dr.		Cr.		Dr.	Cr.
	(e)	125	*(e)*	125	

▌ TRANSACTION *(f)*

Step 1:   The Kitchen Taylor refinished several cabinets, charging the
               customer $400 for the completed work. The customer
               promised to pay The Kitchen Taylor in the near future.

Step 2:   Account?   Fees Earned
               Classification?   Revenue
               Effect?   + $400
               How?   Credit

               Account?   Accounts Receivable
               Classification?   Asset
               Effect?   + $400
               How?   Debit

Step 3:

Accounts Receivable			Fees Earned		
Dr.		Cr.		Dr.	Cr.
(f)	400			*(f)*	400

▌ TRANSACTION *(g)*

Step 1:   The Kitchen Taylor paid $300 monthly rent for a small office
               and storage space.

Step 2:   Account?   Cash
             Classification?   Asset
             Effect?   − $300
             How?   Credit

             Account?   Rent Expense
             Classification?   Expense
             Effect?   + $300
             How?   Debit

Step 3:

	Cash				Rent Expense	
Dr.		Cr.		Dr.		Cr.
	(g)	300	*(g)*	300		

TRANSACTION *(h)*

Step 1:   The Kitchen Taylor received a $100 payment on account from a charge customer.

Step 2:   Account?   Cash
             Classification?   Asset
             Effect?   + $100
             How?   Debit

             Account?   Accounts Receivable
             Classification?   Asset
             Effect?   − $100
             How?   Credit

Step 3:

	Cash				Accounts Receivable	
Dr.		Cr.		Dr.		Cr.
(h)	100				*(h)*	100

TRANSACTION *(i)*

Step 1:   A small repair, costing $25, had to be made on the truck. The Kitchen Taylor promised to pay for this in the near future.

Step 2:   Account?   Repair Expense
              Classification?   Expense
              Effect?   + $25
              How?   Debit

              Account?   Accounts Payable
              Classification?   Liability
              Effect?   + $25
              How?   Credit

Step 3:

Accounts Payable			Repair Expense		
Dr.	Cr.		Dr.		Cr.
	(i)	25	(i)	25	

TRANSACTION (j)

Step 1:   Dennis withdrew $200 in cash from the business for personal
              use.

Step 2:   Account?   Cash
              Classification?   Asset
              Effect?   − $200
              How?   Credit

              Account?   Dennis Taylor, Drawing
              Classification?   Drawing
              Effect?   + $200
              How?   Debit

Step 3:

Cash			Dennis Taylor, Drawing		
Dr.	Cr.		Dr.		Cr.
	(j)	200	(j)	200	

TRANSACTION *(k)*

Step 1:   The Kitchen Taylor determined that $75 of supplies had been used during the month.

Step 2:
Account?	Supplies
Classification?	Asset
Effect?	− $75
How?	Credit

Account?	Supplies Expense
Classification?	Expense
Effect?	+ $75
How?	Debit

Step 3:

Supplies		Supplies Expense	
Dr.	Cr.	Dr.	Cr.
	(k) 75	*(k)* 75	

▮▮▮▮ SUMMARY OF TRANSACTIONS *(a)* THROUGH *(k)*

The following T-accounts summarize our extended analysis of Transactions *(a)* through *(k)*. The account balances have been computed following the procedure described at the beginning of this chapter.

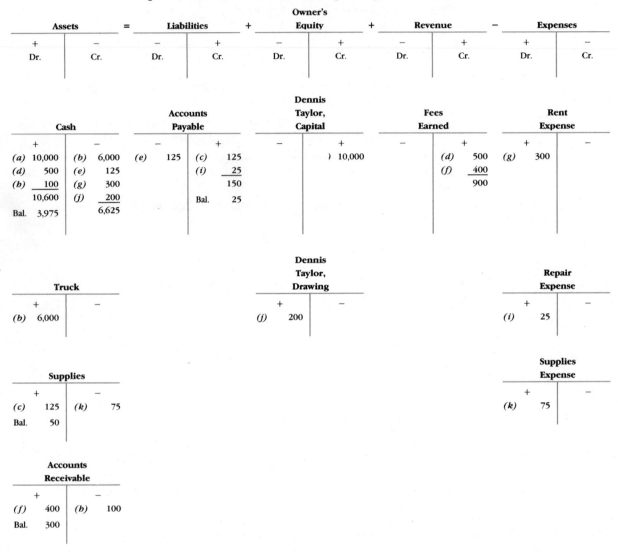

	Assets		=		Liabilities		+	Owner's Equity		+		Revenue		−		Expenses	
+		−		−		+		−	+		−		+		+		−
Dr.		Cr.		Dr.		Cr.		Dr.	Cr.		Dr.		Cr.		Dr.		Cr.

Cash

	+			−	
(a)	10,000		*(b)*	6,000
(d)	500		*(e)*	125
(b)	100		*(g)*	300
	10,600		*(j)*	200
Bal.	3,975			6,625

Accounts Payable

	−			+	
(e)	125		*(c)*	125
			(i)	25
				150
		Bal.	25

Dennis Taylor, Capital

	−			+	
			)	10,000

Fees Earned

	−			+	
			(d)	500
			(f)	400
				900

Rent Expense

	+			−	
(g)	300		

Truck

	+			−	
(b)	6,000		

Dennis Taylor, Drawing

	+			−	
(j)	200		

Repair Expense

	+			−	
(i)	25		

Supplies

	+			−	
(c)	125		*(k)*	75
Bal.	50		

Supplies Expense

	+			−	
(k)	75		

Accounts Receivable

	+			−	
(f)	400		*(b)*	100
Bal.	300		

Chapter Summary

Debits and credits are simply the tools used by accountants to record increases and decreases in the accounts. Debits may be used both to increase and decrease account balances. Credits may also be used both to increase and decrease account balances. Knowing which to use when is determined by account classifications and the accounting equation.

T-accounts are often used by accountants to analyze transactions. The debit side of a T-account is always the left side. The credit side of a T-account is always the right side. The account balance is the difference between total debits and credits and is always written on the side of the account with the larger total.

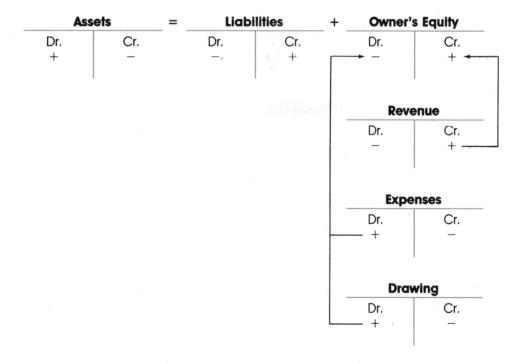

In the next chapter, you will learn to record transactions using a journal and ledger accounts.

Glossary

BALANCE—ACCOUNT
The difference between total debits and total credits. Written on side with larger total.

BALANCE—ACCOUNTING EQUATION
Total debits equal total credits.

CREDIT
Used to increase liability, owner's equity, and revenue accounts. Used to decrease asset, expense, and drawing accounts. Abbreviation: cr.

DEBIT
Used to increase asset, expense, and drawing accounts. Used to decrease liability, owner's equity, and revenue accounts. Abbreviation: dr.

FOOTING
A total placed in small pencil figures at the bottom of a column of figures.

NORMAL BALANCE
The increase side of an account.

T-ACCOUNT
A simple T-shaped account form with debits on the left and credits on the right.

Questions for Discussion

1. What four questions must be answered when analyzing business transactions using debits and credits?

2. What is a T-account? For what are T-accounts used?

3. Debits are used to increase which classifications of accounts?

4. Debits are used to decrease which classifications of accounts?

5. Credits are used to increase which classifications of accounts?

6. Credits are used to decrease which classifications of accounts?

7. Why must total debits always equal total credits?

8. *a.* As the balance on the debit side of an expense account increases, does owner's equity indirectly increase or decrease?

   b. As the balance on the credit side of a revenue account increases, does owner's equity indirectly increase or decrease?

Exercises

EXERCISE 3-1
DEBIT OR CREDIT
(L.O.2)

Indicate whether a debit or credit is needed to accomplish the following:

1. Increase assets.
2. Decrease assets.
3. Increase liabilities.
4. Decrease liabilities.
5. Increase owner's equity.
6. Decrease owner's equity.

7. Increase revenue.
8. Decrease revenue.
9. Increase expenses.
10. Decrease expenses.
11. Increase drawing.
12. Decrease drawing.

EXERCISE 3-2
EFFECT OF DEBIT OR
CREDIT
(L.O.2)

Determine whether the following will increase or decrease the account mentioned:

1. Debit to Accounts Receivable.
2. Credit to Cash.
3. Debit to Rent Expense.
4. Credit to Fees Earned.
5. Credit to Supplies.
6. Debit to Truck.
7. Credit to Accounts Payable.
8. Debit to Supplies Expense.
9. Debit to Diane Wilson, Drawing.
10. Credit to Diane Wilson, Capital.

EXERCISE 3-3
DESCRIBE
TRANSACTIONS
(L.O.1, 2)

Referring to the following T-accounts, describe Transactions *(a)* through *(g):*

	Cash		
Dr.		Cr.	
(a)	20,000	(b)	8,000
(f)	750	(e)	900
		(g)	175

	Accounts Receivable		
Dr.		Cr.	
(c)	1,000	(f)	750

	Truck	
Dr.		Cr.
(b)	8,000	

	Accounts Payable		
Dr.		Cr.	
(g)	175	(d)	175

	Nolan Ross, Capital	
Dr.		Cr.
	(a)	20,000

	Nolan Ross, Drawing	
Dr.		Cr.
(e)	900	

	Fees Earned	
Dr.		Cr.
	(c)	1,000

	Repair Expense	
Dr.		Cr.
(d)	175	

EXERCISE 3-4
EFFECT OF DEBIT OR
CREDIT
(L.O.2, 3)

Determine whether the following transactions will increase or decrease total assets, total liabilities, and owner's equity. Use a format with the following column headings:

Transaction
Number   Assets   Liabilities   Owner's Equity

Transaction
Number
1   Dr. Cash, Cr. Fees Earned.

2   Dr. Accounts Payable, Cr. Cash.

3   Dr. Accounts Receivable, Cr. Fees Earned.

4   Dr. Cash, Cr. Accounts Receivable.

5   Dr. Rent Expense, Cr. Cash.

6   Dr. Supplies, Cr. Cash.

7   Dr. Roberta Kleegon, Drawing; Cr. Cash.

8   Dr. Supplies Expense, Cr. Supplies.

EXERCISE 3-5
TRANSACTION ANALYSIS
(L.O.2, 3)

For each of the following transactions, determine

    a. Accounts?

    b. Classification (asset, liability, owner's equity, revenue, expense, or drawing)?

    c. Effect (+ or −)?

    d. How (dr. or cr.)?

Use the following format:

Transaction Number	Account	Classification	Effect (+ or −)	How (dr. or cr.)

Transaction
Number
1   Purchased supplies on account.

2   Made a sale on account.

3   David Crowe, owner, withdrew cash for personal use.

4   Paid creditor on account.

5   Paid monthly rent.

6   Purchased truck for cash.

7   Received payment on account from charge customer.

8   Recorded used supplies.

EXERCISE 3-6
INCOME STATEMENT
(L.O.1, 2)

On January 31, 19X1, the accounts of Herbert Cohen, M.D., appear as follows:

Cash				Accounts Receivable		
Dr.	Cr.			Dr.	Cr.	
15,000	440			2,250	1,675	
125	660					
1,675	800					

Supplies				Equipment		
Dr.	Cr.			Dr.	Cr.	
450	275			2,580		

Accounts Payable	
Dr.	Cr.
	450
	2,580

Herbert Cohen, Capital	
Dr.	Cr.
	15,000

Herbert Cohen, Drawing	
Dr.	Cr.
800	

Fees Earned	
Dr.	Cr.
	125
	2,250

Supplies Expense	
Dr.	Cr.
275	

Rent Expense	
Dr.	Cr.
660	

Salary Expense	
Dr.	Cr.
440	

Prepare an income statement for the month of January.

EXERCISE 3-7
STATEMENT OF OWNER'S
EQUITY
(L.O.1, 2)

Referring to the information presented in Exercise 3-6, prepare a statement of owner's equity for the month ending January 31, 19X1.

EXERCISE 3-8
BALANCE SHEET
(L.O.1, 2)

Referring to the information presented in Exercise 3-6, prepare a balance sheet as of January 31, 19X1.

Problems—Set A

PROBLEM 3-1A
TRANSACTION ANALYSIS
(L.O.2, 3)

Cleveland Horne, an architect, established a sole proprietorship known as Horne Design Associates. Following are transactions for July 19X1, the first month of operations:

Transaction

a   Cleveland invested $12,000 in his new business.

b   Horne Design Associates paid $7,200 for equipment.

c   Purchased $510 worth of supplies on account.

d   Performed architectural services for a client who paid $2,500 in cash.

e   Paid $350 to a creditor on account.

f   Paid for a small repair to the equipment, $56.

g   Performed architectural services for a customer on account, $1,850.

h   Paid monthly rent, $775.

i   Received a $1,200 payment on account from a charge customer.

j   Paid secretary's salary, $650.

k   Cleveland withdrew $935 for personal use.

l   Determined that $260 worth of supplies had been used during the month.

The following accounts are used by Horne Design Associates:

Cash	Cleveland Horne, Drawing
Accounts Receivable	Fees Earned
Supplies	Rent Expense
Equipment	Repair Expense
Accounts Payable	Salary Expense
Cleveland Horne, Capital	Supplies Expense

INSTRUCTIONS

Analyze each transaction by determining:

    a. Accounts?

    b. Classification (asset, liability, owner's equity, revenue, expense, or drawing)?

    c. Effect (+ or −)?

    d. How (dr. or cr.)?

Use the following columnar format:

Transaction	Account	Classification	Effect (+ or −)	How (dr. or cr.)

PROBLEM 3-2A

T-ACCOUNTS;
FINANCIAL STATEMENTS
(L.O.1, 2)

INSTRUCTIONS

1. Set up T-accounts for all the accounts used by Horne Design Associates in Problem 3-1A.

2. Record the transactions described in Problem 3-1A in the T-accounts. (Note: If Problem 3-1A has been completed, refer to your transaction analysis from Problem 3-1A.)

3. Compute the account balances.

4. For the month of July 19X1, prepare the following financial statements:

    a. Income statement.

    b. Statement of owner's equity.

    c. Balance sheet.

PROBLEM 3-3A

TRANSACTION ANALYSIS
(L.O.2, 3)

Maria Valdez, an accountant, established a sole proprietorship known as Valdez Accounting Services. Following are transactions for the month of September 19X1, the first month of operations:

Transaction

a   Maria invested $5,000 cash in the business.

b   Purchased a new electronic typewriter on account, $750.

c   Billed a customer for accounting services performed on account, $825.

d   Paid $167 for letterhead stationery.

e   Paid $375 to a creditor on account.

f   Performed accounting services for cash, $480.

g   Paid monthly rent, $650.

h   Received payment on account from a charge customer, $500.

i   Prepaid a one-year insurance premium covering the period September 19X1 through August 19X2, $225. (Hint: Insurance, like supplies, is considered an asset as long as it is unused or unexpired.)

j   Purchased typewriter ribbons on account, $36.

k   Maria withdrew $800 for personal use.

l   Paid clerical assistant's salary, $575.

m   Determined that $110 worth of office supplies had been used during the month.

The following accounts are used by Valdez Accounting Services:

Cash	Maria Valdez, Capital
Accounts Receivable	Maria Valdez, Drawing
Office Supplies	Fees Earned
Prepaid Insurance	Rent Expense
Office Equipment	Salary Expense
Accounts Payable	Supplies Expense

INSTRUCTIONS

Analyze each transaction by determining:

     a. Accounts?

     b. Classification (asset, liability, owner's equity, revenue, expense, or drawing)?

     c. Effect (+ or −)?

     d. How (dr. or cr.)?

Use the following format:

Transaction	Account	Classification	Effect (+ or −)	How (dr. or cr.)

PROBLEM 3-4A

T-ACCOUNTS;
FINANCIAL STATEMENTS
(L.O.1, 2)

INSTRUCTIONS

1. Set up T-accounts for all the accounts used by Valdez Accounting Services in Problem 3-3A.

2. Record the transactions described in Problem 3-3A in the T-accounts. (Note: If Problem 3-3A has been completed, refer to your transaction analysis from Problem 3-3A.)

3. Compute the account balances.

4. For the month of September 19X1, prepare the following financial statements:

   a. Income statement.

   b. Statement of owner's equity.

   c. Balance sheet.

Problems—Set B

PROBLEM 3-1B
TRANSACTION ANALYSIS
(L.O.2, 3)

Debra Washington, a financial planner, established a sole proprietorship known as First Financial Services. Following are transactions for July 19X1, the first month of operations:

Transaction

a   Debra invested $6,000 in her new business.

b   Paid $3,600 for equipment.

c   Purchased $255 worth of supplies on account.

d   Performed financial services for a client who paid $1,250 in cash.

e   Paid $175 to a creditor on account.

f   Paid for a small repair to the equipment, $28.

g   Performed financial services for a customer on account, $925.

h   Paid monthly rent, $400.

i   Received a $600 payment on account from a charge customer.

j   Paid secretary's salary, $325.

k   Debra withdrew $500 for personal use.

l   Determined that $130 worth of supplies had been used during the month.

The following accounts are used by First Financial Services:

Cash	Debra Washington, Drawing
Accounts Receivable	Fees Earned
Supplies	Rent Expense
Equipment	Repair Expense
Accounts Payable	Salary Expense
Debra Washington, Capital	Supplies Expense

INSTRUCTIONS

Analyze each transaction by determining:

  a. Accounts?

  b. Classification (asset, liability, owner's equity, revenue, expense, or drawing)?

  c. Effect (+ or −)?

  d. How (dr. or cr.)?

Use the following format:

Transaction	Account	Classification	Effect (+ or −)	How (dr. or cr.)

PROBLEM 3-2B
T-ACCOUNTS;
FINANCIAL STATEMENTS
(L.O.1, 2)

INSTRUCTIONS

1. Set up T-accounts for all the accounts used by First Financial Services in Problem 3-1B.

2. Record the transactions described in Problem 3-1B in the T-accounts. (Note: If Problem 3-1B has been completed, refer to your transaction analysis from Problem 3-1B.)

3. Compute the account balances.

4. For the month of July 19X1, prepare the following financial statements:

  a. Income statement.

  b. Statement of owner's equity.

  c. Balance sheet.

PROBLEM 3-3B
TRANSACTION ANALYSIS
(L.O.2, 3)

John Ricardo, an attorney, established a sole proprietorship known as Ricardo Legal Services. Following are transactions for the month of September 19X1, the first month of operations:

Transaction
a   John invested $6,000 cash in the business.

b   Purchased computer equipment on account, $850.

c   Billed a client for legal services performed on account, $925.

d   Paid $267 for letterhead stationery.

e   Paid $400 to a creditor on account.

f   Performed legal services for cash, $600.

g   Paid monthly rent, $700.

b   Received payment on account from a charge client, $600.

i   Prepaid a one-year insurance premium covering the period September 19X1 through August 19X2, $315. (Hint: Insurance, like supplies, is considered an asset as long as it is unused or unexpired.)

j   Purchased yellow legal paper on account, $42.

k   John withdrew $900 for personal use.

l   Paid part-time assistant's salary, $550.

m   Determined that $95 worth of office supplies had been used during the month.

The following accounts are used by Ricardo Legal Services:

Cash	John Ricardo, Capital
Accounts Receivable	John Ricardo, Drawing
Office Supplies	Fees Earned
Prepaid Insurance	Rent Expense
Computer Equipment	Salary Expense
Accounts Payable	Supplies Expense

INSTRUCTIONS

Analyze each transaction by determining:

a. Accounts?

b. Classification (asset, liability, owner's equity, revenue, expense, or drawing)?

c. Effect (+ or −)?

d. How (dr. or cr.)?

Use the following format:

Transaction	Account	Classification	Effect (+ or −)	How (dr. or cr.)

PROBLEM 3-4B
T-ACCOUNTS;
FINANCIAL STATEMENTS
(L.O.1, 2)

INSTRUCTIONS

1. Set up T-accounts for all the accounts used by Ricardo Legal Services in Problem 3-3B.

2. Record the transactions described in Problem 3-3B in the T-accounts. (Note: If Problem 3-3B has been completed, refer to your transaction analysis from Problem 3-3B.)

3. Compute the account balances.

4. For the month of September 19X1, prepare the following financial statements:

   a. Income statement.

   b. Statement of owner's equity.

   c. Balance sheet.

Mini-Cases

CASE 3-1

Your friend, Michael Roberts, is taking a beginning accounting course. Michael is having some difficulty understanding debits and credits and asks you for assistance. How would you explain debits and credits?

CASE 3-2

You are a self-employed accountant, performing services for a number of clients. One of your clients is sloppy about recording daily transactions, but expects you to prepare accurate financial statements based on the recorded data he submits to you. How would you respond to this situation?

CASE 3-3

DuPage Laundry and Dry Cleaning uses only one revenue account. Revenue, however, is derived from two sources: laundry and dry cleaning. The owner, Ron Maguire, would like more detailed revenue information from his accounting records. What would you suggest?

CHAPTER 4

Journalizing and Posting

L E A R N I N G
O B J E C T I V E S

AFTER STUDYING THIS CHAPTER, YOU SHOULD BE ABLE TO:

1 Record journal entries in a general journal.

2 Post from the journal to the ledger.

3 Prepare a trial balance.

In Chapter 3, you analyzed transactions and recorded the debits and credits in T-accounts. However, T-accounts are only a rough-draft device. You are now ready to study how transactions are formally recorded in the financial records of a business through the use of a journal and a ledger.

▮▮▮▮ THE GENERAL JOURNAL

OBJECTIVE 1
RECORD JOURNAL
ENTRIES IN A GENERAL
JOURNAL

In previous chapters, you learned to analyze, classify, and record transactions using a three-step process. We will continue to use that process in this chapter. However, in Step 3, instead of using T-accounts, we will record a journal entry.

Journal entries are always recorded in a book known as a journal. The journal is often referred to as the book of original entry because this is where the formal recording process begins. The two-column journal (one Debit column and one Credit column) we will be using is known as a general journal. Any transaction, no matter how complex, can be recorded in a general journal. Later in the text we will consider more specialized types of journals.

A separate journal entry must be prepared for each transaction. Each journal entry must:

- Include a debit part and a credit part.

- Balance—meaning the debits must equal the credits.

Balance between debits and credits is necessary if we are to keep the accounting equation in balance. To maintain balance, each journal entry requires the use of at least two accounts: the account being debited and the account being credited. This system is often referred to as double-entry accounting. An entry requiring debits to more than one account and/or credits to more than one account is known as a compound journal entry. As in all journal entries, total debits must equal total credits.

The process of recording journal entries is known as journalizing. To demonstrate how transactions are journalized, let's return to The Kitchen Taylor.

▮ TRANSACTION *(a)*

Step 1:   On January 1, 19X1, Dennis Taylor invested $10,000 cash in his new business in a checking account in the name of The Kitchen Taylor.

Step 2:
Account?	Cash
Classification?	Asset
Effect?	+ $10,000
How?	Debit

Account?   Dennis Taylor, Capital
Classification?   Owner's Equity
Effect?   + $10,000
How?   Credit

Step 3:   Journalize. *(Book the entry)*

GENERAL JOURNAL					Page 1
Date	Description	Post. Ref.	Debit	Credit	
19X1 Jan. 1	Cash *Debit first (always)*		10,000 00		
	Dennis Taylor, Capital			10,000 00	
	To record original investment.				

normal balance of assets - debits.   *normal Balance of liabilities + owner's eq - credit*

||||||||||||||||||||||
C O M M E N T

Journal entries are formal in tone:

● No abbreviations (except the date).

● Complete account titles.

● A fixed format that does not change.

Each item of information recorded in an entry has a certain position in which it is written. There is only one acceptable format. You must be sure to follow it carefully.

Using Transaction *(a)* as an example, let's study the preparation of a journal entry in greater detail.

Enter the date.

GENERAL JOURNAL					Page 1
Date	Description	Post. Ref.	Debit	Credit	
19X1 Jan. 1					

The first date entered at the top of the Date column must be complete: year, month, and day. The year and month need not be repeated unless they change while on this page. However, every entry must contain the day of the month, regardless of how many transactions occurred on the same date. The day of the month not only dates the entry but also serves as a visual cue that a new entry is beginning.

Enter the title of the account to be debited.

GENERAL JOURNAL   Page 1

Date		Description	Post. Ref.	Debit	Credit
19X1 Jan.	1	Cash			

Observe the position in which the account title is written. The debit part of the entry always comes first, and all debit account titles should start at the beginning (left) of the Description column. In a compound entry, all debit account titles would be written in this debit position. Remember, the account title must be complete—not a description of the transaction or an abbreviated version of the title.

Enter the debit amount in the Debit column.

GENERAL JOURNAL   Page 1

Date		Description	Post. Ref.	Debit	Credit
19X1 Jan.	1	Cash		10,000 00	

Note that dollar signs are not used in the journal. Also note that the Posting Reference column is left blank. This will be filled in during the posting process, which will occur later.

Enter the title of the account to be credited.

GENERAL JOURNAL   Page 1

Date		Description	Post. Ref.	Debit	Credit
19X1 Jan.	1	Cash		10,000 00	
		Dennis Taylor, Capital			

Observe the position in which the account title is written. The credit part of the entry always comes second, and all credit account titles are indented about one-half inch from the beginning (left) of the Description column. In a compound entry, all credit account titles are written in this credit position. Anyone scanning the Description column can tell immediately whether an account is being debited or credited by the position in which it is written. Position, or format, communicates information, so it is very important.

Enter the credit amount in the Credit column.

		GENERAL JOURNAL			Page 1
Date		Description	Post. Ref.	Debit	Credit
19X1 Jan.	1	Cash		10,000 00	
		Dennis Taylor, Capital			10,000 00

Again observe that no dollar signs are used and that the Posting Reference column is left blank. A blank Posting Reference column indicates that this information has not yet been transferred to the appropriate account.

Enter a brief explanation of the transaction.

		GENERAL JOURNAL			Page 1
Date		Description	Post. Ref.	Debit	Credit
19X1 Jan.	1	Cash		10,000 00	
		Dennis Taylor, Capital			10,000 00
		(To record original investment.)			

This could prove to be quite helpful in case of an error or if a transaction needed to be reconstructed at a later date. Observe the position in which the explanation is written. It is indented approximately one-half inch to the right of the credit position. Every line of the explanation begins at the same point. An explanation is not a required part of every journal entry. Accountants tend to use explanations only for nonroutine transactions. For beginning students, however, it is a good idea to write an explanation for every journal entry.

After Transactions (a) through (k) have been recorded, The Kitchen Taylor's journal appears as shown in Figure 4-1.

for 6 steps journal

FIGURE 4 - 1

GENERAL JOURNAL

Page 1

Date		Description	Post. Ref.	Debit		Credit	
19X1 Jan.	1	Cash		10,000	00		
		Dennis Taylor, Capital				10,000	00
		To record original investment.					
	3	Truck		6,000	00		
		Cash				6,000	00
		Purchased truck.					
	4	Supplies		125	00		
		Accounts Payable				125	00
		Purchased supplies.					
	7	Cash		500	00		
		Fees Earned				500	00
		Services performed.					
	10	Accounts Payable		125	00		
		Cash				125	00
		Paid creditor on account.					
	15	Accounts Receivable		400	00		
		Fees Earned				400	00
		Services performed.					
	17	Rent Expense		300	00		
		Cash				300	00
		Paid monthly rent.					
	21	Cash		100	00		
		Accounts Receivable				100	00
		Received payment on account.					

▮ **FIGURE 4 - 1** *(concluded)*

	26	Repair Expense			25	00		
		Accounts Payable					25	00
		Small repair to truck.						
	28	Dennis Taylor, Drawing			200	00		
		Cash					200	00
		Withdrawal for personal use.						
	31	Supplies Expense			75	00		
		Supplies					75	00
		Supplies used during January.						

▮▮▮▮ **POSTING TO THE LEDGER**

OBJECTIVE 2
POST FROM THE
JOURNAL TO THE
LEDGER

A **ledger** is simply a group of accounts. We will keep our ledger in book form. In practice, such a book probably would be a loose-leaf binder with a separate page for each account.

CHART OF ACCOUNTS

A **chart of accounts** is displayed at the front of the ledger. The Kitchen Taylor's chart of accounts is shown below.

Chart of Accounts

Assets	Owner's Equity
110 Cash	310 Dennis Taylor, Capital
111 Accounts Receivable	320 Dennis Taylor, Drawing
112 Supplies	**Revenue**
120 Truck	410 Fees Earned
Liabilities	**Expenses**
210 Accounts Payable	510 Rent Expense
	511 Repair Expense
	512 Supplies Expense

This chart shows the arrangement of the accounts within the ledger, as well as the official account titles and account numbers. Every account in the ledger has a number assigned according to a particular numbering system. The numbering system may vary from company to company. However, account numbers generally indicate classifications of accounts and placement within a particular classification.

POSTING

Journalizing transactions is the first step in our recording process. The journal contains information grouped by transaction and arranged in chronological order. The second step in our recording process is to transfer this information from the journal to the ledger. This process is known as posting. As we post to the ledger, this information is sorted by account. How often we post depends on our volume of transactions and our need for timely information. Most companies post daily or weekly.

After completing the journalizing and posting, the same information is in two places and in two different kinds of order:

Journal → Chronological (date) order

Ledger → Account order

This is a very advantageous arrangement. Keep in mind that the recording of data is not the end of the road. If the recorded data are to serve a useful purpose, we must be able to access the data conveniently at a later date. It is sometimes convenient to access information by date, or perhaps we might find it useful to access information in the context of a particular transaction; in such situations, we would refer to the journal. On the other hand, it is sometimes more convenient to access information by account; in that case, we would refer to the ledger.

In posting from the journal, we simply start at the top of the journal page and proceed down the page, line by line. Don't skip around! That greatly increases the potential for error.

After locating the appropriate account in the ledger, the posting procedure consists of five basic steps:

1. Enter the **date.**

2. Enter the **amount.**

3. Enter the new **balance.**

4. Enter the **posting reference** in the ledger account (journal page number).

5. Enter the **posting reference** in the journal (account number).

on Test
2-1 To T accounts
then Book entries - page - 84
31, 33, 62, 85, 89, 90, 91, 92, 93

Observe that the two posting references serve as a cross-reference between the journal and the ledger. The posting reference in the journal looks forward and indicates where we put the data. The posting reference in the ledger account looks backward and indicates where we got the data.

Let's practice our five-step posting procedure. We will begin by posting the debit portion of the entry as shown in Figure 4-2.

FIGURE 4 - 2

GENERAL JOURNAL
Page 1

Date	Description	Post. Ref.	Debit	Credit
19X1 Jan. 1	Cash	110	10,000 00	
	Dennis Taylor, Capital			10,000 00
	To record original investment.			

LEDGER

Account **Cash** Account No. 110

Date	Item	Post. Ref.	Debit	Credit	Balance Debit	Balance Credit
19X1 Jan. 1	Balance	J1	10,000 00		10,000 00	

Next, we will post the credit portion of the entry using the same five-step posting procedure. The posting of the credit is shown in Figure 4-3.

Figure 4-4 shows The Kitchen Taylor's journal and ledger after Transactions *(a)* through *(k)* have been journalized and posted.

|||||||||||||||||||||
C O M M E N T

Since The Kitchen Taylor is a new business, there are no beginning balances in the ledger accounts on January 1. In time, of course, The Kitchen Taylor will have to carry existing balances forward to the top of a new page. A balance that has been carried forward to the top of a new page is marked by writing the word *balance* in the Item column and placing a check mark in the Posting Reference column.

FIGURE 4 - 3

GENERAL JOURNAL

Page 1

Date		Description	Post. Ref.	Debit		Credit	
19X1 Jan.	1	Cash	110	10,000	00		
		Dennis Taylor, Capital	310			10,000	00
		To record original investment.					

①

⑤

LEDGER

②

Account **Dennis Taylor, Capital** ④ Account No. 310

Date		Item	Post. Ref.	Debit		Credit		Balance			
								Debit		Credit	
19X1 Jan.	1		J1			10,000	00	③		10,000	00

FIGURE 4 - 4

GENERAL JOURNAL

Page 1

Date		Description	Post. Ref.	Debit		Credit	
19X1 Jan.	1	Cash	110	10,000	00		
		Dennis Taylor, Capital	310			10,000	00
		To record original investment.					
	3	Truck	120	6,000	00		
		Cash	110			6,000	00
		Purchased truck.					

FIGURE 4 - 4 *(continued)*

4	Supplies	112	125	00				
	Accounts Payable	210					125	00
	Purchased supplies.							
7	Cash	110	500	00				
	Fees Earned	410					500	00
	Services performed.							
10	Accounts Payable	210	125	00				
	Cash	110					125	00
	Paid creditor on account.							
15	Accounts Receivable	111	400	00				
	Fees Earned	410					400	00
	Services performed.							
17	Rent Expense	510	300	00				
	Cash	110					300	00
	Paid monthly rent.							
21	Cash	110	100	00				
	Accounts Receivable	111					100	00
	Received payment on account.							
26	Repair Expense	511	25	00				
	Accounts Payable	210					25	00
	Small repair to truck.							
28	Dennis Taylor, Drawing	320	200	00				
	Cash	110					200	00
	Withdrawal for personal use.							
31	Supplies Expense	512	75	00				
	Supplies	112					75	00
	Supplies used during January.							

FIGURE 4 - 4 (continued)

LEDGER

Account **Cash** _____ Account No. 110

Date		Item	Post. Ref.	Debit		Credit		Balance Debit		Credit
19X1 Jan.	1		J1	10,000	00			10,000	00	
	3		J1			6,000	00	4,000	00	
	7		J1	500	00			4,500	00	
	10		J1			125	00	4,375	00	
	17		J1			300	00	4,075	00	
	21		J1	100	00			4,175	00	
	28		J1			200	00	3,975	00	

Account **Accounts Receivable** _____ Account No. 111

Date		Item	Post. Ref.	Debit		Credit		Balance Debit		Credit
19X1 Jan.	15		J1	400	00			400	00	
	21		J1			100	00	300	00	

Account **Supplies** _____ Account No. 112

Date		Item	Post. Ref.	Debit		Credit		Balance Debit		Credit
19X1 Jan.	4		J1	125	00			125	00	
	31		J1			75	00	50	00	

FIGURE 4 - 4 *(continued)*

Account **Truck**   Account No. 120

Date		Item	Post. Ref.	Debit		Credit		Balance			
								Debit		Credit	
19X1 Jan.	3		J1	6,000	00			6,000	00		

Account **Accounts Payable**   Account No. 210

Date		Item	Post. Ref.	Debit		Credit		Balance			
								Debit		Credit	
19X1 Jan.	4		J1			125	00			125	00
	10		J1	125	00					—0—	
	26		J1			25	00			25	00

Account **Dennis Taylor, Capital**   Account No. 310

Date		Item	Post. Ref.	Debit		Credit		Balance			
								Debit		Credit	
19X1 Jan.	1		J1			10,000	00			10,000	00

Account **Dennis Taylor, Drawing**   Account No. 320

Date		Item	Post. Ref.	Debit		Credit		Balance			
								Debit		Credit	
19X1 Jan.	28		J1	200	00			200	00		

■ FIGURE 4 - 4 *(concluded)*

Account __**Fees Earned**__ _____ Account No. ___410___

Date		Item	Post. Ref.	Debit	Credit	Balance	
						Debit	Credit
19X1 Jan.	7		J1		500 00		500 00
	15		J1		400 00		900 00

Account __**Rent Expense**__ _____ Account No. ___510___

Date		Item	Post. Ref.	Debit	Credit	Balance	
						Debit	Credit
19X1 Jan.	17		J1	300 00		300 00	

Account __**Repair Expense**__ _____ Account No. ___511___

Date		Item	Post. Ref.	Debit	Credit	Balance	
						Debit	Credit
19X1 Jan.	26		J1	25 00		25 00	

Account __**Supplies Expense**__ _____ Account No. ___512___

Date		Item	Post. Ref.	Debit	Credit	Balance	
						Debit	Credit
19X1 Jan.	31		J1	75 00		75 00	

▌▌▌▌ THE TRIAL BALANCE

OBJECTIVE 3
PREPARE A TRIAL
BALANCE

After completing the journalizing and posting for the month, we prepare financial statements that summarize the financial activity for the month. But, before we invest all the time necessary to prepare statements, it would be wise to verify that our accounting equation is in balance—that total debits equal total credits. To check for equality, we prepare a **trial balance** as shown in Figure 4-5.

The trial balance is not a statement. It is a trial to test the overall balance of the debits and credits in the ledger. It is easy to prepare. Simply follow these steps:

1. Make sure that all transactions have been journalized and posted.

2. Take out a sheet of two-column paper—or rule it yourself. You will need one Debit column and one Credit column.

3. At the top, write in a three-line heading: company name, trial balance, and date.

4. Referring to the ledger, write down the title of each account with a balance. Insert the balance in the appropriate column indicating whether it is a debit or credit balance.

▌ **FIGURE 4 - 5**

THE KITCHEN TAYLOR
Trial Balance *as of*
January 31, 19X1

	Debit		Credit	
Cash	3,975	00		
Accounts Receivable	300	00		
Supplies	50	00		
Truck	6,000	00		
Accounts Payable			25	00
Dennis Taylor, Capital			10,000	00
Dennis Taylor, Drawing	200	00		
Fees Earned			900	00
Rent Expense	300	00		
Repair Expense	25	00		
Supplies Expense	75	00		
	10,925	00	10,925	00

5. When all accounts and balances have been listed, total the Debit and Credit columns.

6. Compare the totals and check for balance.

LOCATING ERRORS IN THE TRIAL BALANCE

If the trial balance does not balance, we have made an error that has created an inequality between debits and credits. Now we must locate the error. Before actually beginning the search, some simple calculations can be made that might be helpful.

1. Find the difference between the debit and credit totals to determine how much we are out of balance. We can then scan the amount columns in the journal to see if we might have forgotten to post such a figure.

2. Divide the difference by 2. It is possible that we mistakenly posted a debit as a credit or vice versa.

3. Try dividing the difference by 9. If the difference is *evenly* divisible by 9 (no remainder), there is a high probability that we made one of the following two errors:

   a. Transposition. This occurs when the digits in a number are inadvertently rearranged. For example, the number $427 is rewritten as $247—the digits are all there, but they are transposed in the wrong order.

   b. Slide. This occurs when the decimal point is inserted in the wrong place. For example, the figure $5,245 is incorrectly written as $52.45.

These simple calculations do not tell us the exact nature and location of our error. However, they give us some useful hints and something to watch for as we actually search for the error.

We need to search for the error in an organized fashion. It is usually most efficient to search in reverse order:

1. Re-add the Trial Balance columns.

2. Trace each balance on the trial balance back to the ledger account from which it came.

3. Recompute the balance of each account in the ledger.

4. Trace each posting in each ledger account back to the journal entry from which it came. *Posting Ref.*

5. Check the equality of debits and credits in the journal.

When the error is located, we make the necessary correction and bring the trial balance into balance. We are then ready to prepare financial statements (income statement, statement of owner's equity, and balance sheet).

LIMITATIONS OF A TRIAL BALANCE

Keep in mind that a trial balance only tests the overall equality of debits and credits in the ledger. Any error upsetting this equality will throw the trial balance out of balance. However, it is possible to make other types of errors not affecting the overall equality of debits and credits. For example:

1. Posting the correct debit or credit amount to the wrong account.

2. Failing to journalize or post an entire transaction.

Such errors will not cause the trial balance to be out of balance. A trial balance is extremely useful in detecting errors, but you must remember its limitations.

Chapter Summary

In this chapter, we further refined our process of recording business transactions. We are now able to journalize transactions—make journal entries in a general journal in order to formally record transactions in the financial records of a business. Each transaction requires a separate journal entry. Each entry must:

- Include a debit part and a credit part.
- Balance—the debits must equal the credits.

In addition, journal entries are formal in tone:

- No abbreviations (except the date).
- Complete account titles.
- A fixed format that does not change.

Journalizing is the first step in our recording process. The second step is to transfer the information from the journal to the ledger (a group of accounts). This process is known as *posting*. As we post, the information is sorted by account.

At the end of the month, after all transactions have been journalized and posted, we prepare financial statements that summarize the financial activity for the month. Before preparing statements, however, we want to be sure our accounting equation is in balance—that total debits equal total credits. To check for equality, we prepare a trial balance. Once the trial balance is in balance, we prepare financial statements (income statement, statement of owner's equity, and balance sheet).

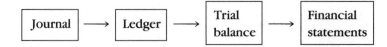

Accounting data flows through a business in an orderly pattern. The above flowchart demonstrates this pattern as studied up to this point.

Glossary

BALANCE—JOURNAL ENTRY

Debits equal credits.

CHART OF ACCOUNTS

A list showing the arrangement of the accounts within the ledger, as well as the official account titles and account numbers.

COMPOUND JOURNAL ENTRY

A journal entry requiring debits and/or credits to more than one account.

DOUBLE-ENTRY ACCOUNTING

A system requiring a minimum of two accounts in each journal entry: the account being debited and the account being credited. This is necessary to keep the accounting equation in balance.

GENERAL JOURNAL

A two-column journal, one Debit column and one Credit column.

JOURNAL

A book in which journal entries are recorded. Frequently referred to as the book of original entry, since this is where the formal recording process begins.

JOURNAL ENTRY

Formally records a transaction in the financial records of a business. Must include a debit part and a credit part. Debits must equal credits.

JOURNALIZING

The process of recording journal entries.

LEDGER

A group of accounts.

POSTING

The process of transferring information from the journal to the ledger.

POSTING REFERENCE

A cross-reference between the journal and the ledger.

SLIDE

An error occurring when a decimal point is inserted in the wrong place.

TRANSPOSITION
An error involving the rearrangement of the digits within a number.

TRIAL BALANCE
A list of accounts and balances to test the overall equality, or balance, of debits and credits in the ledger.

Questions for Discussion

1. Why is the journal often referred to as the book of original entry?

2. Describe how journal entries are formal in tone.

3. What is a compound journal entry?

4. Why must every journal entry balance?

5. Would it be more convenient to use the journal or the ledger in the following?

   a. To access information by account.

   b. To access information in the context of a particular transaction.

6. What are the five basic steps in the posting procedure?

7. What is the purpose of a trial balance?

8. a. How do we test for transpositions and slides?

   b. Give an example of (1) a transposition and (2) a slide.

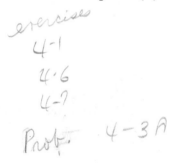

Exercises

EXERCISE 4-1
JOURNAL ENTRIES
(L.O.1)

Chung Company's ledger contains the following accounts: Cash; Accounts Receivable; Supplies; Office Equipment; Accounts Payable; Grace Chung, Capital; Grace Chung, Drawing; Fees Earned; Rent Expense; Utilities Expense; and Miscellaneous Expense. Record the following transactions for July 19X1 in a general journal:

July 1   Purchased $600 worth of supplies for cash.

3   Purchased office equipment on account, $5,500.

7   Paid monthly rent, $700.

8   Performed services on account, $12,000.

12   Paid creditor on account, $5,500.

17   The owner withdrew $2,000 in cash for personal use.

22   Performed services for cash, $1,750.

29   Received payment on account from charge customer, $635.

30   Paid electricity bill, $130.

EXERCISE 4-2
JOURNAL ENTRIES
(L.O.1)

GOULD MEDICAL ASSOCIATES
Chart of Accounts

Assets
110   Cash
111   Accounts Receivable
112   Supplies
113   Equipment

Liabilities
210   Accounts Payable

Owner's Equity
310   Mark Gould, Capital
320   Mark Gould, Drawing

Revenue
410   Professional Fees

Expenses
510   Salary Expense
511   Utilities Expense
512   Repair Expense

Record the following transactions for May 19X2 in a general journal (number the journal page 8):

May 1   Mark Gould, the owner, invested $10,000 cash in the business.

  2   Performed services on account, $5,000.

  3   Performed services for cash, $1,500.

  7   Purchased supplies on account, $1,236.

  10   Received payment on account from charge customer, $5,000.

  14   Paid employees' salaries, $875.

  15   The owner withdrew $2,000 cash for personal use.

  19   Paid electricity bill, $265.

  21   Paid creditor on account, $736.

  25   Paid for small plumbing repair, $40.

  30   Purchased $5,000 worth of equipment, paying $1,000 in cash and the remainder on account.

EXERCISE 4-3
POSTING
(L.O.2)

1. Referring to the chart of accounts given in Exercise 4-2, open up ledger accounts inserting the title and account number for each account.

2. Referring to Exercise 4-2, post from the journal to the ledger.

EXERCISE 4-4
POSTING
(L.O.2)

1. Open up ledger accounts, inserting account title and number, for the following:

Account Title	Account Number
Cash	110
Accounts Receivable	111
Supplies	112
Equipment	120
Accounts Payable	210
Fees Earned	410
Repair Expense	512

2. Post the following journal entries:

GENERAL JOURNAL   Page 1

Date		Description	Post. Ref.	Debit		Credit	
19X8 Jul.	1	Cash		1,000	00		
		Fees Earned				1,000	00
		Services performed.					
	6	Supplies		200	00		
		Acounts Payable				200	00
		Purchased supplies.					
	9	Accounts Receivable		2,500	00		
		Fees earned				2,500	00
		Services performed.					
	14	Accounts Payable		100	00		
		Cash				100	00
		Paid creditor on account.					
	19	Cash		1,500	00		
		Accounts Receivable				1,500	00
		Payment on account.					
	24	Equipment		1,000	00		
		Cash				500	00
		Accounts Payable				500	00
		Purchased equipment.					
	31	Repair Expense		75	00		
		Cash				75	00
		Equipment repair.					

EXERCISE 4-5
TRIAL BALANCE
(L.O.3)

Following is the ledger for Garcia Company as it appears on November 30, 19X5. Prepare a trial balance as of November 30, 19X5.

LEDGER

Account __Cash__   Account No. __110__

Date		Item	Post. Ref.	Debit		Credit		Balance			
								Debit		Credit	
19X5 Nov.	1		J26	18,000	00			18,000	00		
	2		J26			1,200	00	16,800	00		
	3		J26			1,500	00	15,300	00		
	17		J26			500	00	14,800	00		
	20		J26			200	00	14,600	00		
	23		J26			3,000	00	11,600	00		
	28		J26			1,450	00	10,150	00		
	29		J26			3,000	00	7,150	00		
	29		J26	1,800	00			8,950	00		

Account __Accounts Receivable__   Account No. __111__

Date		Item	Post. Ref.	Debit		Credit		Balance			
								Debit		Credit	
19X5 Nov.	2		J26	7,300	00			7,300	00		
	29		J26			1,800	00	5,500	00		
	30		J26	3,700	00			9,200	00		

Account **Supplies**　　　　　　　　　　　　　　　　　Account No. 112

Date		Item	Post. Ref.	Debit		Credit		Balance			
								Debit		Credit	
19X5 Nov.	3		J26	1,500	00			1,500	00		

Account **Office Equipment**　　　　　　　　　　　　Account No. 120

Date		Item	Post. Ref.	Debit		Credit		Balance			
								Debit		Credit	
19X5 Nov.	9		J26	3,500	00			3,500	00		

Account **Truck**　　　　　　　　　　　　　　　　　　Account No. 121

Date		Item	Post. Ref.	Debit		Credit		Balance			
								Debit		Credit	
19X5 Nov.	23		J26	12,000	00			12,000	00		

Account **Accounts Payable**　　　　　　　　　　　　Account No. 210

Date		Item	Post. Ref.	Debit		Credit		Balance			
								Debit		Credit	
19X5 Nov.	9		J26			3,500	00			3,500	00
	17		J26	500	00					3,000	00

Account __Notes Payable__ _____ Account No. ___211___

Date		Item	Post. Ref.	Debit	Credit	Balance	
						Debit	Credit
19X5 Nov.	23		J26		9,000 00		9,000 00

Account __Carol Garcia, Capital__ _____ Account No. ___310___

Date		Item	Post. Ref.	Debit	Credit	Balance	
						Debit	Credit
19X5 Nov.	1		J26		18,000 00		18,000 00

Account __Carol Garcia, Drawing__ _____ Account No. ___320___

Date		Item	Post. Ref.	Debit	Credit	Balance	
						Debit	Credit
19X5 Nov.	29		J26	3,000 00		3,000 00	

Account __Fees Earned__ _____ Account No. ___410___

Date		Item	Post. Ref.	Debit	Credit	Balance	
						Debit	Credit
19X5 Nov.	2		J26		7,300 00		7,300 00
	30		J26		3,700 00		11,000 00

Account **Interest Expense**   Account No. 510

Date		Item	Post. Ref.	Debit		Credit		Balance	
								Debit	Credit
19X5 Nov.	20		J26	200	00			200	00	

Account **Rent Expense**   Account No. 511

Date		Item	Post. Ref.	Debit		Credit		Balance	
								Debit	Credit
19X5 Nov.	2		J26	1,200	00			1,200	00	

Account **Utilities Expense**   Account No. 512

Date		Item	Post. Ref.	Debit		Credit		Balance	
								Debit	Credit
19X5 Nov.	28		J26	1,450	00			1,450	00	

EXERCISE 4-6
EFFECT OF TRIAL
BALANCE ERRORS
(L.O.3)

1. Indicate whether or not each of the following errors would cause the trial balance to be out of balance (yes or no).

   a. A credit of $5,000 to Accounts Payable is posted as a credit of $500 to Accounts Payable.

   b. A debit of $250 to Supplies is posted as a credit of $250 to the Supplies account.

   c. A credit of $1,200 to Accounts Receivable is posted as a credit of $1,200 to Accounts Payable.

   d. A debit of $9,700 to Equipment is posted as a debit of $7,900 to the Equipment account.

e. A journal entry recording a $1,500 withdrawal by the owner is not posted at all.

f. A credit of $8,400 to Fees Earned was posted twice.

2. a. Which of the errors in part 1 involve a transposition?
   b. Which of the errors in part 1 involve a slide?

EXERCISE 4-7
ANSWER QUESTIONS
USING JOURNAL AND
LEDGER
(L.O.1, 2)

Based on the following journal and ledger for Washington Company, determine:

1. The account number of the Accounts Payable account.

2. The amount of money owed to creditors on October 13.

3. The purpose of the October 21 payment of cash.

4. The account title of Account No. 111.

5. The cost of the equipment purchased on October 10.

6. The amount of money owed to creditors as a result of the purchase of equipment.

7. The number of transactions involving cash during October.

GENERAL JOURNAL					Page 11	
Date		Description	Post. Ref.	Debit	Credit	
19X3 Oct.	1	Cash	110	12,000 00		
		Charles Washington, Capital	310		12,000	00
		Investment by owner.				
	2	Cash	110	5,400 00		
		Fees Earned	410		5,400	00
		Services performed.				
	3	Supplies	112	1,000 00		
		Accounts Payable	210		600	00
		Cash	110		400	00
		Purchased supplies.				

	6	Accounts Receivable	111	4,300	00				
		Fees Earned	410				4,300	00	
		Services performed.							
	10	Equipment	120	10,000	00				
		Cash	110				1,000	00	
		Accounts Payable	210				9,000	00	
		Purchased equipment.							
	15	Accounts Payable	210	200	00				
		Cash	110				200	00	
		Payment on account.							
	21	Repair Expense	510	350	00				
		Cash	110				350	00	
		Equipment repair.							
	24	Cash	110	2,000	00				
		Accounts Receivable	111				2,000	00	
		Payment on account.							
	27	Charles Washington, Drawing	320	1,800	00				
		Cash	110				1,800	00	
		Personal use.							

LEDGER

Account __Cash__   Account No. ___110___

Date		Item	Post. Ref.	Debit		Credit		Balance			
								Debit		Credit	
19X3 Oct.	1		J11	12,000	00			12,000	00		
	2		J11	4,500	00			16,500	00		
	3		J11			400	00	16,100	00		
	10		J11			1,000	00	15,100	00		
	15		J11			200	00	14,900	00		
	21		J11			350	00	14,550	00		
	24		J11	2,000	00			16,550	00		
	28		J11			1,800	00	14,750	00		

Account __Accounts Receivable__   Account No. ___111___

Date		Item	Post. Ref.	Debit		Credit		Balance			
								Debit		Credit	
19X3 Oct.	6		J11	4,300	00			4,300	00		
	24		J11			2,000	00	2,300	00		

Account __Supplies__   Account No. ___112___

Date		Item	Post. Ref.	Debit		Credit		Balance			
								Debit		Credit	
19X3 Oct.	3		J11	1,000	00			1,000	00		

Account **Equipment** _____ Account No. 120

Date		Item	Post. Ref.	Debit		Credit		Balance			
								Debit		Credit	
19X3 Oct.	10		J11	10,000	00			10,000	00		

Account **Accounts Payable** _____ Account No. 210

Date		Item	Post. Ref.	Debit		Credit		Balance			
								Debit		Credit	
19X3 Oct.	3		J11			600	00			600	00
	10		J11			9,000	00			9,600	00
	15		J11	200	00					9,400	00

Account **Charles Washington, Capital** _____ Account No. 310

Date		Item	Post. Ref.	Debit		Credit		Balance			
								Debit		Credit	
19X3 Oct.	1		J11			12,000	00			12,000	00

Account **Charles Washington, Drawing** _____ Account No. 320

Date		Item	Post. Ref.	Debit		Credit		Balance			
								Debit		Credit	
19X3 Oct.	27		J11	1,800	00			1,800	00		

Account **Fees Earned**						Account No. 410	
Date	Item	Post. Ref.	Debit	Credit	Balance		
					Debit	Credit	
19X3 Oct. 2		J11		5,400 00		5,400 00	
6		J11		4,300 00		9,700 00	

Account **Repair Expense**						Account No. 510	
Date	Item	Post. Ref.	Debit	Credit	Balance		
					Debit	Credit	
19X3 Oct. 21		J11	350 00		350 00		

EXERCISE 4-8

TRIAL BALANCE;
IDENTIFICATION OF
ERRORS
(L.O.3)

1. Referring to the ledger presented in Exercise 4-7, prepare a trial balance as of October 31, 19X3.

2. *a.* Does it balance?
   b. If not, find and describe the error.

Problems—Set A

Beautiful Costume Rentals was established by Judy Johnson on August 1, 19X1.

Chart of Accounts	
Assets	**Owner's Equity**
110 Cash	310 Judy Johnson, Capital
111 Accounts Receivable	320 Judy Johnson, Drawing
112 Supplies	
113 Prepaid Insurance	**Revenue**
114 Costumes	410 Rental Revenue
Liabilities	**Expenses**
210 Accounts Payable	510 Cleaning Expense
	511 Rent Expense
	512 Salary Expense
	513 Utilities Expense

The following transactions were completed during the first month of operations:

Aug. 1   Judy invested $5,000 cash in the business.

     2   Paid monthly rent, $620.

     3   Purchased $4,000 worth of costumes, paying $500 in cash and the remainder on account.

     7   Rented costumes for cash, $300.

     10   Prepaid a one-year insurance premium covering the period August 10, 19X1, through August 9, 19X2, $432.

     10   Paid creditor on account, $700.

     14   Rented costumes on account, $1,867.

     17   Paid employees' salaries, $430.

18   Received payment on account from charge customer, $219.

20   Purchased supplies for cash, $123.

21   Rented costumes: $800 cash, $400 on account.

24   Had costumes cleaned, agreeing to pay in the near future, $173.

26   Received payment on account from charge customer, $600.

28   Paid creditor on account, $772.

30   Paid electricity bill, $109.

31   Judy withdrew $365 in cash for personal use.

INSTRUCTIONS
Record these transactions in a general journal. Number journal pages beginning with page 1.

PROBLEM 4-2A
POSTING; TRIAL BALANCE; FINANCIAL STATEMENTS
(L.O.2, 3)
(Omit this problem if working papers are not being used.)

The general journal displayed in the workbook shows the entries recorded by Asher Data Services for the month of December 19X8.

INSTRUCTIONS

1. Post the journal to the ledger. (Since Asher Data Services has been in operation for a number of years, the existing balances have already been recorded in the ledger accounts.)

2. Prepare a trial balance as of December 31, 19X8.

3. Prepare financial statements for the year ending December 31, 19X8:

    a. Income statement.

    b. Statement of owner's equity.

    c. Balance sheet.

PROBLEM 4-3A
JOURNAL ENTRIES;
POSTING; TRIAL
BALANCE
(L.O.1–3)

Jackie's Hair Emporium began operations in January 19X1.

Chart of Accounts

Assets
110   Cash
111   Accounts Receivable
112   Supplies
113   Prepaid Insurance
114   Equipment

Liabilities
210   Accounts Payable

Owner's Equity
310   Jackie Williams, Capital
320   Jackie Williams, Drawing

Revenue
410   Hair Care Revenue

Expenses
510   Rent Expense
511   Salary Expense
512   Telephone Expense
513   Utilities Expense

The following transactions were completed during the first month of operations:

Jan. 1   The owner, Jackie Williams, invested $18,000 cash in the business.

  1   Paid monthly rent, $450.

  2   Purchased shampoo, conditioner, and hair color on account, $215.

  3   Purchased $6,000 worth of equipment, paying $1,000 in cash and the remainder on account.

  5   Performed hair care services for cash, $830.

  7   Paid creditor on account, $500.

  10   Performed hair care services on account, $510.

  15   Paid employees' salaries, $325.

  18   Purchased hair dryers on account, $348.

  21   Received payment on account from charge customer, $260.

  22   Paid electricity bill, $175.

  23   Prepaid one-year insurance premium covering the period January 23, 19X1, through January 22, 19X2, $469.

  25   Paid telephone bill, $175.

  26   Performed hair care services: $962 cash, $523 on account.

28   Received payment on account from charge customer, $140.

29   Paid water bill, $82.

31   The owner withdrew $300 in cash for personal use.

INSTRUCTIONS

1. Record the transactions in the general journal.

2. Post the journal to the ledger.

3. Prepare a trial balance as of January 31, 19X1.

PROBLEM 4-4A
JOURNAL ENTRIES;
POSTING; TRIAL
BALANCE
(L.O.1–3)

YANKEE COMPUTER SERVICES
Listing of Account Numbers, Titles,
and Balances as of June 1, 19X8

Number	Title	Balance	
110	Cash	$ 4,750	Dr.
111	Accounts Receivable	1,877	Dr.
112	Supplies	265	Dr.
113	Prepaid Insurance	321	Dr.
114	Computer Equipment	10,500	Dr.
115	Office Furniture	3,175	Dr.
210	Accounts Payable	2,426	Cr.
310	David Yankee, Capital	23,874	Cr.
320	David Yankee, Drawing	18,000	Dr.
410	Fees Earned	20,164	Cr.
510	Rent Expense	3,250	Dr.
511	Salary Expense	281	Dr.
512	Telephone Expense	1,810	Dr.
513	Utilities Expense	2,235	Dr.

The following transactions were completed by Yankee Computer Services during June 19X8:

June 1   Paid monthly rent, $650.

2   Purchased $8,000 worth of computer equipment, paying $1,000 in cash and the remainder on account.

5   Prepaid an insurance premium covering the period June 5, 19X8, through June 4, 19X9, $965.

6   Purchased a desk on account, $475.

11   Performed computer services on account, $2,350.

13   Paid creditor on account, $500.

16   Performed computer services for cash, $1,372.

18   Purchased computer paper on account, $278.

22   Received payment on account from charge customer, $700.

23   The owner invested an additional $5,000 cash in the business.

25   Performed computer services: $1,300 for cash, $2,500 on account.

27   Paid telephone bill, $362.

28   Paid electricity bill, $447.

29   The owner withdrew $1,500 in cash for personal use.

30   Paid employees' salaries, $839.

INSTRUCTIONS

1. For those students not using the working papers:

   a. This company uses a general journal. Number the journal pages beginning with page 41.

   b. Open ledger accounts inserting account titles, numbers, and balances as of June 1, 19X8.

2. Record the transactions in the general journal. (Number journal pages beginning with page 41.)

3. Post the journal to the ledger. (Since Yankee Computer Services has been in business for several years, June 1, 19X8, balances already exist in the ledger accounts.)

4. Prepare a trial balance as of June 30, 19X8.

Problems—Set B

PROBLEM 4-1B
JOURNAL ENTRIES
(L.O.1)

Spotless Cleaning Service was established by Barbara Jensen on August 1, 19X1.

Chart of Accounts

Assets
110 Cash
111 Accounts Receivable
112 Supplies
113 Prepaid Insurance
114 Equipment

Liabilities
210 Accounts Payable

Owner's Equity
310 Barbara Jensen, Capital
320 Barbara Jensen, Drawing

Revenue
410 Cleaning Revenue

Expenses
510 Rent Expense
511 Repair Expense
512 Salary Expense
513 Utilities Expense

The following transactions were completed during the first month of operations:

Aug. 1   Barbara invested $6,000 cash in the business.

2   Paid monthly rent, $675.

3   Purchased $4,200 worth of equipment, paying $800 in cash and the remainder on account.

7   Performed cleaning services for cash, $425.

10   Prepaid a one-year insurance premium covering the period August 10, 19X1, through August 9, 19X2, $397.

10   Paid creditor on account, $675.

14   Performed cleaning services on account, $1,932.

17   Paid employees' salaries, $455.

18   Received payment on account from charge customer, $250.

20   Purchased supplies for cash, $150.

21   Performed cleaning services: $300 cash, $700 on account.

24   Had equipment repaired, agreeing to pay in the near future, $185.

26   Received payment on account from charge customer, $630.

28   Paid creditor on account, $815.

30   Paid electricity bill, $157.

31   Barbara withdrew $280 in cash for personal use.

INSTRUCTIONS

Record these transactions in a general journal. Number journal pages beginning with page 1.

PROBLEM 4-2B
POSTING; TRIAL
BALANCE; FINANCIAL
STATEMENTS
(L.O.2, 3)
(Omit this problem if working papers are not being used.)

The general journal displayed in the workbook shows the entries recorded by Becker Advertising Agency for the month of December 19X8.

INSTRUCTIONS

1. Post the journal to the ledger. (Since Becker Advertising Agency has been in operation for a number of years, the existing balances have already been recorded in the ledger accounts.)

2. Prepare a trial balance as of December 31, 19X8.

3. Prepare financial statements for the year ending December 31, 19X8:

    a. Income statement.

    b. Statement of owner's equity.

    c. Balance sheet.

PROBLEM 4-3B
JOURNAL ENTRIES;
POSTING; TRIAL
BALANCE
(L.O.1–3)

Susan's Dog Grooming began operations in January 19X1.

Chart of Accounts

Assets
110 Cash
111 Accounts Receivable
112 Supplies
113 Prepaid Insurance
114 Equipment

Liabilities
210 Accounts Payable

Owner's Equity
310 Susan Cramer, Capital
320 Susan Cramer, Drawing

Revenue
410 Grooming Revenue

Expenses
510 Rent Expense
511 Salary Expense
512 Telephone Expense
513 Utilities Expense

The following transactions were completed during the first month of operations:

Jan. 1 The owner, Susan Cramer, invested $9,000 cash in the business.

1 Paid monthly rent, $425.

2 Purchased pet shampoo, flea spray, and disinfectant on account, $125.

3 Purchased $3,000 worth of equipment, paying $1,000 in cash and the remainder on account.

5 Performed grooming services for cash, $535.

7 Paid creditor on account, $250.

10 Performed grooming services on account, $480.

15 Paid employees' salaries, $295.

18 Purchased electric hair clippers on account, $88.

21 Received payment on account from charge customer, $195.

22 Paid electricity bill, $120.

23 Prepaid a one-year insurance premium covering the period January 23, 19X1, through January 22, 19X2, $297.

25 Paid telephone bill, $107.

26 Performed grooming services: $562 cash, $339 on account.

28   Received payment on account from charge customer, $115.

29   Paid water bill, $78.

31   The owner withdrew $240 in cash for personal use.

INSTRUCTIONS

1. Record the transactions in the general journal.

2. Post the journal to the ledger.

3. Prepare a trial balance as of January 31, 19X1.

PROBLEM 4-4B
JOURNAL ENTRIES;
POSTING; TRIAL
BALANCE
(L.O.1–3)

POST ACCOUNTING SERVICES
Listing of Account Numbers, Titles,
and Balances as of June 1, 19X8

Number	Title	Balance	
110	Cash	$ 4,675	Dr.
111	Accounts Receivable	1,772	Dr.
112	Supplies	296	Dr.
113	Prepaid Insurance	329	Dr.
114	Equipment	9,640	Dr.
115	Office Furniture	2,900	Dr.
210	Accounts Payable	2,570	Cr.
310	Jan Post, Capital	21,146	Cr.
320	Jan Post, Drawing	17,790	Dr.
410	Fees Earned	21,000	Cr.
510	Rent Expense	3,120	Dr.
511	Salary Expense	198	Dr.
512	Telephone Expense	1,943	Dr.
513	Utilities Expense	2,053	Dr.

The following transactions were completed by Post Accounting Services during June 19X8:

June   1   Paid monthly rent, $725.

2   Purchased $5,200 worth of equipment, paying $1,000 in cash and the remainder on account.

5   Prepaid insurance premium covering the period June 5, 19X8, through June 4, 19X9, $467.

6   Purchased a desk on account, $572.

11   Performed accounting services on account, $2,975.

13   Paid creditor on account, $480.

16   Performed accounting services for cash, $375.

18   Purchased columnar paper on account, $153.

22   Received payment on account from charge customer, $940.

23   The owner invested an additional $3,500 cash in the business.

25   Performed accounting services: $200 for cash, $2,330 on account.

27   Paid telephone bill, $267.

28   Paid electricity bill, $328.

29   The owner withdrew $1,250 in cash for personal use.

30   Paid employees' salaries, $925.

INSTRUCTIONS

1. For those students not using the working papers:

   a. This company uses a general journal. Number the journal pages beginning with page 51.

   b. Open ledger accounts inserting accounting titles, numbers, and balances as of June 1, 19X8.

2. Record the transactions in the general journal. (Number journal pages beginning with page 51.)

3. Post the journal to the ledger. (Since Post Accounting Services has been in business for several years, June 1, 19X8, balances already exist in the accounts.)

4. Prepare a trial balance as of June 30, 19X8.

Mini-Cases

CASE 4-1

You are hired as a consultant to suggest improvements in Hager Corporation's accounting procedures. In looking through their journal, you observe that explanations are never used. What would you suggest relative to the use of explanations in journal entries?

CASE 4-2

Bob Koval owns a travel agency and does his own accounting work. Bob prepares financial statements without ever taking a trial balance. He claims this saves him a lot of time. How would you respond to this situation?

CASE 4-3

You are the sole proprietor of a small business. You notice that your bookkeeper does not always fill in the posting reference columns when posting from the journal to the ledger. How would you respond to this situation?

CHAPTER 5

The Work Sheet and Adjustments

||||||||||||||||||||
L E A R N I N G
O B J E C T I V E S

AFTER STUDYING THIS CHAPTER, YOU SHOULD BE ABLE TO:

1 Describe the purpose of a work sheet.

2 Explain where the work sheet fits into the accounting cycle.

3 Prepare a work sheet.

4 Prepare financial statements directly from the work sheet.

5 Journalize and post adjusting entries.

In previous chapters, you learned to journalize, post, and prepare financial statements. You also learned how to prepare a trial balance to verify the equality of debits and credits before preparing financial statements. In a further attempt to prepare financial statements that are accurate and up to date, this chapter will show you how to prepare a work sheet.

▌▌▌▌ THE PURPOSE OF THE WORK SHEET

OBJECTIVE 1
DESCRIBE THE PURPOSE
OF A WORK SHEET

The **work sheet** is a tool used by accountants to rough draft adjustments and financial statements and also to check for mathematical accuracy. This process of rough drafting helps us organize information as well as detect and correct errors before preparing formal statements and journal entries.

A work sheet is not only useful but it is easy to prepare. You are already familiar with much of what appears on the work sheet. Adjustments and the work sheet format are all that is really new.

▌▌▌▌ PREPARING THE WORK SHEET

OBJECTIVE 2
EXPLAIN WHERE THE
WORK SHEET FITS INTO
THE ACCOUNTING
CYCLE

The work sheet is prepared at the end of the accounting period (for example, month or year) after transactions have been journalized and posted but before financial statements have been prepared. Since the work sheet is a rough-draft document, it is prepared in pencil.

OBJECTIVE 3
PREPARE A WORK SHEET

A work sheet is prepared in seven steps, as follows:

Step 1:   Prepare a three-line heading.

Step 2:   Prepare the trial balance.

Step 3:   Rough draft the adjustments.

Step 4:   Prepare the adjusted trial balance.

Step 5:   Rough draft the income statement and balance sheet.

Step 6:   Total and balance the Income Statement columns.

Step 7:   Total and balance the Balance Sheet columns.

Let's study these seven steps and demonstrate by preparing a year-end work sheet for The Kitchen Taylor.

Step 1:   Prepare a three-line heading containing:

   a. Company name.

   b. Work sheet.

   c. Date.

Step 2:   Prepare the trial balance.

There is nothing new here. We want to verify the equality of debits and credits in the ledger before proceeding to anything else. We will follow the procedures described in Chapter 4 to prepare the trial balance. However, when preparing a work sheet, the trial balance is written up on the work sheet rather than on a separate sheet of two-column paper.

Figure 5-1 shows The Kitchen Taylor's year-end work sheet completed through Step 2.

Step 3:   Rough draft the adjustments.

Adjusting entries are really updating entries. The need to update exists because a few **internal transactions** have occurred but have not yet been recorded (journalized). This is possible because internal transactions do not involve anyone outside the business. It is acceptable to allow these internal transactions to go unrecorded on a daily basis, but we cannot prepare financial statements with incorrect account balances. Therefore, before preparing financial statements, we must adjust or update the accounts in several areas.

In this chapter, we will study the adjustments for supplies, insurance, wages, and depreciation. The need to adjust for supplies was discussed in Chapters 2 and 3, and the need to adjust for insurance was noted briefly in Chapter 3. In those areas, the current discussion will review and reinforce those previous discussions.

a. SUPPLIES   When supplies are purchased, the asset account Supplies is debited (increased). As long as supplies are unused, they are considered to be an asset. Day to day, however, supplies are used. The cost of used supplies is an expense—Supplies Expense.

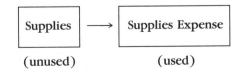

It is not practical to update the accounts (Supplies and Supplies Expense) on a daily basis as the supplies are actually used. Since the dollar amounts involved

FIGURE 5-1

THE KITCHEN TAYLOR
Work Sheet
For the Year Ended December 31, 19X1

Account Title	Trial Balance Debit	Trial Balance Credit	Adjustments Debit	Adjustments Credit
Cash	2,687 00			
Accounts Receivable	1,835 00			
Supplies	842 00			
Prepaid Insurance	1,200 00			
Truck	6,000 00			
Accounts Payable		960 00		
Dennis Taylor, Capital		10,000 00		
Dennis Taylor, Drawing	9,200 00			
Fees Earned		18,500 00		
Rent Expense	3,600 00			
Repair Expense	357 00			
Supplies Expense	75 00			
Utilities Expense	1,564 00			
Wages Expense	2,100 00			
	29,460 00	29,460 00		

in such daily transactions tend to be small, the cost of the paperwork would greatly exceed the benefit of such daily updating. Consequently, we wait until the end of the accounting period to update.

Referring to Figure 5-1, the Trial Balance columns show the Supplies account has a debit balance of $842. However, an inventory, or physical count, of supplies on hand on December 31 indicates that only $310 worth of unused supplies are left in the storeroom. The $532 difference ($842 − $310 = $532) represents the cost of used supplies.

$$\begin{array}{ll} \$842 & \text{Unused—beginning (asset)} \\ -310 & \text{Unused—end (asset)} \\ \hline \$532 & \text{Used (expense)} \end{array}$$

Based on this information, the following accounts must be adjusted:

Adjusted Trial Balance		Income Statement		Balance Sheet	
Debit	**Credit**	**Debit**	**Credit**	**Debit**	**Credit**

- The asset account, Supplies, must be decreased by a credit of $532.
- The Supplies Expense account must be increased by a debit of $532.

Summary:

Supplies		Supplies Expense	
Dr.	Cr.	Dr.	Cr.
842	− 532	+ 532	

|||||||||||||||||||||
C O M M E N T

T-accounts are being used to analyze The Kitchen Taylor's adjustments. After completion of the work sheet, we will journalize the adjustments and post to formal ledger accounts.

■ **FIGURE 5 - 2**

THE KITCHEN TAYLOR
Work Sheet
For the Year Ended December 31, 19X1

Account Title	Trial Balance Debit	Trial Balance Credit	Adjustments Debit	Adjustments Credit
Cash	2,687 00			
Accounts Receivable	1,835 00			
Supplies	842 00			(a) 532 00
Prepaid Insurance	1,200 00			(b) 300 00
Truck	6,000 00			
Accounts Payable		960 00		
Dennis Taylor, Capital		10,000 00		
Dennis Taylor, Drawing	9,200 00			
Fees Earned		18,500 00		
Rent Expense	3,600 00			
Repair Expense	357 00			
Supplies Expense	75 00		(a) 532 00	
Utilities Expense	1,564 00			
Wages Expense	2,100 00		(c) 30 00	
	29,460 00	29,460 00		
Insurance Expense			(b) 300 00	
Wages Payable				(c) 30 00
Depreciation Expense			(d) 1,100 00	
Accumulated Depreciation				(d) 1,100 00
			1,962 00	1,962 00

After adjustment, the December 31 financial statements will include:

Balance Sheet	Income Statement
Supplies $310 (unused)	Supplies expense $532 (used)

As shown in Figure 5-2, all the adjustments are written in the Adjustments columns of the work sheet.

Adjusted Trial Balance		Income Statement		Balance Sheet	
Debit	Credit	Debit	Credit	Debit	Credit

b. INSURANCE   Insurance coverage, like supplies, is always purchased in advance. The cost of the unexpired future coverage is something of value to the business and is recorded as an asset—Prepaid Insurance. As time goes by, however, the coverage is used up (expires). The cost of the expired coverage is now an expense—Insurance Expense.

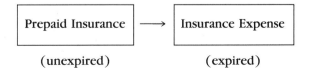

Prepaid Insurance ⟶ Insurance Expense

(unexpired)   (expired)

As with supplies, it is not practical to update the accounts (Prepaid Insurance and Insurance Expense) on a daily basis. Instead, we wait until the end of the accounting period.

Referring to Figure 5-1, the trial balance columns show the Prepaid Insurance account has a debit balance of $1,200. This $1,200 represents the cost of a 2-year, or 24-month, premium paid early in July. By December 31, six months (July through December) of that prepaid coverage has expired.

$$\frac{\$1,200}{24 \text{ months}} = \$50 \text{ per month}$$

$$6 \text{ months} \times \$50 \text{ per month} = \underline{\underline{\$300}}$$

Based on this information, the following accounts must be adjusted:

- The asset account, Prepaid Insurance, must be decreased by a credit of $300.

- The Insurance Expense account must be increased by a debit of $300.

Summary:

Prepaid Insurance		Insurance Expense	
Dr.	Cr.	Dr.	Cr.
1,200	− 300	+ 300	

After adjustment, the December 31 financial statements will include:

Balance Sheet	Income Statement
Prepaid insurance $900 (unexpired)	Insurance expense $300 (expired)

c. WAGES   The Kitchen Taylor, a new business, has only one part-time employee. That employee works a five-day week (Monday through Friday) and is paid $50 per week ($10 per day times five days). Payday is each Friday. The usual payroll entry recorded each Friday is:

```
Wages Expense . . . . . . . . . . . . . . . . . . . . . . .   50
    Cash . . . . . . . . . . . . . . . . . . . . . . . . . .        50
```

Let's assume that December 31 falls on Wednesday. That means three days (Monday, Tuesday, and Wednesday) of this pay period fall in December and two days (Thursday and Friday) fall in January of the next year. As usual, Friday will be payday.

Monday	Tuesday	Wednesday	Thursday	Friday
29	30	31	1	2
	$30 ($10 × 3 days)		$20 ($10 × 2 days)	

Accrual-basis accounting requires that expenses be recorded in the period in which they are incurred regardless of when they are paid. Therefore, the $30 of wages expense incurred on December 29, 30, and 31 must be recorded in December even though the wages will not actually be paid until January 2 of next year. As of December 31, this $30 represents wages expense that has been incurred but not yet paid.

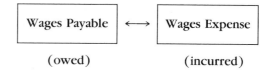

| Wages Payable | ⟷ | Wages Expense |

(owed)　　　　　　　　　　(incurred)

Based on this information, the following adjustment must be recorded on December 31:

- The Wages Expense account must be increased by a debit of $30.

- As of Wednesday, December 31, $30 is owed to the employee. To record this liability, the Wages Payable account must be increased by a credit of $30.

IIIIIIIIIIIIIIIIIIIII
C O M M E N T   Observe that a separate liability account is used to record this liability—Wages Payable. The Accounts Payable account is not used for wages owed to employees.

Summary:

Wages Expense		**Wages Payable**	
Dr.	Cr.	Dr.	Cr.
+30			+30

After adjustment, the December 31 financial statements will include:

Balance Sheet	Income Statement
Wages payable $30 (owed)	Wages expense $30 (incurred)

d. DEPRECIATION   Assets are used to generate revenue. But how long are assets useful? This period of usefulness is referred to as an asset's **useful life.** Useful life varies greatly from asset to asset.

Some assets, such as supplies, are used up quickly. They are used to generate revenue for a period less than a year. Assets with a useful life of one year or less are known as **current assets.** Other assets, such as equipment, are used up more slowly. They are used to generate revenue for a period greater than one year—perhaps 5, 10, 20 years or even longer. Assets that have a useful life of more than one year are known as **plant assets.** Other examples of plant assets include cars, trucks, and buildings.

We know from earlier discussions that as an asset is used, its cost is transferred to an appropriate expense account. To properly match revenue and expense on the income statement, the cost of a plant asset must be spread over its useful life. This process of spreading the cost of a plant asset over its useful life of more than one year is known as **depreciation.**

||||||||||||||||||||||
C O M M E N T

There is one exception—land. Although land is a plant asset, it is not depreciated because it is not used up. Land is considered to be a permanent store of value.

Now that you understand the need to depreciate plant assets, let's consider how to record depreciation.

||||||||||||||||||||||
C O M M E N T

For now, we will not worry about how to compute depreciation. You will be given the dollar amount. At this time, our goal is to understand the nature of depreciation and to correctly record the given amount. In Chapter 18, you will learn how to compute depreciation.

The purchase of a plant asset is recorded with a debit (increase) to an asset account—Equipment, Truck, Building, and so on. As the asset is used up, the cost associated with the used-up portion is transferred to an expense account—Depreciation Expense.

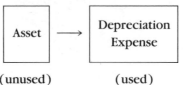

(unused)   (used)

Let's assume The Kitchen Taylor wishes to record $1,100 of depreciation on its truck (plant asset). The following adjustment is recorded on December 31:

- The Depreciation Expense account is increased by a debit of $1,100.

- The $6,000 cost of the truck must be preserved in the Truck account until the truck is discarded, sold, or traded, as required by the principle of historical cost discussed in Chapter 1. Therefore, instead of reducing the asset account directly with a credit of $1,100, it is reduced indirectly by crediting an account known as Accumulated Depreciation. The purpose of the Accumulated Depreciation account is to keep a cumulative record of all the depreciation ever recorded on a particular asset.

||||||||||||||||||||||
C O M M E N T

Accumulated depreciation is a **contra-asset account.** A contra-asset account is contrary to assets—it is a subtraction from assets. The Accumulated Depreciation account (contra asset) has a normal balance on the credit side. As the credit balance in the Accumulated Depreciation account increases, it indirectly decreases total assets.

	Asset	
Dr.		Cr.
+		−

	Accumulated Depreciation	
Dr.		Cr.
−		+

Summary:

	Truck	
Dr.		Cr.
6,000		

Accumulated Depreciation			**Depreciation Expense**	
Dr.	Cr.		Dr.	Cr.
	+1,100		+1,100	

After adjustment, the December 31 financial statements will include:

Balance Sheet			Income Statement
Truck	$6,000		Depreciation expense
Less accumulated depreciation . . .	1,100	$4,900 (unused)	$1,100 (used)

Although unlabeled on the balance sheet, $4,900 is referred to as the **book value** of the truck.

$$\text{Book value} = \text{Cost} - \text{Accumulated depreciation}$$

||||||||||||||||||||||
C O M M E N T

Be careful not to confuse the terms *book value* and *market value*. Book value refers to the undepreciated cost of an asset; book value can only decrease over time. **Market value** refers to the current price of an asset if it were bought or sold today; market value can increase or decrease over time depending on market conditions.

Figure 5-2 shows the work sheet with adjustments *(a)* through *(d)*. Notice that the Debit and Credit columns have been totaled and checked for equality. In studying Figure 5-2, observe the following:

- Adjustments are letter-coded on the work sheet. Later, when the adjustments are journalized, these letter codes make it easy to determine the debits and credits that go together in any one entry. This is particularly convenient in cases of compound journal entries.

- In the Account Title column, some account titles are written below the trial balance accounts. These are accounts that had no balance when the trial balance was taken but are needed in making adjustments. Since they were not included in the trial balance, they are written below. Never write an account title below if it already appears above as part of the trial balance.

Referring to Figure 5-2, observe that the Accumulated Depreciation account appears below the trial balance accounts. This is appropriate in this case because The Kitchen Taylor is a new business and adjustment *(d)* marks the first time that depreciation has ever been recorded on the recently purchased truck. Consequently, the Accumulated Depreciation account had no previous balance and did not appear on the trial balance. However, the next time a trial balance is prepared, the Accumulated Depreciation account will have a $1,100 credit balance and will appear on the trial balance. Therefore, the next time we rough draft the depreciation adjustment on the work sheet, it will not be necessary to write in the Accumulated Depreciation account below the trial balance accounts.

As mentioned earlier, adjusting entries are really updating entries. Situations requiring updating may vary from business to business. Therefore, adjustments may vary from one business to another. In this chapter, you have studied some common types of adjustments. You will study other types in later chapters.

Step 4:   Prepare the adjusted trial balance.

The trial balance and adjustment figures for each account must be combined and extended (carried over) to the Adjusted Trial Balance columns.

- Where there is no adjustment, simply extend the trial balance figure as is. (Figure 5-3 example: Accounts Receivable)

- Where there is a figure in the Adjustments columns but nothing in the Trial Balance columns, simply extend the adjustment figure as is. (Figure 5-3 example: Wages Payable)

- Where there are figures in both the Trial Balance and Adjustments columns, combine as follows:
  Debit and debit: add. (Figure 5-3 example: Wages Expense)
  Credit and credit: add.
  Debit and credit: subtract. (Figure 5-3 example: Supplies)

After all account balances have been extended to the Adjusted Trial Balance columns, the Debit and Credit columns must be totaled and checked for equality.

Figure 5-3 shows the work sheet completed through the Adjusted Trial Balance columns.

█ FIGURE 5 - 3

THE KITCHEN TAYLOR
Work Sheet
For the Year Ended December 31, 19X1

Account Title	Trial Balance Debit		Credit		Adjustments Debit		Credit	
Cash	2,687	00						
Accounts Receivable	1,835	00						
Supplies	842	00					(a) 532	00
Prepaid Insurance	1,200	00					(b) 300	00
Truck	6,000	00						
Accounts Payable			960	00				
Dennis Taylor, Capital			10,000	00				
Dennis Taylor, Drawing	9,200	00						
Fees Earned			18,500	00				
Rent Expense	3,600	00						
Repair Expense	357	00						
Supplies Expense	75	00			(a) 532	00		
Utilities Expense	1,564	00						
Wages Expense	2,100	00			(c) 30	00		
	29,460	00	29,460	00				
Insurance Expense					(b) 300	00		
Wages Payable							(c) 30	00
Depreciation Expense					(d) 1,100	00		
Accumulated Depreciation							(d) 1,100	00
					1,962	00	1,962	00

Adjusted Trial Balance				Income Statement				Balance Sheet			
Debit		Credit		Debit		Credit		Debit		Credit	
2,687	00										
1,835	00										
310	00										
900	00										
6,000	00										
		960	00								
		10,000	00								
9,200	00										
		18,500	00								
3,600	00										
357	00										
607	00										
1,564	00										
2,130	00										
300	00										
		30	00								
1,100	00										
		1,100	00								
30,590	00	30,590	00								

FIGURE 5 - 4

THE KITCHEN TAYLOR
Work Sheet
For the Year Ended December 31, 19X1

Account Title	Trial Balance Debit	Trial Balance Credit	Adjustments Debit	Adjustments Credit
Cash	2,687 00			
Accounts Receivable	1,835 00			
Supplies	842 00			(a) 532 00
Prepaid Insurance	1,200 00			(b) 300 00
Truck	6,000 00			
Accounts Payable		960 00		
Dennis Taylor, Capital		10,000 00		
Dennis Taylor, Drawing	9,200 00			
Fees Earned		18,500 00		
Rent Expense	3,600 00			
Repair Expense	357 00			
Supplies Expense	75 00		(a) 532 00	
Utilities Expense	1,564 00			
Wages Expense	2,100 00		(c) 30 00	
	29,460 00	29,460 00		
Insurance Expense			(b) 300 00	
Wages Payable				(c) 30 00
Depreciation Expense			(d) 1,100 00	
Accumulated Depreciation				(d) 1,100 00
			1,962 00	1,962 00

Step 5:   Rough draft the income statement and balance sheet.

Start at the top of the Adjusted Trial Balance columns and proceed line by line down the columns, extending each balance to either the Income Statement columns or the Balance Sheet columns—never both. Balances are extended as is: debits as debits, credits as credits.

All asset, liability, capital, and drawing account balances are extended from the Adjusted Trial Balance columns to the Balance Sheet columns.

All revenue and expense account balances are extended from the Adjusted Trial Balance columns to the Income Statement columns.

Adjusted Trial Balance		Income Statement		Balance Sheet	
Debit	Credit	Debit	Credit	Debit	Credit
2,687 00				2,687 00	
1,835 00				1,835 00	
310 00				310 00	
900 00				900 00	
6,000 00				6,000 00	
	960 00				960 00
	10,000 00				10,000 00
9,200 00				9,200 00	
	18,500 00		18,500 00		
3,600 00		3,600 00			
357 00		357 00			
607 00		607 00			
1,564 00		1,564 00			
2,130 00		2,130 00			
300 00		300 00			
	30 00				30 00
1,100 00		1,100 00			
	1,100 00				1,100 00
30,590 00	30,590 00				

Figure 5-4 shows The Kitchen Taylor's work sheet completed through Step 5.

||||||||||||||||||||||||
C O M M E N T

Although the drawing account balance is extended to the balance sheet in preparing the work sheet, the drawing account will not appear on the formal balance sheet to be prepared later. Remember, the work sheet is a rough draft. Prior to preparing the formal balance sheet, the statement of owner's equity will be prepared. The drawing account balance will appear on the statement of owner's equity. The up-to-date capital account balance (including the effect of withdrawals by the owner) will then be shown on the formal balance sheet.

FIGURE 5 - 5

THE KITCHEN TAYLOR
Work Sheet
For the Year Ended December 31, 19X1

Account Title	Trial Balance		Adjustments	
	Debit	Credit	Debit	Credit
Cash	2,687 00			
Accounts Receivable	1,835 00			
Supplies	842 00			(a) 532 00
Prepaid Insurance	1,200 00			(b) 300 00
Truck	6,000 00			
Accounts Payable		960 00		
Dennis Taylor, Capital		10,000 00		
Dennis Taylor, Drawing	9,200 00			
Fees Earned		18,500 00		
Rent Expense	3,600 00			
Repair Expense	357 00			
Supplies Expense	75 00		(a) 532 00	
Utilities Expense	1,564 00			
Wages Expense	2,100 00		(c) 30 00	
	29,460 00	29,460 00		
Insurance Expense			(b) 300 00	
Wages Payable				(c) 30 00
Depreciation Expense			(d) 1,100 00	
Accumulated Depreciation				(d) 1,100 00
			1,962 00	1,962 00
Net income				

Step 6: Total and balance the Income Statement columns.

Total both the Income Statement Debit column and Income Statement Credit column. Then find the difference between the debit and credit totals. Since the credits represent revenue and the debits expenses, the difference is equal to net income or loss.

Label the net income or loss in the Account Title column and enter the

Adjusted Trial Balance		Income Statement		Balance Sheet	
Debit	Credit	Debit	Credit	Debit	Credit
2,687 00				2,687 00	
1,835 00				1,835 00	
310 00				310 00	
900 00				900 00	
6,000 00				6,000 00	
	960 00				960 00
	10,000 00				10,000 00
9,200 00				9,200 00	
	18,500 00		18,500 00		
3,600 00		3,600 00			
357 00		357 00			
607 00		607 00			
1,564 00		1,564 00			
2,130 00		2,130 00			
300 00		300 00			
	30 00				30 00
1,100 00		1,100 00			
	1,100 00				1,100 00
30,590 00	30,590 00	9,658 00	18,500 00		
		8,842 00*			
		18,500 00	18,500 00		

*Computation: $18,500 − $9,658 = $8,842

amount as a balancing figure in the Income Statement columns. Total both the Income Statement Debit column and Income Statement Credit column again. The column totals should now be the same.

Figure 5-5 shows The Kitchen Taylor's work sheet completed through Step 6.

■ **FIGURE 5 - 6**

THE KITCHEN TAYLOR
Work Sheet
For the Year Ended December 31, 19X1

Account Title	Trial Balance Debit		Credit		Adjustments Debit		Credit	
Cash	2,687	00						
Accounts Receivable	1,835	00						
Supplies	842	00					(a) 532	00
Prepaid Insurance	1,200	00					(b) 300	00
Truck	6,000	00						
Accounts Payable			960	00				
Dennis Taylor, Capital			10,000	00				
Dennis Taylor, Drawing	9,200	00						
Fees Earned			18,500	00				
Rent Expense	3,600	00						
Repair Expense	357	00						
Supplies Expense	75	00			(a) 532	00		
Utilities Expense	1,564	00						
Wages Expense	2,100	00			(c) 30	00		
	29,460	00	29,460	00				
Insurance Expense					(b) 300	00		
Wages Payable							(c) 30	00
Depreciation Expense					(d) 1,100	00		
Accumulated Depreciation							(d) 1,100	00
					1,962	00	1,962	00
Net income								

Step 7:   Total and balance the Balance Sheet columns.

     Total both the Balance Sheet Debit column and Balance Sheet Credit column. Then find the difference between the debit and credit totals. The difference should be equal to the net income or loss previously computed.
     Enter the net income or loss as a balancing figure in the Balance Sheet

Adjusted Trial Balance		Income Statement		Balance Sheet	
Debit	**Credit**	**Debit**	**Credit**	**Debit**	**Credit**
2,687 00				2,687 00	
1,835 00				1,835 00	
310 00				310 00	
900 00				900 00	
6,000 00				6,000 00	
	960 00				960 00
	10,000 00				10,000 00
9,200 00				9,200 00	
	18,500 00		18,500 00		
3,600 00		3,600 00			
357 00		357 00			
607 00		607 00			
1,564 00		1,564 00			
2,130 00		2,130 00			
300 00		300 00			
	30 00				30 00
1,100 00		1,100 00			
	1,100 00				1,100 00
30,590 00	30,590 00	9,658 00	18,500 00	20,932 00	12,090 00
		8,842 00			8,842 00*
		18,500 00	18,500 00	20,932 00	20,932 00

* Computation: $20,932 − $12,090 = $8,842

columns. Total both the Debit and Credit columns again. The totals of the Balance Sheet Debit and Credit columns should now be the same (but not the same as the totals of the Income Statement columns).

Figure 5-6 shows The Kitchen Taylor's work sheet completed through Step 7, the final step.

At this point, all balance sheet accounts are up to date except for the owner's capital account. This account has not yet been updated to reflect withdrawals by the owner or net income (loss). As you will recall, however, the drawing account balance was extended to the balance sheet as a separate item. That means only the effect of net income (loss) is missing. This is why the balance sheet totals differ by an amount equal to net income (loss).

■■■■ PREPARING THE FINANCIAL STATEMENTS

OBJECTIVE 4
PREPARE FINANCIAL
STATEMENTS DIRECTLY
FROM THE WORK SHEET

Now that the work sheet is complete, we are ready to prepare the formal financial statements. Since the financial statements have already been rough drafted, this is basically a matter of formatting. The information is taken directly from the work sheet and written up in the appropriate statement format.

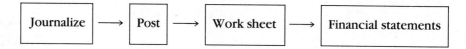

IIIIIIIIIIIIIIIIIIIII
C O M M E N T

All information for the statements comes directly from the work sheet with one exception: an additional investment by the owner. Since a credit to the owner's capital account is recorded at the time the additional investment is made, the capital account balance appearing on the trial balance already includes the investment. However, we cannot tell whether there has been an additional investment by merely looking at the capital account balance on the work sheet. Therefore, when preparing the statement of owner's equity, we must check the owner's capital account in the ledger to determine whether an additional investment has been made. If so, we must pick up two pieces of information from the owner's capital account:

1. The beginning capital account balance. (Remember, the balance on the work sheet is not really the beginning balance, since it includes the investment that was probably made later in the accounting period.)

2. The amount of the additional investment.

Figure 5-7 shows The Kitchen Taylor's financial statements for the year ended December 31, 19X1.

FIGURE 5 - 7

THE KITCHEN TAYLOR
Income Statement
For the Year Ended December 31, 19X1

Revenue:				
Fees earned			$18,500	00
Expenses:				
Rent expense	$ 3,600	00		
Wages expense	2,130	00		
Utilities expense	1,564	00		
Depreciation expense	1,100	00		
Supplies expense	607	00		
Repair expense	357	00		
Insurance expense	300	00		
Total expenses			9,658	00
Net income			$ 8,842	00

THE KITCHEN TAYLOR
Statement of Owner's Equity
For the Year Ended December 31, 19X1

Dennis Taylor, capital, January 1, 19X1			$ -0-	
Add: Investment by Dennis Taylor	$ 10,000	00		
Net income for the year	8,842	00	18,842	00
Subtotal			$ 18,842	00
Deduct: Withdrawals by Dennis Taylor			9,200	00
Dennis Taylor, capital, December 31, 19X1			$ 9,642	00

■ FIGURE 5 - 7 *(concluded)*

THE KITCHEN TAYLOR
Balance Sheet
December 31, 19X1

Assets				
Cash			$ 2,687	00
Accounts receivable			1,835	00
Supplies			310	00
Prepaid insurance			900	00
Truck	$ 6,000	00		
Less accumulated depreciation	1,100	00	4,900	00
Total assets			$ 10,632	00
Liabilities				
Accounts payable	$ 960	00		
Wages payable	30	00		
Total liabilities			$ 990	00
Owner's Equity				
Dennis Taylor, capital			9,642	00
Total liabilities and owner's equity			$ 10,632	00

■■■■ JOURNALIZING AND POSTING THE ADJUSTMENTS

OBJECTIVE 5
JOURNALIZE AND POST
ADJUSTING ENTRIES

Journal entries must be recorded in a journal. Since the work sheet is not a journal, the adjustments rough drafted on the work sheet must now be formally recorded in the journal. Again, this is basically a matter of formatting. The adjustment information, taken directly from the work sheet, is written up in good journal entry format. The need for explanations is eliminated by writing *adjusting entries* in the Description column immediately above the first adjustment.

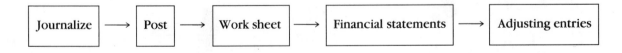

Figure 5-8 shows The Kitchen Taylor's journal after adjustments *(a)* through *(d)* have been recorded.

FIGURE 5 - 8

GENERAL JOURNAL   Page 42

Date		Description	Post. Ref.	Debit	Credit
		Adjusting Entries			
19X1 Dec.	31	Supplies Expense		532 00	
		Supplies			532 00
	31	Insurance Expense		300 00	
		Prepaid Insurance			300 00
	31	Wages Expense		30 00	
		Wages Payable			30 00
	31	Depreciation Expense		1,100 00	
		Accumulated Depreciation			1,100 00

The Kitchen Taylor's adjusting entries must now be posted to the appropriate accounts in the ledger. In posting adjusting entries, the word *Adjusting* is usually written in the Item column of the account. For example, after posting, The Kitchen Taylor's Supplies account appears as follows:

Account **Supplies** _____ Account No. 112

Date		Item	Post. Ref.	Debit	Credit	Balance Debit	Balance Credit
19X1 Dec.	1	Balance	√			842 00	
	31	Adjusting	J42		532 00	310 00	

Chapter Summary

A work sheet is a tool used by accountants to rough draft adjustments and financial statements. This process of rough drafting helps us to organize information as well as detect mathematical errors before preparing formal statements and journal entries.

The work sheet is prepared at the end of the accounting period (month, year, etc.), after transactions have been journalized and posted but before financial statements have been prepared.

To prepare a work sheet:

Step 1:   Prepare a three-line heading.

Step 2:   Prepare the trial balance.

Step 3:   Rough draft the adjustments.

Step 4:   Prepare the adjusted trial balance.

Step 5:   Rough draft the income statement and balance sheet.

Step 6:   Total and balance the Income Statement columns.

Step 7:   Total and balance the Balance Sheet columns.

After the work sheet is completed, formal financial statements are prepared with information taken directly from the work sheet. Then the adjustments, rough drafted on the work sheet, must be journalized and posted.

The accounting cycle, as studied up to this point, is summarized in the following flowchart:

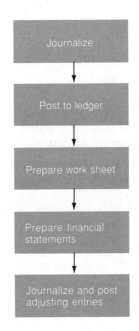

In Chapter 6, we will complete the accounting cycle with closing entries and the post-closing trial balance.

Glossary

ADJUSTING ENTRIES
Entries that update for internal transactions that have occurred but have not yet been recorded (journalized).

BOOK VALUE
Cost minus accumulated depreciation equals book value.

CONTRA-ASSET ACCOUNT
An account that is contrary to assets. It is a subtraction from assets.

CURRENT ASSET
An asset used to generate revenue for a period of one year or less.

DEPRECIATION
The process of spreading the cost of a plant asset over its useful life of more than one year.

INTERNAL TRANSACTION
A transaction occurring within a business that does not involve anyone outside the business.

MARKET VALUE
The current price of an asset if it were bought or sold today.

PLANT ASSET
An asset used to generate revenue for a period greater than one year.

USEFUL LIFE
Period of time over which an asset will help generate revenue.

WORK SHEET
A tool used by accountants to rough draft adjustments and financial statements and also to check for mathematical accuracy.

Questions for Discussion

1. What is the purpose of a work sheet?

2. When is a work sheet prepared?

3. Briefly state the seven steps required to prepare a work sheet.

4. Is the work sheet a formal financial statement? A journal?

5. On the work sheet, why are some account titles written below the trial balance accounts? Would an account title ever be written both above and below?

6. What is the purpose of adjusting entries?

7. Why is it necessary to adjust for the following:

   a. Supplies.
   b. Insurance.
   c. Wages.

8. What is depreciation? How is it recorded?

Exercises

EXERCISE 5-1
ACCOUNTING CYCLE
(L.O.1, 2)

Arrange the following steps in the accounting cycle in their proper order:

    a. Journalize and post adjusting entries.

    b. Prepare a work sheet.

    c. Post to the ledger.

    d. Journalize.

    e. Prepare financial statements.

EXERCISE 5-2
STEPS IN PREPARING A
WORK SHEET
(L.O.3)

Arrange the following steps to prepare a work sheet in their proper order:

    a. Rough draft the adjustments.

    b. Total and balance the Income Statement columns.

    c. Prepare the trial balance.

    d. Rough draft the income statement and balance sheet.

    e. Prepare the adjusted trial balance.

    f. Total and balance the Balance Sheet columns.

    g. Prepare a three-line heading.

EXERCISE 5-3
ADJUSTMENT FOR
SUPPLIES
(L.O.3, 5)

The December 1, 19X1, balance in the Supplies account is $350. On December 31, 19X1, an inventory indicates $185 worth of supplies left unused in the storeroom.

    a. What is the necessary adjusting entry on December 31?

    b. Relative to this situation, the December 31 balance sheet will show what account and balance?

    c. Relative to this situation, the December 31 income statement will show what account and balance?

EXERCISE 5-4
ADJUSTMENT FOR
PREPAID INSURANCE
(L.O.3, 5)

On October 1, 19X1, RMP Company paid a $240 premium for one year of insurance coverage. This future insurance coverage was recorded in the Prepaid Insurance account.

    a. What is the necessary adjusting entry on December 31?

    b. Relative to this situation, the December 31 balance sheet will show what account and balance?

    c. Relative to this situation, the December 31 income statement will show what account and balance?

EXERCISE 5-5
ADJUSTMENT FOR
WAGES
(L.O.3, 5)

Hernandez Associates pays its employees a total of $1,000 for a five-day workweek (Monday through Friday). Payday is each Friday. December 31, 19X1, falls on Tuesday.

    a. What is the necessary adjusting entry on December 31?

    b. Relative to this situation, the December 31 balance sheet will show what account and balance?

    c. Relative to this situation, the December 31 income statement will show what account and balance?

EXERCISE 5-6
ADJUSTMENT FOR
DEPRECIATION
(L.O.3, 5)

On December 31, 19X1, Kim Enterprises wishes to record $650 of depreciation on its equipment.

    a. What is the necessary adjusting entry on December 31?

    b. Relative to this situation, the December 31 balance sheet will show what account and balance?

    c. Relative to this situation, the December 31 income statement will show what account and balance?

EXERCISE 5-7
ADJUSTMENT OF
SELECTED ACCOUNTS
(L.O.3, 5)

Based on the following information, journalize the necessary adjusting entries on September 30.

    a. Used supplies amount to $185.

    b. Expired insurance coverage amounts to $420.

    c. Wages expense incurred but not paid, as of September 30, amounts to $1,150.

    d. Depreciation on the truck amounts to $260.

EXERCISE 5-8
ADJUSTMENT OF
SELECTED ACCOUNTS
(L.O.3, 5)

Based on the following information, journalize the necessary adjusting entries on June 30.

    a. Prior to adjustment, the Supplies account had a balance of $230. On June 30, 19X1, an inventory indicates $105 worth of supplies left unused in the storeroom.

    b. Prior to adjustment, the Prepaid Insurance account had a balance of $470. On June 30, unexpired insurance coverage amounts to only $215.

    c. The payroll each Friday totals $1,500 for a five-day workweek (Monday through Friday). June 30 falls on Thursday.

    d. Depreciation on the building amounts to $1,200.

Problems—Set A

The trial balance and adjustment data for Susan's Pet Motel, a new business, are as follows:

SUSAN'S PET MOTEL
Trial Balance
January 31, 19X1

	Debit	Credit
Cash	1,280 00	
Accounts Receivable	875 00	
Supplies	437 00	
Prepaid Insurance	540 00	
Equipment	5,675 00	
Accounts Payable		790 00
Susan Clingner, Capital		7,433 00
Susan Clingner, Drawing	900 00	
Fees Earned		3,145 00
Advertising Expense	184 00	
Rent Expense	625 00	
Utilities Expense	272 00	
Wages Expense	580 00	
	11,368 00	11,368 00

Adjustment data:

a. Supplies used during January, $295.

b. Insurance expired during January, $45.

c. Wages expense incurred but not yet paid as of January 31, $250.

d. Depreciation on the equipment for January, $90.

INSTRUCTIONS
Complete the work sheet.

PROBLEM 5-2A
FINANCIAL STATEMENTS AND ADJUSTING ENTRIES FROM WORK SHEET (L.O.4, 5)

Following is a completed work sheet for Park Dry Cleaners for the year ended December 31, 19X1:

PARK DRY CLEANERS
Work Sheet
For the Year Ended December 31, 19X1

Account Title	Trial Balance Debit	Trial Balance Credit	Adjustments Debit	Adjustments Credit
Cash	2,315 00			
Accounts Receivable	1,843 00			
Supplies	920 00			(a) 510 00
Prepaid Insurance	1,275 00			(b) 975 00
Equipment	22,500 00			
Accumulated Depreciation		10,600 00		(d) 1,850 00
Accounts Payable		2,571 00		
Ken Park, Capital		20,585 00		
Ken Park, Drawing	19,400 00			
Dry Cleaning Sales		52,500 00		
Advertising Expense	1,580 00			
Rent Expense	9,600 00			
Utilities Expense	3,754 00			
Wages Expense	22,650 00		(c) 340 00	
Miscellaneous Expense	419 00			
	86,256 00	86,256 00		
Supplies Expense			(a) 510 00	
Insurance Expense			(b) 975 00	
Wages Payable				(c) 340 00
Depreciation Expense			(d) 1,850 00	
			3,675 00	3,675 00
Net income				

Adjusted Trial Balance		Income Statement		Balance Sheet	
Debit	Credit	Debit	Credit	Debit	Credit
2,315 00				2,315 00	
1,843 00				1,843 00	
410 00				410 00	
300 00				300 00	
22,500 00				22,500 00	
	12,450 00				12,450 00
	2,571 00				2,571 00
	20,585 00				20,585 00
19,400 00				19,400 00	
	52,500 00		52,500 00		
1,580 00		1,580 00			
9,600 00		9,600 00			
3,754 00		3,754 00			
22,990 00		22,990 00			
419 00		419 00			
510 00		510 00			
975 00		975 00			
	340 00				340 00
1,850 00		1,850 00			
88,446 00	88,446 00	41,678 00	52,500 00	46,768 00	35,946 00
		10,822 00			10,822 00
		52,500 00	52,500 00	46,768 00	46,768 00

INSTRUCTIONS

1. Prepare an income statement.

2. Prepare a statement of owner's equity. (Assume no additional investment by the owner.)

3. Prepare a balance sheet.

4. Journalize the adjustments.

PROBLEM 5-3A
WORK SHEET; FINANCIAL STATEMENTS; ADJUSTING ENTRIES
(L.O.1–5)

The trial balance and year-end adjustment data for Bayne Accounting Services are as follows:

BAYNE ACCOUNTING SERVICES Trial Balance December 31, 19X1	Debit		Credit	
Cash	2,150	00		
Accounts Receivable	5,472	00		
Supplies	830	00		
Prepaid Insurance	975	00		
Equipment	6,500	00		
Accumulated Depreciation			1,200	00
Accounts Payable			2,868	00
Shirley Bayne, Capital			8,178	00
Shirley Bayne, Drawing	7,200	00		
Fees Earned			23,700	00
Advertising Expense	610	00		
Rent Expense	5,400	00		
Utilities Expense	2,080	00		
Wages Expense	4,300	00		
Miscellaneous Expense	429	00		
	35,946	00	35,946	00

Adjustment data:

a. Inventory of supplies on December 31, $327.

b. Insurance expired during the year, $442.

    c. Wages expense incurred but not yet paid as of December 31, $265.

    d. Depreciation on the equipment for the year, $850.

INSTRUCTIONS

1. Complete the work sheet.

2. Prepare an income statement, statement of owner's equity (assume no additional investment by owner), and a balance sheet.

3. Journalize the adjustments.

PROBLEM 5-4A
WORK SHEET; FINANCIAL
STATEMENTS; ADJUSTING
ENTRIES
(L.O.1–5)

The trial balance and year-end adjustment data for Kenwood Travel are as follows:

KENWOOD TRAVEL Trial Balance December 31, 19X1				
	Debit		**Credit**	
Cash	2,542	00		
Accounts Receivable	3,120	00		
Supplies	796	00		
Prepaid Insurance	854	00		
Equipment	10,500	00		
Accumulated Depreciation—Equipment			4,700	00
Building	85,000	00		
Accumulated Depreciation—Building			23,600	00
Land	25,000	00		
Accounts Payable			3,465	00
Mortgage Payable			39,000	00
Karl Kenwood, Capital			42,555	00
Karl Kenwood, Drawing	23,500	00		
Commissions Earned			65,780	00
Advertising Expense	5,925	00		
Utilities Expense	3,042	00		
Wages Expense	18,230	00		
Miscellaneous Expense	591	00		
	179,100	00	179,100	00

Adjustment data:

    a. Inventory of supplies on December 31, $256.

    b. Insurance expired during the year, $610.

    c. Wages expense incurred but not yet paid as of December 31, $438.

    d. Depreciation on the equipment for the year, $1,200.

    e. Depreciation on the building for the year, $1,800.

INSTRUCTIONS

1. Complete the work sheet.

2. Prepare an income statement, statement of owner's equity (assume no additional investment by owner), and a balance sheet.

3. Journalize the adjustments.

Problems—Set B

PROBLEM 5-1B
WORK SHEET
(L.O.1–3)
The trial balance and adjustment data for TLC Day Care Center, a new business, are as follows:

TLC DAY CARE CENTER
Trial Balance
January 31, 19X1

	Debit	Credit
Cash	2,560 00	
Accounts Receivable	1,750 00	
Supplies	874 00	
Prepaid Insurance	1,080 00	
Equipment	11,350 00	
Accounts Payable		1,580 00
Maria Ramirez, Capital		14,866 00
Maria Ramirez, Drawing	1,800 00	
Fees Earned		6,290 00
Advertising Expense	368 00	
Rent Expense	1,250 00	
Utilities Expense	544 00	
Wages Expense	1,160 00	
	22,736 00	22,736 00

Adjustment data:

a. Supplies used during January, $495.

b. Insurance expired during January, $145.

c. Wages expense incurred but not yet paid as of January 31, $550.

d. Depreciation on the equipment for January, $180.

INSTRUCTIONS
Complete the work sheet.

PROBLEM 5-2B
FINANCIAL STATEMENTS
AND ADJUSTING
ENTRIES FROM WORK
SHEET (L.O.4, 5)

Following is a completed work sheet for Highlands Animal Clinic for the year ended December 31, 19X1:

HIGHLANDS ANIMAL CLINIC
Work Sheet
For the Year Ended December 31, 19X1

Account Title	Trial Balance Debit	Trial Balance Credit	Adjustments Debit	Adjustments Credit
Cash	4,630 00			
Accounts Receivable	3,686 00			
Supplies	1,840 00			(a) 1,020 00
Prepaid Insurance	2,550 00			(b) 1,950 00
Equipment	45,000 00			
Accumulated Depreciation		21,200 00		(d) 3,700 00
Accounts Payable		5,142 00		
Ted Harmon, Capital		41,170 00		
Ted Harmon, Drawing	38,800 00			
Professional Fees		105,000 00		
Advertising Expense	3,160 00			
Rent Expense	19,200 00			
Utilities Expense	7,508 00			
Wages Expense	45,300 00		(c) 680 00	
Miscellaneous Expense	838 00			
	172,512 00	172,512 00		
Supplies Expense			(a) 1,020 00	
Insurance Expense			(b) 1,950 00	
Wages Payable				(c) 680 00
Depreciation Expense			(d) 3,700 00	
			7,350 00	7,350 00
Net income				

Adjusted Trial Balance		Income Statement		Balance Sheet	
Debit	**Credit**	**Debit**	**Credit**	**Debit**	**Credit**
4,630 00				4,630 00	
3,686 00				3,686 00	
820 00				820 00	
600 00				600 00	
45,000 00				45,000 00	
	24,900 00				24,900 00
	5,142 00				5,142 00
	41,170 00				41,170 00
38,800 00				38,800 00	
	105,000 00		105,000 00		
3,160 00		3,160 00			
19,200 00		19,200 00			
7,508 00		7,508 00			
45,980 00		45,980 00			
838 00		838 00			
1,020 00		1,020 00			
1,950 00		1,950 00			
	680 00				680 00
3,700 00		3,700 00			
176,892 00	176,892 00	83,356 00	105,000 00	93,536 00	71,892 00
		21,644 00			21,644 00
		105,000 00	105,000 00	93,536 00	93,536 00

INSTRUCTIONS

1. Prepare an income statement.

2. Prepare a statement of owner's equity. (Assume no additional investment by the owner.)

3. Prepare a balance sheet.

4. Journalize the adjustments.

PROBLEM 5-3B
WORK SHEET; FINANCIAL STATEMENTS; ADJUSTING ENTRIES
(L.O.1–5)

The trial balance and year-end adjustment data for Jake's Shoe Repair are as follows:

JAKE'S SHOE REPAIR Trial Balance December 31, 19X1	Debit		Credit	
Cash	4,300	00		
Accounts Receivable	10,944	00		
Supplies	1,660	00		
Prepaid Insurance	1,950	00		
Equipment	13,000	00		
Accumulated Depreciation			2,400	00
Accounts Payable			5,736	00
Jake Lipton, Capital			16,356	00
Jake Lipton, Drawing	14,400	00		
Income from Services			47,400	00
Advertising Expense	1,220	00		
Rent Expense	10,800	00		
Utilities Expense	4,160	00		
Wages Expense	8,600	00		
Miscellaneous Expense	858	00		
	71,892	00	71,892	00

Adjustment data:

a. Inventory of supplies on December 31, $654.

b. Insurance expired during the year, $884.

        c. Wages expense incurred but not yet paid as of December 31, $530.

        d. Depreciation on the equipment for the year, $1,700.

INSTRUCTIONS

1. Complete the work sheet.

2. Prepare an income statement, statement of owner's equity (assume no additional investment by owner), and a balance sheet.

3. Journalize the adjustments.

PROBLEM 5-4B
WORK SHEET; FINANCIAL
STATEMENTS; ADJUSTING
ENTRIES
(L.O.1–5)

The trial balance and year-end adjustment data for Charisma Beauty Boutique are as follows:

CHARISMA BEAUTY BOUTIQUE Trial Balance December 31, 19X1	Debit		Credit	
Cash	5,084	00		
Accounts Receivable	6,240	00		
Supplies	1,592	00		
Prepaid Insurance	1,708	00		
Equipment	21,000	00		
Accumulated Depreciation—Equipment			9,400	00
Building	170,000	00		
Accumulated Depreciation—Building			47,200	00
Land	50,000	00		
Accounts Payable			6,930	00
Mortgage Payable			78,000	00
Marilee Rubin, Capital			85,110	00
Marilee Rubin, Drawing	47,000	00		
Fees Earned			131,560	00
Advertising Expense	11,850	00		
Utilities Expense	6,084	00		
Wages Expense	36,460	00		
Miscellaneous Expense	1,182	00		
	358,200	00	358,200	00

Adjustment data:

    a. Inventory of supplies on December 31, $512.

    b. Insurance expired during the year, $1,220.

    c. Wages expense incurred but not yet paid as of December 31, $876.

    d. Depreciation on the equipment for the year, $2,400.

    e. Depreciation on the building for the year, $1,800.

INSTRUCTIONS

1. Complete the work sheet.

2. Prepare an income statement, statement of owner's equity (assume no additional investment by owner), and a balance sheet.

3. Journalize the adjustments.

Mini-Cases

CASE 5-1

Your friend, Michael, paid a $900 insurance premium for three years of coverage beginning January 1 of this year. He complains to you about all that insurance expense in one year having a terrible effect on his current year's net income. Would you agree?

CASE 5-2

A client is thinking of buying a building. She calls and says she may pay for the building over 5 years rather than over 15 years. That way, she says, she will be able to depreciate the building over a five-year period. She asks for your opinion of her plan.

CASE 5-3

You notice that your new assistant did not journalize any adjusting entries on December 31. When asked about this, he replied: "The adjustments are on the work sheet." How would you respond?

CHAPTER 6

Closing Entries and the Post-Closing Trial Balance

IIIIIIIIIIIIIIIIII
L E A R N I N G
O B J E C T I V E S

AFTER STUDYING THIS CHAPTER, YOU SHOULD BE ABLE TO:

1 Explain the purpose of closing entries.

2 Journalize and post closing entries.

3 Prepare a post-closing trial balance.

4 Describe the concept of fiscal years and interim periods.

5 Describe the similarities and differences between manual and computerized accounting systems.

The <u>accounting cycle,</u> as studied up to this point, is summarized in the following flowchart:

In this chapter, you will learn to complete the basic accounting cycle with closing entries and a post-closing trial balance.

▮▮▮▮ CLOSING ENTRIES

THE NEED FOR CLOSING ENTRIES

OBJECTIVE 1
EXPLAIN THE PURPOSE
OF CLOSING ENTRIES

As you will recall from earlier chapters, revenue, expense, and the owner's drawing account have special relationships to owner's equity. Those relationships are shown in the following chart.

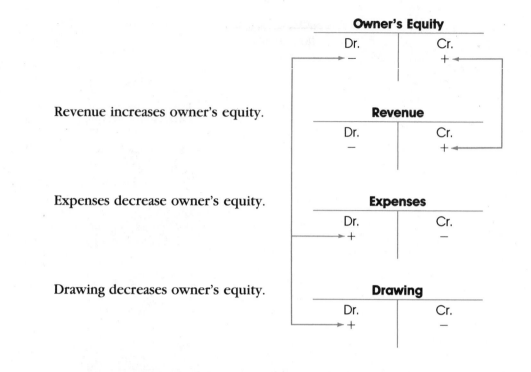

Revenue increases owner's equity.

Expenses decrease owner's equity.

Drawing decreases owner's equity.

Day to day, as revenue, expense, and drawing transactions occur, they are recorded in separate accounts. However, at year-end, the balances in these individual revenue, expense, and drawing accounts must be moved to the owner's capital account.

Why? These accounts are all income statement accounts, except for drawing. As you will recall, an income statement covers a specific period of time—not more than one year. At year-end, these accounts must be cleared (brought to a zero balance) in order to be ready to start accumulating data for the next year. The drawing account, although not an income statement account, also accumulates data for only one year and must be brought to a zero balance at year-end.

HOW TO CLOSE AN ACCOUNT

Closing an account means bringing the account balance to zero. For example, if Account A has a $500 debit balance, it is closed with a $500 credit, leaving a zero balance.

Account A

Dr.		Cr.	
Balance	500	Closing	500

If Account C has an $825 credit balance, it is closed with an $825 debit, leaving a zero balance.

Account C

Dr.		Cr.	
Closing	825	Balance	825

When an account is closed, the debit or credit balance that has been removed is not thrown away but is simply moved to a different account.

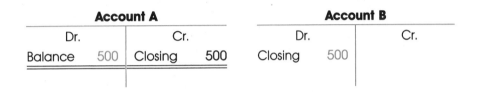

Observe that we have not lost the $500 debit; we have simply moved it from Account A to Account B.

Again, observe that we have not lost the $825 credit; we have moved it from Account C to Account D.

Since revenue, expense, and drawing accounts are closed at the end of each year, they are often referred to as **temporary owner's equity accounts.** They are temporary in the sense that there is no carryover of their balances from one year to the next. They are closed at the end of every year and therefore begin every new year with a zero balance.

On the other hand, balance sheet accounts (assets, liabilities, and capital) are not closed at year-end. Asset, liability, and capital accounts are often referred to as **permanent accounts.** They are permanent in the sense that their year-end balances carry over and become beginning balances in the new year.

THE CLOSING PROCEDURE

The revenue, expense, and drawing accounts are usually closed only once a year—at the end of the company's financial year. The procedure used to close these accounts consists of four steps. *net income affects capital acct.*

Step 1:   Close all revenue accounts to the Income Summary account.

Step 2:   Close all expense accounts to the Income Summary account.

Step 3:   Close the Income Summary account to the owner's capital account.

Step 4:   Close the owner's drawing account to the owner's capital account.

|||||||||||||||||||||| Income Summary is a temporary account used in the closing procedure. It has
C O M M E N T   a balance for only a short time at year-end. It provides a place to summarize
revenue and expense information at year-end. We are then able to transfer a
single summary figure to the owner's capital account.

As shown in Figure 6-1, the basic purpose of the closing procedure is to close the temporary owner's equity accounts to the permanent owner's equity account (capital).

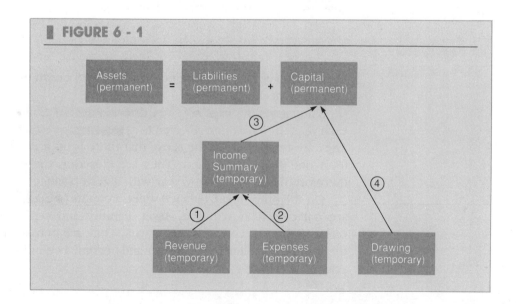

█ FIGURE 6 - 1

In studying Figure 6-1, observe the following:

- Only temporary accounts (revenue, expense, drawing, and Income Summary) are closed at year-end.

- After Steps 1 and 2, the balance in the Income Summary account is equal to net income or loss (revenue minus expenses).

- When the balance in the Income Summary account is closed to capital in Step 3, the net income or loss figure is being transferred to the owner's capital account.

- In Step 4, the drawing account is closed directly to the owner's capital account. Drawing is not closed through the Income Summary account because withdrawals by the owner are not expenses and do not affect net income.

- All temporary account balances are moved to the owner's capital account.

- After the four-step closing procedure is completed, only the permanent accounts (assets, liabilities, and capital) have balances.

PREPARING CLOSING ENTRIES

OBJECTIVE 2
JOURNALIZE AND POST CLOSING ENTRIES

The four-step closing procedure requires four journal entries, known as *closing entries*. To demonstrate the preparation of closing entries, let's return to The Kitchen Taylor.

The information necessary for closing entries can be obtained from either the work sheet or the ledger. Since the information on the work sheet is conveniently arranged for our purposes, we will use the work sheet. Figure 6-2 shows The Kitchen Taylor's year-end work sheet as completed in Chapter 5.

The revenue and expense account balances (after adjustment) are clearly displayed in the Income Statement columns of the work sheet. The drawing account balance is shown in the Balance Sheet Debit column of the work sheet. Using information from the work sheet shown in Figure 6-2, let's prepare closing entries for The Kitchen Taylor.

▌ FIGURE 6 - 2

THE KITCHEN TAYLOR
Work Sheet
For the Year Ended December 31, 19X1

Account Title	Trial Balance		Adjustments	
	Debit	Credit	Debit	Credit
Cash	2,687 00			
Accounts Receivable	1,835 00			
Supplies	842 00			(a) 532 00
Prepaid Insurance	1,200 00			(b) 300 00
Truck	6,000 00			
Accounts Payable		960 00		
Dennis Taylor, Capital		10,000 00		
Dennis Taylor, Drawing	9,200 00			
Fees Earned		18,500 00		
Rent Expense	3,600 00			
Repair Expense	357 00			
Supplies Expense	75 00		(a) 532 00	
Utilities Expense	1,564 00			
Wages Expense	2,100 00		(c) 30 00	
	29,460 00	29,460 00		
Insurance Expense			(b) 300 00	
Wages Payable				(c) 30 00
Depreciation Expense			(d) 1,100 00	
Accumulated Depreciation				(d) 1,100 00
			1,962 00	1,962 00
Net income				

Step 1: Close all revenue accounts to the Income Summary account.

GENERAL JOURNAL Page 43

Date		Description	Post. Ref.	Debit	Credit
19X1 Dec.	31	Fees Earned		18,500 00	
		Income Summary			18,500 00

Adjusted Trial Balance				Income Statement				Balance Sheet			
Debit		Credit		Debit		Credit		Debit		Credit	
2,687	00							2,687	00		
1,835	00							1,835	00		
310	00							310	00		
900	00							900	00		
6,000	00							6,000	00		
		960	00							960	00
		10,000	00							10,000	00
9,200	00							9,200	00		
		18,500	00			18,500	00				
3,600	00			3,600	00						
357	00			357	00						
607	00			607	00						
1,564	00			1,564	00						
2,130	00			2,130	00						
300	00			300	00						
		30	00							30	00
1,100	00			1,100	00						
		1,100	00							1,100	00
30,590	00	30,590	00	9,658	00	18,500	00	20,932	00	12,090	00
				8,842	00					8,842	00
				18,500	00	18,500	00	20,932	00	20,932	00

The picture in T-account form:

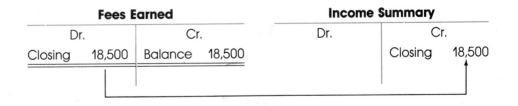

Fees Earned (revenue account) now has a zero balance; it is closed. Its previous $18,500 credit balance has been moved to the Income Summary account. If a company has two or more revenue accounts, Step 1 is accomplished with a compound entry.

Step 2:   Close all expense accounts to the Income Summary account.

Date		Description	Post. Ref.	Debit		Credit	
19X1 Dec.	31	Income Summary		9,658	00		
		Rent Expense				3,600	00
		Repair Expense				357	00
		Supplies Expense				607	00
		Utilities Expense				1,564	00
		Wages Expense				2,130	00
		Insurance Expense				300	00
		Depreciation Expense				1,100	00

GENERAL JOURNAL   Page 43

The picture in T-account form is shown in Figure 6-3.

Each expense account now has a zero balance; they are all closed. Their previous debit balances have all been moved to the Income Summary account. This move is accomplished most efficiently through one compound entry.

FIGURE 6 - 3

Rent Expense				
Dr.		Cr.		
Balance	3,600	Closing	3,600	→

Income Summary			
Dr.		Cr.	
Closing	9,658	Closing	18,500

Repair Expense			
Balance	357	Closing	357

Supplies Expense			
Balance	607	Closing	607

Utilities Expense			
Balance	1,564	Closing	1,564

Wages Expense			
Balance	2,130	Closing	2,130

Insurance Expense			
Balance	300	Closing	300

Depreciation Expense			
Balance	1,100	Closing	1,100

Step 3: Close the Income Summary account to the owner's capital account.

After Steps 1 and 2, the Income Summary account has a credit balance of $8,842 ($18,500 − $9,658).

Income Summary

Closing	9,658	Closing	18,500
(expenses)		(revenue)	
		Balance	8,842
		(net income)	

GENERAL JOURNAL						Page 43	
Date		Description	Post. Ref.	Debit		Credit	
19X1 Dec.	31	Income Summary		8,842	00		
		Dennis Taylor, Capital				8,842	00

The picture in T-account form:

Income Summary					Dennis Taylor, Capital		
Closing	8,842	Balance	8,842			Balance	10,000
						Closing	8,842

The Income Summary account now has a zero balance; it is closed. Its previous $8,842 credit balance, equal to net income, has been moved to the owner's capital account. We have known since Chapter 2 that net income increases capital. It is through this third closing entry that net income actually arrives in the capital account.

It is possible that after Steps 1 and 2, the Income Summary account could have a debit balance. An excess of debits (expenses) over credits (revenue) would indicate a net loss for the period. In this case, the third closing entry would be:

Dec. 31   Dennis Taylor, Capital X
            Income Summary   X

The Income Summary account is closed with a credit exactly equal to its debit balance. Its previous debit balance is moved to capital by debiting the owner's capital account.

Step 4:   Close the owner's drawing account to the owner's capital account.

GENERAL JOURNAL					Page 43	
Date		Description	Post. Ref.	Debit	Credit	
19X1 Dec.	31	Dennis Taylor, Capital		9,200 00		
		Dennis Taylor, Drawing			9,200	00

The picture in T-account form:

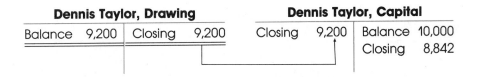

Dennis Taylor, Drawing	**Dennis Taylor, Capital**
Balance 9,200	Closing 9,200	Closing 9,200	Balance 10,000
			Closing 8,842

The drawing account now has a zero balance; it is closed. Its previous $9,200 debit balance has been moved to the owner's capital account.

Figure 6-4 shows The Kitchen Taylor's general journal after closing entries have been journalized and posted. The need for explanations is eliminated by writing *closing entries* in the Description column immediately above the first closing entry.

After the closing entries have been posted, The Kitchen Taylor's capital, drawing, income summary, revenue, and expense accounts appear as shown in Figure 6-5. In looking at the ledger accounts, observe the following details:

- A **balance** that has been **brought forward** to the top of a new page is marked by writing the word *balance* in the Item column and placing a check mark in the Posting Reference column.

- As noted in Chapter 5, postings resulting from adjusting entries are often marked by writing the word *adjusting* in the Item column.

- Although not required, postings resulting from closing entries are often marked by writing the word *closing* in the Item column.

FIGURE 6 - 4

GENERAL JOURNAL

Page 43

Date		Description	Post. Ref.	Debit		Credit	
		Closing Entries					
19X1 Dec.	31	Fees Earned	410	18,500	00		
		Income Summary	330			18,500	00
	31	Income Summary	330	9,658	00		
		Rent Expense	510			3,600	00
		Repair Expense	511			357	00
		Supplies Expense	512			607	00
		Utilities Expense	513			1,564	00
		Wages Expense	514			2,130	00
		Insurance Expense	515			300	00
		Depreciation Expense	516			1,100	00
	31	Income Summary	330	8,842	00		
		Dennis Taylor, Capital	310			8,842	00
	31	Dennis Taylor, Capital	310	9,200	00		
		Dennis Taylor, Drawing	320			9,200	00

FIGURE 6 - 5

Account __Dennis Taylor, Capital__   Account No. ___310___

Date		Item	Post. Ref.	Debit		Credit		Balance Debit		Balance Credit	
19X1 Jan.	1	Balance	✓							10,000	00
Dec.	31	Closing	J43			8,842	00			18,842	00
	31	Closing	J43	9,200	00					9,642	00

FIGURE 6 - 5 *(continued)*

Account **Dennis Taylor, Drawing**   Account No. 320

Date		Item	Post. Ref.	Debit	Credit	Balance Debit	Balance Credit
19X1 Dec.	31	Balance	√			9,200 00	
	31	Closing	J43		9,200 00	—	—

Account **Income Summary**   Account No. 330

Date		Item	Post. Ref.	Debit	Credit	Balance Debit	Balance Credit
19X1 Dec.	31	Closing	J43		18,500 00		18,500 00
	31	Closing	J43	9,658 00			8,842 00
	31	Closing	J43	8,842 00		—	—

Account **Fees Earned**   Account No. 410

Date		Item	Post. Ref.	Debit	Credit	Balance Debit	Balance Credit
19X1 Dec.	31	Balance	√				18,500 00
	31	Closing	J43	18,500 00		—	—

▌ FIGURE 6 - 5 *(continued)*

Account **Rent Expense**   Account No. 510

Date		Item	Post. Ref.	Debit	Credit	Balance	
						Debit	Credit
19X1 Dec.	31	Balance	✓			3,600 00	
	31	Closing	J43		3,600 00	—	—

Account **Repair Expense**   Account No. 511

Date		Item	Post. Ref.	Debit	Credit	Balance	
						Debit	Credit
19X1 Dec.	31	Balance	✓			357 00	
	31	Closing	J43		357 00	—	—

Account **Supplies Expense**   Account No. 512

Date		Item	Post. Ref.	Debit	Credit	Balance	
						Debit	Credit
19X1 Dec.	31	Balance	✓			75 00	
	31	Adjusting	J42	532 00		607 00	
	31	Closing	J43		607 00	—	—

FIGURE 6 - 5 *(continued)*

Account **Utilities Expense**   Account No. 513

Date		Item	Post. Ref.	Debit		Credit		Balance			
								Debit		Credit	
19X1 Dec.	31	Balance	√					1,564	00		
	31	Closing	J43			1,564	00	—		—	

Account **Wages Expense**   Account No. 514

Date		Item	Post. Ref.	Debit		Credit		Balance			
								Debit		Credit	
19X1 Dec.	31	Balance	√					2,100	00		
	31	Adjusting	J42	30	00			2,130	00		
	31	Closing	J43			2,130	00	—		—	

Account **Insurance Expense**   Account No. 515

Date		Item	Post. Ref.	Debit		Credit		Balance			
								Debit		Credit	
19X1 Dec.	31	Adjusting	J42	300	00			300	00		
	31	Closing	J43			300	00	—		—	

▌ **FIGURE 6 - 5**   *(concluded)*

Account __**Depreciation Expense**_____ Account No.____516

Date		Item	Post. Ref.	Debit		Credit		Balance			
								Debit		Credit	
19X1 Dec.	31	Adjusting	J42	1,100	00			1,100	00		
	31	Closing	J43			1,100	00	—		—	

▐▐▐▐ **THE POST-CLOSING TRIAL BALANCE**

OBJECTIVE 3
PREPARE A POST-CLOSING TRIAL BALANCE

After closing entries have been journalized and posted, a post-closing trial balance is prepared. This completes the basic accounting cycle.

The post-closing trial balance is a final check on the overall equality of debits and credits in the ledger. Figures for the post-closing trial balance should come directly from the ledger accounts.

THE KITCHEN TAYLOR
Post-Closing Trial Balance
December 31, 19X1

	Debit		Credit	
Cash	2,687	00		
Accounts Receivable	1,835	00		
Supplies	310	00		
Prepaid Insurance	900	00		
Truck	6,000	00		
Accumulated Depreciation			1,100	00
Accounts Payable			960	00
Wages Payable			30	00
Dennis Taylor, Capital			9,642	00
	11,732	00	11,732	00

Only permanent accounts appear on the post-closing trial balance because all temporary accounts have been closed.

▐▐▐▐ FISCAL YEARS AND INTERIM PERIODS

OBJECTIVE 4
DESCRIBE THE CONCEPT
OF FISCAL YEARS AND
INTERIM PERIODS

The basic accounting cycle is completed over a period of 12 consecutive months. A calendar year consists of 12 consecutive months always beginning in January and ending in December. A fiscal year also consists of 12 consecutive months. However, a fiscal year (financial year) can be any grouping of 12 consecutive months. The most popular fiscal year is the calendar year (January 1 through December 31), but a fiscal year could begin July 1 and end the following June 30, or it could begin October 1 and end the following September 30, for example. A fiscal year usually ends at a slow time of year for the business, allowing extra time for special year-end activities. Once a new business chooses a fiscal year, it must continue to use that same fiscal year in the future. Consistency enables users of financial statements to make year-to-year comparisons.

Any period of time shorter than a fiscal year is known as an interim period. Statements prepared for periods less than a fiscal year (monthly, quarterly, semiannually) are known as interim statements.

▐▐▐▐ A COMPARISON OF MANUAL AND COMPUTERIZED ACCOUNTING SYSTEMS

OBJECTIVE 5
DESCRIBE THE
SIMILARITIES AND
DIFFERENCES BETWEEN
MANUAL AND
COMPUTERIZED
ACCOUNTING SYSTEMS

These days, with all the talk of computerized accounting systems, many students may question the value of studying a manual accounting system. While there is no doubt that the use of computers is growing and that they are tremendously useful in accounting, both manual and computerized accounting systems are based on the same accounting principles and procedures. The difference lies in who will perform the procedures—a person or a computer. Some procedures require analysis and judgment; they must be performed by a person. Other procedures are more mechanical in nature; they may be performed by a person or a computer. Computers may be programmed to perform mechanical tasks with amazing speed and accuracy. Let's consider how a computer might be used in the basic accounting cycle.

JOURNALIZING   Journalizing requires that transactions be analyzed and recorded. Analysis requires thought and judgment:

Should a transaction be recorded?

If so, how?

What accounts are involved?

Should these accounts be debited or credited?

For how much?

Such analysis must be performed by a person. Next, the information must be recorded—entered into the accounting system. The information must be recorded by a person, but how it is recorded depends on whether the system is manual or computerized.

In a manual system, the data would be recorded by a handwritten entry in the journal. In a computerized system, the data would be entered by a person using a keyboard, optical scanner, or some other computer-oriented device. Although the same information is recorded, the data would be entered into a data base rather than a journal. A data base is simply a collection of data or information that is stored within the computer. Once entered, this information may be selected and arranged in many different ways. For example, the data may be arranged and displayed in the form of journal entries.

POSTING TO THE LEDGER   Posting simply involves transferring information from one place to another. In a manual system, the data are transferred from the journal to the ledger. This is a mechanical task that is easily performed by a computer. However, in a computerized system, the information comes from the data base and is arranged in the form of ledger accounts.

PREPARING A TRIAL BALANCE   In a computerized system, it is not necessary to rough draft financial statements, so a work sheet is not needed. However, a trial balance may easily be prepared by a computer.

PREPARING FINANCIAL STATEMENTS   Income statements, statements of owner's equity, and balance sheets are easily prepared by a computer. The computer is programmed to select the appropriate information from the data base and to arrange it in the specified financial statement format.

CONCLUSION   A basic knowledge of accounting is necessary regardless of whether a system is manual or computerized. Although computers perform mechanical tasks with tremendous speed and accuracy, they must still be told what to do and how to do it.

Chapter Summary

Closing an account means bringing the account balance to zero. At the end of every fiscal year, the temporary owner's equity accounts (revenue, expense, and drawing) must be closed to the permanent owner's equity account (capital). The closing procedure, implemented through four closing entries, consists of four steps:

Step 1: Close all revenue accounts to the Income Summary account.

Step 2: Close all expense accounts to the Income Summary account.

Step 3: Close the Income Summary account to the owner's capital account.

Step 4: Close the owner's drawing account to the owner's capital account.

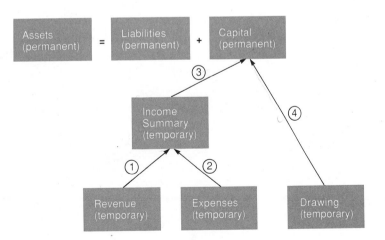

After closing entries have been journalized and posted, a post-closing trial balance is prepared. Only permanent accounts (assets, liabilities, capital) appear on the post-closing trial balance, since all temporary accounts have been closed. This completes the basic accounting cycle.

A basic knowledge of accounting is necessary regardless of whether a system is manual or computerized. Although computers perform mechanical tasks with tremendous speed and accuracy, they must still be told what to do and how to do it.

Glossary

ACCOUNTING CYCLE

The accounting process completed during each fiscal year: journalizing, posting to ledger, preparing a work sheet, financial statements, adjusting entries, closing entries, and a post-closing trial balance.

BALANCE—BROUGHT FORWARD

A balance copied from the bottom of one page to the top of a new page.

CALENDAR YEAR

A year consisting of 12 consecutive months always beginning in January and ending in December.

CLOSED ACCOUNT

An account with a zero balance.

CLOSING ENTRIES

Four entries prepared at the end of the fiscal year to close the temporary owner's equity accounts (revenue, expense, and drawing) to the permanent owner's equity account (capital).

FISCAL YEAR

A financial year consisting of 12 consecutive months. The most popular fiscal year is the calendar year (January through December), but it could be any grouping of 12 consecutive months—for example, July 1 through the following June 30.

INTERIM PERIOD

A period of time shorter than one fiscal year.

INTERIM STATEMENT

A statement prepared for a period less than one fiscal year.

PERMANENT ACCOUNTS

Asset, liability, and capital accounts are permanent in the sense that their year-end balances carry over and become beginning balances in the new fiscal year.

TEMPORARY OWNER'S EQUITY ACCOUNTS

Accounts that accumulate data for only one fiscal year (revenue, expense, and drawing). At the end of each fiscal year, they are closed to capital. They are temporary in the sense that there is no carryover of their balances from one year to the next. They begin every new year with a zero balance.

Questions for Discussion

1. Why are closing entries necessary?

2. Explain how to close an account.

3. Define:
   a. Temporary owner's equity accounts.
   b. Permanent accounts.
   c. Interim period.
   d. Interim statement.

4. Describe the four steps in the closing procedure.

5. Where is the information for closing entries obtained?

6. After the first two closing entries have been journalized and posted, the balance in the Income Summary account could be on either the debit or credit side.
   a. What would a credit balance indicate?
   b. What would a debit balance indicate?

7. Briefly describe the basic accounting cycle.

8. What is the difference between a calendar year and a fiscal year?

9. Describe the basic similarities and differences between manual and computerized accounting systems.

Exercises

Arrange the following steps in the accounting cycle in their proper order:

a. Journalize and post adjusting entries.

b. Prepare a post-closing trial balance.

c. Prepare a work sheet.

d. Post to the ledger.

e. Journalize.

f. Journalize and post closing entries.

g. Prepare financial statements.

Indicate whether each of the following accounts should be closed at year-end (yes or no):

a. Rent Expense.

b. Supplies.

c. Fees Earned.

d. Wendy Mork, Capital.

e. Accounts Payable.

f. Supplies Expense.

g. Wendy Mork, Drawing.

h. Depreciation Expense.

i. Accumulated Depreciation.

j. Prepaid Insurance.

EXERCISE 6-3
INCOME SUMMARY
ACCOUNT
(L.O.1, 2)

After closing entries have been journalized and posted, the Income Summary account appears as follows:

Income Summary

Closing	9,325	Closing	12,580
Closing	3,255		

From this information, answer the following questions:

    a. What is the current balance in the Income Summary account?

    b. What was total revenue?

    c. What were total expenses?

    d. What was the net income or loss? (Be sure to indicate whether the figure represents income or loss.)

EXERCISE 6-4
CLOSING ENTRIES
(L.O.1, 2)

On December 31, after adjusting entries have been journalized and posted, Mitchell Company's ledger contains the following account balances:

	Debit	Credit
Cash	1,300 00	
Accounts Receivable	1,472 00	
Supplies	180 00	
Accounts Payable		1,065 00
Thomas Mitchell, Capital		3,084 00
Thomas Mitchell, Drawing	3,150 00	
Professional Fees		12,400 00
Rent Expense	3,600 00	
Salary Expense	6,500 00	
Miscellaneous Expense	347 00	

Journalize the closing entries.

EXERCISE 6-5
POST-CLOSING TRIAL
BALANCE
(L.O.3)

Assuming the closing entries from Exercise 6-4 have been posted, prepare a post-closing trial balance.

EXERCISE 6-6
CLOSING INCOME
SUMMARY ACCOUNT
(L.O.1, 2)

After the first two closing entries have been journalized and posted, the Income Summary account of Gamon Enterprises (Carla Gamon, owner) appears as follows:

Income Summary	
Closing 28,250	Closing 26,185

Journalize the entry necessary to close the Income Summary account.

EXERCISE 6-7
STATEMENT OF OWNER'S
EQUITY
(L.O.1, 4)

After closing entries have been journalized and posted, the capital account of Romero Company appears as follows:

John Romero, Capital	
19X1	19X1
Dec. 31 Closing 9,500	Jan. 1 Balance 25,460
	Dec. 31 Closing 13,710

Assuming all accounts have normal balances, prepare a statement of owner's equity for the year ended December 31, 19X1.

EXERCISE 6-8
CLOSING ENTRIES
(L.O.1, 2)

Complete the following flowchart to demonstrate the four-step pattern of closing entries.

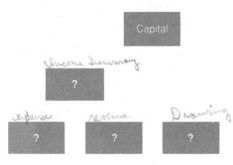

Problems—Set A

PROBLEM 6-1A
CLOSING ENTRIES;
STATEMENT OF OWNER'S
EQUITY
(L.O.1, 2, 4)

On December 31, 19X1, after adjustment, Johnson Company's ledger contains the following account balances:

	Debit	Credit
Cash	1,925 00	
Accounts Receivable	1,430 00	
Supplies	398 00	
Equipment	3,100 00	
Accumulated Depreciation		710 00
Accounts Payable		1,240 00
William Johnson, Capital (Jan. 1, 19X1, bal.)		9,463 00
William Johnson, Drawing	15,700 00	
Income from Services		21,420 00
Advertising Expense	2,150 00	
Rent Expense	6,400 00	
Utilities Expense	1,280 00	
Depreciation Expense	450 00	

INSTRUCTIONS

1. Journalize the closing entries.

2. Prepare a statement of owner's equity for the year ended December 31, 19X1.

PROBLEM 6-2A
ADJUSTING AND
CLOSING ENTRIES;
POST-CLOSING TRIAL
BALANCE (L.O.1–3)

A completed work sheet for Pershing Services is shown below.

INSTRUCTIONS
1. Journalize and post the adjusting entries.
2. Journalize and post the closing entries.
3. Prepare a post-closing trial balance.

PERSHING SERVICES
Work Sheet
For the Year Ended December 31, 19X1

Account Title	Acct. No.	Trial Balance Debit	Trial Balance Credit	Adjustments Debit	Adjustments Credit
Cash	110	2,490 00			
Accounts Receivable	111	3,618 00			
Supplies	112	793 00			(a) 371 00
Prepaid Insurance	113	1,580 00			(b) 836 00
Equipment	114	16,400 00			
Accumulated Depreciation	115		2,600 00		(d) 1,230 00
Accounts Payable	210		3,475 00		
Linda Pershing, Capital	310		21,544 00		
Linda Pershing, Drawing	311	17,580 00			
Service Revenue	410		43,100 00		
Advertising Expense	511	2,350 00			
Rent Expense	514	8,400 00			
Utilities Expense	516	2,985 00			
Wages Expense	517	13,660 00		(c) 1,075 00	
Miscellaneous Expense	518	863 00			
		70,719 00	70,719 00		
Supplies Expense	515			(a) 371 00	
Insurance Expense	513			(b) 836 00	
Wages Payable	211				(c) 1,075 00
Depreciation Expense	512			(d) 1,230 00	
				3,512 00	3,512 00
Net income					

Note: Students not using the working papers should:

a. Number general journal pages beginning with page 63.
b. Open accounts with titles and numbers as shown on the work sheet and Income Summary, No. 312.
c. Insert beginning balances as shown on the trial balance. (Any account not shown on trial balance has a zero balance.)

Adjusted Trial Balance		Income Statement		Balance Sheet	
Debit	Credit	Debit	Credit	Debit	Credit
2,490 00				2,490 00	
3,618 00				3,618 00	
422 00				422 00	
744 00				744 00	
16,400 00				16,400 00	
	3,830 00				3,830 00
	3,475 00				3,475 00
	21,544 00				21,544 00
17,580 00				17,580 00	
	43,100 00		43,100 00		
2,350 00		2,350 00			
8,400 00		8,400 00			
2,985 00		2,985 00			
14,735 00		14,735 00			
863 00		863 00			
371 00		371 00			
836 00		836 00			
	1,075 00				1,075 00
1,230 00		1,230 00	*Inc. Summary*		
73,024 00	73,024 00	31,770 00	43,100 00	41,254 00	29,924 00
		11,330 00			11,330 00
		43,100 00	43,100 00	41,254 00	41,254 00

PROBLEM 6-3A

WORK SHEET;
ADJUSTING AND
CLOSING ENTRIES;
POST-CLOSING TRIAL
BALANCE (L.O.1–3)

A partially completed work sheet for Selitsky and Associates is shown below.

INSTRUCTIONS

1. Complete the work sheet.
2. Journalize and post the adjusting entries.
3. Journalize and post the closing entries.
4. Prepare a post-closing trial balance.

SELITSKY AND ASSOCIATES
Work Sheet
For the Year Ended December 31, 19X1

Account Title	Acct. No.	Trial Balance Debit	Trial Balance Credit	Adjustments Debit	Adjustments Credit
Cash	110	4,218 00			
Accounts Receivable	111	10,730 00			
Supplies	112	1,354 00			(a) 989 00
Prepaid Insurance	113	1,896 00			(b) 1,275 00
Equipment	114	20,155 00			
Accumulated Depreciation	115		5,290 00		(d) 1,630 00
Accounts Payable	210		8,642 00		
Mark Selitsky, Capital	310		24,376 00		
Mark Selitsky, Drawing	311	18,640 00			
Fees Earned	410		76,500 00		
Advertising Expense	511	4,743 00			
Rent Expense	514	9,100 00			
Utilities Expense	517	2,500 00			
Wages Expense	518	39,825 00		(c) 2,300 00	
Repair Expense	515	1,647 00			
		114,808 00	114,808 00		
Supplies Expense	516			(a) 989 00	
Insurance Expense	513			(b) 1,275 00	
Wages Payable	211				(c) 2,300 00
Depreciation Expense	512			(d) 1,630 00	
				6,194 00	6,194 00

Note: Students not using the working papers should:
  a. Number general journal pages beginning with page 53.
  b. Open accounts with titles and numbers as shown in the work sheet and Income Summary, No. 312.
  c. Insert beginning balances as shown on the trial balance. (Any account not shown on trial balance has a zero balance.)

Adjusted Trial Balance		Income Statement		Balance Sheet	
Debit	Credit	Debit	Credit	Debit	Credit
4,218 00					
10,730 00					
365 00					
621 00					
20,155 00					
	6,920 00				
	8,642 00				
	24,376 00				
18,640 00					
	76,500 00				
4,743 00					
9,100 00					
2,500 00					
42,125 00					
1,647 00					
989 00					
1,275 00					
	2,300 00				
1,630 00					
118,738 00	118,738 00				

PROBLEM 6-4A
WORK SHEET; FINANCIAL
STATEMENTS; ADJUSTING
AND CLOSING ENTRIES;
POST-CLOSING TRIAL
BALANCE
(L.O.1–4)

Following is a partially completed work sheet for Payton Legal Services:

Account Title	Trial Balance				Adjustments			
	Debit		Credit		Debit		Credit	
Cash	1,983	00						
Accounts Receivable	2,685	00						
Supplies	597	00						
Prepaid Insurance	1,280	00						
Equipment	12,500	00						
Accumulated Depreciation			1,700	00				
Accounts Payable			2,472	00				
Wanda Payton, Capital			12,619	00				
Wanda Payton, Drawing	26,800	00						
Professional Fees			59,300	00				
Advertising Expense	1,942	00						
Rent Expense	7,300	00						
Utilities Expense	1,268	00						
Salary Expense	18,900	00						
Miscellaneous Expense	836	00						
	76,091	00	76,091	00				

PAYTON LEGAL SERVICES
Work Sheet
For the Year Ended December 31, 19X1

INSTRUCTIONS

1. Complete the work sheet using the following adjustment data:
   a. Supplies on hand, December 31, 19X1, $230.
   b. Expired insurance, $812.
   c. Salary expense incurred but not yet paid as of December 31, 19X1, $1,310.
   d. Depreciation on the equipment, $1,150.

2. Prepare:
   a. An income statement.
   b. A statement of owner's equity.
   c. A balance sheet.

3. Journalize and post the adjusting entries.

4. Journalize and post the closing entries.

5. Prepare a post-closing trial balance.

Note: Students not using the working papers should:
   a. Number general journal pages beginning with page 34.
   b. Open ledger accounts with the following account titles and account numbers:

Cash	110
Accounts Receivable	111
Supplies	112
Prepaid Insurance	113
Equipment	114
Accumulated Depreciation	115
Accounts Payable	210
Salaries Payable	211
Wanda Payton, Capital	310
Wanda Payton, Drawing	311
Income Summary	312
Professional Fees	410
Advertising Expense	511
Depreciation Expense	512
Insurance Expense	513
Rent Expense	514
Salary Expense	515
Supplies Expense	516
Utilities Expense	517
Miscellaneous Expense	518

   c. Insert beginning balances as shown on the trial balance. (Any account not shown on trial balance has a zero balance.)

Problems—Set B

PROBLEM 6-1B
CLOSING ENTRIES;
STATEMENT OF OWNER'S
EQUITY
(L.O.1, 2, 4)

On December 31, 19X1, after adjustment, Raymond Company's ledger contains the following account balances:

	Debit	Credit
Cash	3,850 00	
Accounts Receivable	2,860 00	
Supplies	796 00	
Equipment	6,200 00	
Accumulated Depreciation		1,420 00
Accounts Payable		2,480 00
Sam Raymond, Capital (Jan. 1, 19X1 bal.)		18,926 00
Sam Raymond, Drawing	31,400 00	
Income from Services		42,840 00
Advertising Expense	4,300 00	
Rent Expense	12,800 00	
Utilities Expense	2,560 00	
Depreciation Expense	900 00	

INSTRUCTIONS

1. Journalize the closing entries.

2. Prepare a statement of owner's equity for the year ended December 31, 19X1.

PROBLEM 6-2B   A completed work sheet for Moore Enterprises is shown below.

ADJUSTING AND
CLOSING ENTRIES;
POST-CLOSING TRIAL
BALANCE (L.O.1–3)

INSTRUCTIONS
1. Journalize and post the adjusting entries.
2. Journalize and post the closing entries.
3. Prepare a post-closing trial balance.

MOORE ENTERPRISES
Work Sheet
For the Year Ended December 31, 19X1

Account Title	Acct. No.	Trial Balance Debit	Trial Balance Credit	Adjustments Debit	Adjustments Credit
Cash	110	4,980 00			
Accounts Receivable	111	7,236 00			
Supplies	112	1,586 00			(a) 742 00
Prepaid Insurance	113	3,160 00			(b) 1,672 00
Equipment	114	32,800 00			
Accumulated Depreciation	115		5,200 00		(d) 2,460 00
Accounts Payable	210		6,950 00		
Stanley Moore, Capital	310		43,088 00		
Stanley Moore, Drawing	311	35,160 00			
Service Revenue	410		86,200 00		
Advertising Expense	511	4,700 00			
Rent Expense	514	16,800 00			
Utilities Expense	516	5,970 00			
Wages Expense	517	27,320 00		(c) 2,150 00	
Miscellaneous Expense	518	1,726 00			
		141,438 00	141,438 00		
Supplies Expense	515			(a) 742 00	
Insurance Expense	513			(b) 1,672 00	
Wages Payable	211				(c) 2,150 00
Depreciation Expense	512			(d) 2,460 00	
				7,024 00	7,024 00
Net income					

Note: Students not using the working papers should:

a. Number general journal pages beginning with page 23.

b. Open accounts with titles and numbers as shown on the work sheet and Income Summary, No. 312.

c. Insert beginning balances as shown on the trial balance. (Any account not shown on trial balance has a zero balance.)

Adjusted Trial Balance		Income Statement		Balance Sheet	
Debit	Credit	Debit	Credit	Debit	Credit
4,980 00				4,980 00	
7,236 00				7,236 00	
844 00				844 00	
1,488 00				1,488 00	
32,800 00				32,800 00	
	7,660 00				7,660 00
	6,950 00				6,950 00
	43,088 00				43,088 00
35,160 00				35,160 00	
	86,200 00		86,200 00		
4,700 00		4,700 00			
16,800 00		16,800 00			
5,970 00		5,970 00			
29,470 00		29,470 00			
1,726 00		1,726 00			
742 00		742 00			
1,672 00		1,672 00			
	2,150 00				2,150 00
2,460 00		2,460 00			
146,048 00	146,048 00	63,540 00	86,200 00	82,508 00	59,848 00
		22,660 00			22,660 00
		86,200 00	86,200 00	82,508 00	82,508 00

PROBLEM 6-3B
WORK SHEET;
ADJUSTING AND
CLOSING ENTRIES;
POST-CLOSING TRIAL
BALANCE (L.O.1–3)

A partially completed work sheet for J. Gaines Company is shown below.

INSTRUCTIONS

1. Complete the work sheet.
2. Journalize and post the adjusting entries.
3. Journalize and post the closing entries.
4. Prepare a post-closing trial balance.

J. GAINES COMPANY
Work Sheet
For the Year Ended December 31, 19X1

Account Title	Acct. No.	Trial Balance Debit	Trial Balance Credit	Adjustments Debit	Adjustments Credit
Cash	110	8,436 00			
Accounts Receivable	111	21,460 00			
Supplies	112	2,708 00			(a) 1,978 00
Prepaid Insurance	113	3,792 00			(b) 2,550 00
Equipment	114	40,310 00			
Accumulated Depreciation	115		10,580 00		(d) 3,260 00
Accounts Payable	210		17,284 00		
Jason Gaines, Capital	310		48,752 00		
Jason Gaines, Drawing	311	37,280 00			
Fees Earned	410		153,000 00		
Advertising Expense	511	9,486 00			
Rent Expense	514	18,200 00			
Utilities Expense	517	5,000 00			
Wages Expense	518	79,650 00		(c) 4,600 00	
Repair Expense	515	3,294 00			
		229,616 00	229,616 00		
Supplies Expense	516			(a) 1,978 00	
Insurance Expense	513			(b) 2,550 00	
Wages Payable	211				(c) 4,600 00
Depreciation Expense	512			(d) 3,260 00	
				12,388 00	12,388 00

Note: Students not using the working papers should:
  a. Number general journal pages beginning with page 41.
  b. Open accounts with titles and numbers as shown on the work sheet and Income Summary, No. 312.
  c. Insert beginning balances as shown on the trial balance. (Any account not shown on trial balance has a zero balance.)

Adjusted Trial Balance		Income Statement		Balance Sheet	
Debit	Credit	Debit	Credit	Debit	Credit
8,436 00					
21,460 00					
730 00					
1,242 00					
40,310 00					
	13,840 00				
	17,284 00				
	48,752 00				
37,280 00					
	153,000 00				
9,486 00					
18,200 00					
5,000 00					
84,250 00					
3,294 00					
1,978 00					
2,550 00					
	4,600 00				
3,260 00					
237,476 00	237,476 00				

PROBLEM 6-4B
WORK SHEET; FINANCIAL
STATEMENTS; ADJUSTING
AND CLOSING ENTRIES;
POST-CLOSING TRIAL
BALANCE
(L.O.1–4)

Following is a partially completed work sheet for Bear Accounting Services:

BEAR ACCOUNTING SERVICES
Work Sheet
For the Year Ended December 31, 19X1

Account Title	Trial Balance Debit		Trial Balance Credit		Adjustments Debit		Adjustments Credit	
Cash	3,966	00						
Accounts Receivable	5,370	00						
Supplies	1,194	00						
Prepaid Insurance	2,560	00						
Equipment	25,000	00						
Accumulated Depreciation			3,400	00				
Accounts Payable			4,944	00				
Robert Bear, Capital			25,238	00				
Robert Bear, Drawing	53,600	00						
Professional Fees			118,600	00				
Advertising Expense	3,884	00						
Rent Expense	14,600	00						
Utilities Expense	2,536	00						
Salary Expense	37,800	00						
Miscellaneous Expense	1,672	00						
	152,182	00	152,182	00				

Adjusted Trial Balance		Income Statement		Balance Sheet	
Debit	Credit	Debit	Credit	Debit	Credit

INSTRUCTIONS

1. Complete the work sheet using the following adjustment data:

   a. Supplies on hand, December 31, 19X1, $460.
   b. Expired insurance, $1,624.
   c. Salary expense incurred but not yet paid as of December 31, 19X1, $2,620.
   d. Depreciation on the equipment, $2,300.

2. Prepare:
   a. An income statement.
   b. A statement of owner's equity.
   c. A balance sheet.

3. Journalize and post the adjusting entries.

4. Journalize and post the closing entries.

5. Prepare a post-closing trial balance.

Note: Students not using the working papers should:

   a. Number general journal pages beginning with page 31.

   b. Open ledger accounts with the following account titles and account numbers:

Cash	110
Accounts Receivable	111
Supplies	112
Prepaid Insurance	113
Equipment	114
Accumulated Depreciation	115
Accounts Payable	210
Salaries Payable	211
Robert Bear, Capital	310
Robert Bear, Drawing	311
Income Summary	312
Professional Fees	410
Advertising Expense	511
Depreciation Expense	512
Insurance Expense	513
Rent Expense	514
Salary Expense	515
Supplies Expense	516
Utilities Expense	517
Miscellaneous Expense	518

   c. Insert beginning balances as shown on the trial balance. (Any account not shown on trial balance has a zero balance.)

Mini-Cases

CASE 6-1

Scott Foreman, a friend of yours, says he does not need to make any closing entries because he does not use any temporary accounts. Instead, he records all revenue, expense, and drawing transactions directly in the capital account as they occur. Is this a good idea?

CASE 6-2

Harry, your new accounts receivable clerk, asks, "How is it possible for accounts receivable to be a permanent account? Our customers have to pay in 30 days." What is your reply?

CASE 6-3

Chris Bayne, a client, complains that the post-closing trial balance you prepared is incomplete. Chris says "You left out my drawing account, as well as all the revenue and expense accounts." Did you make a mistake?

Covering Chapters 1–6

Morgan Cleaning Services began operations in October 19X1.

Chart of Acounts

Assets
110 Cash
111 Accounts Receivable
112 Supplies
113 Prepaid Insurance
114 Equipment
115 Accumulated Depreciation—
       Equipment
116 Truck
117 Accumulated Depreciation—
       Truck

Liabilities
210 Accounts Payable
211 Salaries Payable

Owner's Equity
310 Robert Morgan, Capital
320 Robert Morgan, Drawing
330 Income Summary

Revenue
410 Cleaning Revenue

Expenses
510 Advertising Expense
511 Depreciation Expense—
       Equipment
512 Depreciation Expense—Truck
513 Insurance Expense
514 Rent Expense
515 Salary Expense
516 Supplies Expense
517 Telephone Expense
518 Utilities Expense

The following transactions were completed during the first month of operations:

Oct. 1   The owner, Robert Morgan, invested $20,000 cash in the business.

      1   Paid monthly rent, $500.

Oct. 2   Purchased $3,000 worth of equipment, paying $1,000 in cash and the remainder on account.

      3   Purchased soap, cleanser, window cleaner, and other supplies on account, $190.

      5   Purchased a truck for cash, $11,500.

      5   Paid a one-year insurance premium covering the period October 5, 19X1, through October 4, 19X2, $720.

      8   Paid bill for newspaper advertising, $84.

     10   Recorded revenue from cleaning services: $250 cash and $630 on account.

     12   Paid employees' salaries, $365.

     15   Paid creditor on account, $95.

     18   Recorded revenue from cleaning services: $170 cash and $810 on account.

     19   Received payment on account from charge customer, $460.

     22   Paid electricity bill, $78.

     24   Paid creditor on account, $500.

     26   Paid employees' salaries, $410.

     29   Received payment on account from charge customer, $362.

     30   The owner withdrew $250 to pay for personal expenses.

     31   Recorded revenue from cleaning services: $205 cash and $790 on account.

INSTRUCTIONS

1. For those students not using the working papers:
   a. This company uses a general journal. Number the journal pages beginning with page 1.
   b. Open ledger accounts inserting account titles and numbers as indicated on the chart of accounts.

2. Record the October transactions in the general journal.

3. Post the journal to the ledger.

4. Prepare a trial balance using the first two columns of the work sheet.

5. Complete the work sheet using the following adjustment data:

   a. Supplies on hand, October 31, $115.
   b. Expired insurance, $60.
   c. Salary expense incurred but not yet paid as of October 31, $240.
   d. Depreciation on equipment, $75.
   e. Depreciation on truck, $300.

6. Prepare:
   a. An income statement.
   b. A statement of owner's equity.
   c. A balance sheet.

7. Journalize the adjusting entries.

8. Post the adjusting entries.

9. Journalize the closing entries. (Although many businesses close their temporary accounts only at year-end, Robert Morgan has decided to close the accounts on a monthly basis.)

10. Post the closing entries.

11. Prepare a post-closing trial balance.

PART B

Morgan Cleaning Services completed the following transactions during November 19X1:

Nov. 1   Paid monthly rent, $500.

    5   Received payment on account from charge customer, $448.

    9   Paid employees' salaries, $400. Hint: Debit Salary Expense $160 ($400 − 240) and debit Salaries Payable $240—recall October's adjusting entries.

   12   Recorded revenue from cleaning services: $365 cash and $860 on account.

   16   Paid creditor on account, $1,000.

   19   Purchased supplies on account, $72

   21   The owner withdrew $300 to pay for personal expenses.

   23   Paid employees' salaries, $360.

   26   Paid telephone bill, $147.

   26   Paid electricity bill, $98.

   28   Received payment on account from charge customer, $790.

Nov. 30   Recorded revenue from cleaning services: $480 cash and
             $910 on account.

INSTRUCTIONS

12. Record the November transactions in the general journal.

13. Post the journal to the ledger.

14. Prepare a trial balance using the first two columns of the work sheet.

15. Complete the work sheet using the following adjustment data:
    a. Supplies on hand, November 30, $110.
    b. Expired insurance, $60.
    c. Salary expense incurred but not yet paid as of November 30, $235.
    d. Depreciation on equipment, $75.
    e. Depreciation on truck, $300.

16. Prepare:
    a. An income statement.
    b. A statement of owner's equity.
    c. A balance sheet.

17. Journalize the adjusting entries.

18. Post the adjusting entries.

19. Journalize the closing entries.

20. Post the closing entries.

21. Prepare a post-closing trial balance.

Accounting for a Professional Service Business, Cash, and Payroll

||||||||||||||||
CHAPTER

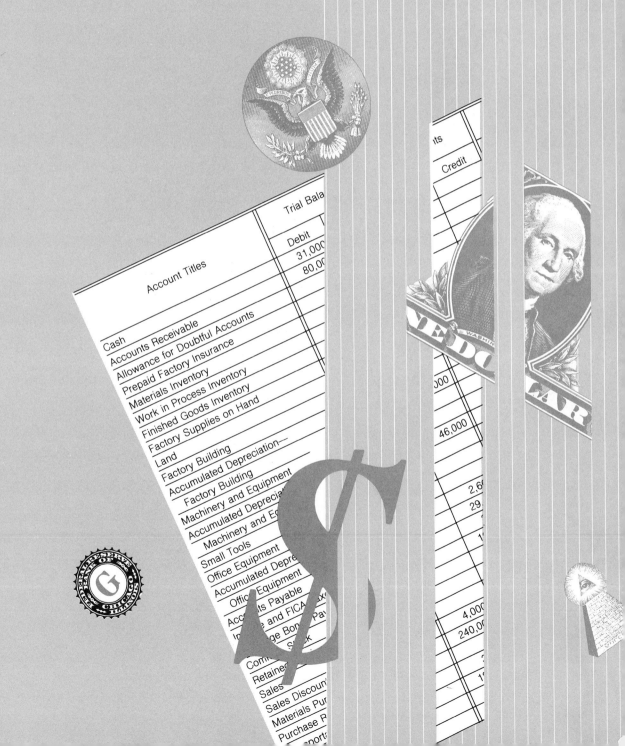

PART 2

CHAPTER 7

Accounting for a Professional Service Business

AFTER STUDYING THIS CHAPTER, YOU SHOULD BE ABLE TO:

1 Define the modified cash basis of accounting.

2 Journalize and post using a combination journal.

3 Prepare a work sheet for a professional service business.

4 Prepare financial statements for a professional service business.

5 Prepare adjusting entries for a professional service business.

6 Prepare closing entries for a professional service business.

In this chapter, you will apply your knowledge of the basic accounting cycle to accounting for a professional service business. As you will recall, a service business sells a skill or technique that has no physical existence. Although The Kitchen Taylor is a service business, refinishing cabinets is generally considered to be a trade rather than a profession. Examples of professional services include the services of public accountants, attorneys, physicians, and architects. As stated in Chapter 1, we assume the use of the accrual basis of accounting throughout the book because accountants generally agree that it results in a more timely measurement of income for most businesses. However, the cash basis of accounting is commonly used by professional service businesses. Before proceeding with our study of a professional service business, let's quickly review these two bases of accounting.

▐▐▐ ACCRUAL VERSUS CASH-BASIS ACCOUNTING

OBJECTIVE 1
DEFINE THE MODIFIED
CASH BASIS OF
ACCOUNTING

Under **accrual-basis accounting**, revenues must be recorded when they are earned regardless of whether the cash has been received. When the service or product has been provided to the customer, the revenue has been earned and must be recorded. Accrual-basis accounting also requires that expenses be recorded in the period in which they are incurred regardless of whether the cash is paid out at that time or later. When we have accepted a product or service from someone else, the expense has been incurred and must be recorded.

Under **cash-basis accounting**, revenues are recorded when the cash is received, and expenses are recorded when the cash is paid out. Recognition of revenues and expenses is tied to the flow of cash.

Let's compare how the same revenue and expense transactions would be handled under each basis.

Transaction	Accrual Basis	Cash Basis
Performed service for customer on account.	Since service was performed, revenue is recorded.	Since cash was not received, revenue is not recorded.
Had office windows washed but have not yet paid the bill.	Since service was accepted from someone else, expense is recorded.	Since cash was not paid out, expense is not recorded.

On a pure cash basis, no adjusting entries would be needed because the flow of cash determines when revenues and expenses are recorded. There is no need to update. However, in recording expenses under the cash basis, exceptions are often made in relation to plant assets. For example, in the case of a building, it would not be reasonable to consider its entire cost as an expense of the year in which it was purchased. The same is true of certain prepaid items such as supplies and insurance. Since these items have useful lives of more than one accounting period, their costs must be spread over their useful lives. This necessitates the recording of adjusting entries for depreciation, used supplies, and expired insurance. The cash basis with these exceptions is referred to as modified-cash-basis accounting. Professional service businesses frequently use the modified cash basis. *Cash base accting of revenues + expenses but take into account a (Plant assets) → buildings, supplies + insurance. vehicles*

▉▉▉▉ EXAMPLE: THE RECORDS OF A PHYSICIAN

To demonstrate the accounting for a professional service business using a modified cash basis, let's look at the records of Robert Miller, M.D. Dr. Miller's chart of accounts is shown below.

Chart of Acounts

Assets
111 Cash
112 Medical Supplies
113 Office Supplies
114 Prepaid Insurance
121 Medical Equipment
122 Accumulated Depreciation—
      Medical Equipment
123 Office Furniture and
      Equipment
124 Accumulated Depreciation—
      Office Furniture and
      Equipment

Liabilities
211 Notes Payable

Owner's Equity
311 R. Miller, Capital
312 R. Miller, Drawing
313 Income Summary

Revenue
411 Professional Fees

Expenses
511 Depreciation Expense—
      Medical Equipment
512 Depreciation Expense—
      Office Furniture and
      Equipment
513 Insurance Expense
514 Laboratory Expense
515 Laundry Expense
516 Medical Supplies Expense
517 Office Supplies Expense
518 Rent Expense
519 Repair Expense
520 Salary Expense
521 Telephone Expense
522 Utilities Expense
523 Miscellaneous Expense

DAILY APPOINTMENT RECORD

Dr. Miller's receptionist prepares the daily appointment record as shown in Figure 7-1. Dr. Miller receives a copy one day in advance so that he can do any necessary preparatory work.

▌ **FIGURE 7 - 1** *really not a journal*

Captures everything they've done for that day *customers journal*

DAILY APPOINTMENT RECORD

DATE   12/15/X8

Time	Patient	Professional Service	Fees	Payments
8:00	Inez Barill			
15	Catherine Colombo			
30	William Johnson			
45				
9:00	Dom Valeria			
15				
30	John Black			
45	Jennifer Cole			
10:00				
15	Lois Sinner			
30				
45	Shirley Bayne			
11:00	Suzanne Farrand			
15				
30	Landi Cohen			
45	Flora Gandolfi			
12:00				
15				
30				
45				
1:00	Emma Bellomo			
15	Nick Urick			
30				
45	Annette Peters			
2:00	Andy Wargo			
15	Helen Wargo			
30				
45	Mike Petrovich			
3:00				
15	Mildred Kadell			
30				
45	Irene Strahotsky			
4:00				
15	Agnes Thompson			
30	Merle Salasnek			
45	Elizabeth Hope			

▌ FIGURE 7 - 2

ROBERT MILLER, M.D.
1717 East 35th Street
Baltimore, Maryland 21218

patients ledger
(to us — individual ledger accts)

Helen Wargo
1523 Kurtz Avenue
Lutherville, MD 21093

Date	Professional Service	Fees	Payments	Balance
6-14-X8	OV	35.00		35.00
6-19-X8	LAB	12.00		47.00
7-8-X8	Payment		47.00	–0–
12-15-X8	OV; X	62.00		62.00
12-15-X8	Payment		62.00	–0–

Pay last amount in balance column.

OV	Office Visit	LAB	Laboratory	M	Medical
HV	Hospital Visit	X	X ray	S	Surgical
				MISC	Miscellaneous

PATIENTS' LEDGER RECORDS

Dr. Miller's receptionist also prepares a separate patient ledger record for each patient as shown in Figure 7-2. Both the fee and payment information recorded in the patients' ledger records are obtained from the daily appointment records. The patients' ledger records are usually kept on cards. Dr. Miller keeps the loose cards in a card file in alphabetical order. This allows for easy insertion and removal of cards. At the end of the month, photocopies of the patients' ledger records are mailed to each patient with an outstanding balance.

PAYMENTS FROM PATIENTS

All payments received from patients, or insurance companies on behalf of patients, are recorded in the Payments column of the daily appointment record on the day they are received. As shown in Figure 7-3, payments received at the time of the scheduled appointment are recorded on the appropriate patient's line. All other payments received on that day (usually through the mail) are recorded at the bottom of the daily appointment record indicating the patient's name and amount.

A receipt is prepared in duplicate for each payment received. One copy

FIGURE 7 - 3

DAILY APPOINTMENT RECORD

DATE   12/15/X8

Time	Patient	Professional Service	Fees	Payments
8:00	Inez Barill	OV	35.00	
15	Catherine Colombo	OV; LAB	77.00	
30	William Johnson	OV; X	64.00	
45				
9:00	Dom Valeria	OV	40.00	40.00
15				
30	John Black	OV; MISC	52.00	
45	Jennifer Cole	OV	40.00	
10:00				
15	Lois Sinner	OV; LAB	59.00	59.00
30				
45	Shirley Bayne	X	30.00	30.00
11:00	Suzanne Farrand	OV; MISC	45.00	
15				
30	Landi Cohen	OV	35.00	
45	Flora Gandolfi	OV; LAB	68.00	
12:00				
15				
30				
45				
1:00	Emma Bellomo	OV; LAB	53.00	
15	Nick Urick	OV; MISC	47.00	47.00
30				
45	Annette Peters	OV; LAB	45.00	
2:00	Andy Wargo	OV	35.00	35.00
15	Helen Wargo	OV; X	62.00	62.00
30				
45	Mike Petrovich	OV	40.00	
3:00				
15	Mildred Kadell	OV	35.00	35.00
30				
45	Irene Strahotsky	OV; LAB	50.00	
4:00				
15	Agnes Thompson	OV	35.00	35.00
30	Merle Salasnek	OV; MISC	56.00	
45	Elizabeth Hope	X	37.00	
	Philip Cottam			129.00
	Minnie Pershing			65.00
	Dorothy Pastor			148.00
			1,040.00	685.00

goes to the patient; the other is kept for Dr. Miller's records. At the end of each day, the cash is deposited in the bank. The entry to record the revenue may be journalized daily or weekly. Dr. Miller's revenue is recorded on a weekly basis. If the office staff is large enough, it is a good idea to separate the responsibility for handling cash from the responsibility for recording payments.

▌▌▌▌▌ THE COMBINATION JOURNAL

OBJECTIVE 2
JOURNALIZE AND POST
USING A COMBINATION
JOURNAL

In most businesses, a few repetitive transactions represent a large portion of the daily accounting activity. The use of a combination journal greatly reduces the time and effort required to journalize and post these transactions. When in use, the combination journal replaces the general journal. Because of its convenience and efficiency, the combination journal is commonly used by professional service businesses.

This increased efficiency is achieved through the use of special columns for frequently used accounts. As shown in Figure 7-4, Dr. Miller uses special columns for the following accounts: Professional Fees; Medical Supplies; R. Miller, Drawing; Laundry Expense; Salary Expense; and Cash. Of course, special columns will vary from business to business due to the varying nature of their daily transactions. To use a special column, only the amount needs to be written in the special column. The column heading does the rest of the work by indicating the title of the account and whether that account is to be debited or credited.

General Debit and Credit columns are used to record debits and credits to accounts that are not used frequently and therefore do not have special columns. In using General columns, we must remember to write in both the account title and the amount of the debit or credit going to that account. Between the special columns and the General Debit and Credit columns, all transactions can be recorded in the combination journal.

|||||||||||||||||||||||
C O M M E N T

Although commonly used in professional service businesses, a combination journal may be used by any business on the accrual, cash, or modified cash basis of accounting.

To demonstrate the use of a combination journal, let's return to Dr. Miller. The following transactions were completed by Dr. Miller during the month of December 19X8. These transactions were recorded in Dr. Miller's combination journal as shown in Figure 7-4.

Dec. 1   Paid monthly rent, $1,250.

2   Purchased medical supplies for cash, $137.

5   Dr. Miller withdrew cash for personal use, $800.

FIGURE 7 - 4

COMBINATION JOURNAL

Date		Account Title	Post. Ref.	General Debit		General Credit		Professional Fees Credit	
19X8									
Dec.	1	Rent Expense	518	1,250	00				
	2	Medical Supplies	—						
	5	R. Miller, Drawing	—						
	5	Professional Fees	—					3,200	00
	8	Telephone Expense	521	95	00				
	8	Utilities Expense	522	120	00				
	9	Laundry Expense	—						
	10	Medical Supplies	—						
	11	Repair Expense	519	27	00				
	12	Salary Expense	—						
	12	R. Miller, Drawing	—						
	12	Professional Fees	—					3,500	00
	15	Laundry Expense	—						
	17	Office Furniture and Equipment	123	159	00				
	18	Medical Supplies	—						
	19	Professional Fees	—					3,760	00
	22	Laundry Expense	—						
	23	R. Miller, Drawing	—						
	26	Salary Expense	—						
	26	Professional Fees	—					2,900	00
	29	Office Supplies	113	245	00				
	30	Laundry Expense	—						
	30	Medical Supplies	—						
	31	Miscellaneous Expense	523	48	00				
	31	Professional Fees	—					850	00
	31	R. Miller, Drawing	—						
	31			1,944	00	–0–		14,210	00
				(✓)		(✓)		(411)	

Page 47

Medical Supplies		R. Miller, Drawing		Laundry Expense		Salary Expense		Cash			
Debit		Debit		Debit		Debit		Debit		Credit	
										1,250	00
137	00									137	00
		800	00							800	00
								3,200	00		
										95	00
										120	00
				143	00					143	00
65	00									65	00
										27	00
						1,350	00			1,350	00
		1,000	00							1,000	00
								3,500	00		
				142	00					142	00
										159	00
155	00									155	00
								3,760	00		
				112	00					112	00
		1,500	00							1,500	00
						1,350	00			1,350	00
								2,900	00		
										245	00
				110	00					110	00
165	00									165	00
										48	00
								850	00		
		1,500	00							1,500	00
522	00	4,800	00	507	00	2,700	00	14,210	00	10,473	00
(112)		(312)		(515)		(520)		(111)		(111)	

Dec.	5	Cash payments from patients totaled $3,200 for the week.
	8	Paid telephone bill, $95.
	8	Paid electricity bill, $120.
	9	Paid laundry bill, $143.
	10	Purchased medical supplies for cash, $65.
	11	Paid for minor repair to typewriter, $27.
	12	Paid employees' salaries, $1,350.
	12	Dr. Miller withdrew cash for personal use, $1,000.
	12	Cash payments from patients totaled $3,500 for the week.
	15	Paid laundry bill, $142.
	17	Purchased new desk chair for cash, $159.
	18	Purchased medical supplies for cash, $155.
	19	Cash payments from patients totaled $3,760 for the week.
	22	Paid laundry bill, $112.
	23	Dr. Miller withdrew cash for personal use, $1,500.
	26	Paid employees' salaries, $1,350.
	26	Cash payments from patients totaled $2,900 for the week.
	29	Purchased office supplies for cash, $245.
	30	Paid laundry bill, $110.
	30	Purchased medical supplies for cash, $165.
	31	Paid magazine subscription, $48.
	31	Cash payments from patients totaled $850 for the period December 29–31.
	31	Dr. Miller withdrew cash for personal use, $1,500.

|||||||||||||||||||||
COMMENT

Observe that in cases where the entire transaction is recorded in special columns, the Account Title column is still filled in with the title that best describes the basic nature of the transaction. The December 2 transaction shown in Figure 7-4 is an example of this type of situation. In such cases, it would also be acceptable to leave the Account Title column blank. Use of the Account Title column is required only when the General Debit or Credit column is used.

POSTING THE COMBINATION JOURNAL

The combination journal requires two types of postings: individual postings and column total postings.

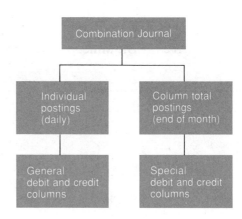

1. INDIVIDUAL POSTINGS Individual postings are necessary where each figure in a column must be posted to a **different** account. In a combination journal, the General Debit and Credit columns are the only columns that are posted individually. These columns are usually posted on a daily basis. The procedure for posting the General Debit and Credit columns is the same procedure used in previous chapters to post the general journal.

||||||||||||||||||||
C O M M E N T

In the Posting Reference column in the combination journal:

- A number indicates that the amount in the General columns has been posted to that account number in the ledger.

- A dash indicates there are no individual postings for the entry on that line.

2. COLUMN TOTAL POSTINGS Column totals are posted where all the figures in a column must be posted to the **same** account. Instead of making many individual postings to the same account, one posting is made at the end of the month with the total. In a combination journal, all the special columns are posted at the end of the month using column totals.

COMBINATION JOURNAL

Date		Account Title	Post. Ref.	General Debit	General Credit	Professional Fees Credit
19X8						
Dec.	1	Rent Expense	518	1,250 00		
	2	Medical Supplies	—			
	5	R. Miller, Drawing	—			
	5	Professional Fees	—			3,200 00
	31	Miscellaneous Expense	523	48 00		
	31	Professional Fees	—			850 00
	31	R. Miller, Drawing	—			
	31			1,944 00	—0—	14,210 00
				(✓)	(✓)	(411)

① ② ⑤

Account	Professional Fees					Account No. 411	
Date		Item	Post. Ref.	Debit	Credit	Balance Debit	Balance Credit
19X8							
Dec.	1	Balance	✓				156,310 00
	31		J47		14,210 00		170,520 00

④ ③

|||||||||||||||||||||||||
C O M M E N T

The overall equality of debits and credits should be verified before posting any column totals. For example, referring to Dr. Miller's journal shown above:

Debit Totals		**Credit Totals**	
General Debit	$ 1,944	General Credit	$ –0–
Medical Supplies Debit . .	522	Professional Fees	
R. Miller, Drawing Debit . .	4,800	Credit	14,210
Laundry Expense Debit . .	507	Cash Credit	10,473
Salary Expense Debit . . .	2,700		$24,683
Cash Debit	14,210		
	$24,683		

Page 47

Medical Supplies		R. Miller, Drawing		Laundry Expense		Salary Expense		Cash			
Debit		Debit		Debit		Debit		Debit		Credit	
										1,250	00
137	00									137	00
		800	00							800	00
								3,200	00		
										48	00
								850	00		
		1,500	00							1,500	00
522	00	4,800	00	507	00	2,700	00	14,210	00	10,473	00
(112)		(312)		(515)		(520)		(111)		(111)	

Observe that the totals of the General Debit and Credit columns must be included in this verification process even though these column totals will not be posted.

To demonstrate the posting of column totals, let's return to Dr. Miller's combination journal as shown above. The following column totals must be posted:

Professional Fees Credit

Medical Supplies Debit

R. Miller, Drawing Debit

Laundry Expense Debit

Salary Expense Debit

Cash Debit

Cash Credit

For practice, the posting of the Professional Fees Credit column total is shown on page 230.

FIGURE 7 - 5

ROBERT MILLER, M.D.
Work Sheet
For the Year Ended December 31, 19X8

Account Title	Trial Balance Debit		Trial Balance Credit		Adjustments Debit		Adjustments Credit	
Cash	5,260	00						
Medical Supplies	6,159	00					(a) 5,264	00
Office Supplies	3,337	00					(b) 2,975	00
Prepaid Insurance	12,350	00					(c)11,400	00
Medical Equipment	47,800	00						
Accum. Dep.—Medical Equipment			22,600	00			(d) 4,000	00
Office Furniture and Equipment	21,940	00						
Accum. Dep.—Office Furn. and Equip.			8,500	00			(e) 2,500	00
Notes Payable			5,000	00				
R. Miller, Capital			31,247	00				
R. Miller, Drawing	75,600	00						
Professional Fees			170,520	00				
Laboratory Expense	6,100	00						
Laundry Expense	5,884	00						
Rent Expense	15,000	00						
Repair Expense	1,851	00						
Salary Expense	31,590	00						
Telephone Expense	1,680	00						
Utilities Expense	1,740	00						
Miscellaneous Expense	1,576	00						
	237,867	00	237,867	00				
Medical Supplies Expense					(a) 5,264	00		
Office Supplies Expense					(b) 2,975	00		
Insurance Expense					(c)11,400	00		
Depreciation Exp.—Medical Equip.					(d) 4,000	00		
Dep. Exp.—Office Furn. and Equip.					(e) 2,500	00		
					26,139	00	26,139	00
Net income								

Adjusted Trial Balance		Income Statement		Balance Sheet	
Debit	Credit	Debit	Credit	Debit	Credit
5,260 00				5,260 00	
895 00				895 00	
362 00				362 00	
950 00				950 00	
47,800 00				47,800 00	
	26,600 00				26,600 00
21,940 00				21,940 00	
	11,000 00				11,000 00
	5,000 00				5,000 00
	31,247 00				31,247 00
75,600 00				75,600 00	
	170,520 00		170,520 00		
6,100 00		6,100 00			
5,884 00		5,884 00			
15,000 00		15,000 00			
1,851 00		1,851 00			
31,590 00		31,590 00			
1,680 00		1,680 00			
1,740 00		1,740 00			
1,576 00		1,576 00			
5,264 00		5,264 00			
2,975 00		2,975 00			
11,400 00		11,400 00			
4,000 00		4,000 00			
2,500 00		2,500 00			
244,367 00	244,367 00	91,560 00	170,520 00	152,807 00	73,847 00
		78,960 00			78,960 00
		170,520 00	170,520 00	152,807 00	152,807 00

The only departure from the usual five-step posting procedure is in Step 5. Observe that in the combination journal, the posting reference for a column total is placed in parentheses below the total rather than in the Posting Reference column. Also note that a check mark is placed in parentheses beneath the totals of the General Debit and Credit columns. A check mark in parentheses indicates the total has not been posted.

||||||||||||||||||||||
C O M M E N T

Using a combination journal, the totals of the Cash Debit and Credit columns are posted to the Cash account at the end of the month. However, most businesses want to know their up-to-date cash balance at various times throughout the month. The current cash balance can be easily computed at any time during the month as follows:

> Beginning cash balance (first day of month)
> Add: Cash debits to date
> Deduct: Cash credits to date
>
> Current cash balance

▮▮▮ PREPARING THE WORK SHEET

OBJECTIVE 3
PREPARE A WORK SHEET
FOR A PROFESSIONAL
SERVICE BUSINESS

The procedures for preparing a work sheet for a professional service business are the same as those described in Chapter 5. Dr. Miller's year-end work sheet is shown in Figure 7-5. Adjustments were based on the following data:

    a. Inventory of medical supplies on December 31, $895.

    b. Inventory of office supplies on December 31, $362.

    c. Insurance expired during the year, $11,400.

    d. Depreciation on the medical equipment, $4,000.

    e. Depreciation on the office furniture and equipment, $2,500.

▮▮▮ FINANCIAL STATEMENTS

OBJECTIVE 4
PREPARE FINANCIAL
STATEMENTS FOR A
PROFESSIONAL SERVICE
BUSINESS

As discussed in Chapter 5, the information for the financial statements is taken directly from the work sheet with one exception: an additional investment by the owner. When preparing the statement of owner's equity, we must check the owner's capital account in the ledger to determine whether an additional investment has been made by the owner. Dr. Miller's financial statements are shown in Figure 7-6.

ROBERT MILLER, M.D.
Income Statement
For the Year Ended December 31, 19X8

Revenue:				
Professional fees			$170,520	00
Expenses:				
Salary expense	$31,590	00		
Rent expense	15,000	00		
Insurance expense	11,400	00		
Laboratory expense	6,100	00		
Laundry expense	5,884	00		
Medical supplies expense	5,264	00		
Depreciation expense—				
medical equipment	4,000	00		
Office supplies expense	2,975	00		
Depreciation expense—office furniture				
and equipment	2,500	00		
Repair expense	1,851	00		
Utilities expense	1,740	00		
Telephone expense	1,680	00		
Miscellaneous expense	1,576	00		
Total expenses			91,560	00
Net income			$ 78,960	00

ROBERT MILLER, M.D.
Statement of Owner's Equity
For the Year Ended December 31, 19X8

R. Miller, capital, January 1, 19X8			$ 31,247	00
Add: Net income for the year			78,960	00
Subtotal			$110,207	00
Deduct: Withdrawals by R. Miller			75,600	00
R. Miller, capital, December 31, 19X8			$ 34,607	00

▮ **FIGURE 7 - 6 *(concluded)***

ROBERT MILLER, M.D. Balance Sheet December 31, 19X8						
Assets						
Cash					$ 5,260	00
Medical supplies					895	00
Office supplies					362	00
Prepaid insurance					950	00
Medical equipment	$47,800	00				
Less accumulated depreciation—						
medical equipment	26,600	00		21,200	00	
Office furniture and equipment	$21,940	00				
Less accumulated depreciation—						
office furniture and equipment	11,000	00		10,940	00	
Total assets					$39,607	00
Liabilities						
Notes payable					$ 5,000	00
Owner's Equity						
R. Miller, capital					34,607	00
Total liabilities and owner's equity					$39,607	00

▮▮▮▮ **ADJUSTING ENTRIES**

OBJECTIVE 5
PREPARE ADJUSTING
ENTRIES FOR A
PROFESSIONAL SERVICE
BUSINESS

The adjustments rough drafted on the work sheet must now be recorded in Dr. Miller's combination journal. As shown in Figure 7-7, the General Debit and Credit columns are used to record adjusting entries.

▮▮▮▮ **CLOSING ENTRIES**

OBJECTIVE 6
PREPARE CLOSING ·
ENTRIES FOR A
PROFESSIONAL SERVICE
BUSINESS

Since December 31 marks the end of Dr. Miller's fiscal year, closing entries must be recorded. The closing procedure used for a professional service business is the same as the closing procedure studied in Chapter 6. The information necessary for closing entries can be obtained from the work sheet.

FIGURE 7 - 7

COMBINATION JOURNAL

Date		Account Title	Post. Ref.	General Debit		General Credit	
		Adjusting Entries					
19X8 Dec.	31	Medical Supplies Expense	516	5,264	00		
		Medical Supplies	112			5,264	00
	31	Office Supplies Expense	517	2,975	00		
		Office Supplies	113			2,975	00
	31	Insurance Expense	513	11,400	00		
		Prepaid Insurance	114			11,400	00
	31	Depreciation Expense—					
		Medical Equipment	511	4,000	00		
		Accumulated Depreciation—					
		Medical Equipment	122			4,000	00
	31	Depreciation Expense—					
		Office Furniture					
		and Equipment	512	2,500	00		
		Accumulated Depreciation—					
		Office Furniture					
		and Equipment	124			2,500	00

As shown in Figure 7-8, the General Debit and Credit columns of the combination journal are used to record closing entries.

▮▮▮▮ OTHER PROFESSIONAL SERVICE BUSINESSES

Although we have used a physician's records as our chapter example, the accounting procedures used in other types of professional service businesses follow the same basic pattern. Just like Dr. Miller, most professional service businesses are on the modified cash basis and most use a combination journal. The special columns in each business' combination journal would vary, but the basic concepts of journalizing and posting are the same. Each business "customizes" its combination journal through its choice of accounts for special

FIGURE 7 - 8

COMBINATION JOURNAL

Date		Account Title	Post. Ref.	General Debit		General Credit	
		Closing Entries					
19X8 Dec.	31	Professional Fees	411	170,520	00		
		Income Summary	313			170,520	00
	31	Income Summary	313	91,560	00		
		Laboratory Expense	514			6,100	00
		Laundry Expense	515			5,884	00
		Rent Expense	518			15,000	00
		Repair Expense	519			1,851	00
		Salary Expense	520			31,590	00
		Telephone Expense	521			1,680	00
		Utilities Expense	522			1,740	00
		Miscellaneous Expense	523			1,576	00
		Medical Supplies Expense	516			5,264	00
		Office Supplies Expense	517			2,975	00
		Insurance Expense	513			11,400	00
		Depreciation Expense— Medical Equipment	511			4,000	00
		Depreciation Expense— Office Furniture and Equipment	512			2,500	00
	31	Income Summary	313	78,960	00		
		R. Miller, Capital	311			78,960	00
	31	R. Miller, Capital	311	75,600	00		
		R. Miller, Drawing	312			75,600	00

columns. Each business also "customizes" its supporting records (i.e., daily appointment record and patients' ledger) to suit its own special needs.

Chapter Summary

A service business sells a skill or technique that has no physical existence. Examples of professional services would include the services of public accountants, attorneys, physicians, and architects.

Most professional service businesses use the modified cash basis of accounting: revenue is recorded when the cash is received, and expenses are recorded when the cash is paid out. Under the pure cash basis, no adjusting entries are necessary. However, under the modified cash basis, adjustments are recorded for depreciation and certain prepaid items such as supplies and insurance.

Most professional service businesses use a combination journal in place of a general journal. The use of a combination journal greatly reduces the time and effort required to journalize and post. This increased efficiency is achieved through the use of special columns for frequently used accounts. Of course, these special columns vary from business to business due to the varying nature of their daily transactions. General Debit and Credit columns are used to record debits and credits to accounts that do not have special columns. Between the special columns and the General columns, all transactions can be recorded in a combination journal.

The combination journal requires two types of postings: individual postings and column total postings.

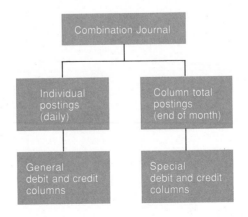

Procedures for preparing a work sheet, financial statements, and adjusting and closing entries are the same as those studied in previous chapters.

Glossary

ACCRUAL-BASIS ACCOUNTING
A system of recording financial information which requires that revenues be recorded when they are earned and expenses be recorded when they are incurred regardless of whether cash has been received or paid.

CASH-BASIS ACCOUNTING
A system of recording financial information which requires that revenues be recorded when the cash is received and expenses be recorded when the cash is paid. No adjusting entries are required.

COMBINATION JOURNAL
A journal with special columns as well as General Debit and Credit columns. It is commonly used by service businesses in place of a general journal because of its greater efficiency in journalizing and posting.

MODIFIED-CASH-BASIS ACCOUNTING
A system of recording financial information which requires that revenues be recorded when the cash is received and expenses be recorded when the cash is paid. However, adjustments are recorded for depreciation and certain prepaid items such as supplies and insurance.

Questions for Discussion

1. Define:
   a. Accrual-basis accounting.
   b. Cash-basis accounting.
   c. Modified-cash-basis accounting.

2. How do special columns make a combination journal more efficient than a general journal?

3. Why might the special columns in a combination journal used by one business be different from the special columns used by another business?

4. Why are General Debit and Credit columns necessary in a combination journal?

5. a. Why must an account title be written in the Account Title column of a combination journal whenever the General Debit or Credit columns are used?
   b. Why is use of the Account Title column optional whenever a special column is used?

6. Describe the two types of postings required in using a combination journal.

7. In the Posting Reference column of a combination journal, what do the following things indicate:
   a. A number.
   b. A dash.

8. Beneath a column total in a combination journal, what do the following things indicate:
   a. A number in parentheses.
   b. A check mark in parentheses.

Exercises

EXERCISE 7-1
MODIFIED CASH BASIS
(L.O.1)

Mork Legal Services uses the modified cash basis of accounting. Indicate whether Mork would record a journal entry for each of the following transactions (yes or no):

    a. Legal services performed on account.

    b. Legal services performed for cash.

    c. Expenses incurred on account.

    d. Expenses incurred for cash.

    e. Payment on account received from client.

    f. Paid creditor on account.

    g. Adjustment for salary expense incurred but not yet paid.

    h. Adjustment for used supplies.

    i. Adjustment for expired insurance.

    j. Adjustment for depreciation on plant assets.

EXERCISE 7-2
POSTING COMBINATION
JOURNAL
(L.O.2)

Powers Architectural Services uses a combination journal that includes the following columns:

    1. General Debit.

    2. General Credit.

    3. Fees Earned Credit.

    4. Janet Powers, Drawing Debit.

    5. Supplies Debit.

    6. Salary Expense Debit.

    7. Miscellaneous Expense Debit.

Using "I" or "CT," indicate whether each of these columns would be posted individually or through a column total.

$$I = \text{Individual posting}$$

$$CT = \text{Column total posting}$$

EXERCISE 7-3
POSTING COMBINATION
JOURNAL
(L.O.2)

Referring to the data given in Exercise 7-2, indicate which columns would be posted daily and which columns would be posted at the end of the month. Use the following letter codes to indicate your answer:

$$D = \text{Daily}$$

$$E = \text{End of the month}$$

EXERCISE 7-4
ADJUSTING ENTRIES
(L.O.5)

Bennett Dental Associates has recorded the following adjusting entries at year-end. For the purposes of this exercise, letters have been used in the Date column.

COMBINATION JOURNAL

Date	Account Title	Post. Ref.	General Debit		General Credit	
	Adjusting Entries					
(a)	Dental Supplies Expense		4,170	00		
	Dental Supplies				4,170	00
(b)	Office Supplies Expense		2,463	00		
	Office Supplies				2,463	00
(c)	Insurance Expense		1,892	00		
	Prepaid Insurance				1,892	00
(d)	Depreciation Expense—					
	Dental Equipment		3,500	00		
	Accumulated Depreciation—					
	Dental Equipment				3,500	00

Describe the purpose of each adjustment.

EXERCISE 7-5

INCOME STATEMENT
(L.O.4)

Referring to the adjusted trial balance presented in Figure 7-9, prepare an income statement for Sarah Roberts, CPA, for the year ended December 31, 19X6.

FIGURE 7 - 9

SARAH ROBERTS, CPA
Adjusted Trial Balance
December 31, 19X6

	Debit		Credit	
Cash	6,460	00		
Office Supplies	1,085	00		
Prepaid Insurance	1,230	00		
Equipment	25,000	00		
Accumulated Depreciation—Equipment			5,200	00
Notes Payable			2,400	00
Sarah Roberts, Capital			23,265	00
Sarah Roberts, Drawing	49,000	00		
Fees Earned			95,000	00
Rent Expense	12,000	00		
Salary Expense	18,200	00		
Telephone Expense	1,500	00		
Utilities Expense	1,800	00		
Supplies Expense	4,600	00		
Insurance Expense	2,890	00		
Depreciation Expense	2,100	00		
	125,865	00	125,865	00

EXERCISE 7-6
STATEMENT OF OWNER'S
EQUITY
(L.O.4)

Referring to the adjusted trial balance presented in Figure 7-9, prepare a statement of owner's equity for Sarah Roberts, CPA, for the year ended December 31, 19X6. Assume there were no additional investments by the owner during 19X6.

EXERCISE 7-7
BALANCE SHEET
(L.O.4)

Referring to the adjusted trial balance presented in Figure 7-9, prepare a year-end balance sheet for Sarah Roberts, CPA.

EXERCISE 7-8
CLOSING ENTRIES
(L.O.6)

Referring to the adjusted trial balance presented in Figure 7-9, prepare closing entries for Sarah Roberts, CPA.

Problems—Set A

Mark Redmond, M.D., uses the following chart of accounts:

Chart of Accounts

Assets
111 Cash
112 Medical Supplies
113 Office Supplies
114 Prepaid Insurance
121 Medical Equipment
122 Accumulated Depreciation—
     Medical Equipment
123 Office Furniture and
     Equipment
124 Accumulated Depreciation—
     Office Furniture and
     Equipment

Liabilities
211 Notes Payable

Owner's Equity
311 M. Redmond, Capital
312 M. Redmond, Drawing
313 Income Summary

Revenue
411 Professional Fees

Expenses
511 Depreciation Expense—
     Medical Equipment
512 Depreciation Expense—Office
     Furniture and Equipment
513 Insurance Expense
514 Laboratory Expense
515 Laundry Expense
516 Medical Supplies Expense
517 Office Supplies Expense
518 Rent Expense
519 Repair Expense
520 Salary Expense
521 Telephone Expense
522 Utilities Expense
523 Miscellaneous Expense

Dr. Redmond uses the modified cash basis of accounting. The following transactions were completed during June 19X3:

June 1   Paid monthly rent, $1,500.

3   Purchased medical supplies for cash, $112.

5   Cash payments from patients totaled $2,900 for the week.

8   Dr. Redmond withdrew cash for personal use, $1,000.

9   Paid electricity bill, $218.

June 11   Paid laundry bill, $157.

12   Paid employees' salaries, $1,400.

12   Cash payments from patients totaled $3,100 for the week.

15   Purchased medical supplies for cash, $314.

16   Dr. Redmond withdrew cash for personal use, $950.

17   Paid telephone bill, $183.

19   Cash payments from patients totaled $2,700 for the week.

19   Paid laundry bill, $132.

22   Purchased medical supplies for cash, $80.

24   Purchased new office desk for cash, $495.

26   Paid employees' salaries, $1,400.

26   Cash payments from patients totaled $3,150 for the week.

29   Paid for small repair to adding machine, $19.

30   Dr. Redmond withdrew cash for personal use, $1,800.

30   Paid laundry bill, $162.

30   Cash payments from patients totaled $1,500 for the period June 29–30.

INSTRUCTIONS

1. For those students not using the working papers:
   a. Dr. Redmond uses a combination journal like the one shown in Figure 7-4, pages 226–27, of this chapter except for the drawing account column which should be titled "M. Redmond, Drawing Debit."
   b. Number the combination journal page 29.

2. Record these transactions in the combination journal.

3. Total the amount columns in the journal.

4. Verify the equality of the debit and credit totals.

PROBLEM 7-2A
COMBINATION
JOURNAL:
JOURNALIZING AND
POSTING
(L.O.1, 2)

Karen Hanson, M.D., uses the modified cash basis of accounting. On January 1, 19X5, the beginning of a new fiscal year, Dr. Hanson's ledger contains the following accounts and balances:

	Debit	Credit
Assets		
111 Cash	3,420	
112 Medical Supplies	908	
113 Office Supplies	425	
114 Prepaid Insurance	1,930	
121 Medical Equipment	18,600	
122 Accumulated Depreciation—Medical Equipment		7,200
123 Automobile	12,500	
124 Accumulated Depreciation—Automobile		4,000
Liabilities		
211 Notes Payable		5,600
Owner's Equity		
311 K. Hanson, Capital		20,983
312 K. Hanson, Drawing		
313 Income Summary		
Revenue		
411 Professional Fees		
Expenses		
511 Depreciation Expense—Medical Equipment		
512 Depreciation Expense—Automobile		
513 Insurance Expense		
514 Laundry Expense		
515 Medical Supplies Expense		
516 Office Supplies Expense		
517 Rent Expense		
518 Salary Expense		
519 Telephone Expense		
520 Utilities Expense		
521 Miscellaneous Expense		

The following transactions were completed during the month of January 19X5:

Jan. 2 Paid monthly rent, $1,400.

3 Dr. Hanson withdrew cash for personal use, $1,200.

4 Paid laundry bill, $171.

5 Cash payments from patients totaled $2,950 for the week.

5 Paid employees' salaries, $1,600.

8 Purchased medical supplies for cash, $290.

Jan. 10   Paid telephone bill, $205.

11   Purchased doctor's scale for cash, $300.

12   Cash payments from patients totaled $3,275 for the week.

12   Dr. Hanson withdrew cash for personal use, $1,300.

15   Paid laundry bill, $169.

16   Purchased medical supplies for cash, $181.

18   Paid electricity bill, $237.

19   Cash payments from patients totaled $3,050 for the week.

19   Paid employees' salaries, $1,600.

22   Purchased office supplies for cash, $52.

23   Paid magazine subscription, $60.

24   Paid laundry bill, $189.

25   Dr. Hanson withdrew cash for personal use, $1,200.

26   Cash payments from patients totaled $2,830 for the week.

29   Purchased medical supplies for cash, $210.

31   Cash payments from patients totaled $982 for the period January 29–31.

INSTRUCTIONS

1. For those students not using the working papers:
   a. Dr. Hanson uses a combination journal like the one shown in Figure 7-4, pages 226–27, of this chapter except for the drawing account column which should be titled "K. Hanson, Drawing Debit." Number the journal page 32.
   b. Open ledger accounts using the titles, account numbers, and January 1, 19X5, balances listed at the beginning of this problem.

2. Record the January transactions in the combination journal.

3. Post from the combination journal to the appropriate ledger accounts.
   a. Individual postings. Since Dr. Hanson has relatively few transactions, we will post the General Debit and Credit columns at the end of each week (January 5, 12, 19, 26, and 31).
   b. Column total postings. Column totals will be posted at the end of the month (January 31) after verifying the equality of the Debit and Credit column totals.

PROBLEM 7-3A
WORK SHEET
(L.O.3)

Martin Accounting Services uses the modified cash basis of accounting. Martin's year-end trial balance and adjustment data are as follows:

MARTIN ACCOUNTING SERVICES
Trial Balance
December 31, 19X9

	Debit	Credit
Cash	4,830 00	
Supplies	6,421 00	
Prepaid Insurance	1,895 00	
Equipment	40,500 00	
Accumulated Depreciation—Equipment		10,500 00
Automobile	12,500 00	
Accumulated Depreciation—Automobile		7,000 00
Notes Payable		6,500 00
T. Martin, Capital		23,240 00
T. Martin, Drawing	42,000 00	
Fees Earned		95,800 00
Rent Expense	11,880 00	
Salary Expense	19,200 00	
Telephone Expense	1,980 00	
Utilities Expense	1,834 00	
	143,040 00	143,040 00

Adjustment data:

a. Inventory of supplies on December 31, 19X9, $796.

b. Insurance expired during the year, $1,450.

c. Depreciation on the equipment, $3,600.

d. Depreciation on the automobile, $4,200.

INSTRUCTIONS
Prepare a work sheet for the year ended December 31, 19X9.

PROBLEM 7-4A
FINANCIAL STATEMENTS,
ADJUSTING ENTRIES,
CLOSING ENTRIES
(L.O.4–6)

A completed work sheet for Pearl Dental Associates is shown in Figure 7-10.

FIGURE 7 - 10

PEARL DENTAL ASSOCIATES
Work Sheet
For the Year Ended December 31, 19X8

Account Title	Trial Balance Debit	Trial Balance Credit	Adjustments Debit	Adjustments Credit
Cash	4,150 00			
Dental Supplies	5,982 00			(a) 4,832 00
Office Supplies	3,469 00			(b) 2,510 00
Prepaid Insurance	2,540 00			(c) 1,950 00
Dental Equipment	46,700 00			
Accum. Dep.—Dental Equip.		19,200 00		(d) 4,200 00
Office Furniture and Equipment	18,500 00			
Accum. Dep.—Office Furn. and Equip.		8,900 00		(e) 2,300 00
Notes Payable		4,000 00		
J. Pearl, Capital		24,836 00		
J. Pearl, Drawing	44,900 00			
Professional Fees		127,300 00		
Laboratory Expense	3,150 00			
Laundry Expense	2,943 00			
Rent Expense	12,000 00			
Repair Expense	921 00			
Salary Expense	34,900 00			
Telephone Expense	1,406 00			
Utilities Expense	1,810 00			
Miscellaneous Expense	865 00			
	184,236 00	184,236 00		
Dental Supplies Expense			(a) 4,832 00	
Office Supplies Expense			(b) 2,510 00	
Insurance Expense			(c) 1,950 00	
Depreciation Exp.—Dental Equip.			(d) 4,200 00	
Dep. Exp.—Office Furn. and Equip.			(e) 2,300 00	
			15,792 00	15,792 00
Net income				

Adjusted Trial Balance		Income Statement		Balance Sheet	
Debit	Credit	Debit	Credit	Debit	Credit
4,150 00				4,150 00	
1,150 00				1,150 00	
959 00				959 00	
590 00				590 00	
46,700 00				46,700 00	
	23,400 00				23,400 00
18,500 00				18,500 00	
	11,200 00				11,200 00
	4,000 00				4,000 00
	24,836 00				24,836 00
44,900 00				44,900 00	
	127,300 00		127,300 00		
3,150 00		3,150 00			
2,943 00		2,943 00			
12,000 00		12,000 00			
921 00		921 00			
34,900 00		34,900 00			
1,406 00		1,406 00			
1,810 00		1,810 00			
865 00		865 00			
4,832 00		4,832 00			
2,510 00		2,510 00			
1,950 00		1,950 00			
4,200 00		4,200 00			
2,300 00		2,300 00			
190,736 00	190,736 00	73,787 00	127,300 00	116,949 00	63,436 00
		53,513 00			53,513 00
		127,300 00	127,300 00	116,949 00	116,949 00

INSTRUCTIONS

1. Prepare an income statement.

2. Prepare a statement of owner's equity. (Assume no additional investment by the owner.)

3. Prepare a balance sheet.

4. Journalize the adjusting entries.

5. Journalize the closing entries.

Problems—Set B

PROBLEM 7-1B
COMBINATION
JOURNAL
(L.O.1, 2)

Susan Collins, M.D., uses the following chart of accounts:

Chart of Accounts

Assets
111 Cash
112 Medical Supplies
113 Office Supplies
114 Prepaid Insurance
121 Medical Equipment
122 Accumulated Depreciation—
    Medical Equipment
123 Office Furniture and
    Equipment
124 Accumulated Depreciation—
    Office Furniture and
    Equipment

Liabilities
211 Notes Payable

Owner's Equity
311 S. Collins, Capital
312 S. Collins, Drawing
313 Income Summary

Revenue
411 Professional Fees

Expenses
511 Depreciation Expense—
    Medical Equipment
512 Depreciation Expense—Office
    Furniture and Equipment
513 Insurance Expense
514 Laboratory Expense
515 Laundry Expense
516 Medical Supplies Expense
517 Office Supplies Expense
518 Rent Expense
519 Repair Expense
520 Salary Expense
521 Telephone Expense
522 Utilities Expense
523 Miscellaneous Expense

Dr. Collins uses the modified cash basis of accounting. The following transactions were completed during March 19X4.

Mar. 1   Purchased medical supplies for cash, $95.

     1   Paid monthly rent, $1,000.

     3   Dr. Collins withdrew cash for personal use, $930.

Mar. 5   Cash payments from patients totaled $2,600 for the week.

      8   Purchased office supplies for cash, $61.

      9   Paid laundry bill, $149.

     10   Paid telephone bill, $173.

     12   Paid employees' salaries, $1,325.

     12   Cash payments from patients totaled $3,100 for the week.

     15   Purchased medical supplies for cash, $298.

     17   Dr. Collins withdrew cash for personal use, $1,400.

     18   Paid laundry bill, $195.

     19   Paid electricity bill, $204.

     19   Cash payments from patients totaled $2,850 for the week.

     22   Purchased new desktop calculator for cash, $112.

     23   Dr. Collins withdrew cash for personal use, $1,000.

     25   Purchased medical supplies for cash, $183.

     26   Cash payments from patients totaled $2,975 for the week.

     26   Paid employees' salaries, $1,325.

     29   Paid laundry bill, $174.

     30   Purchased medical supplies for cash, $102.

     31   Cash payments from patients totaled $1,400 for the period March 29–31.

INSTRUCTIONS

1. For those students not using the working papers:
    a. Dr. Collins uses a combination journal like the one shown in Figure 7-4, pages 226–27, of this chapter except for the drawing account column which should be titled "S. Collins, Drawing Debit."
    b. Number the combination journal page 35.

2. Record these transactions in the combination journal.

3. Total the amount columns in the journal.

4. Verify the equality of the debit and credit totals.

PROBLEM 7-2B
COMBINATION
JOURNAL:
JOURNALIZING AND
POSTING
(L.O.1, 2)

Janice White, M.D., uses the modified cash basis of accounting. On January 1, 19X7, the beginning of a new fiscal year, Dr. White's ledger contains the following accounts and balances.

	Debit	Credit
Assets		
111 Cash	2,980	
112 Medical Supplies	827	
113 Office Supplies	530	
114 Prepaid Insurance	1,600	
121 Medical Equipment	19,500	
122 Accumulated Depreciation—Medical Equipment		6,000
123 Automobile	13,200	
124 Accumulated Depreciation—Automobile		5,100
Liabilities		
211 Notes Payable		7,200
Owner's Equity		
311 J. White, Capital		20,337
312 J. White, Drawing		
313 Income Summary		
Revenue		
411 Professional Fees		
Expenses		
511 Depreciation Expense—Medical Equipment		
512 Depreciation Expense—Automobile		
513 Insurance Expense		
514 Laundry Expense		
515 Medical Supplies Expense		
516 Office Supplies Expense		
517 Rent Expense		
518 Salary Expense		
519 Telephone Expense		
520 Utilities Expense		
521 Miscellaneous Expense		

The following transactions were completed during the month of January 19X7.

Jan. 2 Paid monthly rent, $1,250.

3 Paid laundry bill, $147.

4 Purchased medical supplies for cash, $189.

5 Dr. White withdrew cash for personal use, $1,100.

Jan.   5   Cash payments from patients totaled $2,575 for the week.

       8   Paid electricity bill, $232.

       9   Purchased office supplies for cash, $146.

       9   Paid telephone bill, $173.

      11   Paid laundry bill, $169.

      12   Cash payments from patients totaled $2,650 for the week.

      12   Paid employees' salaries, $1,525.

      15   Dr. White withdrew cash for personal use, $1,500.

      16   Purchased medical microscope for cash, $620.

      19   Cash payments from patients totaled $2,480 for the week.

      22   Purchased medical supplies for cash, $198.

      24   Paid laundry bill, $183.

      25   Dr. White withdrew cash for personal use, $1,000.

      26   Cash payments from patients totaled $2,560 for the week.

      26   Paid employees' salaries, $1,525.

      29   Paid magazine subscription, $52.

      31   Cash payments from patients totaled $1,210 for the week.

INSTRUCTIONS

1. For those students not using the working papers:
   a. Dr. White uses a combination journal like the one shown in Figure 7-4, pages 226–27, of this chapter except for the drawing account column which should be titled "J. White, Drawing Debit." Number the journal page 59.
   b. Open ledger accounts using the titles, account numbers, and January 1, 19X7, balances listed at the beginning of this problem.

2. Record the January transactions in the combination journal.

3. Post from the combination journal to the appropriate ledger accounts.
   a. Individual postings. Since Dr. White has relatively few transactions, we will post the General Debit and Credit columns at the end of each week (January 5, 12, 19, 26, and 31).
   b. Column total postings. Column totals will be posted at the end of the month (January 31) after verifying the equality of the Debit and Credit column totals.

PROBLEM 7-3B
WORK SHEET
(L.O.3)

Sullivan Financial Services uses the modified cash basis of accounting. Sullivan's year-end trial balance and adjustment data are as follows:

SULLIVAN FINANCIAL SERVICES
Trial Balance
December 31, 19X8

	Debit		Credit	
Cash	4,374	00		
Supplies	5,780	00		
Prepaid Insurance	1,700	00		
Office Equipment	36,000	00		
Accumulated Depreciation—Office Equipment			9,450	00
Office Furniture	11,250	00		
Accumulated Depreciation—Office Furniture			6,300	00
Notes Payable			5,800	00
M. Sullivan, Capital			23,130	00
M. Sullivan, Drawing	41,000	00		
Fees Earned			87,200	00
Rent Expense	10,800	00		
Salary Expense	17,250	00		
Telephone Expense	1,782	00		
Utilities Expense	1,650	00		
Miscellaneous Expense	294	00		
	131,880	00	131,880	00

Adjustment data:

    a. Inventory of supplies on December 31, 19X8, $1,718.

    b. Insurance expired during the year, $1,300.

    c. Depreciation on the office equipment, $3,200.

    d. Depreciation on the office furniture, $1,125.

INSTRUCTIONS
Prepare a work sheet for the year ended December 31, 19X8.

FIGURE 7-11

GLENBARD ARCHITECTURAL SERVICES
Work Sheet
For the Year Ended December 31, 19X7

Account Title	Trial Balance				Adjustments			
	Debit		Credit		Debit		Credit	
Cash	3,735	00						
Supplies	2,940	00					(a) 2,084	00
Prepaid Insurance	1,562	00					(b) 1,170	00
Office Equipment	28,000	00						
Accumulated Depreciation—								
Office Equipment			4,500	00			(c) 2,500	00
Office Furniture	7,400	00						
Accumulated Depreciation—								
Office Furniture			2,100	00			(d) 700	00
Notes Payable			2,400	00				
A. Thomas, Capital			25,320	00				
A. Thomas, Drawing	36,000	00						
Fees Earned			82,600	00				
Rent Expense	11,400	00						
Salary Expense	21,900	00						
Telephone Expense	1,780	00						
Utilities Expense	1,894	00						
Miscellaneous Expense	309	00						
	116,920	00	116,920	00				
Supplies Expense					(a) 2,084	00		
Insurance Expense					(b) 1,170	00		
Depreciation Expense—								
Office Equipment					(c) 2,500	00		
Depreciation Expense—								
Office Furniture					(d) 700	00		
					6,454	00	6,454	00
Net income								

Adjusted Trial Balance		Income Statement		Balance Sheet	
Debit	Credit	Debit	Credit	Debit	Credit
3,735 00				3,735 00	
856 00				856 00	
392 00				392 00	
28,000 00				28,000 00	
	7,000 00				7,000 00
7,400 00				7,400 00	
	2,800 00				2,800 00
	2,400 00				2,400 00
	25,320 00				25,320 00
36,000 00				36,000 00	
	82,600 00		82,600 00		
11,400 00		11,400 00			
21,900 00		21,900 00			
1,780 00		1,780 00			
1,894 00		1,894 00			
309 00		309 00			
2,084 00		2,084 00			
1,170 00		1,170 00			
2,500 00		2,500 00			
700 00		700 00			
120,120 00	120,120 00	43,737 00	82,600 00	76,383 00	37,520 00
		38,863 00			38,863 00
		82,600 00	82,600 00	76,383 00	76,383 00

PROBLEM 7-4B
FINANCIAL STATEMENTS,
ADJUSTING ENTRIES,
CLOSING ENTRIES
(L.O.4–6)

A completed work sheet for Glenbard Architectural Services is shown in Figure 7-11.

INSTRUCTIONS

1. Prepare an income statement.

2. Prepare a statement of owner's equity. (Assume no additional investment by owner.)

3. Prepare a balance sheet.

4. Journalize the adjusting entries.

5. Journalize the closing entries.

Mini-Cases

CASE 7-1

Your friend, Jeff Fisher, recently completed medical school and is in the process of setting up his practice. Jeff's accountant has suggested that he use the modified cash basis. Jeff does not think this is a good idea since he does not want to turn away patients who cannot pay in cash at the time the service is performed. Respond to Jeff's concern.

CASE 7-2

Your new client, Mary Higgins, opened a small architectural firm about a year ago. Up to this time, Mary has recorded all the firm's transactions in a two-column general journal. You have suggested that the general journal be replaced with a combination journal. Mary does not see how a journal with so many columns could be easier to work with than a two-column general journal. Explain.

CASE 7-3

Your neighbor, Robert Evans, is a dentist. A friend has just shown Dr. Evans the combination journal that he uses for his legal practice. Dr. Evans, who has been using a general journal, thinks this is a great idea. He tells you that he's planning to use a combination journal identical to his friend's. Comment on his plan.

CHAPTER 8

Internal Control:
Focus on Cash

AFTER STUDYING THIS CHAPTER, YOU SHOULD BE ABLE TO:

1 Explain the basic concept of internal control.

2 Describe the basic forms and procedures related to the use of a checking account.

3 Prepare a bank reconciliation and the related journal entries.

4 Establish, use, and replenish a petty cash fund.

5 Establish and use a change fund.

6 Account for shortages and overages using a Cash Short and Over account.

Every business is concerned with safeguarding its cash from loss or theft. In this chapter, you will study the use of a checking account to safeguard cash. Many of you probably use a personal checking account in managing your own cash. Since many of the procedures involved in opening and maintaining business and personal accounts are similar, much of this discussion may sound familiar. You will also study how to manage cash through the use of special cash funds.

▐▐▐▐ INTERNAL CONTROL

OBJECTIVE 1
EXPLAIN THE BASIC
CONCEPT OF INTERNAL
CONTROL

The procedures used by management to control business operations are known as **internal controls.** The broad topic of internal control can be divided into two subtopics: **internal administrative controls** and **internal accounting controls.**

Although some overlap exists between the two, internal administrative controls are primarily concerned with:

1. Promoting efficiency.

2. Encouraging employee compliance with company policies.

Internal accounting controls are primarily concerned with:

1. Protecting assets.

2. Ensuring the accuracy of accounting data.

We will focus our attention on internal acounting controls specifically dealing with cash. In this discussion, cash will be defined in the broad sense to include currency, coins, checks, bank drafts, and money orders.

▐▐▐▐ CHECKING ACCOUNT

OBJECTIVE 2
DESCRIBE THE BASIC
FORMS AND
PROCEDURES RELATED
TO THE USE OF A
CHECKING ACCOUNT

A checking account is one of the most important ways to safeguard cash. It provides both a secure place to store cash as it flows into the business and a safe way to pay bills. In general, all cash received should be deposited daily into a checking account, and all cash payments should be made by check. Exceptions to this general policy involve the use of special cash funds, which will be discussed later in this chapter. For now, let's review some of the basic forms and procedures related to the use of a checking account.

SIGNATURE CARD

When a checking account is opened, the bank requires that a signature card be signed by each person authorized to sign checks. This card should be signed exactly the way checks will be signed. In the future, the bank can use the signature card to detect forgeries by comparing signatures on checks with signatures on the card. This procedure also limits the number of employees allowed to sign checks and thus reduces the risk of improper disbursements of cash.

DEPOSIT TICKETS

A **deposit ticket** must accompany each deposit. This provides a record of each deposit. Blank deposit tickets are furnished by the bank but must be prepared by the depositor. An example of a deposit ticket is shown in Figure 8-1.

▌ **FIGURE 8 - 1**

DEPOSIT TICKET
WHEATON VALLEY BANK
Wheaton, Illinois

Date: 8–12–XX

Name: The Kitchen Taylor

Address: 2400 Main Street

Wheaton, Illinois 60187

CASH	CURRENCY	85	00
	COIN	3	45
CHECKS—LIST SINGLY			
70-489		650	00
70-492		1,036	50
72-492		134	70
71-220		62	40
TOTAL		1,972	05
Less Cash Received		—	—
NET DEPOSIT		1,972	05

⊕⑆071904821⑆ 7106 37300⑈

Currency, coins, and checks are listed separately on the deposit ticket. Each check being deposited should be identified by its **American Banking Association (ABA) number.** This number is printed in the upper right corner of each check in the form of a fraction. The numerator indicates the city or state and the specific bank; the denominator indicates the Federal Reserve District and the routing number.

$$\frac{70\text{-}482}{719}$$

70—City or state
482—Specific bank
7—Federal Reserve District
19—Routing number

The information contained in the numerator is all that is necessary on the deposit ticket (example: 70-482).

ENDORSEMENTS

The depositor must endorse each check being deposited. The endorsement may be handwritten or stamped on the back of the check. The **endorsement** transfers ownership and guarantees payment of the check.

Figure 8-2 shows a **restrictive endorsement.** Restrictive endorsements protect against theft by restricting further circulation of the check. The check in Figure 8-2 can only be deposited at the indicated bank. It is a good practice to immediately endorse all incoming checks with a restrictive endorsement.

CHECK

A **check** is a document signed by the depositor that orders the bank to pay a certain amount of money to a certain party. The following three parties are named on the face of every check:

1. Drawer—the party who signs the check.

2. Drawee—the drawer's bank.

3. Payee—the party being paid.

Checks are usually attached to a check stub. The amount of each check, the date, the check number, and the payee's name are recorded on the stub. The purpose of each check as well as the previous balance and the new balance in the checking account are also filled in on each stub. The check stub later provides the information necessary for the journal entry to formally record

FIGURE 8 - 2

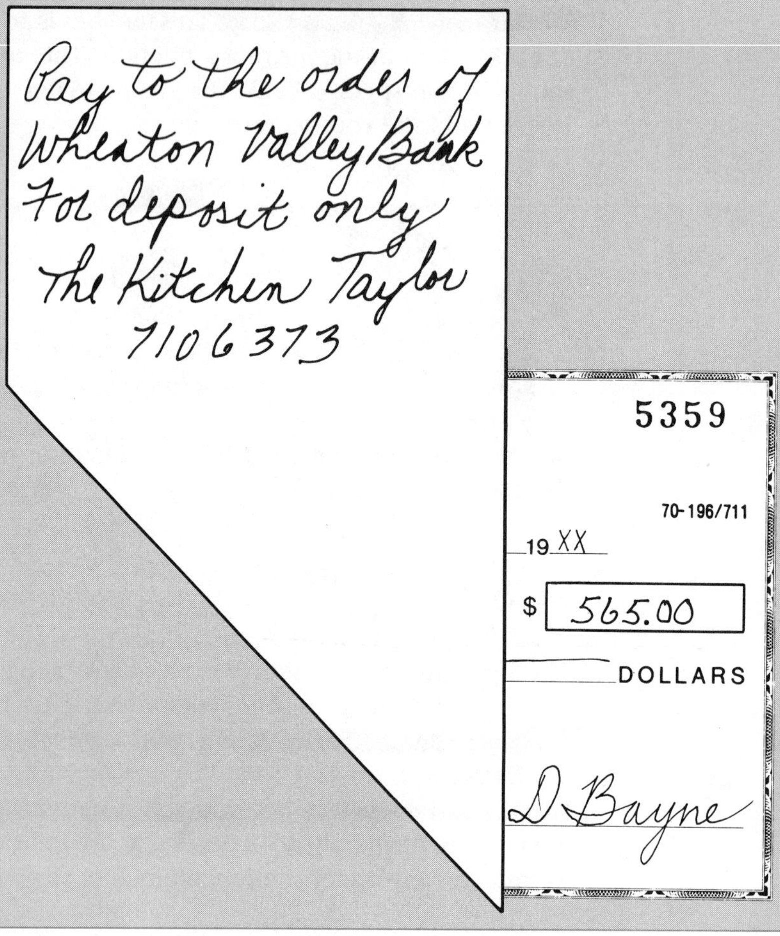

the cash payment each check represents. To avoid omissions, the check stub should be completed before the check is written. This is important since we cannot make a journal entry without the proper information. Figure 8-3 shows a properly written check and check stub.

BANK STATEMENT

Each month a **bank statement** is sent to the depositor. This statement includes the following information:

Balance—beginning of the month.

Additions—deposits and credit memos.

Deductions—checks and debit memos.

Balance—end of the month.

FIGURE 8 - 3

NO. 1426   149.50
DATE AUGUST17, 19XX
TO Baird Co.
FOR Cabinet

Bal. Forward 3,861.55
Amt. Deposited
Total   3,861.55
Amt. this Check 149.50
Balance   3,712.05

THE KITCHEN TAYLOR   1426
2400 Main Street
Wheaton, Ill. 60187   *August 17*, 19XX   70-482/719

PAY TO THE
ORDER OF *Baird Company* $ *149.50*

One hundred forty-nine and 50/100 ——— DOLLARS

WHEATON VALLEY BANK
Wheaton, Illinois 60187
                                        Dennis Taylor
MEMO_____

⑇071904821⑇ ⑇710637300⑇ 1426

Bank credit memos are brief forms, prepared by the bank, explaining additions to the depositor's account for items other than regular deposits. Bank debit memos explain subtractions from the depositor's account for items other than checks written by the depositor.

|||||||||||||||||||||
C O M M E N T

From the bank's point of view, the depositor's account is a liability (credit balance), since the bank owes the depositor the balance in the account. Therefore, the bank records additions to the account with credits and deductions with debits.

Canceled checks are usually returned to the depositor along with the bank statement. These are the checks that have actually been presented to the bank for payment during the period covered by the bank statement. Other checks may have been written but have not yet been presented for payment by the payee. The bank would, of course, have no record of these checks. Figure 8-4 shows a typical bank statement.

BANK RECONCILIATION

THE NEED FOR A BANK RECONCILIATION

OBJECTIVE 3
PREPARE A BANK
RECONCILIATION AND
THE RELATED JOURNAL
ENTRIES

If all cash received is deposited in the checking account and all cash disbursed is paid out of the checking account, the balance in the checking account should be equal to the balance in the depositor's Cash account. On any given day, however, these two balances are rarely the same. Although the difference

FIGURE 8 - 4

WHEATON VALLEY BANK
Wheaton, Illinois

The Kitchen Taylor
2400 Main Street
Wheaton, Illinois 60187

Statement Date: 8-31-XX
Account No.: 7106373
Period Covered:
From 8-1-XX to 8-31-XX

Previous Balance	Checks/Debits	Deposits/Credits	Current Balance
$3,677.25	$3,535.93	$3,769.22	$3,910.54

Checks/Debits		Deposits/Credits	Date	Balance
			08-01	3,677.25
250.00	172.00	380.25	08-01	3,635.50
489.32			08-03	3,146.18
427.00		949.50	08-06	3,668.68
941.60	65.00		08-10	2,662.08
		1,389.47	08-13	4,051.55
190.00 NSF			08-14	3,861.55
149.50	236.00		08-17	3,476.05
83.72			08-20	3,392.33
315.80		1,050.00	08-24	4,126.53
62.79	138.20		08-28	3,925.54
15.00 SC			08-31	3,910.54

Symbols:

CM—Credit Memo
DM—Debit Memo
NSF—Nonsufficient Funds

SC—Service Charge
EC—Error Correction
OD—Overdraft

Please examine this statement carefully. Errors should be reported within ten days.

could be the result of an error, it usually is the result of timing. Sometimes the depositor has access to information before the bank, and other times the bank has access to information before the depositor. When the information becomes known to both the bank and the depositor, the differences disappear. On any given day, the true balance usually lies somewhere between the bank's balance and the depositor's Cash account balance.

Each month when the bank statement is received, the depositor should compare the ending balance according to the bank statement with the Cash account balance as of the same date. To obtain the true or adjusted balance as of the end of the month, the reasons for any difference must be identified. This requires a careful comparison of the bank statement and the depositor's records. This process of bringing the two balances into agreement is known as reconciliation. Each month the depositor should prepare a written bank reconciliation.

Based on the reconciliation, journal entries will be recorded that update or, in the case of errors, correct the depositor's records. The resulting Cash account balance will appear on the balance sheet.

FORMAT OF BANK RECONCILIATION

A bank reconciliation consists of two major sections. Section 1 begins with the balance according to the bank statement as of a given date. Section 2 begins with the Cash account balance according to the depositor's records as of the same date. Both sections end with the same adjusted (or true) balance after reconciliation items have been added and/or deducted. The general format for a bank reconciliation is as follows:

Bank statement balance			$XX
Add: Deposits in transit		$XX	
Bank errors		XX	XX
			$XX
Deduct: Outstanding checks		$XX	
Bank errors		XX	XX
Adjusted balance			$XX
Cash account balance			$XX
Add: Credit memos		$XX	
Depositor errors		XX	XX
			$XX
Deduct: Debit memos		$XX	
Depositor errors		XX	XX
Adjusted balance			$XX

TYPICAL RECONCILIATION ITEMS

Any item appearing on the bank statement but not in the depositor's records is creating a difference and is, therefore, a reconciliation item. Conversely, any item appearing in the depositor's records but not on the bank statement is also a reconciliation item. Let's review some of the most common reconciliation items.

Outstanding checks. These are checks that have been written but have not yet been presented to the bank for payment. These checks were deducted by the depositor when written. The bank has not deducted for these checks, since they have not been presented for payment. On the bank reconciliation, outstanding checks are deducted from the bank statement balance.

Deposits in transit. These are deposits that were made before the end of the month but were not processed by the bank in time to appear on the bank statement. The depositor has already added these deposits to the Cash account; the bank has not. On the bank reconciliation, deposits in transit are added to the bank statement balance.

Service charges. Banks charge for the routine processing of checks and deposits as well as for other special services. Routine charges are frequently based on the number of checks processed or the average daily balance in the account. The bank deducts for service charges on the bank statement. A debit memo explaining the charges is enclosed with the statement. On the bank reconciliation, service charges are deducted from the Cash account balance.

NSF (nonsufficient funds) checks. These are previously deposited checks that have been returned by the bank to the depositor because the drawer's account did not contain enough cash. Notice that these are not checks that the depositor has written. NSF checks are checks written to the depositor by customers. Added by both the bank and the depositor when deposited, NSF checks must be deducted by both when returned. The bank will show NSF checks as deductions on the bank statement. On the bank reconciliation, NSF checks are deducted from the Cash account balance.

Collections. If requested, most banks will collect payments for a depositor on such items as installment sales, charge accounts, and promissory notes. Such collections are added on the bank statement. A credit memo explaining each collection is enclosed with the statement. On the bank reconciliation, collections are added to the Cash account balance.

Errors. In the process of reconciliation, errors are sometimes discovered. On the bank reconciliation, the appropriate adjustment must be made on the side of the party responsible for the error. Whether the adjustment is an addition or a deduction depends on the nature of the error. In the case of a bank error, the depositor should immediately inform the bank of the situation.

FINDING RECONCILIATION ITEMS

To identify reconciliation items, the depositor uses the following procedures:

1. Deposits:
   a. Compare the deposits shown on the bank statement with the deposits in transit shown on last month's reconciliation. All of

last month's deposits in transit should be processed by this time. The bank should be notified if any of these deposits do not appear on the bank statement. Differences in this area usually indicate an error has been made.

    b. Compare the deposits shown on the bank statement with the depositor's records for the current month.
- A deposit missing from the bank statement is treated as a deposit in transit.
- A deposit missing from the depositor's records is treated as an error—an unrecorded deposit.

2. Checks:
    a. Arrange the canceled checks in numerical order by check number. Some bank statements list the canceled checks in check number order indicating breaks in the numerical sequence with an asterisk.
    b. Compare the canceled checks with the outstanding checks shown on last month's reconciliation.
- Checks that have still not been paid are again treated as outstanding checks.

    c. Compare the canceled checks with the depositor's records for the current month.
- Checks that have not been canceled (paid) are treated as outstanding checks.

3. Bank memorandums:
    a. Compare debit memos with the depositor's records for items such as service charges and NSF checks.
- Items not yet recorded by the depositor must be recorded. Such items are deducted from the Cash account balance.

    b. Compare credit memos with the depositor's records for items such as collections.
- Items not yet recorded by the depositor must be recorded. Such items are added to the Cash account balance.

PREPARATION OF A BANK RECONCILIATION

To demonstrate the preparation of a bank reconciliation, let's return to The Kitchen Taylor. The August bank statement (see Figure 8-4) shows a balance of $3,910.54 on August 31. On the same date, The Kitchen Taylor's Cash account balance is $3,032.50. Following the previously described procedures, The Kitchen Taylor identified the following reconciliation items:

1. An August 31 deposit in the amount of $875 is not shown on the bank statement.

2. The following checks have not yet been paid:

No. 1329	. . . .	$ 347.50
No. 1421	. . . .	1,289.00
No. 1430	. . . .	276.54

3. Debit memos:
   a. A service charge amounting to $15 has not been recorded in the journal.
   b. An NSF check for $190 from John Mahoney has not been recorded in the journal.

4. Check No. 1406 for $427 has been recorded in the journal as $472.

Based on this information, the following bank reconciliation is prepared:

THE KITCHEN TAYLOR
Bank Reconciliation
August 31, 19XX

Bank statement balance, August 31		$3,910.54
Add: Deposits in transit		875.00
		$4,785.54
Deduct: Outstanding checks:		
No. 1329	$ 347.50	
No. 1421	1,289.00	
No. 1430	276.54	1,913.04
Adjusted balance		$2,872.50
Cash account balance, August 31		$3,032.50
Add: Error in recording Check No. 1406		
($472 − 427 = $45)		45.00
		$3,077.50
Deduct: Service charge	$ 15.00	
NSF check	190.00	205.00
Adjusted balance		$2,872.50

REQUIRED JOURNAL ENTRIES

Adjustments to the Cash account section of the reconciliation require journal entries to update and/or correct the accounting records. Based on The Kitchen Taylor's bank reconciliation, the following entries are recorded:

GENERAL JOURNAL					Page 72	
Date	Description	Post. Ref.	Debit		Credit	
19XX Aug. 31	Cash		45	00		
	Accounts Payable				45	00
	Error in recording Check No. 1406.					
31	Miscellaneous Expense		15	00		
	Cash				15	00
	Bank service charge.					
31	Accounts Receivable		190	00		
	Cash				190	00
	NSF check from John Mahoney.					

After these entries have been posted, the Cash account balance will be equal to the adjusted or true balance ($2,872.50) on August 31. This is the cash balance that will be shown on the August 31 balance sheet.

Account **Cash**							Account No. 110		
Date	Item	Post. Ref.	Debit		Credit		Balance		
							Debit		Credit
19XX Aug. 31	Balance	✓					3,032	50	
31		J72	45	00			3,077	50	
31		J72			15	00	3,062	50	
31		J72			190	00	2,872	50	

▮▮▮▮ THE PETTY CASH FUND   *is a current asset*

As stated earlier, paying bills by check is an important way to safeguard cash. However, this is not practical in the case of bills for small amounts. For example, writing a check for $0.75 to cover postage due on incoming mail would not make sense. The cost of writing a check for such a small amount would exceed the face amount of the check. Instead, most businesses pay small bills in cash out of a petty cash fund.

The **petty cash fund** is established for a fixed amount. The size of the fund depends on the needs of the business. Day to day, small bills are paid in cash directly out of the fund. Periodically, the fund is replenished, usually on a weekly or monthly basis.

ESTABLISHING THE PETTY CASH FUND

The petty cash fund is established by writing a check for the fixed amount of the fund. Next, the check is cashed, and the cash is placed in a petty cash box.

To demonstrate the accounting for such a transaction, let's assume The Kitchen Taylor decides to establish a $50 petty cash fund. This transaction would be journalized as follows:

			GENERAL JOURNAL						Page 70	
Date			Description	Post. Ref.	Debit			Credit		
19XX July	1	Petty Cash			50	00				
		Cash						50	00	
		To establish a petty cash fund.								

The Petty Cash account is a current asset account. It will appear on the balance sheet immediately below the Cash account. The Petty Cash account will not be debited or credited again unless the business decides to change the fixed size of the fund.

MAKING PAYMENTS FROM THE PETTY CASH FUND

For internal control purposes, one person should be designated as custodian of the petty cash fund. This should be the only person disbursing cash from the fund. The custodian makes payments from the fund based on a company policy describing such things as acceptable purposes for payments and limits on the size of individual payments.

The custodian should prepare a **petty cash voucher** for each payment from the fund. The voucher describes the amount, date, and purpose of each payment. Most petty cash vouchers also categorize the payment by account

FIGURE 8 - 5

PETTY CASH VOUCHER

NO. _____1_____   DATE __July 2, 19xx__

PAID TO ___U.S. Postal Service___ $ _____.65_____

FOR ___Postage Due___

ACCOUNT ___Miscellaneous Expense___

Received by: Approved by custodian:

___J. Avalos___   ___R. Steele___

and require the signatures or initials of the parties making and receiving the payment. Figure 8-5 shows a completed petty cash voucher.

|||||||||||||||||||||||
C O M M E N T

The custodian should be advised that the fund will be balanced on an unannounced basis. To balance the petty cash fund, the supervisor will:

1. Count the cash in the box.

2. Total the petty cash vouchers.

3. Add the cash in the box to the total of the vouchers; this sum should equal the fixed size of the petty cash fund.

In addition to vouchers, some companies use a **petty cash record** to summarize all the petty cash voucher information on a single sheet. The columnar format of the petty cash record makes it convenient to sort voucher information by account. This, in turn, makes it convenient to compile the information needed to replenish the fund at the end of the month. Figure 8-6 shows The Kitchen Taylor's petty cash record for the month of July.

|||||||||||||||||||||
C O M M E N T

Although it resembles a journal, the petty cash record is not a journal. At the end of each month, the information compiled in the petty cash record must be officially recorded in the form of a journal entry. This information will be journalized when the petty cash fund is replenished.

FIGURE 8 - 6

PETTY CASH RECORD
For the Month of July, 19XX

Date	Voucher No.	Explanation	Payments	Supplies	Delivery Expense	Misc. Expense	Sundry Account	Amount
July 1		Established Fund, $50						
2	1	Postage due	.65			.65		
5	2	Ace Delivery Service	4.30		4.30			
8	3	Felt-tip pens	2.75	2.75				
12	4	Withdrawal by owner	10.00				D. Taylor, Draw.	10.00
13	5	Ace Delivery Service	4.75		4.75			
17	6	Scratch pads	3.80	3.80				
19	7	Sent telegram	4.90			4.90		
23	8	Withdrawal by owner	6.50				D. Taylor, Draw.	6.50
27	9	Postage due	.22			.22		
31	10	Small repair	8.50				Repair Expense	8.50
		Totals	46.37	6.55	9.05	5.77		25.00
		Bal., 7-31 $ 3.63						
		Replenished 46.37						
		Bal., 8-1 $50.00						

REPLENISHING THE PETTY CASH FUND

The petty cash fund may be replenished any time cash in the box gets low. However, the fund should always be replenished at the end of the month. This is necessary in order for the monthly financial statements to reflect up-to-date account balances. Remember, payments from the petty cash fund are not journalized until the fund is replenished.

If a petty cash record is used, the information to replenish the fund is taken directly from the petty cash record. Otherwise, the information comes directly from the petty cash vouchers.

Based on the petty cash record shown in Figure 8-6, the replenishment of The Kitchen Taylor's petty cash fund would be recorded as follows.

GENERAL JOURNAL						Page 71	
Date		Description	Post. Ref.	Debit		Credit	
19XX July	31	Supplies		6	55		
		Delivery Expense		9	05		
		Miscellaneous Expense		5	77		
		Dennis Taylor, Drawing		16	50		
		Repair Expense		8	50		
		Cash				46	37
		To replenish petty cash.					

The credit to the Cash account represents a check written in the amount of $46.37. This check is cashed, and the cash is placed in the petty cash box. This brings the fund up to its fixed size ($50). After replenishment on July 31, the actual cash in the box ($50) is equal to the Petty Cash account balance ($50) shown on the July 31 balance sheet.

|||||||||||||||||||||
COMMENT

As noted earlier, replenishing petty cash does not change the fixed size of the fund. Therefore, the replenishment entry does not involve the Petty Cash account.

▊▊▊▊ THE CHANGE FUND

OBJECTIVE 5
ESTABLISH AND USE A
CHANGE FUND

Businesses that regularly receive cash (currency and coin) from customers need to be able to make change. If all cash inflows are deposited into a checking account at the end of each day, an empty cash drawer the following morning could represent a problem. This problem is easily solved by establishing a change fund.

A change fund is a fixed amount of cash that is kept in the cash drawer on a permanent basis for the purpose of making change. How large the fund should be depends on the needs of the individual business. Once the size of the fund has been determined, the business must decide on the denominations of bills and coins to be used in the change fund.

Let's assume The Kitchen Taylor decides to establish a $75 change fund. This transaction would be recorded as follows:

GENERAL JOURNAL				Page 75	
Date	Description	Post. Ref.	Debit	Credit	
19XX Sept. 1	Change Fund		75 00		
	Cash			75 00	
	To establish change fund.				

The credit to the Cash account represents a check written in the amount of $75. This check is cashed, requesting the desired denominations of bills and coins, and the cash is placed in the cash drawer.

At the end of each business day, all the cash in the cash drawer is deposited in the checking account except for the amount in the change fund. The $75 change fund is counted out and placed back in the cash drawer.

The Change Fund account is a current asset account. It will appear on the balance sheet below the Cash account. If the Petty Cash account balance is larger, the Change Fund account will follow the Petty Cash account.

The Change Fund account will not be debited or credited again unless the business decides to change the size of the fund. Otherwise, the $75 balance remains in the account, and the $75 in cash remains in the cash drawer.

|||||||||||||||||||||||
C O M M E N T   The change fund and the petty cash fund are separate funds with separate purposes. The change fund is used to make change for customers. The petty cash fund is used to pay small bills.

████ CASH SHORT AND OVER

OBJECTIVE 6
ACCOUNT FOR
SHORTAGES AND
OVERAGES USING A
CASH SHORT AND OVER
ACCOUNT

Businesses recording large numbers of cash sales generally use a cash register. As each sale is registered, the tape inside the cash register keeps a cumulative record of the day's sales. At the end of the day, the cash in the drawer (minus the change fund) should be equal to the total on the cash register tape. However, even with careful and honest employees, small errors in making change do occur from time to time. Such errors cause the cash in the drawer to be unequal to the total on the tape. If the cash in the drawer is less than the tape total, the difference is referred to as a shortage. On the other hand, if the cash in the drawer is greater than the tape total, the difference is referred to as an overage. An account titled Cash Short and Over is used to record both shortages and overages.

To demonstrate, let's assume the following facts:

$$\begin{aligned} \text{Tape} &= \$360 \\ \text{Cash} &= \underline{358} \\ \text{Shortage} &= \underline{\underline{\$2}} \end{aligned}$$

The cash sales for September 21 would be recorded with the following entry:

GENERAL JOURNAL							Page 77	
Date		Description	Post. Ref.	Debit		Credit		
19XX Sept.	21	Cash		358	00			
		Cash Short and Over		2	00			
		Sales				360	00	

Let's assume the following situation exists on September 22:

$$\begin{aligned} \text{Tape} &= \$415 \\ \text{Cash} &= \underline{416} \\ \text{Overage} &= \underline{\underline{\$1}} \end{aligned}$$

The cash sales for September 22 would be recorded with the following entry:

GENERAL JOURNAL							Page 77	
Date		Description	Post. Ref.	Debit		Credit		
19XX Sept.	22	Cash		416	00			
		Sales				415	00	
		Cash Short and Over				1	00	

||||||||||||||||||||||||

C O M M E N T

The Cash Short and Over account may also be used to account for occasional shortages or overages in the petty cash fund.

Cash Short and Over is an income statement account without a fixed classification. Whether it is reported as revenue or expense depends on its balance as of the statement date. A debit balance, indicating a net shortage, is shown as miscellaneous expense. A credit balance, indicating a net overage, is shown as miscellaneous revenue.

Chapter Summary

In this chapter, we focused our attention on internal accounting controls dealing with cash. These controls are primarily concerned with protecting assets and ensuring the accuracy of accounting data.

A checking account is one of the most important ways to safeguard cash. To use a checking account, the depositor must become familiar with signature cards, deposit tickets, checks, endorsements, and bank statements. Cash receipts should be deposited into a checking account, and cash payments should be made by check.

Due to timing differences and errors, a bank reconciliation should be prepared at the end of each month to obtain the adjusted or true balance. In reconciling the bank statement balance and the checking account balance, the reasons for any differences are identified. Common reconciliation items include outstanding checks, deposits in transit, service charges, NSF checks, collections, and errors.

Adjustments to the Cash account section of the reconciliation require journal entries to update and/or correct the accounting records. After these entries have been journalized and posted, the Cash account balance will be equal to the adjusted or true balance as of the end of the period. This is the Cash account balance that will appear on the balance sheet.

Most businesses pay small bills in cash out of a petty cash fund. This fund is established for a fixed amount and is periodically replenished, usually on a weekly or monthly basis. Payments from the petty cash fund are not formally journalized until the fund is replenished. Replenishing petty cash does not change the fixed size of the fund. Therefore, the replenishment entry does not involve the Petty Cash account. Petty Cash is an asset account and will appear on the balance sheet below Cash.

Businesses that regularly receive cash (currency and coins) from customers need a change fund. A change fund is a fixed amount of cash that is kept in the cash drawer on a permanent basis for the purpose of making change. The Change Fund is an asset account and will appear on the balance sheet below Cash.

Businesses recording large numbers of cash sales generally use a cash register. At the end of the day, the cash in the drawer (minus the change fund) should be equal to the total on the cash register tape. However, small errors in making change do occur from time to time. An account titled Cash Short and Over is used to record both shortages and overages. A debit balance in Cash Short and Over, indicating a net shortage, will be treated as an expense. A credit balance, indicating a net overage, will be treated as revenue.

Glossary

AMERICAN BANKING ASSOCIATION (ABA) NUMBER

The number that is printed in the upper right corner of each check in the form of a fraction. The numerator indicates the city or state and the specific bank; the denominator indicates the Federal Reserve District and the routing number.

BANK RECONCILIATION

The process of bringing the bank statement balance and the Cash account balance into agreement. The resulting balance is known as the adjusted or true balance as of a given date.

BANK STATEMENT

A statement prepared by the bank showing account activity for a specified period of time.

CANCELED CHECKS

Checks that have been presented to the bank for payment. They are usually returned to the depositor along with the bank statement.

CHANGE FUND

A fixed amount of cash kept in the cash drawer on a permanent basis for the purpose of making change.

CHECK

A document signed by the depositor ordering the bank to pay a certain amount of money to a certain party.

DEPOSIT IN TRANSIT

A deposit made before the end of the month but not processed by the bank in time to appear on the bank statement.

DEPOSIT TICKETS

A form supplied by the bank but prepared by the depositor that must accompany each deposit. Currency, coins, and checks being deposited are listed separately.

ENDORSEMENT

A signature or stamp on the back of a check transferring ownership and guaranteeing payment of the check.

INTERNAL ACCOUNTING CONTROLS

Procedures primarily concerned with protecting assets and ensuring the accuracy of accounting data.

INTERNAL ADMINISTRATIVE CONTROLS

Procedures primarily concerned with promoting efficiency and encouraging employee compliance with company policies.

INTERNAL CONTROL

The procedures used by management to control business operations. These can be divided into internal administrative controls and internal accounting controls.

NSF (NONSUFFICIENT FUNDS) CHECK

A previously deposited check that has been returned to the depositor because the drawer's account did not contain enough cash.

OUTSTANDING CHECK

A check that has been written but not yet presented to the bank for payment.

PETTY CASH FUND

A cash fund used to pay small bills.

PETTY CASH RECORD

A columnar form that summarizes all petty cash voucher information on a single sheet.

PETTY CASH VOUCHER

A form prepared for each payment from a petty cash fund. The form contains the amount, date, and purpose of each payment, as well as signatures acknowledging approval and receipt.

RESTRICTIVE ENDORSEMENT

Protects against theft by restricting further circulation of a check.

SERVICE CHARGE

A fee charged by the bank for the routine processing of checks and deposits as well as for other special services.

SIGNATURE CARD

A card that must be signed by each person authorized to sign checks drawn on a particular checking account. The bank uses the card to verify signatures on checks.

Questions for Discussion

1. Define:
   a. Internal control.
   b. Internal accounting control.
   c. Internal administrative control.

2. a. What is a signature card?
   b. Why is it necessary?

3. a. Describe a deposit ticket.
   b. Who prepares the deposit ticket?

4. a. What is the purpose of an endorsement?
   b. Why is it a good practice to immediately endorse all incoming checks with a restrictive endorsement?

5. a. What is a check?
   b. Who are the three parties named on the face of every check?

6. What is the purpose of a bank reconciliation?

7. Name and discuss six common reconciliation items.

8. a. What is the purpose of a petty cash fund?
   b. Describe the duties of the custodian.

9. What is the purpose of a change fund?

10. a. Why would a business need a Cash Short and Over account?
    b. How is the Cash Short and Over account classified on the income statement?

Exercises

Match the following terms with the definitions shown below:

1. Bank reconciliation.
2. Canceled checks.
3. Change fund.
4. Check.
5. Deposit in transit.
6. Endorsement.
7. Internal accounting controls.
8. NSF check.
9. Outstanding check.
10. Petty cash fund.
11. Petty cash voucher.
12. Petty cash record.
13. Restrictive endorsement.

Definitions:

a. Procedures primarily concerned with protecting assets and ensuring the accuracy of accounting data.

b. A document signed by the depositor ordering the bank to pay a certain amount of money to a certain party.

c. A signature or stamp on the back of a check, transferring ownership and guaranteeing payment of the check.

d. A form prepared for each payment from a petty cash fund. The form contains the amount, date, and purpose of each payment, as well as signatures acknowledging approval and receipt.

    e. A deposit made before the end of the month but not processed by the bank in time to appear on the bank statement.

    f. Protects against theft by restricting further circulation of a check.

    g. The process of bringing the bank statement balance and the Cash account balance into agreement. The resulting balance is known as the adjusted or true balance as of a given date.

    h. A cash fund used to pay small bills.

    i. A check that has been written but not yet presented to the bank for payment.

    j. A fixed amount of cash kept in the cash drawer on a permanent basis for the purpose of making change.

    k. Checks that have been presented to the bank for payment. They are usually returned to the depositor along with the bank statement.

    l. A columnar form that summarizes all petty cash voucher information on a single sheet.

    m. A previously deposited check that has been returned to the depositor because the drawer's account did not contain enough cash.

EXERCISE 8-2
RECONCILIATION ITEMS
(L.O.3)

For each of the following reconciliation items indicate:

    a. The section in which the adjustment is recorded (bank statement or Cash account)

    b. Whether the adjustment is added or deducted (+ or −)

Reconciliation Item	*(a)* Adjustment Section	*(b)* Add or Deduct
1. Outstanding check.		
2. Deposit in transit.		
3. Service charge.		
4. NSF check.		
5. Collection.		

EXERCISE 8-3
BANK RECONCILIATION
(L.O.3)

Paragon Products' bank statement shows an ending balance of $2,543.70 on September 30, 19XX. On the same date, Paragon's Cash account balance is $3,209.30. The following reconciliation items have been identified:

- Outstanding checks:

No. 872	. . . . . .	$427.90
No. 885	. . . . . .	618.50

- Deposit in transit, $1,350.

- Bank memo for service charges, $12.

- An NSF check for $350 from Scott Benson has not been recorded.

Prepare a bank reconciliation.

EXERCISE 8-4
RECONCILIATION
ENTRIES
(L.O.3)

Based on the information presented in Exercise 8-3, prepare the necessary journal entries for Paragon Products.

EXERCISE 8-5
RECONCILIATION ITEMS
(L.O.3)

Plum Associates wrote Check No. 1058 to Firenza Company for $927.80. However, this payment on account was recorded as $972.80 in the journal.

1. In preparing Plum Associates bank reconciliation:
   a. In which section would the adjustment be recorded (bank statement or Cash account)?
   b. Would the adjustment be added or deducted?

2. Is a journal entry required? If so, prepare it.

EXERCISE 8-6
PETTY CASH FUND
(L.O.4)

a. Record the following transactions in general journal form:

Oct. 1   Established a petty cash fund, $75.

31   Replenished petty cash based on the following payment information taken from the Petty Cash Record:

Supplies	$27.50
Delivery expense	12.00
Miscellaneous expense . . .	34.75

b. What type of account is petty cash and on what financial statement does it appear? *Current Asset Account (appears on balance sheet right under cash)*

EXERCISE 8-7
CHANGE FUND
(L.O.5)

Bianca Cleaners has decided to establish a change fund in the amount of $50.

a. In general journal form, record the entry to establish the change fund.

b. When will another entry debiting or crediting the Change Fund account be necessary?

    c. At the end of the day, the cash in Bianca's cash drawer totals $542.50. The tape shows sales totaling $497.50. How much cash should be deposited in the checking account.

    d. What type of account is the change fund and on what financial statement does it appear?

EXERCISE 8-8
CASH SHORT AND OVER
(L.O.6)

At the end of the day on July 10, 19XX, the cash in McCaffrey Office Supplies' cash drawer totals $927.35. The cash register tape shows sales totaling $879.52. McCaffrey maintains a $50 change fund.

    a. In general journal form, prepare the entry to record the cash sales for July 10.

    b. How is the Cash Short and Over account reported on the income statement?

Problems—Set A

PROBLEM 8-1A
BANK RECONCILIATION
(L.O.3)

The April bank statement for Ursula's Boutique shows an April 30 balance of $937.57. The April 30 balance in Ursula's Cash account is $1,795.67. Ursula deposits all cash received in a checking account and pays all bills by check. A comparison of the bank statement and accounting records has identified the following reconciliation items:

- Outstanding checks:

No. 1549	$ 85.20
No. 1563	149.50
No. 1571	341.75

- Deposit in transit, $1,824.30.

- Bank debit memo for service charges, $19.

- An NSF check for $240 from Robert Westman has not been recorded.

- Bank credit memo for a charge account collection, $621.75.

- Ursula wrote Check No. 1562 to Applegate Company for $325. However, this payment on account was recorded as $352 in the journal.

INSTRUCTIONS
1. Prepare a bank reconciliation.
2. Record the necessary journal entries in general journal form.

PROBLEM 8-2A
PETTY CASH FUND
(L.O.4)

The following petty cash transactions occurred for Princess Video during the month of June:

June   1   Established a petty cash fund, $75.

        3   Issued Voucher No. 1 for postage due on a letter, $.32.

June 4   Issued Voucher No. 2 for a minor repair to equipment, $7.25.

     7   Issued Voucher No. 3 to Victoria Parsons, owner, for personal use, $10.

    10   Issued Voucher No. 4 to Jiffy Delivery service, $6.50.

    13   Issued Voucher No. 5 for postage due on a parcel, $1.30.

    15   Issued Voucher No. 6 for paper clips and pencils, $5.45.

    17   Issued Voucher No. 7 to Victoria Parsons, owner, for personal use, $8.75.

    20   Issued Voucher No. 8 to send a telegram, $4.95.

    23   Issued Voucher No. 9 for scratch pads, $3.42.

    28   Issued Voucher No. 10 to Jiffy Delivery Service, $5.75.

    30   Replenished the petty cash fund.

INSTRUCTIONS

1. In general journal form, record the entry to establish the petty cash fund.

2. Record all payments from the fund (Voucher Nos. 1 through 10) in the petty cash record.
   - Students not using working papers should draw up a petty cash record as illustrated in Figure 8-6, page 276, of this chapter.

3. In general journal form, record the entry to replenish the petty cash fund on June 30.

PROBLEM 8-3A
CHANGE FUND; CASH
SHORT AND OVER
(L.O.5, 6)

The following selected transactions for Crane Books occurred during the month of September:

Sept. 1   Established a change fund, $50.

     6   Recorded cash sales: total cash in drawer, $225.42; cash register tape, $175.42.

    10   Recorded cash sales: total cash in drawer, $254.80; cash register tape, $207.80.

    17   Recorded cash sales: total cash in drawer, $347.62; cash register tape, $293.46.

    23   Recorded cash sales: total cash in drawer, $315.29; cash register tape, $262.90.

    30   Recorded cash sales: total cash in drawer, $297.85; cash register tape, $241.15.

INSTRUCTIONS

1. Record these transactions in general journal form. (Use general journal page 87.)

2. Post to the Cash Short and Over account (Account No. 59).

3. *a.* What is the September 30 balance in the Cash Short and Over account?
   b. How will the Cash Short and Over account be reported on the September income statement?

PROBLEM 8-4A
BANK RECONCILIATION
(L.O.3)

The August bank statement for Mikey's Garage shows an August 31 balance of $2,137.71. Mikey's August 31 Cash account balance is $1,809.61. Mikey deposits all cash received in a checking account and pays all bills by check. A comparison of the bank statement and accounting records has identified the following reconciliation items:

● The following checks have been written but have not been presented for payment:

No. 2439	$846.35
No. 2467	219.20
No. 2488	781.50

● A deposit in the amount of $1,652.84 was mailed to the bank on August 30. This deposit does not appear on the August bank statement.

● Bank debit memo for routine processing of checks, $9.

● Bank debit memo for printing new checks, $18.50.

● A previously deposited check from Claire Greenspan was returned by the bank because Greenspan's account did not contain enough cash to cover the check, $436.

● Bank credit memo for a charge account collection, $615.39.

● Mikey wrote Check No. 2475 to Danza Motors for $97.40. However, this payment on account was recorded as $79.40 in the journal.

INSTRUCTIONS

1. Prepare a bank reconciliation.

2. Record the necessary journal entries in general journal form.

3. What is Mikey's true Cash account balance on August 31?

Problems—Set B

PROBLEM 8-1B
BANK RECONCILIATION
(L.O.3)

The November bank statement for Bob's Diner shows a November 30 balance of $1,016.62. The November 30 balance in Bob's Cash account is $1,044.25. Bob deposits all cash received in a checking account and pays all bills by check. A comparison of the bank statement and accounting records has identified the following reconciliation items:

- Outstanding checks:

No. 1227	$ 97.25
No. 1249	293.47
No. 1264	182.50

- Deposit in transit, $1,084.20.

- Bank debit memo for service charges, $15.

- An NSF check for $112 from Carl East has not been recorded.

- Bank credit memo for a charge account collection, $574.35.

- Bob wrote Check No. 1260 to Mitchell Products for $215. However, this payment on account was recorded as $251 in the journal.

INSTRUCTIONS

1. Prepare a bank reconciliation.

2. Record the necessary journal entries in general journal form.

PROBLEM 8-2B
PETTY CASH FUND
(L.O.4)

The following petty cash transactions occurred for Zip Copy Service during the month of July:

July 1   Established a petty cash fund, $80.

     2   Issued Voucher No. 1 for minor repair to equipment, $8.50.

     6   Issued Voucher No. 2 for pens and tape, $4.99.

July 8   Issued Voucher No. 3 to Calvin Webster, owner, for personal use, $8.

10   Issued Voucher No. 4 for postage due on a letter, $0.43.

13   Issued Voucher No. 5 to send a telegram, $5.60.

15   Issued Voucher No. 6 for scratch pads, $4.30.

19   Issued Voucher No. 7 to Calvin Webster, owner, for personal use, $10.00.

20   Issued Voucher No. 8 to Jake's Delivery Service, $5.60.

21   Issued Voucher No. 9 for postage due on a parcel, $2.15.

29   Issued Voucher No. 10 to Jake's Delivery Service, $5.

31   Replenished the petty cash fund.

INSTRUCTIONS

1. In general journal form, record the entry to establish the petty cash fund.

2. Record all payments from the fund (Voucher Nos. 1 through 10) in the petty cash record.
   - Students not using working papers should draw up a petty cash record as illustrated in Figure 8-6, page 276, of this chapter.

3. In general journal form, record the entry to replenish the petty cash fund on July 31.

PROBLEM 8-3B
CHANGE FUND; CASH
SHORT AND OVER
(L.O.5, 6)

The following selected transactions for Carol's Gift Shop occurred during the month of July:

July 1   Established a change fund, $75.

7   Recorded cash sales: total cash in drawer, $450.84; cash register tape, $375.84.

12   Recorded cash sales: total cash in drawer, $509.60; cash register tape, $436.50.

18   Recorded cash sales: total cash in drawer, $695.24; cash register tape, $615.20.

24   Recorded cash sales: total cash in drawer, $630.58; cash register tape, $560.68.

31   Recorded cash sales: total cash in drawer, $595.70; cash register tape, $518.65.

INSTRUCTIONS

1. Record these transactions in general journal form. (Use general journal page 74.)

2. Post to the Cash Short and Over account (Account No. 58).

3. *a.* What is the July 31 balance in the Cash Short and Over account?
   b. How will the Cash Short and Over account be recorded on the July income statement?

PROBLEM 8-4B
BANK RECONCILIATION
(L.O.3)

The March bank statement for Ann's Dress Shop shows a March 31 balance of $1,735.56. Ann's March 31 Cash account balance is $1,711.60. Ann deposits all cash received in a checking account and pays all bills by check. A comparison of the bank statement and accounting records has identified the following reconciliation items:

- The following checks have been written but have not been presented for payment:

No. 1476	$192.50
No. 1492	817.25
No. 1493	468.53

- A deposit in the amount of $1,568.42 was mailed to the bank on March 29. This deposit does not appear on the March bank statement.

- Bank debit memo for routine processing of checks, $12.

- Bank debit memo for printing new checks, $21.50.

- A previously deposited check from Beth Elgot was returned by the bank because Elgot's account did not contain enough cash to cover the check, $346.

- Bank credit memo for a charge account collection, $547.60.

- Ann wrote Check No. 1451 to Tarra Company for $82.75. However, this payment on account was recorded as $28.75 in the journal.

INSTRUCTIONS

1. Prepare a bank reconciliation.

2. Record the necessary journal entries in general journal form.

3. What is Ann's true Cash account balance on March 31?

Mini-Cases

CASE 8-1

Your new client, Jerry Eberhart, established a petty cash fund about six months ago. When you asked Mr. Eberhart for a copy of the petty cash voucher form, he stated that petty cash vouchers were not used. "We don't need anything that fancy. We simply pay out the cash, and when the cash in the box gets low, we throw in a few bucks," said Mr. Eberhart. When you asked how the debit portion of the replenishment entry was determined without a voucher, he replied: "We always debit Miscellaneous Expense." Comment on Mr. Eberhart's petty cash procedure.

CASE 8-2

Your neighbor, Maxine, owns her own business. As checks are received, Maxine places them in an envelope she keeps in her desk. After several accumulate she endorses the checks and deposits them in her checking account. Maxine's new accountant is unhappy with these procedures and has suggested several changes. Maxine is reluctant to change. Knowing you are an accountant, she asks for your opinion.

CASE 8-3

Your friend, Carol, claims it only takes her five minutes to reconcile her business checking account. "I don't prepare a written reconciliation," says Carol. "I simply debit or credit my Cash account to bring it into agreement with the ending bank statement balance. After all, the bank never makes any errors and all the adjustments would be on my side anyway." Comment on Carol's method of bank reconciliation.

CHAPTER 9

Payroll: Employee Earnings and Deductions

||||||||||||||||||
L E A R N I N G
O B J E C T I V E S

AFTER STUDYING THIS CHAPTER, YOU SHOULD BE ABLE TO:

1 Distinguish between an employee and an independent contractor.

2 Describe the various bases for employee compensation.

3 Compute total earnings.

4 Determine employee deductions.

5 Compute net pay.

6 Prepare a payroll register.

7 Record the payroll entry.

8 Maintain employee earnings records.

In previous chapters, whenever employees were paid, we simply debited Wages Expense and credited Cash. But that is only part of the story. The computation and recording of a payroll involves considerably more detail. In this chapter and the next, you will study payroll accounting in greater depth.

▮▮▮▮ EMPLOYEES VERSUS INDEPENDENT CONTRACTORS

OBJECTIVE 1
DISTINGUISH BETWEEN AN EMPLOYEE AND AN INDEPENDENT CONTRACTOR

There are two types of people who perform services for a company. An **employee** is one who works under the control and direction of an employer, such as secretaries, receptionists, bookkeepers, and managers. On the other hand, an **independent contractor** is hired by a company to do a specific job but does not work under the company's control or direction. The independent contractor is told what needs to be accomplished but not how to accomplish it. Examples might include doctors, lawyers, plumbers, and various types of repair persons.

The difference between employees and independent contractors is an important legal and accounting distinction. Employees are on the company payroll, and employers are required by law to deduct certain payroll taxes from their earnings. Independent contractors are not on the company payroll, and employers are not required to deduct payroll taxes from their fees. Based on this distinction, payroll accounting deals only with the relationship between employers and employees.

▮▮▮▮ EMPLOYEE COMPENSATION

OBJECTIVE 2
DESCRIBE THE VARIOUS BASES FOR EMPLOYEE COMPENSATION

The earnings of employees are frequently referred to as compensation. Although employees are usually paid in cash, compensation can take the form of meals, lodging, or property. We will assume our employees are compensated in cash. Most compensation is based on wages, salary, piecework, or commissions.

WAGES

The earnings of employees who are paid on an hourly basis are referred to as **wages.** In most cases, a 40-hour week is considered a regular workweek for such employees. Hours worked through 40 are considered regular hours and are paid at a regular hourly rate. The wages paid for regular hours are known as **regular earnings.** Hours worked in excess of 40 in one workweek are considered overtime hours and are paid at an overtime rate per hour. The overtime rate is usually one and a half times the regular hourly rate and is frequently referred to as time and a half. In some instances, overtime on Sundays and holidays is paid at double or even triple the regular hourly rate. The wages paid for overtime hours are known as **overtime earnings.**

▌ **FIGURE 9 - 1**

TIME CARD

Employee: Kevin Barker
Pay Period Ending: July 18, 19XX

Day	In	Out	In	Out	Hours Reg.	Hours O.T.
M	7:55	12:01	12:59	5:00	8	
T	7:59	12:00	1:00	5:01	8	
W	7:57	12:02	12:55	6:02	8	1
T	7:58	12:05	12:58	7:00	8	2
F	7:57	12:00	12:59	5:05	8	
S	8:59	1:05				4
S						
Total					40	7

In small businesses, hourly workers keep a handwritten record of hours worked. In larger businesses, however, time clocks are used. Each worker has a time card that is punched as the worker comes and goes. Figure 9-1 shows a time card for Kevin Barker.

SALARY

Managerial, administrative, and professional employees (for example, engineers, accountants, or attorneys) are usually paid a fixed amount per week, month, or year. This amount is referred to as a salary. A salary is usually not tied to a specific number of hours, although basic salary is sometimes increased with overtime pay for hours worked in excess of 40 during one week.

PIECEWORK

In some situations, employees are paid per unit produced. This used to be a common practice in the garment industry. Cutters and sewers were paid based on the number of garments made rather than on the number of hours worked. However, this is relatively uncommon in today's workplace.

COMMISSIONS

Employees involved in the sale of a product are often paid on a commission basis. Their earnings are equal to a percentage of their sales. Frequently, sales employees are paid on a combination salary plus commission basis. Under such an arrangement, the employee is paid a base salary plus a commission on sales.

▮▮▮▮ COMPUTATION OF TOTAL EARNINGS

OBJECTIVE 3
COMPUTE TOTAL
EARNINGS

To demonstrate the computation of total earnings, let's return to Kevin Barker's time card. Kevin is paid on an hourly basis. His regular hourly rate is $10 per hour. In this textbook, we will assume overtime to be hours worked in excess of 40 in one workweek. We will also assume the overtime rate to be one and a half times the regular hourly rate. Kevin's overtime rate per hour is computed as follows:

$$\text{Regular hourly rate} \times 1.5 = \text{Overtime rate per hour}$$
$$\$10 \qquad \times 1.5 = \qquad \$15$$

Looking back to Figure 9-1, we see that Kevin has worked a total of 47 hours for the workweek ended July 18, 19XX. This means Kevin has worked 40 regular hours plus 7 overtime hours. Kevin's total earnings are computed as follows:

Regular earnings		Overtime earnings		Total earnings
40 × $10 = $400	+	7 × $15 = $105	=	$505

Total earnings are often referred to as *gross pay.*

▮▮▮▮ DEDUCTIONS

OBJECTIVE 4
DETERMINE EMPLOYEE
DEDUCTIONS

Unfortunately, total earnings are not what employees actually take home. Various deductions must be subtracted from total earnings. In general, payroll deductions fall into two categories: required and voluntary. Employers are required by law to withhold federal income taxes and FICA taxes (social security) from the earnings of most employees. In some areas, withholding for state and city income taxes may also be required. Voluntary deductions are for items like U.S. savings bonds, insurance, union dues, charitable contributions, pension plans, and credit union savings and loan payments. Voluntary deductions are usually made at the employee's request or as the result of a labor agreement. Let's consider the required deductions more carefully.

FEDERAL INCOME TAX

Since 1913, when the Sixteenth Amendment to the U.S. Constitution was passed, the federal government has been taxing the income of workers. However, it has only been since 1943 that employers have been required by law to withhold federal income tax from employees' earnings.

When hired, all employees must complete a Form W-4 for their employer. On this form, the employee indicates his or her marital status and number of withholding allowances. Figure 9-2 shows Kevin Barker's Form W-4.

Based on the information in the employee's Form W-4, the employer is able to use tables provided by the Internal Revenue Service to determine the amount to be withheld from each employee's paycheck for federal income tax. Figure 9-3 shows a sample withholding table for married employees who are paid weekly.

Since Kevin Barker is paid weekly and his W-4 indicates he is married, the table in Figure 9-3 is appropriate to use in determining his deduction. Kevin's wages (total earnings, $505) are "at least $500, but less than $510," and he has claimed three withholding allowances on his W-4. Based on this information, the table indicates $62 should be withheld from Kevin's earnings for federal income tax.

|||||||||||||||||||||||||

COMMENT

A **withholding allowance** exempts a portion of an employee's earnings from income tax. In general, an employee is allowed one allowance for him/herself, one for a spouse who doesn't claim an allowance, and one for each additional dependent.

█ **FIGURE 9 - 2**

- - - - - - - - - - - - - - - **Cut here and give the certificate to your employer. Keep the top portion for your records.** - - - - - - - - - - - - - - - -

Form **W-4** Department of the Treasury Internal Revenue Service	**Employee's Withholding Allowance Certificate** ▶ **For Privacy Act and Paperwork Reduction Act Notice, see reverse.**	OMB No. 1545-0010

1 Type or print your first name and middle initial   Last name
  Kevin   Barker

2 Your social security number
  462–50–7534

Home address (number and street or rural route)
  112 Underwood Court

City or town, state, and ZIP code
  Wheaton, IL 60187

3 Marital Status
☐ Single   ☒ Married
☐ Married, but withhold at higher Single rate.
Note: *If married, but legally separated, or spouse is a nonresident alien, check the Single box.*

4 Total number of allowances you are claiming (from line G above or from the Worksheets on back if they apply) . . . . | **4** | 3

5 Additional amount, if any, you want deducted from each pay . . . . | **5** | $

6 I claim exemption from withholding because (check boxes below that apply):
  a ☐ Last year I did not owe any Federal income tax and had a right to a full refund of **ALL** income tax withheld, **AND**
  b ☐ This year I do not expect to owe any Federal income tax and expect to have a right to a full refund of **ALL** income tax withheld.
  c If both **a** and **b** apply and you satisfy the additional conditions outlined above under "Exemption From Withholding," enter the year effective and "EXEMPT" here. Do not complete lines 4 and 5 above . . . . . ▶ | Year
19

7 Are you a full-time student? (**Note:** *Full-time students are **not** automatically exempt.*) | ☐ Yes   ☐ No

Under penalties of perjury, I certify that I am entitled to the number of withholding allowances claimed on this certificate or, if claiming exemption from withholding, that I am entitled to claim the exempt status.
Employee's signature ▶ *Kevin Barker*   **Date** ▶ November 9   , 19XX

8 Employer's name and address (**Employer: Complete 8, 9, and 10 only if sending to IRS**) | **9** Office code | **10** Employer identification number

FICA TAX

Under the provisions of the Federal Insurance Contributions Act (FICA), both the employee and the employer must pay social security taxes. These taxes support a variety of programs that include pension, disability, survivor's benefits, and health care for retired persons. We will consider the employee's contribution in this chapter. The employer's contribution will be covered in Chapter 10.

Computation of the employee's contribution involves two things. One is a tax rate. The second is a limit on earnings that are subject to the tax during any one calendar year. This limit is commonly known as *maximum earnings.* Both the rate and the maximum are determined by the U.S. Congress and are subject to change. In recent years, changes have been frequent. In this text, we will assume a 7.5 percent tax rate on maximum earnings of $50,000.

||||||||||||||||||||||||

C O M M E N T

Once an employee's cumulative earnings are equal to $50,000, additional earnings will not be subject to FICA tax for the remainder of that calendar year. However, on January 1 of the next year, earnings will again be subject to FICA tax until the $50,000 limit is reached next year. Since the maximum earnings figure is higher than the average employee's total annual earnings, most employees will pay FICA tax all year.

The employee's FICA tax deduction is computed by multiplying FICA taxable earnings by the FICA tax rate.

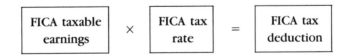

Let's demonstrate the computation by returning to Kevin Barker. As you will recall, Kevin's total earnings for the current weekly pay period are $505. To compute Kevin's FICA tax deduction, we must also know Kevin's cumulative earnings as of the end of the previous pay period. Let's assume Kevin has earned $13,635 as of the end of the previous pay period. We can quickly see that Kevin is far below the $50,000 maximum. Therefore, all of Kevin's current week's earnings are subject to FICA tax. Kevin's FICA tax deduction is computed as follows:

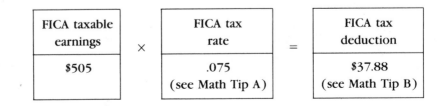

FIGURE 9 - 3

MARRIED Persons—**WEEKLY** Payroll Period

And the wages are—		And the number of withholding allowances claimed is—										
At least	But less than	0	1	2	3	4	5	6	7	8	9	10
		The amount of income tax to be withheld shall be—										
210	220	21	18	15	12	9	7	4	2	0	0	0
220	230	22	19	17	14	11	8	6	3	1	0	0
230	240	24	21	18	15	12	9	7	4	2	0	0
240	250	26	22	19	16	14	11	8	6	3	1	0
250	260	27	24	21	18	15	12	9	7	4	2	0
260	270	29	25	22	19	16	13	11	8	5	3	1
270	280	30	27	24	21	18	15	12	9	7	4	2
280	290	32	29	25	22	19	16	13	10	8	5	3
290	300	34	30	27	24	21	18	15	12	9	7	4
300	310	35	32	28	25	22	19	16	13	10	8	5
310	320	37	33	30	27	23	20	18	15	12	9	6
320	330	39	35	32	28	25	22	19	16	13	10	8
330	340	40	37	33	30	27	23	20	17	14	12	9
340	350	42	38	35	32	28	25	22	19	16	13	10
350	360	44	40	37	33	30	27	23	20	17	14	11
360	370	46	42	38	35	31	28	25	22	19	16	13
370	380	48	44	40	36	33	30	26	23	20	17	14
380	390	49	46	42	38	35	31	28	25	21	19	16
390	400	51	47	44	40	36	33	30	26	23	20	17
400	410	53	49	46	42	38	35	31	28	25	21	18
410	420	55	51	47	44	40	36	33	29	26	23	20
420	430	58	53	49	45	42	38	34	31	28	24	21
430	440	60	55	51	47	43	40	36	33	29	26	23
440	450	62	57	53	49	45	42	38	34	31	28	24
450	460	64	60	55	51	47	43	40	36	33	29	26
460	470	66	62	57	53	49	45	41	38	34	31	27
470	480	69	64	60	55	51	47	43	39	36	32	29
480	490	71	66	62	57	53	49	45	41	37	34	31
490	500	73	68	64	59	55	51	47	43	39	36	32

MATH TIP

A. To convert a percent to a decimal:

Step 1: Move the decimal point two places to the left.

FIGURE 9 - 3 (concluded)

MARRIED Persons—**WEEKLY** Payroll Period

And the wages are—		And the number of withholding allowances claimed is—										
At least	But less than	0	1	2	3	4	5	6	7	8	9	10
		The amount of income tax to be withheld shall be—										
500	510	76	71	66	62	57	52	49	45	41	37	34
510	520	78	73	68	64	59	55	50	47	43	39	35
520	530	81	76	71	66	61	57	52	48	45	41	37
530	540	83	78	73	68	64	59	54	50	46	43	39
540	550	86	81	75	70	66	61	57	52	48	45	41
550	560	88	83	78	73	68	63	59	54	50	46	43
560	570	91	86	80	75	70	66	61	56	52	48	44
570	580	93	88	83	78	72	68	63	59	54	50	46
580	590	96	91	85	80	75	70	65	61	56	52	48
590	600	98	93	88	83	77	72	68	63	59	54	50
600	610	101	96	90	85	80	75	70	65	61	56	52
610	620	104	98	93	88	82	77	72	67	63	58	54
620	630	106	101	95	90	85	80	75	70	65	61	56
630	640	109	103	98	93	87	82	77	72	67	63	58
640	650	112	106	100	95	90	85	80	74	70	65	60
650	660	115	109	103	98	92	87	82	77	72	67	63
660	670	118	112	106	100	95	90	85	79	74	69	65
670	680	120	115	109	103	97	92	87	82	77	72	67
680	690	123	117	112	106	100	95	90	84	79	74	69
690	700	126	120	114	109	103	97	92	87	82	76	71
700	710	129	123	117	111	106	100	95	89	84	79	74
710	720	132	126	120	114	108	103	97	92	87	81	76
720	730	135	129	123	117	111	105	100	94	89	84	79
730	740	139	132	126	120	114	108	102	97	92	86	81
740	750	142	135	128	123	117	111	105	99	94	89	84
750	760	145	138	131	125	120	114	108	102	97	91	86
760	770	148	142	135	128	122	117	111	105	99	94	89
770	780	152	145	138	131	125	119	114	108	102	97	91
780	790	155	148	141	134	128	122	116	111	105	99	94
790	800	158	151	145	138	131	125	119	113	108	102	96

Step 2: Drop the percentage sign.

Example: 7.5% = .075

B. When necessary, we will round to the nearest penny following standard rounding rules:

- If the number in the third decimal place is 5 or more, add one penny.
  Example: $505 × .075 = $37.875 = $37.88

- If the number in the third decimal place is 4 or less, simply drop it.
  Example: $417 × .052 = $21.684 = $21.68

VOLUNTARY DEDUCTIONS

As mentioned earlier, voluntary deductions are usually made at the employee's request or as the result of a labor agreement. Let's assume Kevin Barker's voluntary deductions include the following:

Health insurance	$10.50 per week
Union dues	3.00 per week

TOTAL DEDUCTIONS

Kevin Barker's total deductions for the week ended July 18 are computed as follows:

Federal income tax	$ 62.00
FICA tax	37.88
Health insurance	10.50
Union dues	3.00
Total deductions	$113.38

FIGURE 9 - 4

PAYROLL REGISTER
For the Week Ended July 18, 19XX

Employee	Total Hrs.	Hrly. Rate	Earnings			Cumulative Total Previous Period
			Reg.	O.T.	Total	
Barker, Kevin	47	10.00	400.00	105.00	505.00	13,635.00
Grant, Mary	42	10.50	420.00	31.50	451.50	14,123.50
Hill, Charles	40	5.00	200.00		200.00	4,100.00
Karr, James	40	8.75	350.00		350.00	11,542.30
Lamb, Carol	43	9.00	360.00	40.50	400.50	6,870.00
Roth, Gary	40	15.75	630.00		630.00	16,380.00
Totals			2,360.00	177.00	2,537.00	

▍▍▍▍ COMPUTATION OF NET PAY

OBJECTIVE 5
COMPUTE NET PAY

Kevin Barker's net pay for the week ended July 18 is computed as follows:

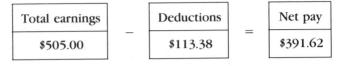

Total earnings		Deductions		Net pay
$505.00	$-$	$113.38	$=$	$391.62

Net pay is also known as *take-home pay.* Net pay is the amount that actually appears on the face of the employee's paycheck.

▍▍▍▍ PAYROLL REGISTER

OBJECTIVE 6
PREPARE A PAYROLL
REGISTER

A payroll register is a multicolumn form that aids in organizing, computing, and summarizing payroll data. The payroll register also aids in verifying the mathematical accuracy of the payroll before the payroll entry is recorded and paychecks issued.

Figure 9-4 shows a completed payroll register for the week ending July 18, 19XX. Observe that Kevin Barker is the first employee. The previously described procedures used for Kevin Barker were also used to compute the earnings, deductions, and net pay for all the other employees.

Taxable Earnings		Deductions						Net Pay	Check Number
FICA	Unemployment	Federal Income Tax	FICA	Health Insurance	Union Dues	Total			
505.00		62.00	37.88	10.50	3.00	113.38		391.62	427
451.50		60.00	33.86	8.00	3.00	104.86		346.64	428
200.00	200.00	22.00	15.00		3.00	40.00		160.00	429
350.00		33.00	26.25	9.20	3.00	71.45		278.55	430
400.50	130.00	54.00	30.04	9.00	3.00	96.04		304.46	431
630.00		82.00	47.25	12.35	3.00	144.60		485.40	432
2,537.00	330.00	313.00	190.28	49.05	18.00	570.33		1,966.67	

TAXABLE EARNINGS

In the center of the payroll register shown in Figure 9-4, you will observe a pair of columns headed Taxable Earnings. In this pair of columns, we compute those earnings subject to FICA tax and those earnings subject to unemployment taxes. *Notice that we are not computing the actual taxes—only the earnings subject to these taxes.* It is necessary to do this for each employee because FICA and unemployment taxes have calendar-year maximums. Although the maximum amounts are the same for everyone, employees may reach those maximums at different times during the year. This is due to differences in such variables as wage rates, hours, and length of employment.

We keep track of earnings subject to FICA and unemployment taxes separately because each has a different maximum.

TAXABLE EARNINGS—FICA   As you will recall, we are assuming maximum earnings of $50,000 for FICA tax purposes. Once an employee's cumulative earnings equal $50,000, further earnings will not be subject to FICA tax for the remainder of the calendar year. Since none of the employees shown in our sample payroll register have cumulative earnings anywhere close to $50,000, all of their current week's earnings are subject to FICA tax.

TAXABLE EARNINGS—UMEMPLOYMENT   Both the federal and state governments levy unemployment taxes. Since these taxes are paid by employers, they will be studied in greater detail in Chapter 10. For now, we will limit our discussion to earnings subject to these taxes.

Both federal and state unemployment taxes involve maximum earnings' limits. In this text, we will assume maximum earnings of $7,000 for both. Once an employee's cumulative earnings are equal to $7,000, further earnings will not be subject to unemployment taxes for the remainder of the calendar year. However, on January 1 of the next year, earnings will again be subject to unemployment taxes until the limit is reached.

Referring to our sample payroll register, Kevin Barker, Mary Grant, James Karr, and Gary Roth all have cumulative earnings that exceed the $7,000 maximum. Therefore, none of their current week's earnings are subject to unemployment taxes.

Charles Hill, on the other hand, has cumulative earnings of only $4,100. Therefore, all of Hill's current week's earnings are subject to unemployment taxes.

Carol Lamb's cumulative earnings as of the end of the previous pay period total $6,870—very close to the $7,000 maximum. Since Lamb is only $130 away from the maximum ($7,000 − $6,870 = $130), only $130 of her current week's earnings will be subject to unemployment taxes. None of Lamb's earnings for the remainder of the calendar year will be subject to unemployment taxes.

VERIFICATION OF MATHEMATICAL ACCURACY

Before recording the payroll entry or issuing paychecks, the amount columns should be totaled (except for the Hourly Rate column and Cumulative Total column). These totals should be cross-verified as follows:

Earnings:		
Regular	$2,360.00	
Overtime	177.00	
Total		$2,537.00
Deductions:		
Federal income tax	$ 313.00	
FICA	190.28	
Health insurance	49.05	
Union dues	18.00	
Total		570.33
Net pay		$1,966.67

Unfortunately, the Taxable Earnings columns cannot be cross-verified. These two column totals will be used in Chapter 10 to compute the employer's payroll tax expense.

▌▌▌▌ RECORDING THE PAYROLL

The payroll register, as you will recall, is not a journal. Once the payroll register is complete, the payroll must be formally recorded in the journal. The payroll register column headings and totals provide the information for the journal entry.

The payroll for the week ended July 18, 19XX, is recorded as follows:

GENERAL JOURNAL				Page 70		
Date	Description	Post. Ref.	Debit		Credit	
19XX July 18	Wages Expense		2,537	00		
	Federal Income Tax Payable				313	00
	FICA Tax Payable				190	28
	Health Insurance Payable				49	05
	Union Dues Payable				18	00
	Wages Payable				1,966	67
	To record weekly payroll.					

Total earnings represent wages expense to the company. The amounts withheld from employees are recorded in various liability accounts. They will remain liabilities until they are actually paid. The net pay is also considered to be a liability (wages payable) until the payroll is actually paid.

▐▐▐ PAYING THE PAYROLL

Most companies do not use their regular checking account to write individual employee paychecks. Instead, most companies use a separate payroll checking account. In this case, one check is written on the regular checking account for an amount equal to the total net pay (wages payable). The entry for this is shown below.

GENERAL JOURNAL				Page 70		
Date	Description	Post. Ref.	Debit		Credit	
19XX July 18	Wages Payable		1,966	67		
	Cash				1,966	67
	Paid wages for week ended July 18.					

This check is deposited in the payroll checking account. Then, individual employee paychecks are written on the payroll checking account. This procedure tends to simplify the monthly bank reconciliation.

FIGURE 9 - 5

```
EARNINGS          DEDUCTIONS      NET PAY
Reg.    400.00    FIT    62.00    391.62
O.T.    105.00    FICA   37.88
Tot.    505.00    Ins.   10.50
                  Dues    3.00
Cum. 14,140.00    Tot.  113.38
```

Payroll Account   **427**
THE KITCHEN TAYLOR
2400 Main Street   July 18, 19 XX   70-482/719
Wheaton, Illinois 60187

PAY TO THE
ORDER OF   Kevin Barker $ 391.62

Three hundred ninety one and 62/100-----------DOLLARS

WHEATON VALLEY BANK

Wheaton, Illinois 60187

MEMO   *Dennis Taylor*

⑈071904821⑈   427

Figure 9-5 shows Kevin Barker's paycheck. Attached to the check is a stub showing earnings, deductions, and net pay for the current pay period. Kevin's stub also shows cumulative total earnings for the year to date. When Kevin cashes his paycheck, he detaches the stub and keeps it for his own records.

▮▮▮▮ EMPLOYEE EARNINGS RECORD

OBJECTIVE 8
MAINTAIN EMPLOYEE
EARNINGS RECORDS

Employers are required by law to keep an **employee earnings record** for each employee. The information for this record comes from the payroll register. At the end of every pay period, each employee earnings record must be updated. Figure 9-6 shows a portion of Kevin Barker's employee earnings record.

FIGURE 9 - 6

EMPLOYEE EARNINGS RECORD

Kevin Barker
112 Underwood Court
Wheaton, IL 60187

Phone: 555-7462

Soc. Sec. No: 462-50-7534
Date of Birth: June 17, 1960
Sex: Male
Marital Status: Married
Allowances (W-4): 3

Employee No. 27
Date Hired: May 5, 1984
Date Terminated:
Rate per Hour: $10.00

Period Ended 19XX	Total Hours	Earnings			Cumulative Total	Deductions					Net Pay	Check Number
		Reg.	O.T.	Total		Federal Income Tax	FICA	Health Insurance	Union Dues	Total		
July 3	40	400.00		400.00	13,190.00	42.00	30.00	10.50	3.00	85.50	314.50	415
July 11	43	400.00	45.00	445.00	13,635.00	49.00	33.38	10.50	3.00	95.88	349.12	421
July 18	47	400.00	105.00	505.00	14,140.00	62.00	37.88	10.50	3.00	113.38	391.62	427

Chapter Summary

The earnings of employees who are paid on an hourly basis are referred to as wages. A 40-hour workweek is usually considered a regular workweek for such employees. Hours worked through 40 are considered regular hours and are paid at a regular hourly rate. Hours worked in excess of 40 in one workweek are usually considered overtime hours and are paid at an overtime rate per hour. The overtime rate is usually one and a half times the regular hourly rate. Total earnings equal regular earnings plus overtime earnings.

Payroll deductions fall into two general categories: required and voluntary. Employers are required to withhold federal income tax and FICA taxes from the earnings of most employees. Voluntary deductions are usually made at the employee's request or as the result of a labor agreement. They include deductions for such items as U.S. savings bonds, insurance, union dues, charitable contributions, pension plans, and credit union savings and loan payments.

Total earnings minus total deductions equals net pay. Net pay is also known as take-home pay and is the amount that appears on the face of the employee's paycheck.

A payroll register is a multicolumn form that aids in organizing, computing, and summarizing payroll data. It also aids in verifying the mathematical accuracy of the payroll before an entry is recorded or paychecks issued. The payroll register is not a journal. Its column headings and totals provide the information for the journal entry to record the payroll.

Employers are required to keep an employee earnings record for each employee. The information for this record comes from the payroll register.

Glossary

EMPLOYEE

A person who works under the control and direction of an employer.

EMPLOYEE EARNINGS RECORD

A form containing payroll data for an individual employee.

INDEPENDENT CONTRACTOR

A person hired by a company to do a specific job, but who does not work under the control or direction of the company.

NET PAY

Total earnings minus total deductions equal net pay; also known as *take-home pay.*

OVERTIME EARNINGS

Earnings for hours worked in excess of 40 in one workweek. The overtime rate per hour is usually one and a half times the regular hourly rate.

PAYROLL REGISTER

A multicolumn form that aids in organizing, computing, and summarizing payroll data.

REGULAR EARNINGS

Earnings for 40 or less hours per workweek.

SALARY

A fixed amount per week, month, or year paid to managerial, administrative, and professional employees.

TOTAL EARNINGS

Regular earnings plus overtime earnings equal total earnings; often referred to as *gross pay.*

WAGES

The earnings of an employee who is paid on an hourly basis.

WITHHOLDING ALLOWANCE

Exempts a portion of an employee's earnings from federal income tax.

Questions for Discussion

1. What is the difference between an employee and an independent contractor?

2. Why must each newly hired employee complete a Form W-4 for his or her employer?

3. What is a withholding allowance?

4. For which taxes are employers required by law to withhold from employee earnings?

5. Which taxes involve both rates and maximum earnings?

6. What is the purpose of the payroll register?

7. How does the payroll register differ from the employee earnings record?

8. Why are the Taxable Earnings columns necessary on the payroll register?

Exercises

EXERCISE 9-1
DEFINITIONS
(L.O.1–8)

Match the following terms with the definitions shown below:

D **1.** Employee.

H **2.** Independent contractor.

B **3.** Net pay.

E **4.** Overtime earnings.

a **5.** Regular earnings.

g **6.** Salary.

i **7.** Total earnings.

C **8.** Wages.

f **9.** Withholding allowance.

K **10.** Employee earnings record.

J **11.** Payroll register.

Definitions:

   a. Earnings for 40 or less hours per workweek.

   b. The result of total earnings minus total deductions; also known as take-home pay.

   c. The earnings of an employee who is paid on an hourly basis.

   d. A person who works under the control and direction of an employer.

   e. Earnings for hours worked in excess of 40 in one workweek.

   f. Exempts a portion of an employee's earnings from federal income tax.

   g. A fixed amount per week, month, or year paid to managerial, administrative, and professional employees.

b. A person hired by a company to do a specific job, but who does not work under the control or direction of the company.

i. The result of regular earnings plus overtime earnings; often referred to as gross pay.

j. A multicolumn form that aids in organizing, computing, and summarizing payroll data.

k. A form containing payroll data for an individual employee.

EXERCISE 9-2
PAYROLL REGISTER
(L.O.3, 6)

Complete the following partial payroll register:

Employee	Total Hours	Regular Hourly Rate	Earnings Regular	Overtime	Total
A	45	$9.50			
B	42	8.00			
C	48	7.90			
D	41	6.25			
E	43	8.75			

EXERCISE 9-3
FEDERAL INCOME TAX
DEDUCTION
(L.O.4)

Using the following information and the table in Figure 9-3, pages 302–303, determine the amount to be withheld for federal income tax purposes for each of the following employees:

Employee	Weekly Earnings	Marital Status	Withholding Allowance	Federal Income Tax
A	$735	Married	4	
B	452	Married	1	
C	517	Married	3	
D	710	Married	5	
E	680	Married	2	

EXERCISE 9-4
FICA DEDUCTION
(L.O.4)

Assuming an FICA tax rate of 7.5 percent on maximum earnings of $50,000, compute the amount that should be withheld for FICA tax purposes for each of the following employees:

Employee	Total Earnings Current Pay Period	Cumulative Earnings Previous Pay Period	FICA
A	$ 815	$24,530	
B	562	18,726	
C	1,300	51,000	
D	1,250	49,500	
E	1,072	49,890	

EXERCISE 9-5
PAYROLL
CALCULATIONS
(L.O.3–5)

Maria Chavez worked a total of 46 hours this week. Maria's regular hourly rate is $9.50 per hour. Determine the following:

   a. Regular earnings.

   b. Overtime earnings.

   c. Total earnings.

   d. Federal income tax assuming Maria is married with two withholding allowances. Use the table in Figure 9-3, pages 302–303.

   e. FICA assuming a rate of 7.5 percent on maximum earnings of $50,000. Maria's cumulative earnings at the end of the previous pay period amounted to $18,500.

   f. Net pay.

EXERCISE 9-6
PAYROLL ENTRY
(L.O.7)

The figures that follow are column totals taken from Becker Company's payroll register for the week ended June 12.

Earnings:		
Regular	$5,749.50	
Overtime	837.62	
Total		$6,587.12
Deductions:		
Federal income tax	$ 815.00	
FICA	494.03	
Health insurance	562.75	
Union dues	95.00	
Total		1,966.78
Net pay		$4,620.34

Prepare the entry to record this payroll.

EXERCISE 9-7
TAXABLE EARNINGS
(L.O.6)

Assuming maximum earnings of $50,000 for FICA and maximum earnings of $7,000 for unemployment tax purposes, determine taxable earnings for the following employees:

	Total Earnings Current	Cumulative Earnings Previous	Taxable Earnings	
Employee	Pay Period	Pay Period	FICA	Unemployment
A	$ 430	$ 6,250		
B	868	10,800		
C	539	6,850		
D	967	24,900		
E	1,350	53,650		

EXERCISE 9-8
CROSS-VERIFY REGISTER
(L.O.6)

Shown below is the totals line from Wing Products payroll register.

Employee	Total Hrs.	Hrly. Rate	Earnings			Cumulative Total Previous Period
			Reg.	O.T.	Total	
Totals			7,256.00	929.50	8,185.50	

Taxable Earnings		Deductions					Net Pay
FICA	Unemployment	Federal Income Tax	FICA	Health Insurance	Union Dues	Total	
7,960.35	987.00	647.00	597.03	99.50	56.00	1,425.53	6,785.97

1399.53

a. Cross-verify the totals to check for mathematical accuracy.

b. Does cross-verification indicate any errors? *yes*

Problems—Set A

The following payroll information pertains to Debra Jackson, an employee of Emery Enterprises:

			TIME CARD			
Employee:	Debra Jackson					
Pay Period Ending:	August 21, 19XX					

Day	In	Out	In	Out	Reg.	O.T.
					Hours	
M	7:56	12:00	12:59	5:01	8	
T	7:52	12:01	12:58	6:00	8	1
W	7:55	12:00	12:59	5:05	8	
T	7:59	12:02	12:57	6:02	8	1
F	7:55	12:01	12:58	5:00	8	
S	8:59	12:00				3
S						
Total					40	5

Employee data:

> Regular hourly rate, $12.
> Married.
> Withholding allowances, 2.
> Cumulative earnings at end of previous pay period, $14,200.
> Voluntary deductions:
>> Health insurance, $12.
>> Pension plan, $16.

Additional data:

> Federal income tax: Use the table in Figure 9-3, pages 302–303.
> FICA: 7.5 percent on $50,000 maximum.

INSTRUCTIONS

Determine the following for Debra Jackson:

 a. Regular earnings. 480

 b. Overtime earnings. 90

 c. Total earnings. 570

 d. Federal income tax. 83

 e. FICA. 42.75

 f. Total deductions. 28

 g. Net pay. 416.25

PROBLEM 9-2A
PAYROLL REGISTER AND
ENTRY
(L.O.3–7)

An incomplete payroll register for Pronto Products is shown in the working papers and also on page 320. Pronto pays its its employees weekly.

Employee data:

 All employees are married.
 Withholding allowances:
  Allen, 2.
  Carter, 1.
  Frigo, 4.
  Lujak, 5.
  Prada, 3.

Additional data:

 Federal income tax: Use the table in Figure 9-3, pages 302–303.
 FICA: 7.5 percent on $50,000 maximum.
 Unemployment: Maximum earnings, $7,000.

INSTRUCTIONS

1. Complete the payroll register.

2. Prepare the entry to record the payroll.

PAYROLL REGISTER
For the Week Ended May 12, 19XX

Employee	Total Hrs.	Hrly. Rate	Earnings Reg.	Earnings O.T.	Earnings Total	Cumulative Total Previous Period
Allen, John	40	6.75				4,860.00
Carter, Ann	48	8.90				7,150.40
Frigo, Paul	44	9.00				6,480.50
Lujak, Fred	41	10.50				7,560.00
Prada, Ray	45	12.00				6,900.00

Taxable Earnings FICA	Taxable Earnings Unemployment	Federal Income Tax	FICA	Health Insurance	Union Dues	Total	Net Pay
				9.25	3.75		
				10.50	3.75		
				10.20	3.75		
				12.10	3.75		
				12.60	3.75		

PROBLEM 9-3A
PAYROLL REGISTER AND ENTRIES
(L.O.3–7)

The following incomplete payroll register is for Meyer Services which pays its employees weekly:

PAYROLL REGISTER
For the Week Ended April 18, 19XX

Employee	Total Hrs.	Hrly. Rate	Earnings Reg.	Earnings O.T.	Earnings Total	Cumulative Total Previous Period
Adams, Jill	45	8.60				5,423.45
Frank, Joe	40	9.20				5,671.30
Kral, Mark	43	11.50				6,800.00
Lang, Gail	47	13.80				8,400.00
Marx, Gary	40	7.75				4,341.20

Taxable Earnings FICA	Taxable Earnings Unemployment	Deductions Federal Income Tax	Deductions FICA	Deductions Savings Bonds	Deductions Pension Plan	Deductions Total	Net Pay
				20.00	17.20		
				10.00	18.40		
				25.00	23.00		
				25.00	27.60		
					15.50		

Employee data:

All employees are married.

Withholding allowances:

Adams, 1.

Frank, 3.

Kral, 4.

Lang, 2.

Marx, 1.

Additional data:

> Federal income tax: Use the table in Figure 9-3, pages 302–303.
> FICA: 7.5 percent on $50,000 maximum.
> Unemployment: Maximum earnings, $7,000.

INSTRUCTIONS

1. Complete the payroll register.

2. Prepare the entry to record the payroll.

3. This company has a separate payroll checking account. On April 18, one check is written on the regular checking account for an amount equal to the total net pay. Record the appropriate entry in the general journal.

PROBLEM 9-4A
PAYROLL REGISTER AND
ENTRIES
(L.O.3–7)

An incomplete payroll register for Lark Office Products is shown in the working papers and on page 323. Lark pays its employees weekly.

Employee data:

> All employees are married.
> Withholding allowances:
> > Brill, 5.
> > Graf, 3.
> > Jared, 4.
> > Lamas, 1.
> > Witt, 4.

Additional data:

> Federal income tax: Use the table in Figure 9-3, pages 302–303.
> FICA: 7.5 percent on $50,000 maximum.
> Unemployment: Maximum earnings, $7,000.

INSTRUCTIONS

1. Complete the payroll register.

2. Prepare the entry to record the payroll.

3. This company has a separate payroll checking account. On July 23, one check is written on the regular checking account for an amount equal to the total net pay. Record the appropriate entry in the general journal.

PAYROLL REGISTER
For the Week Ended July 23, 19XX

Employee	Total Hrs.	Hrly. Rate	Earnings Reg.	Earnings O.T.	Earnings Total	Cumulative Total Previous Period
Brill, Jane	42	12.50	500	37.50	537.50	15,421.32
Graf, John	40	11.75	470	—	470.00	6,850.00
Jared, Henry	47	9.60	384	100.80	484.80	11,520.00
Lamas, Joe	40	8.50	340	—	340.00	3,518.41
Witt, Barry	43	13.00	520	58.50	578.50	15,611.72
			2214.00	196.80	2410.80	

Taxable Earnings FICA	Taxable Earnings Unemployment	Deductions Federal Income Tax	Deductions FICA	Deductions Health Insurance	Deductions Pension Plan	Deductions Total	Net Pay
537.50		59.00	40.31	21.50	25.00	145.81	391.69
470.00	320.00	55.00	35.25	21.10	23.50	134.85	335.15
484.80		53.00	36.36	19.75	19.20	128.31	356.49
340.00	340.00	38.00	25.50	16.50	17.00	97.00	243.00
578.50		51.00	43.39	22.50	26.00	142.89	435.61
2410.80	660.00	256.00	180.81	101.35	110.70	648.86	1761.94

Problems—Set B

The following payroll information pertains to Janet Johnson, an employee of Magnum Associates:

					TIME CARD	

Employee: Janet Johnson
Pay Period Ending: October 14, 19XX

Day	In	Out	In	Out	Hours	
					Reg.	O.T.
M	7:59	12:00	12:58	5:02	8	
T	7:54	12:02	12:59	5:04	8	
W	7:56	12:01	12:59	5:01	8	
T	7:58	12:00	12:59	7:00	8	2
F	7:55	12:00	12:58	6:00	8	1
S						
S						
Total					40	3

Employee data:

Regular hourly rate, $11.
Married.
Withholding allowances, 1.
Cumulative earnings at end of previous pay period, $13,100.
Voluntary deductions:
Health insurance, $10.
Pension plan, $14.

Additional data:

Federal income tax: Use the table in Figure 9-3, pages 302–303.
FICA: 7.5 percent on $50,000 maximum.

INSTRUCTIONS
Determine the following for Janet Johnson:

a. Regular earnings.

b. Overtime earnings.

c. Total earnings.

d. Federal income tax.

e. FICA.

f. Total deductions.

g. Net pay.

PROBLEM 9-2B
PAYROLL REGISTER AND
ENTRY
(L.O.3–7)

An incomplete payroll register for Bench Company is shown in the working papers and also on page 326. Bench pays its employees weekly.

Employee data:
All employees are married.
Withholding allowances:
Ahern, 3.
Drake, 2.
Grant, 4.
Mann, 5.
Tasker, 1.

Additional data:
Federal income tax: Use the table in Figure 9-3, pages 302–303.
FICA: 7.5 percent on $50,000 maximum.
Unemployment: Maximum earnings, $7,000.

INSTRUCTIONS
1. Complete the payroll register.

2. Prepare the entry to record the payroll.

PAYROLL REGISTER
For the Week Ended June 5, 19XX

Employee	Total Hrs.	Hrly. Rate	Earnings			Cumulative Total Previous Period
			Reg.	O.T.	Total	
Ahern, Paul	40	7.25				5,800.00
Drake, Gail	42	8.40				7,210.50
Grant, Jeff	45	9.50				6,375.10
Mann, Mary	47	12.50				10,500.00
Tasker, Jay	41	11.60				6,750.00

Taxable Earnings		Deductions					Net Pay
FICA	Unemployment	Federal Income Tax	FICA	Health Insurance	Union Dues	Total	
				9.50	4.10		
				10.25	4.10		
				10.40	4.10		
				12.00	4.10		
				11.90	4.10		

PROBLEM 9-3B
PAYROLL REGISTER AND
ENTRIES
(L.O.3–7)

The following incomplete payroll register is for Merrill Associates which pays its employees weekly:

PAYROLL REGISTER
For the Week Ended March 29, 19XX

Employee	Total Hrs.	Hrly. Rate	Earnings Reg.	Earnings O.T.	Earnings Total	Cumulative Total Previous Period
Carr, James	44	8.40				5,151.34
Jones, Carl	40	8.85				6,210.15
Lake, Mona	40	11.75				6,850.00
Varga, Max	41	7.90				4,534.60
Wall, Gail	45	10.80				7,425.80

Taxable Earnings FICA	Taxable Earnings Unemployment	Deductions Federal Income Tax	Deductions FICA	Deductions Savings Bonds	Deductions Pension Plan	Deductions Total	Net Pay
				15.00	17.20		
					17.70		
				10.00	23.50		
					15.80		
				15.00	21.60		

Employee data:

All employees are married.

Withholding allowances:

Carr, 2.

Jones, 3.

Lake, 4.

Varga, 1.

Wall, 2.

Additional data:

Federal income tax: Use the table in Figure 9-3, pages 302–303.
FICA: 7.5 percent on $50,000 maximum.
Unemployment: Maximum earnings, $7,000.

INSTRUCTIONS

1. Complete the payroll register.

2. Prepare the entry to record the payroll.

3. This company has a separate payroll checking account. On March 29, one check is written on the regular checking account for an amount equal to the total net pay. Record the appropriate entry in the general journal.

PROBLEM 9-4B
PAYROLL REGISTER AND
ENTRIES
(L.O.3–7)

An incomplete payroll register for Mark Computer Services is shown in the working papers and also on page 329. Mark pays its employees weekly.

Employee data:

All employees are married.
Withholding allowances:
Ardis, 5.
Farrel, 2.
King, 3.
Norris, 1.
Zima, 4.

Additional data:

Federal income tax: Use the table in Figure 9-3, pages 302–303.
FICA: 7.5 percent on $50,000 maximum.
Unemployment: Maximum earnings, $7,000.

INSTRUCTIONS

1. Complete the payroll register.

2. Prepare the entry to record the payroll.

3. This company has a separate payroll checking account. On August 8, one check is written on the regular checking account for an amount equal to the total net pay. Record the appropriate entry in the general journal.

PAYROLL REGISTER
For the Week Ended August 8, 19XX

Employee	Total Hrs.	Hrly. Rate	Earnings			Cumulative Total Previous Period
			Reg.	O.T.	Total	
Ardis, Carol	43	14.00				18,065.89
Farrel, Paula	40	13.25				6,775.00
King, Jason	45	12.60				16,872.50
Norris, Pat	40	10.00				5,938.10
Zima, Frank	42	9.30				11,718.25

Taxable Earnings		Deductions					Net Pay
FICA	Unemployment	Federal Income Tax	FICA	Health Insurance	Pension Plan	Total	
				25.40	28.00		
				24.00	26.50		
				24.85	25.20		
				18.00	20.00		
				19.75	18.60		

Mini-Cases

CASE 9-1

Sarah, your company's switchboard operator, has requested that you treat her as an independent contractor for payroll purposes. "No payroll deductions would be the equivalent of a gigantic raise for me," says Sarah, "and it wouldn't cost you an extra penny!" Respond to Sarah's request.

CASE 9-2

Felicia Stern, an employee, has come to see you about withholding for federal income tax. Felicia requests that you stop deducting federal income tax from her paycheck. She would prefer to pay the Internal Revenue Service directly on April 15 when she files her annual tax return. Respond to Felicia's request.

CASE 9-3

Your friend, Pat, is self-employed. Pat's new accountant has complained that the company payroll is not being handled properly because there are no W-4 forms on file for any of the employees. The former accountant is now deceased, and Pat has no idea how the payroll was computed in the past. Knowing you are an accountant, Pat asks: "Why are these W-4s necessary?" Respond.

CHAPTER 10

Payroll: Employer Taxes and Other Responsibilities

AFTER STUDYING THIS CHAPTER, YOU SHOULD BE ABLE TO:

1 Compute the employer's payroll taxes.

2 Record the employer's payroll tax expense.

3 Record the payment of the employer's payroll taxes.

4 Compute and record the premium for workers' compensation insurance.

In Chapter 9, you learned to record payroll taxes levied (imposed) on the employee. The employee pays these taxes out of his/her earnings through payroll deductions. These deductions appear as liabilities on the employer's balance sheet until the amounts are paid to the appropriate parties. In this chapter, we will focus our attention on payroll taxes levied on the employer. These taxes, paid by the employer, appear as expenses on the employer's income statement.

EMPLOYER'S PAYROLL TAXES

OBJECTIVE 1
COMPUTE THE
EMPLOYER'S PAYROLL
TAXES

Three payroll taxes are levied on the employer:

1. FICA tax (employer's contribution).
2. Federal unemployment tax.
3. State unemployment tax.

Although these taxes are based on the total earnings of employees, they are paid by the employer. As discussed in Chapter 9, all three of these taxes involve both a tax rate and a calendar-year limit on earnings subject to the tax, known as a *maximum*.

The payroll register is the basic source of information in computing the employer's payroll taxes. As shown in Figure 10-1, the payroll register contains a pair of columns labeled Taxable Earnings. The total of the Taxable Earnings—FICA column is used to compute the employer's FICA tax. The total of the

FIGURE 10 - 1

PAYROLL REGISTER
For the Week Ended July 18, 19XX

Employee	Total Hours	Hourly Rate	Earnings			Cumulative Total Previous Period
			Regular	O.T.	Total	
Barker, Kevin	47	10.00	400.00	105.00	505.00	13,635.00
Grant, Mary	42	10.50	420.00	31.50	451.50	14,123.50
Hill, Charles	40	5.00	200.00		200.00	4,100.00
Karr, James	40	8.75	350.00		350.00	11,542.30
Lamb, Carol	43	9.00	360.00	40.50	400.50	6,870.00
Roth, Gary	40	15.75	630.00		630.00	16,380.00
Totals			2,360.00	177.00	2,537.00	

Taxable Earnings—Unemployment column is used to compute both the federal and state unemployment taxes.

FICA TAX

As you will recall, the FICA tax (social security) supports a variety of programs that include pension, disability, survivor's benefits, and health care for retired persons.

Equal amounts of FICA tax are paid by both the employee and the employer. In this textbook, we are assuming an FICA tax rate of 7.5 percent on the first $50,000 earned by each employee. The employee's 7.5 percent contribution was discussed in Chapter 9 and appears as a deduction on the payroll register. The employer must match each employee's contribution with an additional 7.5 percent contribution.

Referring to the taxable earnings section of the payroll register shown in Figure 10-1, the employer's contribution is computed as follows:

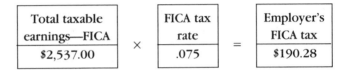

Total taxable earnings—FICA		FICA tax rate		Employer's FICA tax
$2,537.00	×	.075	=	$190.28

Taxable Earnings		Deductions					Net Pay	Check Number
FICA	Unemployment	Federal Income Tax	FICA	Health Insurance	Union Dues	Total		
505.00		62.00	37.88	10.50	3.00	113.38	391.62	427
451.50		60.00	33.86	8.00	3.00	104.86	346.64	428
200.00	200.00	22.00	15.00		3.00	40.00	160.00	429
350.00		33.00	26.25	9.20	3.00	71.45	278.55	430
400.50	130.00	54.00	30.04	9.00	3.00	96.04	304.46	431
630.00		82.00	47.25	12.35	3.00	144.60	485.40	432
2,537.00	330.00	313.00	190.28	49.05	18.00	570.33	1,966.67	

190.28   2.64
17.82

|||||||||||||||||||||||
C O M M E N T

The $50,000 FICA maximum is the earnings limit per employee. The total of the Taxable Earnings—FICA column represents the total earnings subject to tax for all the company's employees. Therefore, the total of the Taxable Earnings—FICA column could be greater than $50,000.

FEDERAL UNEMPLOYMENT TAX

Unemployment taxes provide temporary financial support for unemployed workers. This is accomplished through a joint federal-state effort. The funds raised by the federal unemployment tax are used to cover the costs of administering the various state programs.

The federal unemployment tax is paid by the employer only. In this textbook, we are assuming a federal unemployment tax rate of .8 percent on the first $7,000 earned by each employee.

Referring to the taxable earnings section of the payroll register shown in Figure 10-1, the federal unemployment tax is computed as follows:

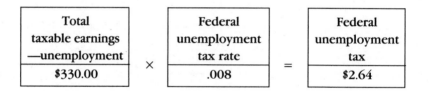

Total taxable earnings —unemployment		Federal unemployment tax rate		Federal unemployment tax
$330.00	×	.008	=	$2.64

MATH TIP

A. To convert a percent to a decimal:

Step 1: Move the decimal point two places to the left.

Step 2: Drop the percentage sign.
    Example: .8% = .008

B. When necessary, we will round to the nearest penny following standard rounding rules:

• If the number in the third decimal place is 5 or more, add one penny.

• If the number in the third decimal place is 4 or less, simply drop it. ▪

STATE UNEMPLOYMENT TAX

The funds raised by the state unemployment tax are used to pay unemployment benefits. Rates and benefits vary from state to state.

In most states, the state unemployment tax is paid by the employer only.

In this textbook, we are assuming a state unemployment tax rate of 5.4 percent on the first $7,000 earned by each employee.

Again referring to the taxable earnings section of the payroll register shown in Figure 10-1, the state unemployment tax is computed as follows:

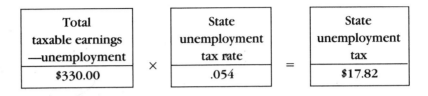

Total taxable earnings —unemployment		State unemployment tax rate		State unemployment tax
$330.00	×	.054	=	$17.82

|||||||||||||||||||||
C O M M E N T

Remember, the $7,000 federal and state unemployment tax maximum is the limit per employee. The total of the Taxable Earnings—Unemployment column could be greater than $7,000.

In summary, the employer's payroll taxes on the July 18 payroll are as follows:

FICA tax	$190.28
Federal unemployment tax	2.64
State unemployment tax	17.82
Total employer's payroll taxes . . .	$210.74

▮▮▮▮ RECORDING THE EMPLOYER'S PAYROLL TAX EXPENSE

OBJECTIVE 2
RECORD THE
EMPLOYER'S PAYROLL
TAX EXPENSE

Now that the employer's payroll taxes have been computed, they must be recorded in the journal. The following entry records the employer's taxes on the July 18 payroll:

GENERAL JOURNAL				Page 70			
Date		Description	Post. Ref.	Debit		Credit	
19XX July	18	Payroll Tax Expense		210	74		
		FICA Tax Payable				190	28
		Federal Unemployment Tax Payable				2	64
		State Unemployment Tax Payable				17	82
		To record the employer's payroll taxes.					

The Payroll Tax Expense account will appear on the income statement as an operating expense. Since these taxes are not being paid on July 18, they are recorded as liabilities. They will appear on the balance sheet as liabilities until they are paid.

▌▌▌▌ TAX PAYMENTS

FEDERAL INCOME TAX AND FICA TAX

OBJECTIVE 3
RECORD THE PAYMENT
OF THE EMPLOYER'S
PAYROLL TAXES

Both the employer and employee FICA taxes and the amounts withheld from employees for federal income tax are paid together. Figure 10-2 shows a summary of deposit rules and due dates taken from *Circular E, Employer's Tax Guide.*

▌ FIGURE 10 - 2

SUMMARY OF DEPOSIT RULES FOR SOCIAL SECURITY TAXES AND WITHHELD FEDERAL INCOME TAX

Deposit Rules	Deposit Due
1. If at the end of the quarter, your total un-deposited taxes for the quarter are less than $500:	1. No deposit is required. You may pay the taxes due to IRS with Form 941 or you may deposit them by the due date of Form 941.
2. If at the end of any month, your total un-deposited taxes are less than $500:	2. No deposit is required. You may carry the taxes over to the following month.
3. If at the end of any month, your total un-deposited taxes are $500 or more but less than $3,000:	3. Within 15 days after the end of the month. (No deposit is required if you were re-quired to make a deposit for an eighth monthly period during the month under Rule 4. However, if this occurs in the last month of the quarter, deposit any bal-ance due by the due date of Form 941.)
4. If at the end of any eighth monthly period (the 3rd, 7th, 11th, 15th, 19th, 22nd, 25th, and last day of each month), your total undeposited taxes are $3,000 or more:	4. Within three banking days after the end of that eighth monthly period.

|||||||||||||||||||||
C O M M E N T

Circular E, Employer's Tax Guide, published by the Internal Revenue Service, is available free of charge to all employers. This publication provides employers with a good source of basic payroll tax information. It discusses such information as tax rates, forms, due dates, and payments, etc. It also contains withholding tables for federal income tax and social security (FICA).

Due dates vary according to the dollar amounts involved. In general, the larger the dollar amount, the sooner the amount will have to be paid. Payments are deposited at a Federal Reserve Bank or some other authorized bank using deposit Form 8109 which is supplied by the Internal Revenue Service. A completed Form 8109 is shown in Figure 10-3.

‖‖‖‖‖‖‖‖‖‖‖‖‖‖‖‖‖

C O M M E N T

Just as each employee must have a social security number, every employer must have an **employer identification number** (EIN). This number must be included on all reports, forms, or correspondence submitted to the Internal Revenue Service (IRS) pertaining to payroll taxes. It is also required on all items submitted to the Social Security Administration (SSA).

Each payment is recorded with the following entry:

Federal Income Tax Payable XX	
FICA Tax Payable XX	
Cash	XX

At the end of each calendar quarter, the employer must file a Form 941.

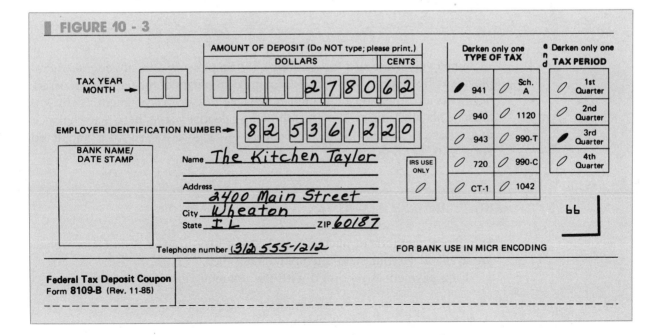

FIGURE 10 - 3

Calendar Quarter	Form 941 Due Date
January 1–March 31	April 30
April 1—June 30	July 31
July 1–September 30	October 31
October 1–December 31	January 31

On Form 941, the employer shows the federal income tax (employee) and FICA tax (employer and employee) liabilities for the quarter, payments already deposited, and any resulting balance due or overpayment. Figure 10-4 shows a completed Form 941.

FEDERAL UNEMPLOYMENT TAX

Due dates for the payment of federal unemployment tax vary according to amount. In general, if the accumulated liability at the end of a calendar quarter is more than $100, the tax payment is due by the last day of the month following the end of the calendar quarter (April 30, July 31, October 31, and January 31). If the accumulated liability is less than $100, it is not due until January 31 of the following calendar year. Again, *Circular E* provides the details. Deposit Form 8109, supplied by the IRS, is used to make the deposit at a Federal Reserve Bank or other authorized bank.

Each payment is recorded with the following entry:

```
Federal Unemployment Tax Payable . . . . . . . . . . . . .  XX
    Cash . . . . . . . . . . . . . . . . . . . . . . . . . . .       XX
```

Employers must also file a Form 940, Employer's Annual Federal Unemployment Tax Return. This form is an annual summary of the liability incurred, payments already deposited, and any balance due or overpayment. Form 940 must be filed by January 31 of the following calendar year if there is any balance due; otherwise, it must be filed by February 10. Figure 10-5 shows a completed Form 940.

STATE UNEMPLOYMENT TAX

Due dates, methods of payment, and forms vary from state to state. Details are available at your state unemployment office.

Each payment is recorded with the following entry:

```
State Unemployment Tax Payable . . . . . . . . . . . . . . .  XX
    Cash . . . . . . . . . . . . . . . . . . . . . . . . . . .       XX
```

FIGURE 10 - 4

Form **941**
(Rev. July 1987)
Department of the Treasury
Internal Revenue Service

4141

Employer's Quarterly Federal Tax Return
For Paperwork Reduction Act Notice, see page 2.
Please type or print.

OMB No. 1545-0029
Expires: 8-31-88

Your name, address, employer identification number, and calendar quarter of return. (If not correct, please change.)

Name (as distinguished from trade name)	Date quarter ended
Dennis Taylor Trade name, if any	September 30, 19XX Employer identification number
The Kitchen Taylor Address and ZIP code	82-5361220
2400 Main Street Wheaton, IL 60187	

T
FF
FD
FP
I
T

1 1 1   2   3 3 3 3 3   4 4 4

If address is different from prior return, check here ☐

IRS Use

5 5 5   6   7   8 8 8 8 8   9 9 9   10 10 10 10 10 10 10 10 10

If you are not liable for returns in the future, check here . . . ☐   Date final wages paid . . . .

Complete for First Quarter Only

1a Number of employees (except household) employed in the pay period that includes March 12th	**1a**	6
b If you are a subsidiary corporation AND your parent corporation files a consolidated Form 1120, enter parent corporation employer identification number (EIN) . . **1b** —		
2 Total wages and tips subject to withholding, plus other compensation	**2**	30,444 00
3 Total income tax withheld from wages, tips, pensions, annuities, sick pay, gambling, etc.	**3**	3,756 47
4 Adjustment of withheld income tax for preceding quarters of calendar year (see instructions) . .	**4**	0
5 Adjusted total of income tax withheld	**5**	3,756 47
6 Taxable social security wages paid . . . . . $ ___30,444 00_ x 15.0%(.15) . . .	**6**	4,566 60
7a Taxable tips reported . . . . $ _____ x 7.5% (.075) .	**7a**	
b Tips deemed to be wages (see instructions) . . $ _____ x 7.5% (.075) .	**7b**	
c Taxable hospital insurance wages paid . . $ _____ x 2.9% (.029) .	**7c**	
8 Total social security taxes (add lines 6, 7a, 7b, and 7c)	**8**	4,566 60
9 Adjustment of social security taxes (see instructions for required explanation)	**9**	0
10 Adjusted total of social security taxes (see instructions)	**10**	4,566 60
11 Backup withholding (see instructions)	**11**	
12 Adjustment of backup withholding tax for preceding quarters of calendar year	**12**	
13 Adjusted total of backup withholding	**13**	
14 Total taxes (add lines 5, 10, and 13)	**14**	8,323 07
15 Advance earned income credit (EIC) payments, if any	**15**	
16 Net taxes (subtract line 15 from line 14). **This must equal line IV below** (plus line IV of Schedule A (Form 941) if you have treated backup withholding as a separate liability).	**16**	8,323 07
17 Total deposits for quarter, including overpayment applied from a prior quarter, from your records .	**17**	8,323 07
18 Balance due (subtract line 17 from line 16). This should be less than $500. Pay to IRS	**18**	0
19 If line 17 is more than line 16, enter overpayment here ___ $ _____ and check if to be: ☐ Applied to next return **OR** ☐ Refunded.		

Record of Federal Tax Liability (Complete if line 16 is $500 or more.) See the instructions under rule 4 for details before checking these boxes.
Check only if you made eighth-monthly deposits using the 95% rule ☐   Check only if you are a first time 3-banking-day depositor ☐

Tax liability *(Do not show Federal tax deposits here.)*

Date wages paid		First month of quarter		Second month of quarter		Third month of quarter
1st through 3rd	A	695.47	I	679.80	Q	
4th through 7th	B		J		R	705.21
8th through 11th	C	689.20	K	701.25	S	
12th through 15th	D		L	681.93	T	695.41
16th through 19th	E	693.56	M		U	689.40
20th through 22nd	F		N	695.06	V	
23rd through 25th	G	702.39	O		W	
26th through the last	H		P		X	694.39
Total liability for month	I	2,780.62	II	2,758.04	III	2,784.41
IV Total for quarter (add lines *I*, *II*, and *III*)						8,323.07

Under penalties of perjury, I declare that I have examined this return, including accompanying schedules and statements, and to the best of my knowledge and belief, it is true, correct, and complete.

Signature *Dennis Taylor*   Title Owner   Date 10/31/XX

▌ **FIGURE 10 - 5**

Form **940**	**Employer's Annual Federal**	OMB No. 1545-0028

Department of the Treasury
Internal Revenue Service

Employer's Annual Federal Unemployment (FUTA) Tax Return
► For Paperwork Reduction Act Notice, see page 2.

OMB No. 1545-0028

	T	
	FF	
	FD	
	FP	
	I	
	T	

Name (as distinguished from trade name)

If incorrect, make any necessary change. ►

Dennis Taylor
Trade name, if any

The Kitchen Taylor
Address and ZIP code

2400 Main Street
Wheaton, IL 60187

Calendar year
19XX

Employer identification number
82-5361220

A Did you pay all required contributions to state unemployment funds by the due date of Form 940? (See instructions if none required.)   [x] **Yes** [ ] **No**
If you checked the "Yes" box, enter the amount of contributions paid to state unemployment funds .   ► $ 217 | 20

B Are you required to pay contributions to only one state?   [x] **Yes** [ ] **No**
If you checked the "Yes" box: (1) Enter the name of the state where you are required to pay contributions   ►   Illinois
(2) Enter your state reporting number(s) as shown on state unemployment tax return.   ►   21-675463

C If any part of wages taxable for FUTA tax is exempt from state unemployment tax, check the box. (See the Specific Instructions on page 2.)   [ ]

Part I   Computation of Taxable Wages and Credit Reduction (to be completed by all taxpayers)

1	Total payments (including exempt payments) during the calendar year for services of employees	**1**	131,924	00
2	Exempt payments. (Explain each exemption shown, attaching additional sheets if necessary.) ►	**2** Amount paid		
3	Payments for services of more than $7,000. Enter only the excess over the first $7,000 paid to individual employees not including exempt amounts shown on line 2. Do not use the state wage limitation.	**3** 89,924 00		
4	Total exempt payments (add lines 2 and 3)	**4**	89,924	00
5	**Total taxable wages** (subtract line 4 from line 1). (If any part is exempt from state contributions, see instructions.)►	**5**	42,000	00
6	Additional tax resulting from credit reduction for unpaid advances to the state listed below (by two-letter Postal Service abbreviation). Enter the wages included on line 5 above for that state and multiply by the rate shown. (See the instructions.) Enter the credit reduction amount here and in Part II, line 2, or Part III, line 4: PA _____ x .015= ►	**6**		

Part II   Tax Due or Refund (Complete if you checked the "Yes" boxes in both questions A and B and did not check the box in C, above.)

1	FUTA tax. Multiply the wages in Part I, line 5, by .008 and enter here	**1**	336	00
2	Enter amount from Part I, line 6	**2**		
3	**Total FUTA tax** (add lines 1 and 2)	**3**	336	00
4	Minus: Total FUTA tax deposited for the year, including any overpayment applied from a prior year (from your records)	**4**	336	00
5	**Balance due** (subtract line 4 from line 3). This should be $100 or less. Pay to IRS ►	**5**	-0-	
6	Overpayment (subtract line 3 from line 4). Check if it is to be: [ ] Applied to next return, or [ ] Refunded ►	**6**		

Part III   Tax Due or Refund (Complete if you checked the "No" box in either question A or B or you checked the box in C, above. Also complete Part V.)

1	Gross FUTA tax. Multiply the wages in Part I, line 5, by .062	**1**		
2	Maximum credit. Multiply the wages in Part I, line 5, by .054	**2**		
3	Enter the smaller of the amount in Part V, line 11, or Part III, line 2	**3**		
4	Enter amount from Part I, line 6	**4**		
5	**Credit allowable** (subtract line 4 from line 3). (If zero or less, enter 0.)	**5**		
6	**Total FUTA tax** (subtract line 5 from line 1)	**6**		
7	Minus: Total FUTA tax deposited for the year, including any overpayment applied from a prior year (from your records)	**7**		
8	**Balance due** (subtract line 7 from line 6). This should be $100 or less. Pay to IRS ►	**8**		
9	Overpayment (subtract line 6 from line 7). Check if it is to be: [ ] Applied to next return, or [ ] Refunded ►	**9**		

Part IV   Record of Quarterly Federal Tax Liability for Unemployment Tax (Do not include state liability.)

Quarter	First	Second	Third	Fourth	Total for Year
Liability for quarter	80.00	85.00	83.00	88.00	336.00

If you will not have to file returns in the future, write "Final" here (see general instruction "Who Must File") and sign the return.   ►

Under penalties of perjury, I declare that I have examined this return, including accompanying schedules and statements, and to the best of my knowledge and belief, it is true, correct, and complete, and that no part of any payment made to a state unemployment fund claimed as a credit was or is to be deducted from the payments to employees.

Signature ► *Dennis Taylor*   Title (Owner, etc.) ► Owner   Date ► 2/10/XX

Form **940** (1987)

▊▊▊▊ WAGE AND TAX STATEMENT (FORM W-2)

In addition to providing information to the government, employers are required to provide each employee with an annual wage and tax statement. This information is reported on a Form W-2 which must be furnished to each employee by January 31. Form W-2 shows wages paid, federal income tax withheld, and FICA tax withheld during the preceding year. The employee earnings record provides the information for each employee's W-2 form.

The employer submits a copy of each employee's W-2 form to the Social Security Administration. In addition, each employee attaches a copy of Form W-2 to his/her federal income tax return. Figure 10-6 shows a completed Form W-2.

▊▊▊▊ WORKERS' COMPENSATION INSURANCE

OBJECTIVE 4
COMPUTE AND
RECORD THE PREMIUM
FOR WORKERS'
COMPENSATION
INSURANCE

Workers' compensation insurance protects workers in case of job-related illness or accident. Most states require employers to carry workers' compensation insurance. The employer usually has the option of contributing to a state insurance fund or acquiring coverage from a state-approved private plan.

The employer normally pays the cost of this coverage. Premiums vary according to the level of risk. For example, a factory job would involve greater risk than a clerical job. A company's accident history would also be taken into consideration.

▊ FIGURE 10 - 6

1 Control number	**22222**	For Paperwork Reduction Act Notice, see back of Copy D. OMB No. 1545-0008	For Official Use Only ▶		
2 Employer's name, address, and ZIP code			3 Employer's identification number 82–5361220		4 Employer's state I.D. number 21–675463
The Kitchen Taylor 2400 Main Street Wheaton, IL 60187			5 Statutory employee ☐ Deceased ☐ Pension plan ☐ Legal rep. ☐	942 emp. ☐ Subtotal ☐ Deferred compensation ☐ Void ☐	
			6 Allocated tips	7 Advance EIC payment	
8 Employee's social security number 462–50–7534	9 Federal income tax withheld $2,600.00		10 Wages, tips, other compensation $26,380.00	11 Social security tax withheld $1,978.50	
12 Employee's name (first, middle, last) Kevin Barker			13 Social security wages $26,380.00	14 Social security tips None	
112 Underwood Court Wheaton, IL 60187			16 (See Instr. for Forms W-2/W-2P)	16a Fringe benefits incl. in Box 10	
			17 State income tax	18 State wages, tips, etc.	19 Name of state
15 Employee's address and ZIP code			20 Local income tax	21 Local wages, tips, etc.	22 Name of locality

Form **W-2** Wage and Tax Statement **1988**

Copy A For Social Security Administration   Dept. of the Treasury—IRS

The premium is usually paid at the beginning of the year based on the estimated payroll for the year. To demonstrate, let's assume the payroll is estimated to be $185,000 and the insurance rate is .25 percent. The estimated premium is computed as follows:

Estimated payroll		Insurance rate		Estimated premium
$185,000	×	.0025	=	$462.50

MATH TIP

As described earlier, .25 percent is converted to a decimal by (1) moving the decimal point two places to the left and (2) dropping the percentage sign.

$$.25\% = .0025$$

The following entry records the payment of the estimated premium on January 10:

GENERAL JOURNAL					Page 62	
Date	Description	Post. Ref.	Debit		Credit	
19XX Jan. 10	Prepaid Insurance		462	50		
	Cash				462	50
	To record payment of workers'					
	compensation insurance premium.					

At year-end, when the actual payroll is known, the exact premium is computed. Continuing with our example, let's assume the actual payroll amounts to $192,000. The additional premium is computed as follows:

Step 1:

Actual payroll		Insurance rate		Exact premium
$192,000	×	.0025	=	$480.00

Step 2:

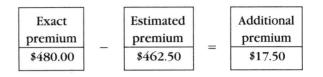

Exact premium	−	Estimated premium	=	Additional premium
$480.00		$462.50		$17.50

The liability for the additional premium is recorded as part of the regular year-end adjustment for expired insurance.

GENERAL JOURNAL						Page 105	
Date	Description	Post. Ref.	Debit		Credit	
19XX Dec. 31	Insurance Expense		480	00		
	Prepaid Insurance				462	50
	Insurance Payable				17	50

The additional premium is normally paid in January along with the following year's estimated premium. On the other hand, if the exact premium turns out to be less than the estimated premium, the company receives a refund for the difference.

Chapter Summary

Three payroll taxes are levied on the employer:

1. FICA tax—employer's contribution. (Assume: 7.5 percent on $50,000 maximum.)

2. Federal unemployment tax. (Assume: .8 percent on $7,000 maximum.)

3. State unemployment tax. (Assume: 5.4 percent on $7,000 maximum.)

All three of these taxes involve both a tax rate and a calendar-year limit on earnings subject to the tax. The taxable earnings section of the payroll register provides the earnings information necessary to compute these taxes.

Matching amounts of FICA tax are paid by both the employee and the employer. The employer's contribution is computed as follows:

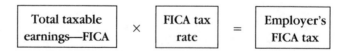

Federal unemployment tax is paid by the employer only. It is computed as follows:

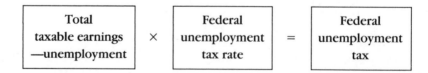

State unemployment tax is paid by the employer only. It is computed as follows:

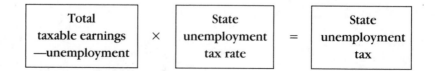

After the employer's payroll taxes have been computed, they must be recorded in the journal. The total is debited to the Payroll Tax Expense account. The individual taxes are recorded as liabilities until they are paid. As the liabilities are paid, the liability accounts are debited and Cash is credited.

Both the employer and employee FICA taxes and the amounts withheld from employees for federal income tax are paid together. The due dates vary according to the dollar amounts involved; *Circular E* provides the details. A Form 941 must be filed quarterly relative to these taxes and payments.

Due dates for the payment of federal unemployment tax also vary according to amount; again, *Circular E* provides details. A Form 940 must be filed annually relative to this tax.

Due dates, methods of payment, and forms for the payment of state unemployment tax vary from state to state. Details are available at your state unemployment office.

Employers are required to provide each employee with an annual wage and tax statement. This information is reported on a Form W-2 which must be furnished to each employee by January 31.

Most states require employers to carry workers' compensation insurance. The employer normally pays the cost of this coverage. An estimated premium is paid at the beginning of the year. At year-end, the exact premium is determined and the appropriate adjustment is recorded.

Glossary

CIRCULAR E

Employer's Tax Guide published by the Internal Revenue Service. It discusses the tax rates, forms, due dates, payments, etc. It also contains withholding tables for federal income tax and FICA.

EMPLOYER IDENTIFICATION NUMBER

A number assigned by the Internal Revenue Service that must be included on all employer reports, forms, or correspondence submitted to the IRS.

FEDERAL UNEMPLOYMENT TAX

Funds raised by this tax are used to cover the cost of administering the various state unemployment programs. This tax is paid by the employer only.

FICA TAX

This tax supports a variety of programs that include pension, disability, survivor's benefits, and health care for retired persons. It is paid by both the employee and the employer.

FORM 940

An annual form, filed by the employer, summarizing the federal unemployment tax liability incurred, payments already deposited, and any balance due or overpayment.

FORM 941

A quarterly form, filed by the employer, showing federal income tax (employee) and FICA tax (employee and employer) liabilities, payments, and any resulting balance due or overpayment.

FORM 8109

A deposit form, supplied by the IRS, used to deposit all federal tax payments (federal income tax, FICA, federal unemployment tax) at a Federal Reserve Bank or other authorized bank.

FORM W-2

An annual wage and tax statement, prepared by the employer, which must be furnished to each employee by January 31. This form shows wages paid, federal income tax withheld, and FICA tax withheld during the preceding calendar year.

QUARTER

A time period consisting of three months. Calendar quarters end March 31, June 30, September 30, and December 31.

STATE UNEMPLOYMENT TAX

The funds raised by this tax are used to pay state unemployment benefits. In most states, this tax is paid by the employer only.

WORKERS' COMPENSATION INSURANCE

Most states require employers to carry this insurance which protects workers in case of job-related illness or accident. The employer pays the cost of this coverage.

Questions for Discussion

1. *a.* Name the three payroll taxes levied on the employer.
   b. Earnings information needed to compute these taxes comes from what section of the payroll register?

2. Assuming a $50,000 FICA tax maximum, how is it possible that the total of the Taxable Earnings—FICA column of the payroll register could be greater than $50,000?

3. A Form 941:
   a. Is filed by whom?
   b. How often?
   c. Requires information about which tax(es)?

4. A Form 940:
   a. Is filed by whom?
   b. How often?
   c. Requires information about which tax(es)?

5. A Form W-2:
   a. Is prepared by whom?
   b. For whom?
   c. Contains what information?

6. *a.* What is the purpose of workers' compensation insurance?
   b. Who pays the premium?

7. Describe the general process of computing and recording the workers' compensation insurance premium.

8. Briefly describe the contents of *Circular E.*

Exercises

Match the following terms with the definitions shown below:

1. *Circular E.*

2. Employer identification number.

3. Federal unemployment tax.

4. FICA tax.

5. Form 940.

6. Form 941.

7. Form W-2.

8. Quarter.

9. State unemployment tax.

10. Workers' compensation insurance.

Definitions:

 a. An annual wage and tax statement, prepared by the employer, which must be furnished to each employee by January 31. This form shows wages paid, federal income tax withheld, and FICA tax withheld during the preceding calendar year.

 b. A time period consisting of three months.

 c. Funds raised by this tax are used to cover the cost of administering the various state unemployment programs. This tax is paid by the employer only.

 d. Most states require employers to carry this insurance which protects workers in case of job-related illness or accident. The employer pays the cost of this coverage.

e. A quarterly form, filed by the employer showing federal income tax (employee) and FICA tax (employee and employer) liabilities, payments, and any resulting balance due or overpayment.

f. A number assigned by the Internal Revenue Service that must be included on all employer reports, forms, or correspondence submitted to the IRS.

g. The funds raised by this tax are used to pay state unemployment benefits. This tax is paid by the employer only.

h. This tax supports a variety of programs that include pension, disability, survivor's benefits, and health care for retired persons. It is paid by both the employee and the employer.

i. *Employer's Tax Guide* published by the Internal Revenue Service. It discusses tax rates, forms, due dates, payments, etc. It also contains withholding tables for federal income tax and FICA.

j. An annual form, filed by the employer, summarizing the federal unemployment tax liability incurred, payments already deposited, and any balance due or overpayment.

EXERCISE 10-2
COMPUTE AND
RECORD PAYROLL
TAXES
(L.O.1, 2)

For the pay period ending April 21, 19XX, Archer Company's payroll register shows taxable earnings as follows:

Total taxable earnings—FICA $5,650
Total taxable earnings—unemployment . . 3,940

Additional data:
FICA tax: 7.5 percent on $50,000 maximum.
Federal unemployment tax: .8 percent on $7,000 maximum.
State unemployment tax: 5.4 percent on $7,000 maximum.

a. Compute the employer's:

1. FICA tax.

2. Federal unemployment tax.

3. State unemployment tax.

b. Prepare the entry to record the employer's payroll tax expense.

EXERCISE 10-3
PAYMENT OF FICA AND
FEDERAL INCOME TAX
(L.O.3)

On June 30, Straka Company's ledger shows the following selected account balances:

FICA Tax Payable . . . . $ 2,250
Federal Income Tax Payable   2,135
Federal Unemployment Tax Payable   120
State Unemployment Tax Payable   810
Wages Payable   10,500
Payroll Tax Expense   12,330
Wages Expense   90,000

Prepare the June 30 entry to record the payment of the liabilities for FICA and federal income tax.

EXERCISE 10-4
PAYMENT OF FEDERAL AND STATE UNEMPLOYMENT TAXES
(L.O.3)

Referring to the information given in Exercise 10-3:

a. Prepare the July 31 entry to record the payment of the liability for federal unemployment tax.

b. Prepare the July 31 entry to record the payment of the liability for state unemployment tax.

EXERCISE 10-5
COMPUTE WAGES AND PAYROLL TAX EXPENSE
(L.O.1, 2)

The payroll records of Kurtzman Associates show the following information on January 31, the end of their first month of operations:

Employee	Cumulative Earnings
A	3,200
B	2,450
C	5,690

Additional data:
FICA tax: 7.5 percent on $50,000 maximum.
Federal unemployment tax: .8 percent on $7,000 maximum.
State unemployment tax: 5.4 percent on $7,000 maximum.

Assuming the accounts are up to date:

a. What is the balance in the Wages Expense account on January 31?

b. What is the balance in the Payroll Tax Expense account?

EXERCISE 10-6
ESTIMATED WORKERS' COMPENSATION PREMIUM
(L.O.4)

On January 10, Parrant Products estimates its payroll for the coming year will total $145,000. The workers' compensation insurance rate assigned to Parrant is .65 percent.

a. Compute the estimated premium for workers' compensation insurance.

   b. Prepare the entry to record the payment of the estimated premium
       on January 10.

EXERCISE 10-7
EXACT WORKERS'
COMPENSATION
PREMIUM
(L.O.4)

On December 31, Parrant Products determines that its actual payroll for the
past year amounts to $152,000. In reference to Exercise 10-6:

   a. Compute the exact premium for workers' compensation insurance.

   b. Compute the additional premium.

   c. Record the liability for the additional premium as part of the regular
       year-end adjustment for expired insurance.

Problems—Set A

The payroll records of Harrelson Company show the following information for the weekly pay period ending April 28:

Employee	Total Earnings Current Pay Period	Cumulative Earnings Previous Pay Period
Arnold	$295.00	$4,250.00
Bauer	405.82	6,173.50
Crawford	526.30	8,421.30
Drake	381.75	5,948.00
Eckman	456.00	6,825.00

Additional data:

FICA tax: 7.5 percent on $50,000 maximum.
Federal unemployment tax: .8 percent on $7,000 maximum.
State unemployment tax: 5.4 percent on $7,000 maximum.

INSTRUCTIONS
1. Compute for each employee:
   a. Taxable earnings—FICA.
   b. Taxable earnings—unemployment.

2. Compute:
   a. Total taxable earnings—FICA.
   b. Total taxable earnings—unemployment.

3. Prepare the entry to record the employer's payroll tax expense for the pay period ending April 28.

**PROBLEM
10-2A**

ENTRIES FOR PAYROLL
AND EMPLOYER'S
PAYROLL TAXES
(L.O.1, 2)

Shown below is the totals line from Farbman Enterprises's payroll register for the pay period ending July 25.

| | | | | PAYROLL REGISTER For the Week Ended July 25, 19XX | | | |
| | | | Earnings | | | |
Employee	Total Hours	Hourly Rate	Regular	O.T.	Total	Cumulative Total Previous Period
Totals			8,425.00	947.50	9,372.50	

| Taxable Earnings | | Deductions | | | | Net Pay |
FICA	Unemployment	Federal Income Tax	FICA	Union Dues	Total	
9,372.50	985.00	995.00	702.94	64.00	1,761.94	7,610.56

Additional data:

FICA tax: 7.5 percent on $50,000 maximum.
Federal unemployment tax: .8 percent on $7,000 maximum.
State unemployment tax: 5.4 percent on $7,000 maximum.

INSTRUCTIONS

1. Prepare the entry to record the payroll.

2. Prepare the entry to record the employer's payroll tax expense for the pay period ending July 25.

PROBLEM 10-3A

ENTRIES FOR PAYROLL, PAYROLL TAXES, AND PAYMENT OF NET PAY (L.O.1, 2)

The figures shown below are column totals taken from Farra Company's payroll register for the pay period ended May 7.

Earnings:		
Regular.		$11,500.00
Overtime		1,675.20
Total		$13,175.20
Taxable earnings:		
FICA	$13,175.20	
Unemployment	8,670.00	
Deductions:		
Federal income tax		$ 1,630.00
FICA		988.14
Health insurance		1,125.50
Pension plan		660.00
Total		4,403.64
Net pay		$ 8,771.56

Additional data:

FICA tax: 7.5 percent on $50,000 maximum.
Federal unemployment tax: .8 percent on $7,000 maximum.
State unemployment tax: 5.4 percent on $7,000 maximum.

INSTRUCTIONS

1. Prepare the entry to record the payroll.

2. Prepare the entry to record the employer's payroll tax expense for the pay period ending May 7.

3. This company has a separate payroll checking account. On May 7, one check is written on the regular checking account for an amount equal to the total net pay. Prepare the appropriate journal entry.

PROBLEM 10-4A

ENTRIES FOR PAYROLL, PAYROLL TAXES, AND PAYMENT OF NET PAY AND PAYROLL TAXES (L.O.1–3)

Shown on page 356 is the totals line from Grace Products' payroll register for the monthly pay period ending December 31, 19X1. Grace Products is a new business that opened on December 1, 19X1.

PAYROLL REGISTER
For the Month Ended December 31, 19X1

| Employee | Total Hours | Hourly Rate | Earnings | | | Cumulative Total Previous Period |
			Regular	O.T.	Total	
Totals			8,924.00	952.40	9,876.40	

| Taxable Earnings | | Deductions | | | | Net Pay |
FICA	Unemployment	Federal Income Tax	FICA	Union Dues	Total	
9,876.40	9,876.40	964.00	740.73	82.00	1,786.73	8,089.67

Additional data:

FICA tax: 7.5 percent on $50,000 maximum.
Federal unemployment tax: .8 percent on $7,000 maximum.
State unemployment tax: 5.4 percent on $7,000 maximum.

INSTRUCTIONS

1. Prepare the entry to record the monthly payroll.

2. Prepare the entry to record the employer's payroll tax expense for the pay period ending December 31, 19X1.

3. This company has a separate payroll checking account. On December 31, 19X1, one check is written on the regular checking account for an amount equal to the total net pay. Prepare the appropriate journal entry.

Note: Grace Products is a new business. December 31, 19X1, ends its first month in operation. Therefore, the column totals on the monthly payroll register are also the totals for the calendar year ending December 31, 19X1.

4. Prepare the January 15, 19X2, entry to record the payment of the liabilities for FICA and federal income tax.

5. Prepare the January 31, 19X2, entry to record the payment of the liabilities for federal unemployment tax.

6. Prepare the January 31, 19X2, entry to record the payment of the liability for state unemployment tax.

PROBLEM 10-5A
WORKERS' COMPENSATION INSURANCE (L.O.4)

On January 2, 19X1, Hope Enterprises estimates its payroll for the coming year will total $250,000. The workers' compensation insurance rate assigned to Hope is .45 percent.

INSTRUCTIONS

1. Compute the estimated premium for worker's compensation insurance.

2. Prepare the entry to record the payment of the estimated premium on January 2, 19X1.

On December 31, 19X1, Hope Enterprises determines that its actual payroll for the past year amounts to $265,000.

INSTRUCTIONS

3. Compute the exact premium for workers' compensation insurance.

4. Compute the additional premium.

5. Record the liability for the additional premium as a part of the regular year-end adjustment for expired insurance.

Problems—Set B

The payroll records of Jacklin Company show the following information for the weekly pay period ending May 12:

Employee	Total Earnings Current Pay Period	Cumulative Earnings Previous Pay Period
Atkins	$383.90	$6,142.50
Brown	560.00	8,974.00
Carrol	410.00	3,792.10
Dartley	456.50	6,780.00
Eckles	401.25	5,981.75

Additional data:

FICA tax: 7.5 percent on $50,000 maximum.
Federal unemployment tax: .8 percent on $7,000 maximum.
State unemployment tax: 5.4 percent on $7,000 maximum.

INSTRUCTIONS
1. Compute for each employee:
   a. Taxable earnings—FICA.
   b. Taxable earnings—unemployment.

2. Compute:
   a. Total taxable earnings—FICA.
   b. Total taxable earnings—unemployment.

3. Prepare the entry to record the employer's payroll tax expense for the pay period ending May 12.

PROBLEM 10-2B

ENTRIES FOR PAYROLL AND EMPLOYER'S PAYROLL TAXES (L.O.1, 2)

Shown below is the totals line from Kanges Associates' payroll register for the pay period ending August 10.

PAYROLL REGISTER For the Week Ended August 10, 19XX						
Employee	Total Hours	Hourly Rate	Earnings			Cumulative Total Previous Period
			Regular	O.T.	Total	
Totals			6,475.00	432.50	6,907.50	

Taxable Earnings		Deductions				Net Pay
FICA	Unemployment	Federal Income Tax	FICA	Union Dues	Total	
6,907.50	875.00	829.00	518.06	52.00	1,399.06	5,508.44

Additional data:

FICA tax: 7.5 percent on $50,000 maximum.
Federal unemployment tax: .8 percent on $7,000 maximum.
State unemployment tax: 5.4 percent on $7,000 maximum.

INSTRUCTIONS

1. Prepare the entry to record the payroll.

2. Prepare the entry to record the employer's payroll tax expense for the pay period ending August 10.

PROBLEM 10-3B

ENTRIES FOR PAYROLL, PAYROLL TAXES, AND PAYMENT OF NET PAY (L.O.1, 2)

The figures shown below are column totals taken from Barton Company's payroll register for the pay period ended June 9.

Earnings:		
Regular.		$10,370.00
Overtime		1,230.00
Total		$11,600.00
Taxable earnings:		
FICA	$11,600.00	
Unemployment	7,240.00	
Deductions:		
Federal income tax		$ 1,740.00
FICA		870.00
Health insurance		1,090.50
Pension plan		638.00
Total		4,338.50
Net pay		$ 7,261.50

Additional data:

FICA tax: 7.5 percent on $50,000 maximum.
Federal unemployment tax: .8 percent on $7,000 maximum.
State unemployment tax: 5.4 percent on $7,000 maximum.

INSTRUCTIONS

1. Prepare the entry to record the payroll.

2. Prepare the entry to record the employer's payroll tax expense for the pay period ending June 9.

3. This company has a separate payroll checking account. On June 9, one check is written on the regular checking account for an amount equal to the total net pay. Prepare the appropriate journal entry.

PROBLEM 10-4B

ENTRIES FOR PAYROLL, PAYROLL TAXES, AND PAYMENT OF NET PAY AND PAYROLL TAXES (L.O.1–3)

Shown on page 361 is the totals line from Keller Products' payroll register for the monthly pay period ending December 31, 19X1. Keller Products is a new business that opened on December 1, 19X1.

PAYROLL REGISTER
For the Month Ended December 31, 19X1

| Employee | Total Hours | Hourly Rate | Earnings | | | Cumulative Total Previous Period |
			Regular	O.T.	Total	
Totals			7,842.00	678.00	8,520.00	

| Taxable Earnings | | Deductions | | | | Net Pay |
FICA	Unemployment	Federal Income Tax	FICA	Union Dues	Total	
8,520.00	8,520.00	812.00	639.00	72.00	1,523.00	6,997.00

Additional data:

FICA tax: 7.5 percent on $50,000 maximum.
Federal unemployment tax: .8 percent on $7,000 maximum.
State unemployment tax: 5.4 percent on $7,000 maximum.

INSTRUCTIONS

1. Prepare the entry to record the monthly payroll.

2. Prepare the entry to record the employer's payroll tax expense for the pay period ending December 31, 19X1.

3. This company has a separate payroll checking account. On December 31, 19X1, one check is written on the regular checking account for an amount equal to the total net pay. Prepare the appropriate journal entry.

Note: Keller Products is a new business. December 31, 19X1, ends its first month in operation. Therefore, the column totals on the monthly payroll register are also the totals for the calendar year ending December 31, 19X1.

4. Prepare the January 15, 19X2, entry to record the payment of the liabilities for FICA and federal income tax.

5. Prepare the January 31, 19X2, entry to record the payment of the liability for federal unemployment tax.

6. Prepare the January 31, 19X2, entry to record the payment of the liability for state unemployment tax.

PROBLEM 10-5B
WORKERS' COMPENSATION INSURANCE
(L.O.4)

On January 3, 19X1, Grant Company estimates its payroll for the coming year will total $315,000. The workers' compensation insurance rate assigned to Grant is .35 percent.

INSTRUCTIONS

1. Compute the estimated premium for workers' compensation insurance.

2. Prepare the entry to record the payment of the estimated premium on January 3, 19X1.

On December 31, 19X1, Grant Company determines that its actual payroll for the past year amounts to $324,000.

INSTRUCTIONS

3. Compute the exact premium for workers' compensation insurance.

4. Compute the additional premium.

5. Record the liability for the additional premium as a part of the regular year-end adjustment for expired insurance.

Mini-Cases

CASE 10-1

Your friend, Jack, has his own business. All smiles, Jack tells you that one of his employees no longer wants to be part of the U.S. Social Security Program. "Isn't that great! Now I won't have to pay a matching amount for that employee," says Jack. Does Jack have cause for jubilation?

CASE 10-2

Mr. Harvey, your new employer, does not want you to prepare W-2 forms for employees. "It's a waste of time and money! Let them use their check stubs," says Mr. Harvey. Respond.

CASE 10-3

You have just completed your first payroll for Mrs. Grant, a new client. Payroll register in hand, she angrily points to the total of the Taxable Earnings—Unemployment column saying: "This $9,200 column total can't be correct! Only the first $7,000 of earnings are subject to unemployment taxes." Respond to Mrs. Grant's comments.

Accounting for a Merchandising Business

||||||||||||||||
CHAPTER

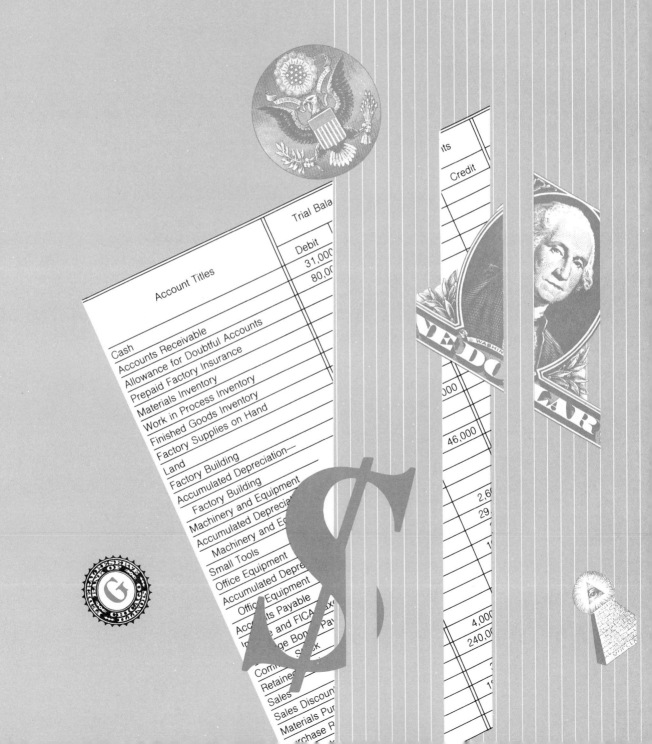

PART 3

Merchandising Business: Accounting for Sales

AFTER STUDYING THIS CHAPTER, YOU SHOULD BE ABLE TO:

1 Describe the nature of a merchandising business.

2 Use an accounts receivable ledger.

3 Describe the concept of special journals.

4 Describe the use of a sales invoice in recording sales transactions.

5 Journalize and post using a sales journal.

6 Record sales tax.

7 Record sales returns and allowances.

In previous chapters, we have focused our attention on accounting for businesses that sell a service. In this chapter, you will apply your knowledge of the accounting cycle to businesses that sell a product. You will also be introduced to subsidiary ledgers and special journals. These new tools will allow you to record more accounting information with less time and effort.

▌▌▌ A MERCHANDISING BUSINESS

OBJECTIVE 1
DESCRIBE THE NATURE
OF A MERCHANDISING
BUSINESS

Businesses that sell products can be divided into two groups: manufacturing businesses and merchandising businesses. A manufacturing business makes the products that it sells. You will study a manufacturing business in Chapter 29. A merchandising business purchases the product ready-made from a supplier and then resells this ready-made product to its customers. Units purchased by a merchandising business for resale are referred to as merchandise. Such items as office supplies or equipment are not merchandise because they are not purchased for resale. They are purchased to be used by the business. However, an office supply or equipment company would consider office supplies or equipment to be merchandise, since the company purchases these items for resale.

In this chapter, Dennis Taylor decides that it is more profitable to sell ready-made kitchen cabinets than to refinish old cabinets. In other words, The Kitchen Taylor is becoming a merchandising business. To The Kitchen Taylor, cabinets are merchandise.

▌▌▌ THE ACCOUNTS RECEIVABLE LEDGER

OBJECTIVE 2
USE AN ACCOUNTS
RECEIVABLE LEDGER

In the past, you have recorded transactions involving accounts receivable by simply debiting or crediting the Accounts Receivable account. The balance in the Accounts Receivable account indicated the total amount owed to a business by all its charge customers. Common sense tells us that this accounts receivable information is not adequate. A business must know its charge customers by name. Sales on account and payments received on account must be identified with a customer name. This information can be added to our existing accounting system through the use of an accounts receivable ledger.

Up to this time, we have worked with only one ledger or book of accounts. Since we had only one, we simply referred to it as the ledger. That ledger will now become known as the *general ledger.* The Accounts Receivable account found in the general ledger will now be referred to as a control or controlling account. The Accounts Receivable account will continue to function as it has in the past; it will contain only summary information. The accounts receivable ledger, another book of accounts, will provide the detail. The accounts receivable ledger will contain a separate account for each charge customer. This ledger is a subsidiary ledger. The entire accounts receivable ledger supports or explains just one general ledger account—the Accounts Receivable (control) account. The Accounts Receivable account is a controlling account because it *controls* the accounts receivable ledger.

must balance

As you will recall, all of the accounts in the general ledger are numbered. In the accounts receivable ledger, however, the accounts are kept in alphabetical order by customer name without account numbers. From now on, we will automatically assume every company has an accounts receivable ledger.

JOURNALIZING

The use of an accounts receivable ledger adds only one step to our journalizing process. Whenever the Accounts Receivable account is debited or credited, the specific customer's name must also be written in the Description column of the journal. For example, let's assume that on January 22, The Kitchen Taylor sold $1,200 worth of kitchen cabinets to William Dexter on account. Assuming the use of an accounts receivable ledger, this transaction is recorded as follows:

		GENERAL JOURNAL			Page 45
Date		**Description**	**Post. Ref.**	**Debit**	**Credit**
19XX Jan.	22	Accounts Receivable—William Dexter		1,200 00	
		Sales			1,200 00

IIIIIIIIIIIIIIIIIIIII
C O M M E N T   Sales is a revenue account title commonly used by merchandising businesses.

POSTING

After a debit or credit to Accounts Receivable has been recorded in the general journal, it must be posted two places:

1. The Accounts Receivable (control) account in the general ledger.

2. The customer's account in the accounts receivable ledger.

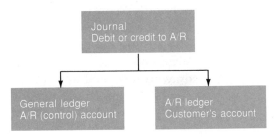

Using this procedure, Figure 11-1 shows how the debit portion of the entry shown earlier would be posted.

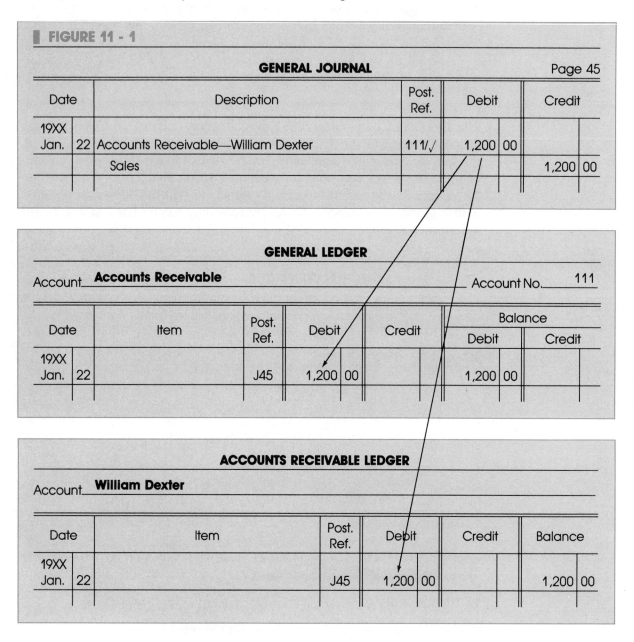

▌ **FIGURE 11 - 1**

Observe the following points relative to Figure 11-1:

● The Posting Reference column in the general journal must accommodate two debit posting references. This is accomplished by drawing a slanted line across the column, thereby creating two compartments on the same line.

- Since the customers' accounts in the accounts receivable ledger are not numbered, a check mark is placed in the Posting Reference column of the journal rather than an account number. This check mark indicates that this item has been posted to the customer's account in the subsidiary ledger.

- The Balance column in the accounts receivable ledger account is not labeled debit or credit. It is assumed to be a normal balance. In the case of accounts receivable, a debit balance is assumed. An abnormal balance would be indicated by placing parentheses around the figure in the Balance column.

THE SCHEDULE OF ACCOUNTS RECEIVABLE

After all journalizing and posting is completed, the debits and credits in the Accounts Receivable (control) account should equal the debits and credits in the accounts receivable ledger. In other words, the balance in the Accounts Receivable (control) account should equal the total of all the customer account balances in the accounts receivable ledger. To verify this equality of debits and credits, accountants prepare a schedule of accounts receivable. This schedule is usually prepared at the end of the month before statements of account are mailed to charge customers. The schedule of accounts receivable lists each charge customer's name and account balance; this information is taken directly from the accounts receivable ledger. The total accounts receivable as shown on the schedule is then compared with the balance in the Accounts Receivable (control) account in the general ledger. The two figures should agree; if not, an error has been made.

Using T-accounts to demonstrate, let's assume The Kitchen Taylor's accounts receivable ledger appears as follows on January 31, 19XX:

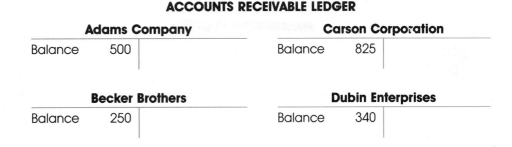

ACCOUNTS RECEIVABLE LEDGER

Adams Company		Carson Corporation	
Balance 500		Balance 825	

Becker Brothers		Dubin Enterprises	
Balance 250		Balance 340	

From the accounts receivable ledger, the following schedule of accounts receivable is prepared:

THE KITCHEN TAYLOR Schedule of Accounts Receivable January 31, 19XX		
Adams Company	$ 500	00
Becker Brothers	250	00
Carson Corporation	825	00
Dubin Enterprises	340	00
Total accounts receivable	$ 1,915	00

The total accounts receivable shown on the schedule is then compared with the January 31 balance in the Accounts Receivable (control) account in the general ledger.

GENERAL LEDGER

Accounts Receivable 111

19XX
Jan. 31   Balance   1,915

Since the total of the schedule of accounts receivable and the balance in the Accounts Receivable account are the same ($1,915), we know there is overall equality between the debits and credits in the subsidiary ledger and the controlling account. Later in this chapter, you will learn to use an accounts receivable ledger in conjunction with a special journal.

▊▊▊ SPECIAL JOURNALS

OBJECTIVE 3
DESCRIBE THE CONCEPT
OF SPECIAL JOURNALS

Up to this point, all transactions have been recorded in a two-column general journal. Although effective, this is not an efficient way to handle repetitive types of transactions.

You have probably observed that sales on account, purchases on account, receipts of cash, and payments of cash occur over and over again. In most businesses, these four types of transactions represent over 90 percent of the daily activity. If the recording and posting of these repetitive types of transactions could be sped up, the savings in time and effort would be substantial. This increased efficiency can be accomplished through the use of special journals.

In this and the next couple of chapters, you will be introduced to four special journals. Each of these special journals will accommodate only specific types of transactions.

Journal	Transaction
Sales journal	Sales of merchandise on account
Purchases journal	Purchases of merchandise on account
Cash receipts journal	All receipts of cash
Cash payments journal	All payments of cash

Any transaction that does not fit into a special journal will be recorded in the general journal. *It is important to note that a transaction is recorded in only one journal.* Since we will ultimately be working with five journals (four special journals and one general journal), *a choice must be made for each transaction.* In this chapter, we will focus our attention on the sales journal. The information necessary to record a transaction in the sales journal comes from a sales invoice. So, before studying the sales journal, let's consider the sales invoice more carefully.

THE SALES INVOICE

OBJECTIVE 4
DESCRIBE THE USE OF A
SALES INVOICE IN
RECORDING SALES
TRANSACTIONS

When a transaction occurs, a business document containing all the relevant information must be prepared. In the case of a sale of merchandise, a sales invoice must be prepared. Figure 11-2 shows a sales invoice prepared by The Kitchen Taylor.

FIGURE 11 - 2

THE KITCHEN TAYLOR   **INVOICE NO. 824**
2400 Main Street
Wheaton, Illinois 60187

Sold to: Dubin Enterprises   Date: February 4, 19XX
           5100 Springdale Avenue
           Western Springs, Illinois 60558   Terms: Net 30 days

Quantity	Description	Unit Price	Total
3	XJ-12 Cabinets	175.00	525.00
1	#428 Hardware	19.00	19.00
			544.00

The sales **invoice** contains the customer's name and address, invoice number, date, description of the merchandise, and the selling price. The terms shown on the invoice are the seller's terms of credit. Net 30 days, or n/30, means the full invoice amount is due 30 days from the invoice date. If the seller is offering a discount to the purchaser for early payment, the terms might read 2/10, n/30. This means a 2 percent discount may be deducted if the invoice is paid within 10 days of the invoice date; the full amount is due in 30 days. These terms of credit will be studied in greater detail in Chapter 13.

Sales invoices are usually prepared with multiple copies. An invoice prepared in triplicate might be distributed as follows:

Copy 1 . . . . . . Customer
Copy 2 . . . . . . Accounting department
Copy 3 . . . . . . Shipping department

The copy received by the accounting department provides the information necessary for the accountant to journalize the transaction.

▌▌▌▌ THE SALES JOURNAL

JOURNALIZING

OBJECTIVE 5
JOURNALIZE AND POST
USING A SALES
JOURNAL

Special journals speed things up by making the repetitive portion of an entry into a permanent part of the journal. This is done through the use of column headings. For example, every sale on account requires a debit to Accounts Receivable and a credit to Sales. In a sales journal, this is made permanent through the use of a special Dr. Accounts Receivable, Cr. Sales column. This eliminates the need to rewrite this information each time a sale on account is recorded in the sales journal. To demonstrate, let's consider The Kitchen Taylor's sales journal.

sales on account

SALES JOURNAL				Page 17	
Date	Customer's Name	Invoice Number	Post. Ref.	Dr. Accts. Rec. Cr. Sales	
19XX Feb. 4	Dubin Enterprises	824		544	00
9	Adams Company	825		237	00
12	Carson Corporation	826		846	00
18	Becker Brothers	827		1,250	00
25	Dubin Enterprises	828		372	00
28	Carson Corporation	829		629	00

In studying The Kitchen Taylor's sales journal, observe the following:

- The **sales journal** accommodates only one type of transaction: a sale of merchandise on account. *What if you have a cash sale? go to general journal or cash receipts*

- The portion of the entry that never changes (debit Accounts Receivable and credit Sales) is made permanent through use of a column heading. Since the debit and credit amounts are always the same, this can all be done in a single column.

- The accountant needs to enter only the information that changes: the date, customer's name, invoice number, and the amount of the sale.

- Each transaction requires only one line.

- No explanations are necessary since every transaction represents a sale on account.

POSTING

In accordance with our basic accounting cycle, all journal entries must be posted to the appropriate ledger accounts. However, all special journals require two types of postings:

1. **Individual postings.** These postings are necessary where each figure in a column must be posted to a *different* account. These items are usually posted on a daily basis.

2. **Column total postings.** Column totals are posted where all the figures in a column must be posted to the *same* account. Instead of making many individual postings to the same account, one posting is made at the end of the month with the total.

Let's demonstrate by posting The Kitchen Taylor's sales journal.

1. **Individual postings.** The Kitchen Taylor uses an accounts receivable ledger. This means that each debit to Accounts Receivable must be posted to the individual customer's account in the accounts receivable ledger. After posting, the sales journal and the accounts receivable ledger appear as shown in Figures 11-3 and 11-4.

|||||||||||||||||||||
C O M M E N T   Observe the check marks in the Posting Reference column of the sales journal. They indicate that these amounts have been posted to the individual customer's accounts in the accounts receivable ledger.

■ FIGURE 11 - 3

		SALES JOURNAL			Page 17	
Date		Customer's Name	Invoice Number	Post. Ref.	Dr. Accts. Rec. Cr. Sales	
19XX Feb.	4	Dubin Enterprises	824	√	544	00
	9	Adams Company	825	√	237	00
	12	Carson Corporation	826	√	846	00
	18	Becker Brothers	827	√	1,250	00
	25	Dubin Enterprises	828	√	372	00
	28	Carson Corporation	829	√	629	00

■ FIGURE 11 - 4

ACCOUNTS RECEIVABLE LEDGER

Account **Adams Company**

Date		Item	Post. Ref.	Debit		Credit		Balance	
19XX Feb.	1	Balance	√					500	00
	9		S17	237	00			737	00

Account **Becker Brothers**

Date		Item	Post. Ref.	Debit		Credit		Balance	
19XX Feb.	1	Balance	√					250	00
	18		S17	1,250	00			1,500	00

FIGURE 11 - 4 (concluded)

Account__**Carson Corporation**_____

Date		Item	Post. Ref.	Debit		Credit		Balance	
19XX									
Feb.	1	Balance	√					825	00
	12		S17	846	00			1,671	00
	18		S17	629	00			2,300	00

Account__**Dubin Enterprises**_____

Date		Item	Post. Ref.	Debit		Credit		Balance	
19XX									
Feb.	1	Balance	√					340	00
	4		S17	544	00			884	00
	25		S17	372	00			1,256	00

|||||||||||||||||||||||
C O M M E N T

Observe that the posting references in the accounts receivable ledger begin with the letter S. This indicates the posted information came from page 17 of the sales journal.

2. **Column total postings.** As the column heading indicates, all the figures in the amount column must be posted as a debit to the Accounts Receivable (control) account and also as a credit to the Sales account. This can be accomplished easily with the following steps.

a. Total the amount column.

b. Post the total as a debit to the Accounts Receivable account in the general ledger.

c. Post the total as a credit to the Sales account in the general ledger.

After posting, the sales journal and the Accounts Receivable and Sales accounts appear as shown in Figures 11-5 and 11-6.

||||||||||||||||||||||
C O M M E N T

Observe the placement of the posting reference in the sales journal. The posting reference for a column total is placed below the total in parentheses. The debit posting reference is always written below and to the left. The credit posting reference is always written below and to the right.

FIGURE 11 - 5

		SALES JOURNAL			Page 17
Date		Customer's Name	Invoice Number	Post. Ref.	Dr. Accts. Rec. Cr. Sales
19XX Feb.	4	Dubin Enterprises	824	√	544 00
	9	Adams Company	825	√	237 00
	12	Carson Corporation	826	√	846 00
	18	Becker Brothers	827	√	1,250 00
	25	Dubin Enterprises	828	√	372 00
	28	Carson Corporation	829	√	629 00
	28				3,878 00
					(111) (411)

FIGURE 11 - 6

GENERAL LEDGER

Account **Accounts Receivable (Control)**   Account No. **111**

Date		Item	Post. Ref.	Debit	Credit	Balance Debit	Balance Credit
19XX Feb.	1	Balance	√			1,915 00	
	28		S17	3,878 00		5,793 00	

Account **Sales**   Account No. **411**

Date		Item	Post. Ref.	Debit	Credit	Balance Debit	Balance Credit
19XX Feb.	1	Balance	√				2,950 00
	28		S17		3,878 00		6,828 00

FIGURE 11 - 7

A/R LEDGER

Adams Company

Bal.	500
	237

SALES JOURNAL Page 17

Date	Customer's Name	Inv. No.	Post. Ref.	Dr. Accts. Rec. Cr. Sales	
19XX Feb. 4	Dubin Enterprises	824	√	544	00
9	Adams Company	825	√	237	00
12	Carson Corporation	826	√	846	00
18	Becker Brothers	827	√	1,250	00
25	Dubin Enterprises	828	√	372	00
28	Carson Corporation	829	√	629	00
28				3,878	00
				(111)	(411)

Becker Company

Bal.	250
	1,250

Carson Corporation

Bal.	825
	846
	629

Dubin Enterprises

Bal.	340
	544
	372

GENERAL LEDGER

Account **Accounts Receivable (Control)** Account No. 111

Date	Item	Post. Ref.	Debit	Credit	Balance Debit	Balance Credit
19XX Feb. 1	Balance	√			1,915 00	
28		S17	3,878 00		5,793 00	

Account **Sales** Account No. 411

Date	Item	Post. Ref.	Debit	Credit	Balance Debit	Balance Credit
19XX Feb. 1	Balance	√				2,950 00
28		S17		3,878 00		6,828 00

Figure 11-7 shows the overall flow of information from the sales journal to both the accounts receivable ledger and the general ledger. In the next section of this chapter, we will customize the sales journal to accommodate the needs of a business that collects sales tax.

▐▐▐▐ **SALES TAX**

OBJECTIVE 6
RECORD SALES TAX

A **wholesale business** sells merchandise to another business. A **retail business** sells merchandise to the end user (final consumer). Many states and local municipalities levy a **sales tax** on retail sales. This tax is actually paid by the retail customer, but the retail seller acts as a collection agent for the taxing authority. At the time of the sale, the seller charges the customer for the tax and later remits the cash to the appropriate taxing authority.

Once the seller has charged the customer for the sales tax, the tax becomes a liability (Sales Tax Payable) of the seller. The seller now owes the sales tax to the taxing authority. This liability must be recorded when the sale is recorded.

Since special journals are tailored to meet special needs, a retailer's sales journal should be designed to accommodate the recording of sales tax. To demonstrate, let's assume that on May 2 a retailer makes a $200 sale on account, Invoice No. 947, to Ida Chambers. A 5 percent sales tax is applicable. As shown below, this transaction is recorded in a slightly expanded version of the sales journal.

		SALES JOURNAL					Page 34
Date	Customer's Name	Invoice Number	Post. Ref.	Accounts Receivable Debit	Sales Tax Payable Credit	Sales Credit	
19XX May 2	Ida Chambers	947		210 00	10 00	200 00	

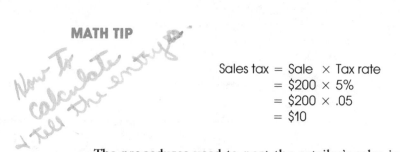

MATH TIP

$$\text{Sales tax} = \text{Sale} \times \text{Tax rate}$$
$$= \$200 \times 5\%$$
$$= \$200 \times .05$$
$$= \$10$$

The procedures used to post the retailer's sales journal are the same as those described earlier.

1. **Individual postings.** Only the Accounts Receivable Debit column needs to be posted individually. Each debit to Accounts Receivable must be posted to the individual customer's account in the accounts receivable ledger. These amounts are usually posted daily.

2. **Column total postings.** At the end of the month, all three amount columns are totaled. Then, as the column headings indicate:
   a. Post the total of the Accounts Receivable Debit column to the Accounts Receivable (control) account in the general ledger.
   b. Post the total of the Sales Tax Payable Credit column to the Sales Tax Payable account in the general ledger.
   c. Post the total of the Sales Credit column to the Sales account in the general ledger.

▌▌▌▌ SALES RETURNS AND ALLOWANCES

OBJECTIVE 7
RECORD SALES RETURNS
AND ALLOWANCES

When previously sold merchandise is returned, sales must be reduced. However, most businesses do not reduce the Sales account directly with a debit. Instead, most businesses record a **sales return** by debiting an account titled Sales Returns and Allowances. This account is known as a contra-revenue or **contra-sales account.** On the income statement, it is subtracted from sales in arriving at **net sales.**

For example:

THE KITCHEN TAYLOR Income Statement For the Year Ended December 31, 19XX		
Sales		$100,000	00
Less: Sales returns and allowances		2,500	00
Net sales		$ 97,500	00

The Sales Returns and Allowances account is also used in situations where previously sold merchandise is discovered to be defective but is not returned to the seller. Instead, the seller "allows" for the damage by reducing the price. A **sales allowance** is usually recorded with a debit to the Sales Returns and Allowances account.

Since sales returns and allowances have a negative impact on revenue, most businesses keep a careful watch over these types of transactions. Although the Sales account could be debited directly, the use of a separate contra account makes it easier to monitor the volume of returns and allowances.

In these situations, the seller prepares a business document known as a **credit memorandum.** The word *credit* refers to the credit that will reduce the customer's accounts receivable when this transaction is journalized. Figure 11-8 shows a credit memorandum prepared by The Kitchen Taylor.

▮ **FIGURE 11 - 8**

THE KITCHEN TAYLOR
2400 Main Street
Wheaton, Illinois 60187

CREDIT MEMORANDUM
NO. 62

Credit to: Dubin Enterprises
            5100 Springdale Avenue
            Western Springs, Illinois 60558

Date: February 10, 19XX

Terms: Net 30 days

Your account is being credited as follows:

| 1 | XJ-12 Cabinet | 175.00 |

The return described in Credit Memorandum No. 62, as shown in Figure 11-8, is journalized as follows:

GENERAL JOURNAL					Page 48		
Date		Description	Post. Ref.	Debit		Credit	
19XX Feb.	10	Sales Returns and Allowances		175	00		
		Accounts Receivable—Dubin Enterprises				175	00
		Credit Memorandum No. 62.					

|||||||||||||||||||||

C O M M E N T

Observe that this entry was recorded in the general journal. This type of transaction will not fit into any of our special journals.

If the customer was charged for sales tax when the sale was recorded (retail sale), then the Sales Tax Payable account must also be reduced in case of a return or allowance. For example, assume the merchandise sold to Ida Chambers earlier in this chapter is returned on May 9 for credit. The return is recorded as follows:

GENERAL JOURNAL						Page 65	
Date		Description	Post. Ref.	Debit		Credit	
19XX May	9	Sales Returns and Allowances		200	00		
		Sales Tax Payable		10	00		
		Accounts Receivable—Ida Chambers				210	00

In Chapter 12, you will study these transactions from the purchaser's point of view.

Chapter Summary

In this chapter, we turned our attention to a business that sells a product. A business that purchases ready-made merchandise from a supplier and resells it to its customers is known as a *merchandising business.*

In the context of a merchandising business, you learned how to use an accounts receivable ledger to record and access information about charge customers. The sales journal was also introduced. The use of this special journal will allow you to journalize and post sales on account more efficiently.

By the end of Chapter 13 you will be working with the following special journals:

Journal	Transaction
Sales journal	Sales of merchandise on account
Purchases journal	Purchases of merchandise on account
Cash receipts journal	All receipts of cash
Cash payments journal	All payments of cash

Any transaction that does not fit into a special journal is recorded in the general journal. One such transaction would be a sales return or allowance not involving cash. Rather than reduce the Sales account directly, a contra-sales account is used. This account is titled Sales Returns and Allowances. On the income statement, the Sales Returns and Allowances account is subtracted from Sales in arriving at net sales.

In Chapter 12, you will study these transactions from the purchaser's point of view.

Glossary

credit accounts receivable — you owe.

ACCOUNTS RECEIVABLE LEDGER

should Balance

A subsidiary ledger containing a separate account for each charge customer. This ledger supports or explains one general ledger account—the Accounts Receivable (control) account.

CASH PAYMENTS JOURNAL

A special journal used to record all payments of cash.

CASH RECEIPTS JOURNAL

A special journal used to record all receipts of cash.

CONTRA-SALES ACCOUNT

A debit-balance account that appears on the income statement as a subtraction from sales. Also referred to as a contra-revenue account.

CONTROLLING ACCOUNT

A general ledger account containing summary information, which is supported by a subsidiary ledger.

CREDIT MEMORANDUM

A business document prepared by the seller containing information relevant to a sales return or allowance. The word *credit* refers to the credit that will reduce the customer's account receivable.

INVOICE

A business document prepared by the seller and containing all the relevant information about a sale. It is usually prepared with multiple copies. The accounting department receives one of these copies.

MERCHANDISE

Units purchased by a merchandising business for resale to its customers.

MERCHANDISING BUSINESS

A business that purchases a ready-made product from a supplier and resells it to its own customers.

NET SALES

Sales minus contra-sales accounts result in net sales.

PURCHASES JOURNAL

A special journal used to record the purchase of merchandise on account.

RETAIL BUSINESS
A business that sells merchandise to the end user (final consumer).

SALES ALLOWANCE
A reduction in the price of previously sold merchandise. The seller "allows" for defective merchandise by reducing the price.

SALES JOURNAL
A special journal used to record sales of merchandise on account.

SALES RETURN
The return of previously sold merchandise to the seller.

SALES TAX
A tax on retail sales levied by a state or local municipality. It is paid by the retail customer but collected by the retail seller for the taxing authority.

SPECIAL JOURNAL
A journal designed to facilitate the recording and posting of repetitive transactions. The repetitious portion of an entry is made a permanent part of the journal through the use of column headings.

SUBSIDIARY LEDGER
A group of accounts that supports or explains one general ledger account (controlling account).

WHOLESALE BUSINESS
A business that sells merchandise to another business.

Questions for Discussion

1. What is the difference between a merchandising business and a service business?

2. How is merchandise different from supplies?

3. Describe the relationship between the Accounts Receivable (control) account and the accounts receivable ledger.

4. Why are special journals helpful?

5. The sales journal accommodates what type(s) of transaction(s)?

6. Describe the two types of postings required by all special journals. Be sure to indicate when these postings occur.

7. Who levies, pays, and collects a sales tax?

8. Describe the difference between a sales allowance and a sales return.

9. *a.* What is the normal balance (debit or credit) in the Sales Returns and Allowances account?
   b. Why is the Sales Returns and Allowances account referred to as a contra-sales account?

Exercises

EXERCISE 11-1
DEFINITIONS
(L.O.1–7)

Match the following terms with the definitions shown below:

1. Contra-sales account.
2. Merchandise.
3. Sales allowance.
4. Retail business.
5. Controlling account.
6. Merchandising business.
7. Subsidiary ledger.
8. Wholesale business.
9. Net sales.
10. Sales return.

Definitions:

a. A general ledger account containing summary information, which is supported by a subsidiary ledger.

b. A business that purchases a ready-made product from a supplier and resells it to its own customers.

c. A debit-balance account that appears on the income statement as a subtraction from sales. Also referred to as a contra-revenue account.

d. A business that sells merchandise to another business.

e. A business that sells merchandise to the end user (final consumer).

f. Units purchased by a merchandising business for resale to its customers.

g. The return of previously sold merchandise to the seller.

h. The result of sales minus contra-sales accounts.

i. A reduction in the price of previously sold merchandise. The seller "allows" for defective merchandise by reducing the price.

j. A group of accounts that supports or explains one general ledger account (controlling account).

EXERCISE 11-2
DESCRIBE
TRANSACTIONS
(L.O.1, 7)

Describe the transactions indicated by the following T-accounts:

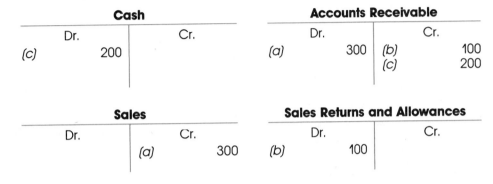

	Cash		
Dr.		Cr.	
(c)	200		

	Accounts Receivable		
Dr.		Cr.	
(a)	300	*(b)*	100
		(c)	200

	Sales		
Dr.		Cr.	
		(a)	300

	Sales Returns and Allowances		
Dr.		Cr.	
(b)	100		

EXERCISE 11-3
SCHEDULE OF
ACCOUNTS RECEIVABLE;
CONTROL ACCOUNT
(L.O.2)

Santiago Brothers' accounts receivable ledger appears as follows:

Account **Ackerman Company**

Date		Item	Post. Ref.	Debit	Credit	Balance
19XX June	1	Balance	✓			300 00
	8		S27	155 00		455 00

Account **Fagan Enterprises**

Date		Item	Post. Ref.	Debit	Credit	Balance
19XX June	1	Balance	✓			823 00
	15		S28	246 00		1,069 00

Account **Romano Corporation**

Date		Item	Post. Ref.	Debit	Credit	Balance
19XX June	1	Balance	✓			137 00
	12		S27	75 00		212 00

Account **Tann and Associates**

Date		Item	Post. Ref.	Debit	Credit	Balance
19XX June	1	Balance	✓			546 00
	24		S28	198 00		744 00

a. Prepare a schedule of accounts receivable as of June 30, 19XX.

b. The balance in the Accounts Receivable (control) account should be what amount?

EXERCISE 11-4
SELECTING PROPER JOURNAL
(L.O.3)

Match the journals with the appropriate transactions.

1. Sales journal.

2. Purchases journal.

3. Cash receipts journal.

4. Cash payments journal.

5. General journal.

a. All receipts of cash.

b. Any transaction that does not fit into a special journal.

c. All sales of merchandise on account.

d. All payments of cash.

e. All purchases of merchandise on account.

EXERCISE 11-5
ENTRIES FOR ACCOUNTS RECEIVABLE TRANSACTIONS
(L.O.2, 7)

Assuming the use of an accounts receivable ledger, record the following transactions in general journal form:

a. Sold merchandise on account to Charles Wang Company, Invoice No. 427, $540.

    b. Issued Credit Memorandum No. 47 to Charles Wang Company to allow for damaged merchandise, $75.

    c. Received check in full payment of the Charles Wang Company account.

EXERCISE 11-6
ENTRIES FOR
ACCOUNTS RECEIVABLE
TRANSACTIONS
(L.O.2, 6, 7)

Assuming the use of an accounts receivable ledger, record the following transactions in general journal form:

    a. Sold merchandise on account to John Moreno, Invoice No. 651, $175 plus 5 percent sales tax.

    b. Issued Credit memorandum No. 68 to John Moreno for $50 of returned merchandise plus sales tax.

    c. Received check in full payment of the John Moreno account.

EXERCISE 11-7
ENTRY FOR
TRANSACTION USING
DOCUMENT
(L.O.4)

Using the following business document, record the transaction in general journal form on the books of The Kitchen Taylor:

THE KITCHEN TAYLOR
2400 Main Street
Wheaton, Illinois 60187

INVOICE NO. 835

Sold to: Williams Company
           20524 Gardendale
           Wheaton, Illinois 60187

Date: June 17, 19XX

Terms: Net 30 days

Quantity	Description	Unit Price	Total
6	WRJ-76 Cabinets	82.00	492.00
1	CMJ-76 Cabinet	57.00	57.00
			549.00

EXERCISE 11-8
ENTRY FOR
TRANSACTION USING
DOCUMENT
(L.O.7)

Using the following business document, record the transaction in general journal form on the books of The Kitchen Taylor:

THE KITCHEN TAYLOR
2400 Main Street
Wheaton, Illinois 60187

CREDIT MEMORANDUM
NO. 69

Credit to: Sirpella Corporation
1724 Rosemont Drive
Glen Ellyn, Illinois 60137

Date: February 15, 19XX

Terms: Net 30 days

Your account is being credited as follows:

| 1 | #430 Hardware | 22.00 |

Problems—Set A

PROBLEM 11-1A
POSTING; SCHEDULE OF ACCOUNTS RECEIVABLE (L.O.2, 5)

(Omit this problem if working papers are not being used.)

A sales journal for Castillo Products is shown in the working papers.

INSTRUCTIONS

1. Post to the accounts receivable ledger.

2. Post to the general ledger.

3. Prepare a schedule of accounts receivable.

PROBLEM 11-2A
JOURNALIZE AND POST USING SALES JOURNAL AND ACCOUNTS RECEIVABLE LEDGER; SCHEDULE OF ACCOUNTS RECEIVABLE (L.O.2, 3, 5, 7)

Asta Electronics, a new business, completed the following transactions during July 19XX.

July 1 Sold merchandise on account to Schirmer, Inc., Invoice No. 1, $157.60.

4 Sold merchandise on account to Carlson Brothers, Invoice No. 2, $835.46.

7 Sold merchandise on account to Barill Associates, Invoice No. 3, $650.

8 Sold merchandise on account to Marlett Corporation, Invoice No. 4, $518.25.

11 Issued Credit Memorandum No. 1 to Carlson Brothers for merchandise returned, $75.

14 Sold merchandise on account to Barill Associates, Invoice No. 5, $75.42.

15 Sold merchandise on account to Schirmer, Inc., Invoice No. 6, $294.60.

17 Sold merchandise on account to Marlett Corporation, Invoice No. 7, $375.

July 21   Issued Credit Memorandum No. 2 to Schirmer, Inc., for merchandise returned, $65.

     24   Sold merchandise on account to Carlson Brothers, Invoice No. 8, $1,749.58.

     27   Sold merchandise on account to Barill Associates, Invoice No. 9, $776.

     31   Issued Credit Memorandum No. 3 to Marlett Corporation for merchandise returned, $47.50.

INSTRUCTIONS

1. For those students not using the working papers:
   a. This company uses a sales journal (as illustrated on page 374) and a general journal. Number the sales journal page 1 and the general journal page 1.
   b. Open ledger accounts as follows:

GENERAL LEDGER

Account Title	Account No.
Accounts Receivable	112
Sales	410
Sales Returns and Allowances	411

ACCOUNTS RECEIVABLE LEDGER

Account Title

Barill Associates
Carlson Brothers
Marlett Corporation
Schirmer, Inc.

2. Record these transactions in the appropriate journal.
   a. Post to the accounts receivable ledger daily.
   b. Post the general journal daily.

3. Post the sales journal column total at the end of the month.

4. Prepare a schedule of accounts receivable.

PROBLEM 11-3A

JOURNALIZE AND POST USING SALES JOURNAL AND ACCOUNTS RECEIVABLE LEDGER; SCHEDULE OF ACCOUNTS RECEIVABLE (L.O.2, 3, 5, 7)

Polonus Enterprises completed the following transactions during November 19XX:

Nov. 3   Sold merchandise on account to Ambrust Corporation, Invoice No. 251, $742.

     5   Sold merchandise on account to Richardson Labs, Invoice No. 252, $257.40.

Nov.   8   Issued Credit Memorandum No. 37 to Ambrust Corporation for merchandise returned, $42.

11   Sold merchandise on account to Hager Corporation, Invoice No. 253, $463.50.

13   Sold merchandise on account to Marine Products, Invoice No. 254, $547.25.

16   Sold merchandise on account to Richardson Labs, Invoice No. 255, $340.

18   Issued Credit Memorandum No. 38 to Hager Corporation for merchandise returned, $55.

20   Sold merchandise on account to Marine Products, Invoice No. 256, $387.75.

23   Sold merchandise on account to Ambrust Corporation, Invoice No. 257, $839.

24   Issued Credit Memorandum No. 39 to Richardson Labs for merchandise returned, $24.50.

27   Sold merchandise on account to Hager Corporation, Invoice No. 258, $983.25.

30   Sold merchandise on account to Marine Products, Invoice No. 259, $837.

INSTRUCTIONS

1. For those students not using the working papers:
   a. This company uses a sales journal (as illustrated on page 374) and a general journal. Number the sales journal page 59 and the general journal page 16.
   b. Open ledger accounts as follows:

GENERAL LEDGER

Account Title	Account No.	Balance
Accounts Receivable	112	$ 1,342.50
Sales	410	39,746.25
Sales Returns and Allowances	411	415.37

ACCOUNTS RECEIVABLE LEDGER

Account Title	Balance
Ambrust Corporation	$117.22
Hager Corporation	373.47
Marine Products	565.69
Richardson Labs	286.12

2. Record these transactions in the appropriate journal.
   a. Post to the accounts receivable ledger daily.
   b. Post the general journal daily.

3. Post the sales journal column total at the end of the month.

4. Prepare a schedule of accounts receivable.

**PROBLEM
11-4A**

JOURNALIZE AND POST
USING SALES JOURNAL
AND ACCOUNTS
RECEIVABLE LEDGER;
SCHEDULE OF
ACCOUNTS RECEIVABLE
(L.O.2, 3, 5–7)

Jack's Videoland is a retail business selling a wide variety of home-video products. The state levies a 5 percent sales tax that must be collected by all retailers. Although most of Jack's sales are for cash, a few customers have charge accounts. Charge sales for February 19XX were as follows:

Feb. 1   Sold a 25-inch color television on account to Theresa Kapoor, Invoice No. 624, $595 plus sales tax.

   6   Sold a video recorder on account to Karen Tucker, Invoice No. 647, $499 plus sales tax.

   11   Sold blank video cassettes on account to Alan Bergeson, Invoice No. 659, $60 plus sales tax.

   16   Issued Credit Memorandum No. 46 to Theresa Kapoor to allow for a scratch on the television cabinet (Invoice No. 624), $50 plus sales tax.

   20   Sold a video camera on account to Robert Zelenka, Invoice No. 672, $650 plus sales tax.

   25   Sold a 45-inch television on account to Kathy Davidson, Invoice No. 689, $2,495 plus sales tax.

   28   Issued Credit Memorandum No. 47 to Alan Bergeson for the return of two broken video cassettes (Invoice No. 659), $10 plus sales tax.

INSTRUCTIONS

1. For those students not using the working papers:
   a. This company uses a sales journal (as illustrated on page 380) and a general journal. Number the sales journal page 71 and the general journal page 29.
   b. Open ledger accounts as follows:

GENERAL LEDGER

Account Title	Account No.	Balance
Accounts Receivable	11	$ 1,243.56
Sales Tax Payable	21	792.75
Sales	40	20,575.50
Sales Returns and Allowances	41	342.17

ACCOUNTS RECEIVABLE LEDGER

Account Title	Balance
Alan Bergeson	$ 85.12
Kathy Davidson	247.75
Theresa Kapoor	569.90
Karen Tucker	172.40
Robert Zelenka	168.39

2. Record these transactions in the appropriate journal.
   a. Post to the accounts receivable ledger daily.
   b. Post the general journal daily.

3. Post the sales journal column totals at the end of the month.

4. Prepare a schedule of accounts receivable.

Problems—Set B

PROBLEM 11-1B

POSTING; SCHEDULE OF ACCOUNTS RECEIVABLE (L.O.2, 5)

(Omit this problem if working papers are not being used.)

A sales journal for Mantia Company is shown in the working papers.

INSTRUCTIONS

1. Post to the accounts receivable ledger.

2. Post to the general ledger.

3. Prepare a schedule of accounts receivable.

PROBLEM 11-2B

JOURNALIZE AND POST USING SALES JOURNAL AND ACCOUNTS RECEIVABLE LEDGER; SCHEDULE OF ACCOUNTS RECEIVABLE (L.O.2, 3, 5, 7)

Landi Limited, a new business, completed the following transactions during June 19XX.

June 2 Sold merchandise on account to Elgot Company, Invoice No. 1, $315.20.

3 Sold merchandise on account to Ada Enterprises, Invoice No. 2, $1,670.92.

6 Sold merchandise on account to Zak Industries, Invoice No. 3, $1,300.

7 Sold merchandise on account to Helman Corporation, Invoice No. 4, $1,036.50.

10 Issued Credit Memorandum No. 1 to Ada Enterprises for merchandise returned, $150.

13 Sold merchandise on account to Zak Industries, Invoice No. 5, $150.84.

14 Sold merchandise on account to Elgot Company, Invoice No. 6, $589.20.

18 Sold merchandise on account to Helman Corporation, Invoice No. 7, $750.

June 20   Issued Credit Memorandum No. 2 to Elgot Company for merchandise returned, $85.

23   Sold merchandise on account to Ada Enterprises, Invoice No. 8, $947.85.

28   Sold merchandise on account to Zak Industries, Invoice No. 9, $667.

30   Issued Credit Memorandum No. 3 to Helman Corporation for merchandise returned, $74.25.

INSTRUCTIONS

1. For those students not using the working papers:
   a. This company uses a sales journal (as illustrated on page 374) and a general journal. Number the sales journal page 1 and the general journal page 1.
   b. Open ledger accounts as follows:

GENERAL LEDGER

Account Title	Account No.
Accounts Receivable	112
Sales	410
Sales Returns and Allowances	411

ACCOUNTS RECEIVABLE LEDGER

Account Title

Ada Enterprises
Elgot Company
Helman Corporation
Zak Industries

2. Record these transactions in the appropriate journal.
   a. Post to the accounts receivable ledger daily.
   b. Post the general journal daily.

3. Post the sales journal column total at the end of the month.

4. Prepare a schedule of accounts receivable.

PROBLEM 11-3B

JOURNALIZE AND POST USING SALES JOURNAL AND ACCOUNTS RECEIVABLE LEDGER; SCHEDULE OF ACCOUNTS RECEIVABLE (L.O.2, 3, 5, 7)

Wood Associates completed the following transactions during August 19XX:

Aug.	4	Sold merchandise on account to Bader Corporation, Invoice No. 512, $247.
	6	Sold merchandise on account to Tasker Company, Invoice No. 513, $428.50.
	9	Issued Credit Memorandum No. 72 to Bader Corporation for merchandise returned, $34.
	12	Sold merchandise on account to Grant Corporation, Invoice No. 514, $365.45.
	14	Sold merchandise on account to Lemont Industries, Invoice No. 515, $472.55.
	17	Sold merchandise on account to Tasker Company, Invoice No. 516, $403.
	19	Issued Credit Memorandum No. 73 to Grant Corporation for merchandise returned, $27.
	21	Sold merchandise on account to Lemont Industries, Invoice No. 517, $573.87.
	24	Sold merchandise on account to Bader Corporation, Invoice No. 518, $398.
	25	Issued Credit Memorandum No. 74 to Tasker Company for merchandise returned, $37.25.
	28	Sold merchandise on account to Grant Corporation, Invoice No. 519, $829.35.
	31	Sold merchandise on account to Lemont Industries, Invoice No. 520, $738.

INSTRUCTIONS

1. For those students not using the working papers:

    a. This company uses a sales journal (as illustrated on page 374) and a general journal. Number the sales journal page 95 and the general journal page 34.

    b. Open ledger accounts as follows:

GENERAL LEDGER

Account Title	Account No.	Balance
Accounts Receivable	112	$ 1,532.75
Sales	410	42,899.50
Sales Returns and Allowances . . .	411	472.14

ACCOUNTS RECEIVABLE LEDGER

Account Title	Balance
Bader Corporation	$471.50
Grant Corporation	214.29
Lemont Industries	175.46
Tasker Company	671.50

2. Record these transactions in the appropriate journal.

    a. Post to the accounts receivable ledger daily.

    b. Post the general journal daily.

3. Post the sales journal column total at the end of the month.

4. Prepare a schedule of accounts receivable.

PROBLEM 11-4B

JOURNALIZE AND POST USING SALES JOURNAL AND ACCOUNTS RECEIVABLE LEDGER; SCHEDULE OF ACCOUNTS RECEIVABLE (L.O.2, 3, 5–7)

DuPage Sporting Goods is a retail business selling a wide range of sports products. The state levies a 4 percent retail sales tax that must be collected by all retailers. Although most of DuPage's sales are for cash, a few customers have charge accounts. Charge sales for March 19XX were as follows:

Mar. 2   Sold a 10-speed bicycle on account to Paul Sherman, Invoice No. 705, $250 plus sales tax.

     5   Sold cross-country skis on account to Judy Ficks, Invoice No. 720, $165 plus sales tax.

    12   Sold a set of weights on account to Harry Barker, Invoice No. 731, $128 plus sales tax.

    17   Issued Credit Memorandum No. 58 to Paul Sherman to allow for a dented fender on the bicycle (Invoice No. 705), $25 plus sales tax.

    21   Sold a rowing machine on account to Megan Park, Invoice No. 745, $220 plus sales tax.

    26   Sold a snorkel mask on account to Mike Walters, Invoice No. 767, $45 plus sales tax.

    31   Issued Credit Memorandum No. 61 to Harry Barker for the return of a weight set (Invoice No. 731), $128 plus sales tax.

INSTRUCTIONS

1. For those students not using the working papers:

    a. This company uses a sales journal (as illustrated on page 380) and a general journal. Number the sales journal page 83 and the general journal page 26.

b. Open ledger accounts as follows:

GENERAL LEDGER

Account Title	Account No.	Balance
Accounts Receivable	11	$ 1,475.50
Sales Tax Payable	21	864.22
Sales	40	27,857.60
Sales Returns and Allowances	41	410.87

ACCOUNTS RECEIVABLE LEDGER

Account Title	Balance
Harry Barker	$147.50
Judy Ficks	562.48
Megan Park	394.67
Paul Sherman	89.90
Mike Walters	280.95

2. Record these transactions in the appropriate journal.
   a. Post to the accounts receivable ledger daily.
   b. Post the general journal daily.

3. Post the sales journal column totals at the end of the month.

4. Prepare a schedule of accounts receivable.

Mini-Cases

CASE 11-1

Your friend, Jennifer, owns an architectural firm. She complains that her book-keeper often posts to the wrong account in the accounts receivable ledger. These posting errors go undetected, resulting in customers receiving incorrect statements of their account. Jennifer thinks she has this problem solved: "I'm insisting that a schedule of accounts receivable be prepared every month before the statements of account are mailed to customers." Will this solve Jennifer's problem? Why?

CASE 11-2

You have suggested the use of a sales journal to your new client, Richard Moy. Mr. Moy doesn't understand how a journal that accommodates only one type of transaction could save much time or effort. How would you respond?

CASE 11-3

Marge Flashing, your new employer, does not use an accounts receivable ledger. Instead, two files of customer invoices are kept:

1. Unpaid invoices in alphabetical order by customer name.

2. Paid invoices in alphabetical order by customer name.

When Mrs. Flashing wants to know how much a customer currently owes, she refers to the unpaid invoice file. Mrs. Flashing is skeptical of your suggestion to add an accounts receivable ledger. How would you convince her that an accounts receivable ledger would be an improvement?

Merchandising Business: Accounting for Purchases

AFTER STUDYING THIS CHAPTER, YOU SHOULD BE ABLE TO:

1 Describe the purchasing process.

2 Record the purchase of merchandise on account.

3 Use an accounts payable ledger.

4 Journalize and post using a purchases journal.

5 Record purchases returns and allowances.

6 Record transportation charges.

In Chapter 11, you were introduced to a merchandising business. However, the discussion was limited to the selling activities of a merchandising business. In Chapter 12, we will shift our attention to the purchasing activities of a merchandising business. After studying the purchasing process, you will learn to use an accounts payable ledger and a purchases journal as well as how to record other purchase-related transactions.

THE PURCHASING PROCESS

OBJECTIVE 1
DESCRIBE THE
PURCHASING PROCESS

Purchasing procedures often vary based on the size of the business. Our discussion describes the typical purchasing process for a moderate to large-sized firm. This process is illustrated in Figure 12-1.

Generally, departmental requests to buy merchandise must be in writing. The form used for such requests is known as a purchase requisition. As shown in Figure 12-2, the purchase requisition is sent to the purchasing department and indicates what is needed and when it is needed. After the purchase requisition has been approved, the purchasing department prepares a purchase order, as shown in Figure 12-3, which is sent to a supplier. A copy of the purchase order is also sent to the purchaser's accounting department. The purchase order is an offer to purchase the requested goods from the supplier. If the offer is accepted, the supplier will prepare an invoice like the one shown in Figure 12-4. This invoice is sent to the purchaser's accounting department about the time the goods are shipped. The accounting department compares the purchase order with the invoice to be sure the company is being billed for what was ordered and that the price is correct. After comparing the purchase order with the invoice, the accounting department makes a journal entry to record the purchase.

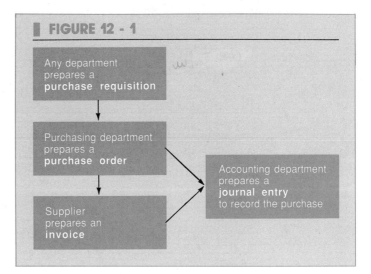

FIGURE 12 - 1

Any department prepares a **purchase requisition**

Purchasing department prepares a **purchase order**

Supplier prepares an **invoice**

Accounting department prepares a **journal entry** to record the purchase

FIGURE 12 - 2

THE KITCHEN TAYLOR   **PURCHASE REQUISITION NO. H534**
2400 Main Street
Wheaton, Illinois 60187

To: Purchasing Department   Date Requested: Oct. 20, 19XX

From: Hardware Department   Date Required: Nov. 20, 19XX

Quantity	Description
200	Magnetic door latch sets, 1" width

Requested by: *C. Colombo*   Approved by: *W. Johnson*

Date Ordered: Oct. 26, 19XX   P.O. No. 1283

FIGURE 12 - 3

THE KITCHEN TAYLOR   **PURCHASE ORDER NO. 1283**
2400 Main Street
Wheaton, Illinois 60187

To: Franklin Products   Date: Oct. 26, 19XX
      5370 Park Boulevard   FOB: Shipping Point
      Glen Ellyn, Illinois 60137   Terms: 2/10, n/30

Quantity	Description	Unit Price	Total
200	Magnetic door latch sets, 1" width	1.05	210.00

Ordered by: *Emma Frank*

▌ **FIGURE 12 - 4**

FRANKLIN PRODUCTS   **INVOICE NO. 849**
5370 Park Boulevard
Glen Ellyn, Illinois 60137

Sold to: The Kitchen Taylor   Date: Nov. 1, 19XX
           2400 Main Street   Terms: 2/10, n/30
           Wheaton, Illinois 60187   F.O.B.:   Shipping Point
                                       P.O. No.: 1283

Quantity	Description	Unit Price	Total
200	Magnetic door latch sets, 1″ width	1.05	210.00

*invoice is key when booking
liabilities under accrual system*

▌▌▌▌ THE PURCHASES ACCOUNT

OBJECTIVE 2
RECORD THE PURCHASE
OF MERCHANDISE ON
ACCOUNT

As you will recall, The Kitchen Taylor is now a merchandising business selling cabinets and related hardware. Whenever The Kitchen Taylor purchases merchandise from a supplier, an account titled Purchases is debited. This account has a narrow scope of activity. The Purchases account is used only for the purchase of merchandise. *(expense)*

|||||||||||||||||||||
C O M M E N T

As you learned in Chapter 11, a merchandising business does not make the product it sells. It purchases the product from a supplier, and then resells this product to its own customers. Units purchased by a merchandising business for resale are referred to as merchandise.

Based on the invoice shown in Figure 12-4, The Kitchen Taylor's accountant makes the following entry to record the purchase of merchandise on account:

	GENERAL JOURNAL			Page 59	
Date	Description	Post. Ref.	Debit	Credit	
19XX Nov. 3	Purchases		210 00		
	Accounts Payable			210 00	

The Purchases account is a temporary account. At year-end, it will be closed along with all the other temporary accounts (revenue, expense, drawing). In Chapter 15, we will consider the placement of the Purchases account on the income statement.

THE ACCOUNTS PAYABLE LEDGER

OBJECTIVE 3
USE AN ACCOUNTS
PAYABLE LEDGER

In Chapter 11, you were introduced to the concept of a controlling account and a subsidiary ledger. You applied that concept to accounts receivable. Now we will apply that concept to accounts payable.

In the past, you recorded transactions involving accounts payable by simply debiting or crediting the Accounts Payable account. The resulting balance in the Accounts Payable account indicated the total amount owed to all creditors. This information, although useful, is not adequate. Just as a business must be able to identify its charge customers, a business must also know how much it owes to each of its creditors. Another subsidiary ledger, called the **accounts payable ledger,** conveniently adds this information to our accounting system.

The Accounts Payable account in the general ledger will now be referred to as a control or controlling account. As in the past, the Accounts Payable account contains only summary information. The accounts payable ledger provides the necessary detail. It contains a separate account for each creditor. As in the accounts receivable ledger, the accounts payable ledger accounts are kept in alphabetical order.

When journalizing, the creditor's name must be indicated whenever the Accounts Payable account is debited or credited. In posting, all debits and credits to Accounts Payable must be posted to the Accounts Payable (control) account in the general ledger and to the creditor's account in the accounts payable ledger.

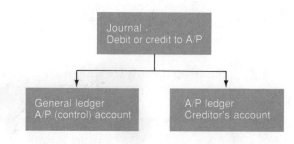

After all journalizing and posting is completed, the balance in the Accounts Payable (control) account should equal the total of the creditor account balances in the accounts payable ledger. To verify this equality of debits and credits, a schedule of accounts payable is usually prepared at the end of each month. We'll demonstrate the preparation of a schedule of accounts payable later in this chapter.

From now on, we will assume every company has both an accounts receivable ledger and an accounts payable ledger.

▮▮▮▮ THE PURCHASES JOURNAL

JOURNALIZING

OBJECTIVE 4
JOURNALIZE AND POST
USING A PURCHASES
JOURNAL

In a merchandising business, purchases of merchandise on account occur frequently. Each purchase requires a debit to the Purchases account and a credit to the Accounts Payable account. As noted in Chapter 11, a special journal for purchases greatly reduces the time and effort required to record and post such repetitive transactions. Through the use of a Dr. Purchases, Cr. Accounts Payable column, the repetitious portion of the entry is made into a permanent part of the journal. To demonstrate, let's consider The Kitchen Taylor's purchases journal:

	PURCHASES JOURNAL					Page 12	
Date	Supplier's Name	Invoice Number	Invoice Date	Terms	Post. Ref.	Dr. Purchases Cr. Accts. Pay.	
19XX Nov. 3	Franklin Products	849	11/1	2/10, n/30		210	00
8	Avery Industries	4517	11/5	1/10, n/30		2,632	00
15	Saroya Corporation	923	11/12	n/30		871	00
21	Kavan Manufacturing	A556	11/19	2/10, n/30		1,560	00
25	Franklin Products	893	11/22	2/10, n/30		975	00
30	Saroya Corporation	941	11/26	n/30		1,624	00

In studying The Kitchen Taylor's purchases journal, observe the following:

- The **purchases journal** accommodates only one type of transaction: the purchase of merchandise on account.

- The portion of the entry that never changes (debit Purchases, credit Accounts Payable) is made permanent through the use of a column heading. Since the debit and credit amounts are always the same, this can all be done in a single column.

- The accountant needs to enter only the information that changes: the date, supplier's name, invoice number and date, terms, and the amount of the purchase.

- Each transaction requires only one line.

- No explanations are necessary since every transaction represents a purchase of merchandise on account.

POSTING

As indicated in Chapter 11, all special journals require two types of postings. Let's demonstrate by posting The Kitchen Taylor's purchases journal.

1. **Individual postings.** These postings are necessary where each figure in a column must be posted to a *different* account. These items are usually posted on a daily basis. Since The Kitchen Taylor uses an accounts payable ledger, each credit to Accounts Payable must be posted to the individual creditor's account in the accounts payable ledger. After posting, the purchases journal and the accounts payable ledger appear as shown in Figures 12-5 and 12-6.

||||||||||||||||||||||
C O M M E N T

The check marks in the Posting Reference column of the purchases journal indicate that these amounts have been posted to the individual creditor's accounts in the accounts payable ledger.

▌ FIGURE 12 - 5

PURCHASES JOURNAL   Page 12

Date		Supplier's Name	Invoice Number	Invoice Date	Terms	Post. Ref.	Dr. Purchases Cr. Accts. Pay.	
19XX Nov.	3	Franklin Products	849	11/1	2/10, n/30	√	210	00
	8	Avery Industries	4517	11/5	1/10, n/30	√	2,632	00
	15	Saroya Corporation	923	11/12	n/30	√	871	00
	21	Kavan Manufacturing	A556	11/19	2/10, n/30	√	1,560	00
	25	Franklin Products	893	11/22	2/10, n/30	√	975	00
	30	Saroya Corporation	941	11/26	n/30	√	1,624	00

ACCOUNTS PAYABLE LEDGER

Account __Avery Industries__

Date		Item	Post. Ref.	Debit	Credit	Balance
19XX Nov.	1	Balance	√			241 00
	8		P12		2,632 00	2,873 00

Account __Franklin Products__

Date		Item	Post. Ref.	Debit	Credit	Balance
19XX Nov.	1	Balance	√			372 00
	3		P12		210 00	582 00
	25		P12		975 00	1,557 00

Account __Kavan Manufacturing__

Date		Item	Post. Ref.	Debit	Credit	Balance
19XX Nov.	1	Balance	√			93 00
	21		P12		1,560 00	1,653 00

Account __Saroya Corporation__

Date		Item	Post. Ref.	Debit	Credit	Balance
19XX Nov.	1	Balance	√			117 00
	15		P12		871 00	988 00
	30		P12		1,624 00	2,612 00

Observe that the posting references in the accounts payable ledger begin with the letter *P*. This indicates the posted information came from the purchases journal.

2. Column total postings. Column totals are posted when all the figures in a column must be posted to the *same* account. Rather than making many individual postings to the same account, one posting is made at the end of the month with the total. As the column heading in the purchases journal indicates, the column total must be posted as a debit to the Purchases account in the general ledger and as a credit to the Accounts Payable (control) account in the general ledger. After posting, the purchases journal and the Accounts Payable and Purchases accounts appear as shown in Figures 12-7 and 12-8.

The posting reference for a column total posting is placed in parentheses below the total. The debit posting reference is written below and to the left. The credit posting reference is written below and to the right.

▌ **FIGURE 12 - 7**

PURCHASES JOURNAL   Page 12

Date		Supplier's Name	Invoice Number	Invoice Date	Terms	Post. Ref.	Dr. Purchases Cr. Accts. Pay.	
19XX Nov.	3	Franklin Products	849	11/1	2/10, n/30	✓	210	00
	8	Avery Industries	4517	11/5	1/10, n/30	✓	2,632	00
	15	Saroya Corporation	923	11/12	n/30	✓	871	00
	21	Kavan Manufacturing	A556	11/19	2/10, n/30	✓	1,560	00
	25	Franklin Products	893	11/22	2/10, n/30	✓	975	00
	30	Saroya Corporation	941	11/26	n/30	✓	1,624	00
	30						7,872	00
							(501)	(210)

FIGURE 12 - 8

GENERAL LEDGER

Account **Accounts Payable**   Account No. 210

Date		Item	Post. Ref.	Debit	Credit	Balance Debit	Balance Credit
19XX Nov.	1	Balance	✓				823 00
	30		P12		7,872 00		8,695 00

Account **Purchases**   Account No. 501

Date		Item	Post. Ref.	Debit	Credit	Balance Debit	Balance Credit
19XX Nov.	1	Balance	✓			35,800 00	
	30		P12	7,872 00		43,672 00	

Figure 12-9 shows the flow of information from the purchases journal to the accounts payable ledger and the general ledger.

PURCHASES JOURNAL

Page 12

Date		Supplier's Name	Invoice Number	Invoice Date	Terms	Post. Ref.	Dr. Purchases Cr. Accts. Pay.	
19XX Nov.	3	Franklin Products	849	11/1	2/10, n/30	√	210	00
	8	Avery Industries	4517	11/5	1/10, n/30	√	2,632	00
	15	Saroya Corporation	923	11/12	n/30	√	871	00
	21	Kavan Manufacturing	A556	11/19	2/10, n/30	√	1,560	00
	25	Franklin Products	893	11/22	2/10, n/30	√	975	00
	30	Saroya Corporation	941	11/26	n/30	√	1,624	00
	30						7,872	00
							(501) (210)	

ACCOUNTS PAYABLE LEDGER

GENERAL LEDGER

▐▐▐▐ THE SCHEDULE OF ACCOUNTS PAYABLE

After all journalizing and posting is completed, a schedule of accounts payable is prepared. As mentioned earlier, this schedule verifies the equality of debits and credits in the Accounts Payable account and the accounts payable ledger. On November 30, The Kitchen Taylor prepared the following schedule of accounts payable from information taken directly from the accounts payable ledger shown in Figure 12-6:

THE KITCHEN TAYLOR Schedule of Accounts Payable November 30, 19XX		
Avery Industries	$2,873	00
Franklin Products	1,557	00
Kavan Manufacturing	1,653	00
Saroya Corporation	2,612	00
Total accounts payable	$8,695	00

The total accounts payable shown on this schedule ($8,695) should be equal to the November 30 balance in the Accounts Payable (control) account in the general ledger ($8,695) shown in Figure 12-8.

▐▐▐▐ PURCHASES RETURNS AND ALLOWANCES

OBJECTIVE 5
RECORD PURCHASES
RETURNS AND
ALLOWANCES

To the purchaser, a return of merchandise to the supplier is a **purchase return.** An allowance granted by the supplier to the purchaser for damaged but usable merchandise is a **purchase allowance.** The purchaser records such transactions by crediting an account titled Purchases Returns and Allowances. This account is known as a **contra-purchases account.** On the income statement, the Purchases Returns and Allowances account is subtracted from the Purchases account in arriving at net purchases. In Chapter 15, we will consider its presentation on the income statement in greater detail.

||||||||||||||||||||
C O M M E N T

To the purchaser, a return of merchandise to the seller is a purchase return. To the seller, this returned merchandise represents a sales return. These transactions are opposite sides of the same coin.

To demonstrate the accounting for a purchase return, let's assume that The Kitchen Taylor returns a portion of the merchandise purchased from

Saroya Corporation on November 30. This was a purchase on account that has not yet been paid. The Kitchen Taylor receives a copy of the following credit memo from Saroya Corporation.

SAROYA CORPORATION   **CREDIT MEMORANDUM NO. 143**
2610 Eastern Avenue
Wheaton, Illinois 60187

Credit to: The Kitchen Taylor   Date: Dec. 7, 19XX
             2400 Main Street
             Wheaton, Illinois 60187   Terms: N/30

Your account is being credited as follows:

1   Model A-46 Cabinet   150.00

To record this purchase return, The Kitchen Taylor makes the following entry:

Date		Description	Post. Ref.	Debit		Credit	
		GENERAL JOURNAL				Page 59	
19XX Dec.	9	Accounts Payable—Saroya Corporation		150	00		
		Purchases Returns and Allowances				150	00
		Credit Memorandum No. 143.					

The debit to Accounts Payable—Saroya Corporation reduces the amount owed to Saroya Corporation. The credit to Purchases Returns and Allowances reduces net purchases on the income statement.

|||||||||||||||||||
C O M M E N T   Observe that this entry was recorded in the general journal. This type of transaction will not fit into any of our special journals.

▌▌▌▌ TRANSPORTATION CHARGES

When a business purchases merchandise, or any other asset, transportation charges must be considered. Does the seller pay the transportation charges or does the purchaser pay the transportation charges? In negotiating the purchase, this question must be settled.

If the seller is to pay, the invoice will indicate that the transportation terms are **FOB destination.** This means the goods will be shipped free on board (FOB) to the purchaser's place of business (destination). If the purchaser is to pay, the invoice will indicate **FOB shipping point.** This means that the purchaser must pay to transport the goods from the seller's place of business (shipping point).

Either way, the purchaser will ultimately pay the transportation charges. If the terms are FOB destination, the purchaser will pay indirectly through a higher purchase price. If the terms are FOB shipping point, the purchaser pays the carrier directly or is billed by the seller for the cost of transportation.

From an accounting point of view, the transportation charges are considered to be part of the cost of the item being purchased. For example, let's assume that on July 17, The Kitchen Taylor purchases $1,200 worth of merchandise on account, FOB destination. The following entry is made to record the purchase.

July 17	Purchases	1,200	
	Accounts Payable		1,200

In this case, we can assume that the cost of transportation is part of the $1,200 purchase price that is debited to the Purchases account.

Let's try another example. This time, let's assume that on August 19, The Kitchen Taylor purchases $800 worth of merchandise on account, FOB shipping point. This transaction is recorded as follows:

Aug. 19	Purchases	800	
	Accounts Payable		800

On August 20, the merchandise is received. On arrival, The Kitchen Taylor pays the carrier $50 in cash to cover the cost of transportation. This transaction is journalized as follows:

Aug. 20	Purchases	50	
	Cash		50

Observe that the cost of transportation is debited to the Purchases account. It is considered to be part of the cost of the merchandise.

Let's try another example. On September 21, The Kitchen Taylor purchases office equipment on account, $775, FOB shipping point.

Sept. 21   Office Equipment 775

Accounts Payable   775

The office equipment is received on September 23. On arrival, The Kitchen Taylor pays the carrier $65 in cash to cover the cost of transportation.

Sept. 23   Office Equipment 65

Cash   65

The cost of transportation is considered to be part of the cost of the office equipment. The transportation charges are therefore debited to the Office Equipment account.

Some businesses prefer to record the transportation charges on purchases of merchandise in a separate account titled Freight-In or Transportation-In. In this case, the balance in the Freight-In account is added to the balance in the Purchases account to determine the delivered cost of the merchandise. In this text, we will follow the previously described procedure of debiting the Purchases account for the cost of transporting merchandise.

Chapter Summary

In this chapter, we studied the purchasing activities of a merchandising business. The purchasing process is summarized in the following flowchart:

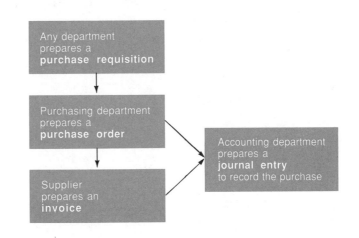

Purchases of merchandise are recorded by debiting the Purchases account. This is a temporary account that will be closed to the capital account at year-end.

Through the use of an accounts payable ledger, we can conveniently keep track of how much we owe to each of our creditors. The Accounts Payable (control) account in the general ledger contains summary information, while the accounts payable ledger provides the detail. At the end of the month, a schedule of accounts payable is prepared to verify the equality of debits and credits in the Accounts Payable (control) account and the accounts payable ledger.

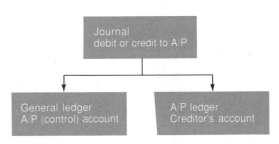

In a merchandising business, purchases of merchandise on account occur frequently. Each time, the Purchases account is debited and the Accounts Payable account is credited. A purchases journal greatly reduces the time and effort required to record and post this repetitive transaction.

A return or allowance for damaged merchandise is recorded with a credit to the Purchases Returns and Allowances account. This account is known as a contra-purchases account. On the income statement, the Purchases Returns and Allowances account is subtracted from the Purchases account in arriving at net purchases.

In negotiating a purchase, transportation terms must be considered. If the seller is to pay, the invoice indicates FOB destination. If the purchaser is to pay, the invoice indicates FOB shipping point. From an accounting point of view, transportation charges are considered to be part of the cost of the item being purchased.

Glossary

ACCOUNTS PAYABLE LEDGER

A subsidiary ledger containing a separate account for each creditor. This ledger supports or explains one general ledger account—the Accounts Payable (control) account.

CONTRA-PURCHASES ACCOUNT

A credit-balance account that appears on the income statement as a subtraction from purchases in arriving at net purchases.

FOB DESTINATION

The goods are shipped free on board (FOB) to the purchaser's place of business (destination). The seller pays the transportation charges.

FOB SHIPPING POINT

The purchaser pays to transport goods from the seller's place of business (shipping point).

INVOICE

A business document prepared by the seller containing all the relevant information about a sale. To the seller it is a sales invoice. To the purchaser it is a purchase invoice.

NET PURCHASES

Purchases minus contra-purchases accounts.

PURCHASE ALLOWANCE

A reduction in the price of previously purchased merchandise. The seller "allows" for defective merchandise by reducing the price to the purchaser.

PURCHASE ORDER

An offer to purchase goods from a supplier.

PURCHASE REQUISITION

A form used by departments to request the purchase of necessary items. It is sent to the purchasing department.

PURCHASE RETURN

The return of previously purchased merchandise to the supplier.

PURCHASES JOURNAL

A special journal used to record the purchase of merchandise on account.

Questions for Discussion

1. What is the purpose of the following?
   a. Purchase requisition.
   b. Purchase order.
   c. Purchase invoice.

2. The Purchases account:
   a. Is used to record what type of transaction?
   b. Has a normal balance on the _____ (debit or credit) side.
   c. Is a _____ (temporary or permanent) account.

3. Describe the relationship between the Accounts Payable (control) account and the accounts payable ledger.

4. The purchases journal accommodates what type(s) of transaction(s)?

5. In posting a purchases journal, what must be posted individually and usually on a daily basis?

6. In posting a purchases journal:
   a. To which account(s) is the column total posted?
   b. When is the column total posted?

7. The Purchases Returns and Allowances account:
   a. Is used to record what type(s) of transaction(s)?
   b. Has a normal balance on the _____ (debit or credit) side.
   c. Is _____ (added or subtracted) from the _____ account in arriving at net purchases.

8. Who pays the transportation charges under the following terms?
   a. FOB destination?
   b. FOB shipping point?

Exercises

Match the following terms with the definitions shown below:

1. FOB destination.
2. Net purchases.
3. Accounts payable ledger.
4. Purchase allowance.
5. Purchases journal.
6. FOB shipping point.
7. Purchase order.
8. Purchase return.
9. Contra-purchases account.
10. Purchase requisition.

Definitions:

a. The return of previously purchased merchandise to the supplier.

b. A form used by departments to request the purchase of necessary items. It is sent to the purchasing department.

c. Terms indicating that goods will be shipped free on board to the purchaser's place of business. The seller will pay the transportation charges.

d. A credit-balance account that appears on the income statement as a subtraction from purchases in arriving at net purchases.

e. An offer to purchase goods from a supplier.

f. A reduction in the price of previously purchased merchandise. The seller "allows" for defective merchandise by reducing the price to the purchaser.

g. Result of purchases minus contra-purchases accounts.

h. Terms indicating the purchaser must pay to transport goods from the seller's place of business.

i. A subsidiary ledger containing a separate account for each creditor.

j. A special journal used to record the purchase of merchandise on account.

EXERCISE 12-2
ENTRIES FOR PURCHASE
AND SALE USING
INVOICE
(L.O.2)

Assuming the following invoice represents the purchase and sale of merchandise on account, record the transaction in general journal form on the books of:

a. Norville Products.
b. Webster Corporation.

WEBSTER CORPORATION	**INVOICE NO. 538**
455 Raintree Court	
Lutherville, Maryland 21093	

| Sold to: | Norville Products 1717 Beach Road Baltimore, Maryland 21204 | Date: February 5, 19XX Terms: Net 30 days FOB: Shipping point P.O. No: 284 |

Quantity	Description	Unit Price	Total
145	#M-56 Metal hooks	1.36	197.20

EXERCISE 12-3
ENTRIES FOR
MERCHANDISE RETURN
USING CREDIT
MEMORANDUM
(L.O.5)

Assuming the following credit memo represents the return of merchandise on account, record the transaction on the books of:

a. Suarez Company.
b. Maple Corporation.

SUAREZ COMPANY
245 Seaton Road
Riverdale, New York 10463

CREDIT MEMORANDUM NO. 172

Credit to: Maple Corporation
            4760 Fulton Street
            Berkeley, California 94705

Date: Aug. 14, 19XX

Terms: Net 30 days

Your account is being credited as follows:

| 1 | Model K-47 Motor | 185.00 |

EXERCISE 12-4
DESCRIBE
TRANSACTIONS
(L.O.2, 5)

Describe the transactions indicated by the following T-accounts:

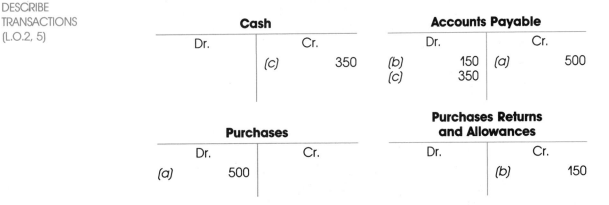

Cash		
Dr.	Cr.	
	(c)	350

Accounts Payable				
Dr.		Cr.		
(b)	150	(a)	500	
(c)	350			

Purchases		
Dr.	Cr.	
(a)	500	

Purchases Returns and Allowances		
Dr.	Cr.	
	(b)	150

EXERCISE 12-5
SCHEDULE OF
ACCOUNTS PAYABLE
(L.O.3)

Garnet Company's accounts payable ledger appears as follows:

Account **Aronson Enterprises**

Date		Item	Post. Ref.	Debit	Credit	Balance
19XX Sept.	1	Balance	√			1,235 00
	19		P22		225 00	1,460 00

Account **Lim and Associates**

Date		Item	Post. Ref.	Debit	Credit	Balance
19XX Sept.	1	Balance	✓			760 00
	8		P21		142 00	902 00

Account **Palmer Products**

Date		Item	Post. Ref.	Debit	Credit	Balance
19XX Sept.	1	Balance	✓			315 00
	12		P21		109 00	424 00

Account **Romero Corporation**

Date		Item	Post. Ref.	Debit	Credit	Balance
19XX Sept.	1	Balance	✓			1,571 00
	24		P22		350 00	1,921 00

a. Prepare a schedule of accounts payable dated September 30, 19XX.

b. The balance in the Accounts Payable (control) account should be what amount?

EXERCISE 12-6
ENTRIES FOR PURCHASE
AND RETURN OF
MERCHANDISE
(L.O.5)

Assuming the use of an accounts payable ledger, record the following transactions in general journal form:

a. Purchased merchandise on account from Diamond Brothers, Invoice No. 927, $425.

b. Returned defective merchandise to Diamond Brothers, $50.

c. Issued check to Diamond Brothers in settlement of the account.

EXERCISE 12-7
TRANSPORTATION
CHARGES
(L.O.6)

Assuming the use of an accounts payable ledger, record the following transactions in general journal form:

a. Purchased merchandise on account from Gilman Enterprises, $370, FOB shipping point.

b. Paid transportation charges related to purchase from Gilman Enterprises, $25.

c. Purchased office equipment on account from Solarz Corporation, $995, FOB shipping point.

d. Paid transportation charges related to purchase from Solarz Corporation, $65.

EXERCISE 12-8
SELECT PROPER
JOURNAL
(L.O.4, 5)

Indicate which journal (sales journal, purchases journal, or general journal) would be used to record each of the following transactions:

a. Purchase of merchandise on account.

b. Purchase return not involving cash.

c. Sale of merchandise on account.

d. Sales return not involving cash.

Problems—Set A

(Omit this problem if working papers are not being used.)

PROBLEM 12-1A
POSTING; SCHEDULE OF ACCOUNTS PAYABLE
(L.O.3, 4)

A purchases journal for Lemke Corporation, a new business, is shown in the working papers.

INSTRUCTIONS

1. Post to the accounts payable ledger.

2. Post to the general ledger.

3. Prepare a schedule of accounts payable.

PROBLEM 12-2A
PURCHASES JOURNAL; ACCOUNTS PAYABLE LEDGER; SCHEDULE OF ACCOUNTS PAYABLE
(L.O.2–5)

Miller Company, a new business, completed the following purchase-related transactions during April 19XX:

Apr. 1   Purchased merchandise on account from Lazlo Corporation, Invoice No. 1265, dated March 28, terms 1/10, n/30, $238.50.

3   Purchased merchandise on account from Garris Products, Invoice No. 739, dated April 1, terms 2/10, n/30, $727.33.

6   Purchased office equipment on account from Hargett Electronics, Invoice, No. A504, dated April 4, terms net 30, $1,450.75.

8   Received Credit Memorandum No. 38 from Lazlo Corporation for merchandise returned, $125.

12   Purchased merchandise on account from Wolf Corporation, Invoice No. 2783, dated April 9, terms net 30, $987.50.

15   Purchased merchandise on account from Garris Products, Invoice No. 768, dated April 13, terms 2/10, n/30, $695.

Apr. 17   Received Credit Memorandum No. 124 from Wolf Corporation for merchandise returned, $227.

19   Purchased office supplies on account from Hargett Electronics, Invoice No. A563, dated April 16, terms net 30, $172.50.

23   Purchased merchandise on account from Lazlo Corporation, Invoice No. 1309, dated April 21, terms 1/10, n/30, $1,342.35.

25   Purchased merchandise on account from Wolf Corporation, Invoice No. 2804, dated April 22, terms net 30, $899.

28   Received Credit Memorandum No. 46 from Garris Products for merchandise returned, $350.

30   Purchased merchandise on account from Lazlo Corporation, Invoice No. 1321, dated April 27, terms 1/10, n/30, $289.47.

INSTRUCTIONS

1. For those students not using the working papers:
   a. This company uses a purchases journal (as illustrated on page 409) and a general journal. Number the purchases journal page 1 and the general journal page 1.

   b. Open ledger accounts as follows:

GENERAL LEDGER

Account Title	Account No.
Office Supplies	112
Office Equipment	120
Accounts Payable	210
Purchases	501
Purchases Returns and Allowances	502

ACCOUNTS PAYABLE LEDGER

Account Title
Garris Products
Hargett Electronics
Lazlo Corporation
Wolf Corporation

2. Record these transactions in the appropriate journal.
   a. Post to the accounts payable ledger daily.
   b. Post the general journal daily.

3. Post the Purchases Journal column total at the end of the month.

4. Prepare a schedule of accounts payable.

PROBLEM 12-3A
SPECIAL JOURNALS;
SUBSIDIARY LEDGERS
(L.O.2–5)

Hernandez Enterprises, a new business, completed the following transactions during July 19XX:

July 1   Purchased merchandise on account from Kramer Corporation, Invoice No. 995, dated June 28, terms net 30, $472.18.

3   Sold merchandise on account to Park Products, Invoice No. 1, $250.

5   Purchased supplies on account from Safran Brothers, Invoice No. 1438, dated July 2, terms 1/10, n/30, $135.50.

7   Sold merchandise on account to Arlington Industries, Invoice No. 2, $369.82.

10   Issued Credit Memorandum No. 1 to Park Products for merchandise returned, $54.

12   Purchased merchandise on account from Berra Company, Invoice No. 2130, dated July 10, terms 2/10, n/30, $1,250.

15   Received Credit Memorandum No. 96 from Kramer Corporation for merchandise returned, $72.35.

17   Sold merchandise on account to Arlington Industries, Invoice No. 3, $297.65.

18   Purchased merchandise on account from Berra Company, Invoice No. 2164, dated July 16, terms 2/10, n/30, $249.50.

20   Issued Credit Memorandum No. 2 to Arlington Industries for merchandise returned, $87.

22   Purchased merchandise on account from Kramer Corporation, Invoice No. 1023, dated July 19, terms net 30, $427.35.

26   Sold merchandise on account to Towas Corporation, Invoice No. 4, $762.

31   Received Credit Memorandum No. 107 from Berra Company for merchandise returned, $47.50.

INSTRUCTIONS

1. For those students not using the working papers:
   a. This company uses a sales journal (as illustrated on page 374 of Chapter 11), a purchases journal (as illustrated on page 409 of this chapter), and a general journal. Number the sales journal page 1, the purchases journal page 1, and the general journal page 1.
   b. Open ledger accounts as follows:

GENERAL LEDGER

Account Title	Account No.
Accounts Receivable	112
Supplies	115
Accounts Payable	210
Sales	410
Sales Returns and Allowances	411
Purchases	501
Purchases Returns and Allowances	502

ACCOUNTS RECEIVABLE LEDGER

Account Title
Arlington Industries
Park Products
Towas Corporation

ACCOUNTS PAYABLE LEDGER

Account Title
Berra Company
Kramer Corporation
Safran Brothers

2. Record these transactions in the appropriate journal.
   a. Post to the accounts receivable ledger daily.
   b. Post to the accounts payable ledger daily.
   c. Post the general journal daily.

3. Post the Sales Journal column total at the end of the month.

4. Post the Purchases Journal column total at the end of the month.

5. Compute net sales as of July 31.

6. Compute net purchases as of July 31.

**PROBLEM
12-4A**

SPECIAL JOURNALS;
SUBSIDIARY LEDGERS;
SCHEDULES OF
ACCOUNTS RECEIVABLE
AND ACCOUNTS
PAYABLE
(L.O.2–5)

Clarence Products completed the following transactions during August 19XX:

Aug. 1   Purchased merchandise on account from Karol Corporation, Invoice No. 923, dated July 28, terms 2/10, n/30, $1,537.50.

4   Sold merchandise on account to Kikta Enterprises, Invoice No. 6751, $1,250.

6   Purchased supplies on account from Target Products, Invoice No. 1247, dated August 4, terms net 30, $227.45.

9   Sold merchandise on account to Canyon Corporation, Invoice No. 6752, $1,989.27.

11   Issued Credit Memorandum No. 307 to Kikta Enterprises for merchandise returned, $175.

14   Purchased merchandise on account from Zappa Corporation, Invoice No. 2561, dated August 12, terms 1/10, n/30, $823.61.

17   Received Credit Memorandum No. 129 from Karol Corporation for merchandise returned, $237.

19   Sold merchandise on account to Merritt Company, Invoice No. 6753, $918.25.

20   Purchased merchandise on account from Karol Corporation, Invoice No. 969, dated August 17, terms 2/10, n/30, $758.32.

22   Issued Credit Memorandum No. 308 to Canyon Corporation for merchandise returned, $326.50.

25   Purchased merchandise on account from Zappa Corporation, Invoice No. 2597, dated August 23, terms 1/10, n/30, $246.75.

28   Sold merchandise on account to Kikta Enterprises, Invoice No. 6754, $1,865.30.

31   Received Credit Memorandum No. 118 from Zappa Corporation for merchandise returned, $95.

INSTRUCTIONS
1. For those students not using the working papers:
   a. This company uses a sales journal (as illustrated on page 374 of Chapter 11), a purchases journal (as illustrated on page 409 of this chapter), and a general journal. Number the sales journal page 47, the purchases journal page 39, and the general journal page 18.

b. Open ledger accounts as follows:

GENERAL LEDGER

Account Title	Account No.	Balance
Accounts Receivable	112	$ 3,686.67 dr.
Supplies	115	472.50 dr.
Accounts Payable	210	2,832.78 cr.
Sales	410	54,671.50 cr.
Sales Returns and Allowances	411	5,142.35 dr.
Purchases	501	25,732.67 dr.
Purchases Returns and Allowances	502	2,146.50 cr.

ACCOUNTS RECEIVABLE LEDGER

Account Title	Balance
Canyon Corporation	$ 1,750.32
Kikta Enterprises	864.10
Merritt Company	1,072.25

ACCOUNTS PAYABLE LEDGER

Account Title	Balance
Karol Corporation	$ 1,295.42
Target Products	108.65
Zappa Corporation	1,428.71

2. Record these transactions in the appropriate journal.
   a. Post to the accounts receivable ledger daily.
   b. Post to the accounts payable ledger daily.
   c. Post the general journal daily.

3. Post the Sales Journal column total at the end of the month.

4. Post the Purchases Journal column total at the end of the month.

5. Prepare a schedule of accounts receivable.

6. Prepare a schedule of accounts payable.

Problems—Set B

PROBLEM 12-1B

POSTING; SCHEDULE OF ACCOUNTS PAYABLE (L.O.3, 4)

(Omit this problem if working papers are not being used.)

A purchases journal for Sotak Corporation, a new business, is shown in the working papers.

INSTRUCTIONS

1. Post to the accounts payable ledger.

2. Post to the general ledger.

3. Prepare a schedule of accounts payable.

PROBLEM 12-2B

PURCHASES JOURNAL; ACCOUNTS PAYABLE LEDGER; SCHEDULE OF ACCOUNTS PAYABLE (L.O.2–5)

Baxter Company, a new business, completed the following purchase-related transactions during March 19XX:

Mar. 1   Purchased merchandise on account from Marks Corporation, Invoice No. 1056, dated February 28, terms 1/10, n/30, $327.50.

3   Purchased merchandise on account from Charly Products, Invoice No. 541, dated March 1, terms 2/10, n/30, $641.25.

6   Purchased office equipment on account from Johnson Electronics, Invoice No. C453, dated March 4, terms net 30, $1,532.25.

8   Received Credit Memorandum No. 29 from Marks Corporation for merchandise returned, $142.

12   Purchased merchandise on account from Star Corporation, Invoice No. 2841, dated March 9, terms net 30, $239.86.

15   Purchased merchandise on account from Charly Products, Invoice No. 573, dated March 13, terms 2/10, n/30, $561.

Mar. 17   Received Credit Memorandum No. 129 from Star Corporation for merchandise returned, $198.

19   Purchased office supplies on account from Johnson Electronics, Invoice No. C479, dated March 16, terms net 30, $129.25.

23   Purchased merchandise on account from Marks Corporation, Invoice No. 1082, dated March 21, terms 1/10, n/30, $1,291.87.

25   Purchased merchandise on account from Star Corporation, Invoice No. 2893, dated March 22, terms net 30, $486.

28   Received Credit Memorandum No. 73 from Charly Products for merchandise returned, $162.

30   Purchased merchandise on account from Marks Corporation, Invoice No. 1108, dated March 27, terms 1/10, n/30, $199.50.

INSTRUCTIONS

1. For those students not using the working papers:
   a. This company uses a purchases journal (as illustrated on page 409) and a general journal. Number the purchases journal page 1 and the general journal page 1.
   b. Open ledger accounts as follows:

GENERAL LEDGER

Account Title	Account No.
Office Supplies	112
Office Equipment	120
Accounts Payable	210
Purchases	501
Purchases Returns and Allowances	502

ACCOUNTS PAYABLE LEDGER

Account Title

Charly Products
Johnson Electronics
Marks Corporation
Star Corporation

2. Record these transactions in the appropriate journal.
   a. Post to the accounts payable ledger daily.
   b. Post the general journal daily.

3. Post the Purchases Journal column total at the end of the month.

4. Prepare a schedule of accounts payable.

**PROBLEM
12-3B**
SPECIAL JOURNALS;
SUBSIDIARY LEDGERS
(L.O.2–5)

Governess Enterprises, a new business, completed the following transactions during January 19XX:

Jan. 3   Purchased merchandise on account from Landon Corporation, Invoice No. 989, dated January 2, terms net 30, $681.27.

4   Sold merchandise on account to Kapp Products, Invoice No. 1, $347.

6   Purchased supplies on account from Spring Brothers, Invoice No. 8431, dated January 4, terms 1/10, n/30, $129.25.

8   Sold merchandise on account to Big River Industries, Invoice No. 2, $698.23.

11   Issued Credit Memorandum No. 1 to Kapp Products for merchandise returned, $41.

13   Purchased merchandise on account from Buggs Company, Invoice No. 3120, dated January 12, terms 2/10, n/30, $1,735.

15   Received Credit Memorandum No. 84 from Landon Corporation for merchandise returned, $51.70.

16   Sold merchandise on account to Big River Industries, Invoice No. 3, $486.90.

18   Purchased merchandise on account from Buggs Company, Invoice No. 3162, dated January 16, terms 2/10, n/30, $318.75.

21   Issued Credit Memorandum No. 2 to Big River Industries for merchandise returned, $70.

23   Purchased merchandise on account from Landon Corporation, Invoice No. 1017, dated January 20, terms net 30, $815.37.

27   Sold merchandise on account to Rally Corporation, Invoice No. 4, $998.

31   Received Credit Memorandum No. 123 from Buggs Company for merchandise returned, $78.90.

INSTRUCTIONS

1. For those students not using the working papers:
   a. This company uses a sales journal (as illustrated on page 374 of Chapter 11), a purchases journal (as illustrated on page 409 of this chapter), and a general journal. Number the sales journal page 1, the purchases journal page 1, and the general journal page 1.
   b. Open ledger accounts as follows:

GENERAL LEDGER

Account Title	Account No.
Accounts Receivable	112
Supplies	115
Accounts Payable	210
Sales	410
Sales Returns and Allowances	411
Purchases	501
Purchases Returns and Allowances	502

ACCOUNTS RECEIVABLE LEDGER

Account Title
Big River Industries
Kapp Products
Rally Corporation

ACCOUNTS PAYABLE LEDGER

Account Title
Buggs Company
Landon Corporation
Spring Brothers

2. Record these transactions in the appropriate journal.
   a. Post to the accounts receivable ledger daily.
   b. Post to the accounts payable ledger daily.
   c. Post the general journal daily.

3. Post the Sales Journal column total at the end of the month.

4. Post the Purchases Journal column total at the end of the month.

5. Compute net sales as of January 31.

6. Compute net purchases as of January 31.

PROBLEM 12-4B

SPECIAL JOURNALS;
SUBSIDIARY LEDGERS;
SCHEDULES OF
ACCOUNTS RECEIVABLE
AND ACCOUNTS
PAYABLE
(L.O.2–5)

Tennyson Products completed the following transactions during November 19XX:

Nov. 1   Purchased merchandise on account from Aiken Corporation, Invoice No. 832, dated October 27, terms 2/10, n/30, $1,273.25.

3   Sold merchandise on account to Mikva Enterprises, Invoice No. 5495, $1,675.

5   Purchased supplies on account from Marris Products, Invoice No. 2741, dated November 3, terms net 30, $542.72.

8   Sold merchandise on account to Darren Corporation, Invoice No. 5496, $1,879.61.

10   Issued Credit Memorandum No. 296 to Mikva Enterprises for merchandise returned, $192.

14   Purchased merchandise on account from Sarko Corporation, Invoice No. 8972, dated November 11, terms 1/10, n/30, $363.28.

16   Received Credit Memorandum No. 157 from Aiken Corporation for merchandise returned, $184.

18   Sold merchandise on account to Sparton Company, Invoice No. 5497, $998.50.

20   Purchased merchandise on account from Aiken Corporation, Invoice No. 867, dated November 18, terms 2/10, n/30, $578.46.

21   Issued Credit Memorandum No. 297 to Darren Corporation for merchandise returned, $229.34.

24   Purchased merchandise on account from Sarko Corporation, Invoice No. 8994, dated November 22, terms 1/10, n/30, $465.72.

27   Sold merchandise on account to Mikva Enterprises, Invoice No. 5498, $2,135.48.

30   Received Credit Memorandum No. 106 from Sarko Corporation for merchandise returned, $39.

INSTRUCTIONS

1. For those students not using the working papers:
   a. This company uses a sales journal (as illustrated on page 374 of Chapter 11), a purchases journal (as illustrated on page 409 of this chapter), and a general journal. Number the sales journal page 65, the purchases journal page 41, and the general journal page 23.

b. Open ledger accounts as follows:

GENERAL LEDGER

Account Title	Account No.	Balance
Accounts Receivable	112	$ 3,257.72 dr.
Supplies	115	361.28 dr.
Accounts Payable	210	3,045.07 cr.
Sales	410	63,957.40 cr.
Sales Returns and Allowances	411	6,280.95 dr.
Purchases	501	34,675.69 dr.
Purchases Returns and Allowances	502	3,257.94 cr.

ACCOUNTS RECEIVABLE LEDGER

Account Title	Balance
Darren Corporation	$ 1,435.47
Mikva Enterprises	723.50
Sparton Company	1,098.75

ACCOUNTS PAYABLE LEDGER

Account Title	Balance
Aiken Corporation	$ 1,054.52
Marris Products	119.25
Sarko Corporation	1,871.30

2. Record these transactions in the appropriate journal.
    a. Post to the accounts receivable ledger daily.
    b. Post to the accounts payable ledger daily.
    c. Post the general journal daily.

3. Post the Sales Journal column total at the end of the month.

4. Post the Purchases Journal column total at the end of the month.

5. Prepare a schedule of accounts receivable.

6. Prepare a schedule of accounts payable.

Mini-Cases

CASE 12-1

Your friend, Pat, owns a successful merchandising concern. Her accountant has complained about not receiving copies of purchase orders from the purchasing department. Since the accounting department receives the purchase invoice from the supplier, Pat doesn't understand why they would need a copy of the purchase order. Explain.

CASE 12-2

Your purchasing agent has received two price quotations on the same merchandise.

Supplier A: $275 per unit, FOB destination.
Supplier B: $265 per unit, FOB shipping point.

Why might Supplier A be the better choice even though the price per unit is higher?

CASE 12-3

Your client, Jill Barrington, owns a cleaning service. She has observed that a friend, who owns a record store, uses a purchases journal. Jill wants to know why you haven't suggested a purchases journal for her business. Explain.

CHAPTER 13

Merchandising Business: Accounting for Cash

AFTER STUDYING THIS CHAPTER, YOU SHOULD BE ABLE TO:

1 Compute trade discounts.

2 Compute and record cash discounts.

3 Record credit card sales.

4 Journalize and post using a cash receipts journal.

5 Journalize and post using a cash payments journal.

In Chapters 11 and 12, you learned to use a sales journal and a purchases journal. In this chapter, we will extend the special journal concept to transactions involving the inflow and outflow of cash. In addition to the cash receipts journal and the cash payments journal, you will also study trade discounts, cash discounts, and credit card sales.

▮▮▮▮ TRADE DISCOUNTS

OBJECTIVE 1
COMPUTE TRADE
DISCOUNTS

Some manufacturers and wholesalers distribute catalogs to their customers listing their products and prices. These prices, however, are not selling prices. They are known as **list prices.** The actual selling price consists of the list price minus an amount known as a **trade discount.** *no entry*

| List price | − | Trade discount | = | Selling price |

The use of a trade discount allows the seller to change the selling price without having to reprint the catalog. The list price printed in the catalog remains fixed, but the trade discount and consequently the selling price can be changed as often as necessary. Since printing and distributing a catalog is an expensive process, the use of trade discounts represents quite a savings to the seller.

To demonstrate the use of a trade discount, let's assume product KX-16 is currently selling at a list price of $1,000 less a 15 percent trade discount. The selling price is computed as follows:

List price	$1,000
Less 15% trade discount	
($1,000 × .15)	−150
Selling price	$ 850

MATH TIP

To calculate a trade discount, the discount must be converted from a percent to either a decimal or a fraction. Since most people prefer to use decimals, we will convert to a decimal. As studied in earlier chapters, this is accomplished in two steps:

Step 1:   Move the decimal point two places to the left.

Step 2:   Drop the percent sign.

For example, let's convert 25% from a percent to a decimal.

Step 1:   .25.%

Step 2:   .25

The trade discount will not appear in the accounts of either the purchaser or the seller. Trade discounts are only used to compute the selling price, which is the significant figure to the accountant.

To continue with the example, the purchaser of one unit of product KX-16 records this purchase of merchandise on account as follows:

19XX								
Jan.	14	Purchases			850	00		
		Accounts Payable					850	00

The seller records this sale of merchandise on account as follows:

19XX								
Jan.	14	Accounts Receivable			850	00		
		Sales					850	00

Observe that the trade discount does not appear on the books of either the purchaser or the seller.

▐▐▐▐ CASH DISCOUNTS

OBJECTIVE 2
COMPUTE AND
RECORD CASH
DISCOUNTS

The seller determines not only who will receive credit but also the **credit terms.** As mentioned in Chapter 11, these terms are displayed on the invoice in an abbreviated format. For example, "net 30 days," or "n/30," means the full invoice amount is due 30 days from the invoice date; "n/EOM" means the full amount is due by the end of the month. The time between the invoice date and the date full payment is due is known as the **credit period.**

||||||||||||||||||||
C O M M E N T

Usually the term *net* refers to a figure after deductions. However, when used to describe credit terms, the word *net* refers to the full amount.

To encourage charge customers to pay quickly, a seller may offer the purchaser a **cash discount.** This is an amount that may be deducted from the bill if it is paid within a specified time known as the **discount period.** For example, credit terms of 2/10, n/30 indicate that a 2 percent discount may be deducted if the invoice is paid within 10 days of the invoice date or the full amount is due 30 days from the invoice date.

To the seller, the cash discount is a **sales discount.** To the purchaser, the cash discount is a **purchases discount.**

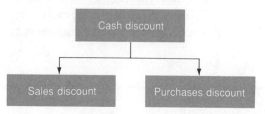

The seller records sales discounts in an account titled Sales Discount. The Sales Discount account is a contra-revenue or contra-sales account. It appears on the income statement of the seller as a subtraction from sales in arriving at **net sales.**

The purchaser records purchases discounts in an account titled Purchases Discount. The Purchases Discount account is a contra-purchases account. It appears on the income statement of the purchaser as a subtraction from purchases in arriving at **net purchases.**

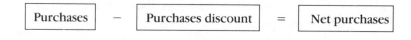

To demonstrate the accounting, let's consider the purchase/sale of merchandise described by the following invoice:

THE KITCHEN TAYLOR		INVOICE NO. 875	
2400 Main Street			
Wheaton, Illinois 60187			
Sold to: Adams Company		**Date:** March 10, 19XX	
217 Liberty Avenue		**FOB:** Destination	
La Grange, Illinois 60525		**Terms:** 2/10, n/30	
Quantity	**Description**	**Unit Price**	**Total**
2	RJ-76 Cabinets	250.00	500.00

The purchaser and seller record the following entries related to this invoice:

PURCHASER'S BOOKS (Adams Company)		SELLER'S BOOKS (The Kitchen Taylor)	
To record purchase:		To record sale:	
Purchases 500		Accounts Receivable 500	
Accounts Payable	500	Sales	500
To record payment within 10 days:		To record receipt of payment:	
Accounts Payable 500		Cash 490	
Cash	490	Sales Discount 10	
Purchases Discount	10	Accounts Receivable	500

Computations:
Cash discount = $500 × .02 = $10
Cash payment = $500 − $10 = $490

|||||||||||||||||||||
C O M M E N T

Observe that both the purchaser and the seller record the purchase/sale at the full invoice amount. The discount is recorded when the invoice is paid.

The cash discount is always computed after subtracting any returns or allowances. Also, the cash discount is not allowed on transportation charges. If an invoice includes transportation charges, the discount is figured only on the merchandise portion of the bill.

To demonstrate, let's assume that on May 12, The Kitchen Taylor purchased merchandise on account from Avery Industries for $650 plus transportation charges of $25, terms 1/15, n/30. This transaction is recorded with the following entry:

19XX							
May	12	Purchases			675	00	
		Accounts Payable—Avery Industries					675	00

On May 18, The Kitchen Taylor returned $50 of damaged merchandise to Avery Industries. This purchase return is recorded as follows:

19XX							
May	18	Accounts Payable—Avery Industries			50	00	
		Purchases Returns and Allowances					50	00

On May 27, the last day of the discount period, The Kitchen Taylor paid Avery Industries the amount due. The computations for the amount to be paid are as follows:

a. $675 A/P (Merchandise, $650 + Transportation, $25)
    − 50 Less returned merchandise
    $625 A/P balance (Merchandise, $600 + Transportation, $25)
b. $600 Merchandise only
    ×.01
    $6.00 Purchases discount
c. $625 A/P balance
    − 6 Less purchases discount
    $619 Cash payment

The payment is recorded with the following entry:

19XX								
May	27	Accounts Payable—Avery Industries			625	00		
		Cash					619	00
		Purchases Discount					6	00

Notice that the purchases discount is recorded when the invoice is paid.

▌▌▌▌ CREDIT CARD SALES

OBJECTIVE 3
RECORD CREDIT CARD
SALES

Many retailers allow customers the convenience of paying for their merchandise with credit cards. This allows customers to consolidate their purchases. Instead of writing many separate checks to different stores, the customer may charge all these purchases to one account, receive one statement, and write only one check to the credit card company.

This is also a convenience to the retailer. The credit card company guarantees prompt payment to the retailer, thus relieving the retailer of the burden and risk of having to collect from individual customers. The credit card company bills and collects from the individual customers. For this service, the credit card company charges the retailer a fee. This fee is generally between 2 and 5 percent of the invoice amount.

If the credit card is a **bank credit card** (such as Visa or MasterCard), the retailer deposits the credit card invoices at the bank just like cash. The retailer's bank account is immediately increased by the amount of the invoices less the credit card fee.

To demonstrate the accounting for such a transaction, let's assume that Damon Clothiers deposits bankcard invoices totaling $1,961 (sales of $1,850 plus 6 percent sales tax) into its account at the bank. The bank charges a 5 percent credit card fee. Damon treats these bankcard sales as cash sales and records the deposit as follows:

19XX								
June	14	Cash			1,862	95		
		Credit Card Expense			98	05		
		Sales					1,850	00
		Sales Tax Payable					111	00

Computations:
  Sales tax payable = $1,850 × .06 = $111
  Credit card expense = ($1,850.00 + 111.00 = $1,961.00) × .05 = $98.05
  Cash = $1,961.00 − $98.05 = $1,862.95

Nonbank credit cards (such as American Express or Diners Club) are also commonly used. In this case, the retailer mails the credit card invoices to the credit card company. Usually within 30 days, the retailer receives a check from the credit card company for the total amount of the invoices less the credit card fee.

To demonstrate the accounting, let's assume that Damon Clothiers makes nonbank credit card sales totaling $1,590 (sales of $1,500 plus 6 percent sales tax). Damon records these sales with the following entry:

19XX								
Nov.	9	Accounts Receivable—Credit Card Co.			1,590	00		
		Sales					1,500	00
		Sales Tax Payable					90	00

Computation:
  Sales tax payable = $1,500 × .06 = $90

The credit card company charges a 5 percent fee. When the check from the nonbank credit card company is received, Damon makes the following entry:

19XX								
Nov.	30	Cash			1,510	50		
		Credit Card Expense			79	50		
		Accounts Receivable—Credit Card Co.					1,590	00

Computations:
  Credit card expense = $1,590 × .05 = $79.50
  Cash = $1,590.00 − $79.50 = $1,510.50

▮▮▮▮ THE CASH RECEIPTS JOURNAL

In Chapters 11 and 12, you learned to record purchases and sales more efficiently through the use of special journals. The cash receipts journal, another special journal, provides a more efficient way of recording receipts of cash.

JOURNALIZING

OBJECTIVE 4
JOURNALIZE AND POST USING A CASH RECEIPTS JOURNAL

When in use, all transactions involving the inflow of cash are recorded in the **cash receipts journal.** The sales and purchases journals have only one amount column because each accommodates only one type of transaction. The cash receipts journal is a multicolumn journal because many types of transactions involve the receipt of cash. Common examples are cash sales and cash payments received from charge customers. Less common examples include additional cash investments made by the owner and cash refunds received on purchase returns. The cash receipts journal must be able to handle all the possibilities.

Like all special journals, the cash receipts journal is customized to meet the needs of the user through the choice of accounts for special columns. To make these choices, the daily transactions of a business must be analyzed to determine the types of transactions involving the receipt of cash that occur frequently. Since every transaction recorded in this journal will require a debit to the Cash account, a special Cash Debit column will be a part of every cash receipts journal. However, other special columns are chosen to accommodate the high-volume transactions of the individual business.

Too many special columns would make the journal cumbersome to use. We do not want special columns for accounts that are used infrequently. A Sundry Accounts Credit column gives us the ability to credit any account for which we do not have a special column. Whenever the Sundry Accounts Credit column is used, the title of the account to be credited must be written in the Account Credited column. This is important because each credit in the Sundry Accounts Credit column will probably be going to a different account. In order to post, we must know the account title for each credit in the column.

Figure 13-1 shows a typical cash receipts journal for a retail business. The following transactions have been recorded in this journal:

June 1 Sold merchandise for cash, $100 plus 6 percent sales tax.

    Computations:

        Sales tax = $100 \times .06 = $6

        Cash = $100 + $6 = $106

    4 Sold merchandise, $500 plus 6 percent sales tax; customer used a bank credit card charging a fee equal to 5 percent of sales plus tax.

    Computations:

        Sales tax = $500 \times .06 = $30

        Credit card expense = $530.00 \times .05 = $26.50

        Cash = $530.00 - $26.50 = $503.50

post individual

CASH RECEIPTS JOURNAL

Date		Account Credited	Post. Ref.	Sundry Accounts Credit	Accounts Receivable Credit	Sales Credit	Sales Tax Payable Credit	Credit Card Expense Debit	Cash Debit
19XX June	1	Sales				100 00	6 00		106 00
	4	Sales				500 00	30 00	26 50	503 50
	7	Mark Sullivan			232 50				232 50
	11	Jan Davis, Capital		5,000 00					5,000 00
	15	Sales				1,250 00	75 00	66 25	1,258 75
	18	Magic Charge			1,500 00			75 00	1,425 00
	21	Sales				95 00	5 70		100 70
	24	Purchases Returns and Allowances		75 18					75 18
	27	Michael Hojnacki			527 95				527 95
	30	Easy Charge			2,000 00			100 00	1,900 00

June 7 Received payment on account from Mark Sullivan, a charge customer, $232.50.

11 Jan Davis, the owner, invested an additional $5,000 cash in the business.

15 Sold merchandise, $1,250 plus 6 percent sales tax; customer used a bank credit card charging a fee equal to 5 percent of sales plus tax.

Computations:
Sales tax = $1,250 × .06 = $75
Credit card expense = $1,325.00 × .05 = $66.25
Cash = $1,325.00 − $66.25 = $1,258.75

18 Received a $1,425 check from Magic Charge. This check covered nonbank credit card invoices totaling $1,500 less their $75 fee.

21 Sold merchandise for cash, $95 plus 6 percent sales tax.

Computations:
Sales tax = $95.00 × .06 = $5.70
Cash = $95.00 + $5.70 = $100.70

24 Received a $75.18 cash refund on merchandise returned to a supplier. (No cash discount was involved in the original purchase.)

27 Received payment on account from Michael Hojnacki, a charge customer, $527.95.

30 Received a $1,900 check from Easy Charge. This check covered nonbank credit card invoices totaling $2,000 less their $100 fee.

In studying the cash receipts journal, observe the following:

● All transactions involving the inflow of cash are recorded in the cash receipts journal.

● The portion of frequently occurring entries that never changes is made permanent through the use of column headings (Accounts Receivable Credit; Sales Credit; Sales Tax Payable Credit; Credit Card Expense Debit; Cash Debit).

● The accountant needs to enter only the information that changes: the date, account credited, and the dollar amounts.

● The Account Credited column is used for three things:
1. To specify the title of the account to be credited whenever the Sundry Accounts Credit column is used.
2. To specify the customer's name whenever the Accounts Receivable Credit column is used.

3. The word *Sales* is written in the Account Credited column whenever a cash sale or a sale using a bank credit card is recorded.

POSTING

As indicated in Chapter 11, all special journals require two types of postings.

1. **Individual postings.** These postings are necessary where each figure in a column must be posted to a *different* account. These items are usually posted on a daily basis. In our cash receipts journal, the following columns must be posted individually:

   a. Sundry Accounts Credit. These credits are posted to various accounts in the general ledger.

   b. Accounts Receivable Credit. These credits are posted to the customers' accounts in the accounts receivable ledger.

2. **Column total postings.** Column totals are posted when all the figures in a column must be posted to the *same* account. Rather than making many individual postings to the same account, one posting is made at the end of the month with the column total. As the column headings in our cash receipts journal indicate, the following column totals must be posted:

   a. Accounts Receivable Credit. This credit total is posted to the Accounts Receivable (control) account in the general ledger.

   b. Sales Credit. This credit total is posted to the Sales account in the general ledger.

   c. Sales Tax Payable Credit. This credit total is posted to the Sales Tax Payable account in the general ledger.

   d. Credit Card Expense Debit. This debit total is posted to the Credit Card Expense account in the general ledger.

   e. Cash Debit. This debit total is posted to the Cash account in the general ledger.

Before posting any totals, the equality of debits and credits should be verified. Using column totals from the cash receipts journal shown in Figure 13-2, the debits and credits are verified as follows:

Debit Totals		Credit Totals	
Credit Card Expense	$ 267.75	Sundry Accounts	$ 5,075.18
Cash	11,129.58	Accounts Receivable	4,260.45
		Sales	1,945.00
	$11,397.33	Sales Tax Payable	116.70
			$11,397.33

This process is known as crossfooting the journal.

FIGURE 13 - 2

CASH RECEIPTS JOURNAL

Page 72

Date	Account Credited	Post. Ref.	Sundry Accounts Credit	Accounts Receivable Credit	Sales Credit	Sales Tax Payable Credit	Credit Card Expense Debit	Cash Debit
19XX June 1	Sales	—			100 00	6 00		106 00
4	Sales	—			500 00	30 00	26 50	503 50
7	Mark Sullivan	✓		232 50				232 50
11	Jan Davis, Capital	310	5,000 00					5,000 00
15	Sales	—			1,250 00	75 00	66 25	1,258 75
18	Magic Charge	✓		1,500 00			75 00	1,425 00
21	Sales	—			95 00	5 70		100 70
24	Purchases Returns and Allowances	502	75 18					75 18
27	Michael Hojnacki	✓		527 95				527 95
30	Easy Charge	✓		2,000 00			100 00	1,900 00
30			5,075 18	4,260 45	1,945 00	116 70	267 75	11,129 58
			(✓)	(111)	(410)	(220)	(515)	(110)

After posting, the cash receipts journal and the related general ledger and accounts receivable ledger accounts appear as shown in Figures 13-2, 13-3, and 13-4.

||||||||||||||||||||||
C O M M E N T

In the Posting Reference column in the cash receipts journal:

- A dash indicates there are no individual postings for the entry on that line.
- A check mark indicates the amount in the Accounts Receivable Credit column has been posted to the individual customer's account in the accounts receivable ledger.
- A number indicates that the amount in the Sundry Accounts Credit column has been posted to that account number in the general ledger.

▌ **FIGURE 13 - 3**

PARTIAL GENERAL LEDGER

Account __**Cash**__   Account No. ____110

Date		Item	Post. Ref.	Debit	Credit	Balance Debit	Balance Credit
19XX June	1	Balance	✓			2,475 30	
	30		CR72	11,129 58		13,604 88	

Account __**Accounts Receivable (Control)**__   Account No. ____111

Date		Item	Post. Ref.	Debit	Credit	Balance Debit	Balance Credit
19XX June	1	Balance	✓			4,672 45	
	30		CR72		4,260 45	412 00	

FIGURE 13 - 3   *(continued)*

Account __Sales Tax Payable__   Account No. __220__

Date		Item	Post. Ref.	Debit	Credit	Balance	
						Debit	Credit
19XX June	1	Balance	√				149 50
	30		CR72		116 70		266 20

Account __Jan Davis, Capital__   Account No. __310__

Date		Item	Post. Ref.	Debit	Credit	Balance	
						Debit	Credit
19XX June	1	Balance	√				65,689 20
	11		CR72		5,000 00		70,689 20

Account __Sales__   Account No. __410__

Date		Item	Post. Ref.	Debit	Credit	Balance	
						Debit	Credit
19XX June	1	Balance	√				15,390 00
	30		CR72		1,945 00		17,335 00

FIGURE 13 - 3   *(concluded)*

Account **Purchases Returns and Allowances**   Account No. 502

Date		Item	Post. Ref.	Debit	Credit	Balance Debit	Balance Credit
19XX June	1	Balance	√				295 35
	24		CR72		75 18		370 53

Account **Credit Card Expense**   Account No. 515

Date		Item	Post. Ref.	Debit	Credit	Balance Debit	Balance Credit
19XX June	1	Balance	√			1,508 20	
	30		CR72	267 75		1,775 95	

||||||||||||||||||||||||||
COMMENT

Observe that the posting references in the ledger accounts begin with CR. This indicates the posted information came from the cash receipts journal.

FIGURE 13 - 4

ACCOUNTS RECEIVABLE LEDGER

Account **Easy Charge**

Date		Item	Post. Ref.	Debit	Credit	Balance
19XX June	1	Balance	√			2,302 00
	30		CR72		2,000 00	302 00

FIGURE 13 - 4 *(concluded)*

Account **Michael Hojnacki**

Date		Item	Post. Ref.	Debit	Credit	Balance
19XX						
June	1	Balance	✓			637 95
	27		CR72		527 95	110 00

Account **Magic Charge**

Date		Item	Post. Ref.	Debit	Credit	Balance
19XX						
June	1	Balance	✓			1,500 00
	18		CR72		1,500 00	——

Account **Mark Sullivan**

Date		Item	Post. Ref.	Debit	Credit	Balance
19XX						
June	1	Balance	✓			232 50
	7		CR72		232 50	——

JOURNALIZING AND POSTING—A WHOLESALE BUSINESS

Let's look at another example of a cash receipts journal. Figure 13-5 shows a typical cash receipts journal for a wholesale business. The following transactions have been recorded in this journal:

July 1   Received check from Calico Corporation in payment of Invoice No. 2579, $560 (merchandise) less a 2 percent discount.

   Computations:

   Discount = $560.00 × .02 = $11.20

   Cash = $560.00 − $11.20 = $548.80

   5   Sold old equipment for cash at cost, $469.50.

   8   Cash sales for first week of July, $2,347.65.

CASH RECEIPTS JOURNAL

Date	Account Credited	Post. Ref.	Sundry Accounts Credit	Accounts Receivable Credit	Sales Credit	Sales Discount Debit	Cash Debit
19XX July							
1	Calico Corporation			560 00		11 20	548 80
5	Equipment		469 50				469 50
8	Sales				2,347 65		2,347 65
10	Kelly and Sons			350 00			350 00
15	Sales				2,482 30		2,482 30
19	Lopez Company			875 00		8 20	866 80
20	Kowalski Company			213 00			213 00
22	Sales				2,657 89		2,657 89
25	Goldberg Associates			382 00		7 20	374 80
28	Purchases Returns and Allowances		65 00				65 00
31	Sales				2,569 75		2,569 75

July 10 Received check from Kelly and Sons in payment of Invoice No. 2588, $350, no discount.

15 Cash sales for second week of July, $2,482.30.

19 Received check from Lopez Company in payment of Invoice No. 2601, $875 ($820 merchandise plus $55 transportation) less a 1 percent cash discount.

Computations:
Discount = $820.00 × .01 = $8.20
Cash = $875.00 − $8.20 = $866.80

20 Received a check from Kowalski Company in payment of Invoice No. 2617, $248 (merchandise) less Credit Memorandum No. 243, $35 (recorded earlier), no discount.

Computation:
Cash = $248 − $35 = $213

22 Cash sales for third week of July, $2,657.89.

25 Received a check from Goldberg Associates in payment of Invoice No. 2623, $382 ($360 merchandise plus $22 transportation) less a 2 percent cash discount.

Computations:
Discount = $360.00 × .02 = $7.20
Cash = $382.00 − $7.20 = $374.80

28 Received a $65 cash refund on merchandise returned to a supplier. (No cash discount was involved in the original purchase.)

31 Cash sales for fourth week of July, $2,569.75.

This journal is posted following the procedures described earlier in the chapter.

1. Individual postings (daily):
   a. Sundry Accounts Credit. These credits are posted to the Equipment account and the Purchases Returns and Allowances account in the general ledger.
   b. Accounts Receivable Credit. These credits are posted to the customers' accounts in the accounts receivable ledger.
2. Column total postings (end of month):
   a. Accounts Receivable Credit. This credit total is posted to the Accounts Receivable (control) account in the general ledger.
   b. Sales Credit. This credit total is posted to the Sales account in the general ledger.
   c. Sales Discount Debit. This debit total is posted to the Sales Discount account in the general ledger.
   d. Cash Debit. This debit total is posted to the Cash account in the general ledger.

▓▓▓ THE CASH PAYMENTS JOURNAL

JOURNALIZING

When in use, all transactions involving the outflow of cash are recorded in the **cash payments journal.** This journal is also a multicolumn journal because there are many types of transactions that involve the paying out of cash.

Like all special journals, the cash payments journal is customized to meet the needs of the user through the choice of accounts for special columns. Since every transaction recorded in this journal will require a credit to the Cash account, a special Cash Credit column will be a part of every cash payments journal. Other special columns are chosen to accommodate the frequently occurring transactions of the individual business.

A Sundry Accounts Debit column enables the user to debit any account for which there is not a special column. The title of the account to be debited must be written in the Account Debited column whenever the Sundry Accounts Debit column is used.

Figure 13-6 shows a typical cash payments journal for a wholesale business. The following transactions have been recorded in this journal:

Aug. 1   Paid monthly rent, Check No. 420, $900.

3   Paid Gardella Company, a creditor, on account, Check No. 421, $739.50.

7   Paid telephone bill, Check No. 422, $84.75.

11   Paid Lanson Corporation, a creditor, on account, Check No. 423, $450 (merchandise) less 2 percent discount.

      Computations:
        Discount = $450 × .02 = $9
        Cash = $450 − $9 = $441

15   Purchased equipment for cash, Check No. 424, $1,595.

18   Paid transportation charges on equipment purchased on August 15, Check No. 425, $125.

20   Voided Check No. 426.

22   Paid Lutz Company, a creditor, on account, Check No. 427, $835 ($790 merchandise, $45 transportation) less a 1 percent cash discount.

      Computations:
        Discount = $790.00 × .01 = $7.90
        Cash = $835.00 − $7.90 = $827.10

26   Paid for minor repair, Check No. 428, $37.50.

31   Paid Crenshaw Brothers, a creditor, on account, Check No. 429, $79.95.

FIGURE 13 - 6

CASH PAYMENTS JOURNAL

Page 93

Date		Check No.	Account Debited	Post. Ref.	Sundry Accounts Debit	Accounts Payable Debit	Purchases Discount Credit	Cash Credit
19XX Aug.	1	420	Rent Expense		900 00			900 00
	3	421	Gardella Company			739 50		739 50
	7	422	Telephone Expense		84 75			84 75
	11	423	Lanson Corporation			450 00	9 00	441 00
	15	424	Equipment		1,595 00			1,595 00
	18	425	Equipment		125 00			125 00
	20	426	Void					
	22	427	Lutz Company			835 00	7 90	827 10
	26	428	Repair Expense		37 50			37 50
	31	429	Crenshaw Brothers			79 95		79 95

|||||||||||||||||||||| All check numbers must be listed in consecutive order. Even voided checks must
C O M M E N T be listed (see August 20, Check No. 426). This assures greater control over the outflow of cash.

POSTING

The cash payments journal is posted following the procedures described earlier in the chapter.

1. Individual postings (daily):
   a. Sundry Accounts Debit. These debits are posted to various general ledger accounts.
   b. Accounts Payable Debit. These debits are posted to creditors' accounts in the accounts payable ledger.

2. Column total postings (end of month):
   a. Accounts Payable Debit. This debit total is posted to the Accounts Payable account in the general ledger.
   b. Purchases Discount Credit. This credit total is posted to the Purchases Discount account in the general ledger.
   c. Cash Credit. This credit total is posted to the Cash account in the general ledger.

In posting the cash payments journal, the posting references in the ledger accounts begin with CP.

Chapter Summary

Some manufacturers and wholesalers use trade discounts to change the selling price of a product without having to reprint an entire catalog.

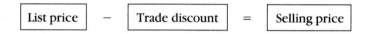

$$\boxed{\text{List price}} \quad - \quad \boxed{\text{Trade discount}} \quad = \quad \boxed{\text{Selling price}}$$

A cash discount is another type of discount offered by many sellers. The purpose of a cash discount is to encourage charge customers to pay promptly. For example, credit terms of 2/10, n/30 indicate that a 2 percent discount may be deducted if the invoice is paid within 10 days of the invoice date or the full amount is due in 30 days. The cash discount is not allowed on transportation charges and is always computed after subtracting any returns or allowances. To the seller, the cash discount is a sales discount. To the purchaser, the cash discount is a purchases discount.

Many retailers allow customers the convenience of paying with credit cards. This is also a convenience to the retailer. The credit card company guarantees prompt payment, and the retailer is relieved of the burden and risk of having to collect from individual customers. Of course, the credit card company charges the retailer a fee for this service. Visa and MasterCard are examples of bank credit cards. American Express and Diners Club are examples of nonbank credit cards.

Special journals allow us to journalize and post with greater efficiency. You are now able to work with the following special journals:

Journal	Transaction	Abbreviation
Sales journal	Sales of merchandise on account	S
Purchases journal	Purchases of merchandise on account	P
Cash receipts journal	All receipts of cash	CR
Cash payments journal	All payments of cash	CP

Any transaction that does not fit into a special journal is recorded in the general journal (abbreviation J).

Glossary

BANK CREDIT CARD

A credit card used by retail customers to pay for merchandise. The retailer collects cash from the bank rather than individual customers. The bank deducts a fee for this service. Visa and MasterCard are common examples.

CASH DISCOUNT

A discount offered by the seller to encourage charge customers to pay promptly.

CASH PAYMENTS JOURNAL

A special journal used to record all outflows of cash.

CASH RECEIPTS JOURNAL

A special journal used to record all inflows of cash.

CREDIT PERIOD

The time between the invoice date and the date full payment is due.

CREDIT TERMS

Terms of payment determined by the seller.

CROSSFOOTING

The process of proving the equality of debit and credit column totals.

DISCOUNT PERIOD

A specified time during which a cash discount may be taken.

LIST PRICE

A fixed price that is listed in a catalog. The list price minus a trade discount equals the selling price.

NET PURCHASES

Purchases minus contra-purchases accounts (such as Purchases Discount and Purchases Returns and Allowances).

NET SALES

Sales minus contra-sales accounts (such as Sales Discount and Sales Returns and Allowances).

NONBANK CREDIT CARD

A credit card used by retail customers to pay for merchandise. The retailer collects cash from the credit card company rather than individual customers. The credit card company deducts a fee for this service. American Express and Diners Club are common examples.

PURCHASES DISCOUNT

The term used to describe a cash discount from the purchaser's point of view.

SALES DISCOUNT

The term used to describe a cash discount from the seller's point of view.

TRADE DISCOUNT

A discount used by sellers to change the selling price of a product without having to reprint an entire catalog. The list price minus the trade discount equals the selling price.

Questions for Discussion

1. *a.* What is the purpose of a trade discount?
   b. How do trade discounts fit into the accounting process?

2. *a.* What is the purpose of a cash discount?
   b. To the seller, a cash discount is a _____ discount.
   c. To the purchaser, a cash discount is a _____ discount.

3. Explain the following credit terms:
   a. n/30.
   b. 1/15, n/30.
   c. n/EOM.

4. Explain how credit cards can be a convenience to the following:
   a. Customer.
   b. Retailer.

5. Explain what the following items indicate when written in the Posting Reference column of a special journal:
   a. A dash.
   b. A check mark.
   c. A number.

6. In constructing special journals, how are accounts for special columns selected?

7. Even though special journals may vary in detail from company to company:
   a. Every cash receipts journal will have what special column?
   b. Every cash payments journal will have what special column?

8. What is the purpose of a sundry accounts column in a special journal?

9. The Purchases Discount account:
   a. Is _____ (added or subtracted) to/from the _____ account in arriving at net purchases.
   b. Has a normal balance on the _____ (debit or credit) side.
   c. Is a _____ (temporary or permanent) account.

10. The Sales Discount account:
   a. Is _____ (added or subtracted) to/from the _____ account in arriving at net sales.
   b. Has a normal balance on the _____ (debit or credit) side.
   c. Is a _____ (temporary or permanent) account.

Exercises

EXERCISE 13-1
TRADE DISCOUNT
(L.O.1)

L & K Products sells one unit of product MW-42 at a list price of $565 less a 10 percent trade discount.

   a. Compute the trade discount.

   b. What is the selling price?

   c. In general journal form, record the sale.

EXERCISE 13-2
CASH DISCOUNT
(L.O.2)

For each purchase described below, determine the cash payment necessary to settle the account assuming that all available cash discounts are taken.

Trans-action	Invoice Date	Credit Terms	Date Paid	FOB	Merchandise	Trans-portation	Returns and Allowances
A	May 1	n/30	May 25	Shipping point	$300	$18	$50
B	8	2/10, n/30	18	Destination	875		
C	12	1/10, n/30	22	Destination	460		72
D	16	2/10, n/30	25	Shipping point	940	55	60
E	18	1/10, n/30	30	Shipping point	294	32	

EXERCISE 13-3
SELECT PROPER
JOURNAL
(L.O.4, 5)

Captiva Company uses the following journals:

   Sales journal.
   Purchases journal.
   Cash payments journal.
   Cash receipts journal.
   General journal.

Indicate in which journal each of the following transactions should be recorded:

1. Purchased merchandise on account.

2. Paid creditor on account.

3. Sold merchandise on account.

4. Received a payment on account from a charge customer.

5. Issued a credit memo for damaged merchandise returned by a customer.

6. Purchased merchandise for cash.

7. Paid the monthly rent.

8. Sold merchandise for cash.

9. Recorded adjusting entries.

10. Recorded closing entries.

EXERCISE 13-4

ENTRIES FOR SALES
TRANSACTIONS USING
CREDIT CARDS
(L.O.3)

In general journal form, record the following transactions for Mary Ellen's Dress Shop:

1. Deposited bank credit card invoices totaling $2,140 (sales of $2,000 plus 7 percent sales tax) into its account at the bank. The bank charged a 4 percent fee.

2. Made nonbank credit card sales totaling $1,979.50 (sales of $1,850 plus 7 percent sales tax). The invoices were submitted to Quick Charge for payment.

3. Received a check from Quick Charge for $1,900.32 covering invoices totaling $1,979.50 less their $79.18 fee (4 percent).

EXERCISE 13-5

ENTRIES FOR PURCHASE
AND SALE FROM
INVOICE
(L.O.2)

GILBERTE CORPORATION 907 Salem Lane Westport, CN 06880		INVOICE NO. 9672	
Sold to: Devine Enterprises 456 Crescent Road Oneonta, NY 13820		Date: 9/21/XX Terms: 1/10, n/30 FOB: Shipping point	
Quantity	**Description**	**Unit Price**	**Total**
500	Part No. 347-T	2.35	1,175.00

a. In reference to Invoice No. 9672, record the following transactions on the books of Devine Enterprises in general journal form:
1. The purchase of merchandise on account.
2. The payment on account within the 10-day discount period.

b. In reference to Invoice No. 9672, record the following transactions on the books of Gilberte Corporation in general journal form:
1. The sale of merchandise on account.
2. The receipt of payment within the discount period.

EXERCISE 13-6
ENTRIES FOR PURCHASE, RETURN, PAYMENT WITH DISCOUNT
(L.O.2)

Record the following transactions in general journal form:

1. Purchased merchandise on account from R & J Company; 2/10, n/30; FOB destination; $872.

2. Returned defective merchandise to R & J Company for credit, $50.

3. Issued check to R & J Company in settlement of the account within the discount period.

EXERCISE 13-7
ENTRIES FOR SALE, RETURN, PAYMENT WITH DISCOUNT
(L.O.2)

Record the following transactions in general journal form:

1. Sold merchandise on account to Cheetah Corporation; 1/10, n/30; FOB destination; $1,200.

2. Issued credit memo to Cheetah Corporation for the return of damaged merchandise, $80.

3. Received check from Cheetah Corporation in settlement of their account within the discount period.

EXERCISE 13-8
CASH DISCOUNT
(L.O.2)

CLINGNER PRODUCTS		**INVOICE NO. 8479**	
894 Ridge Road			
Fort Thomas, KY 41075			

Sold to:	Blanchard Company	Date:	4/12/XX
	20335 Lehman Street	Terms:	2/10, n/30
	Eau Claire, WI 54701	FOB:	Shipping point

Quantity	Description	Unit Price	Total
250	Part No. 198-Q	7.15	1,787.50
	Transportation charges		185.00
			1,972.50

Blanchard Company received a bill from Clingner Products indicating Blanchard still owes $3.70 on Invoice No. 8479 (as shown). Blanchard claims they paid this invoice promptly within the 10-day discount period with Check No. 745 in the amount of $1,933.05. Does Blanchard Company owe Clingner Products an additional $3.70? Explain.

Problems—Set A

During October 19XX, Craft Products, a retail business, completed the selected transactions that follow. The state levies a 5 percent sales tax on retail sales.

Partial Chart of Accounts

Cash
Accounts Receivable
Sales Tax Payable
Richard Craft, Capital
Sales
Purchases Returns and Allowances
Credit Card Expense

Oct. 1   Sold merchandise for cash, $1,250 plus sales tax.

3   Sold merchandise, $800 plus sales tax; customer used a bank credit card charging a fee equal to 4 percent of sales plus tax.

6   Received payment on account from Robert Carson, a charge customer, $542.75.

10   Richard Craft, the owner, invested an additional $4,000 cash in the business.

14   Sold merchandise, $925 plus sales tax; customer used a bank credit card charging a fee equal to 4 percent of sales plus tax.

17   Received a check from Magic Charge, $1,140. This check covered nonbank credit card invoices totaling $1,200 less their $60 fee.

20   Sold merchandise for cash, $165 plus sales tax.

23   Received a cash refund on merchandise returned to a supplier, $54.30. (No cash discount was involved in the original purchase.)

Oct. 27   Received payment on account from Dixie Conrad, a charge customer, $672.

   31   Received a check from Easy Charge, $1,520. This check covered nonbank credit card invoices totaling $1,600 less their $80 fee.

INSTRUCTIONS

1. For those students not using the working papers:
   a. This company uses a cash receipts journal as shown on page 449.
   b. Number this journal page 46.

2. Record these transactions in the cash receipts journal.

3. Total the amount columns in the journal.

4. Verify the equality of the debit and credit totals.

5. Rule the journal.

PROBLEM 13-2A
CASH PAYMENTS JOURNAL
(L.O.2, 5)

The Top Shop, a retail business, completed the following selected transactions during February 19XX:

```
┌─────────────────────────────────────┐
│       Partial Chart of Accounts      │
│                                      │
│   Cash                               │
│   Accounts Payable                   │
│   Purchases                          │
│   Purchases Discount                 │
│   Rent Expense                       │
│   Repair Expense                     │
│   Utilities Expense                  │
│                                      │
└─────────────────────────────────────┘
```

Feb.   1   Paid monthly rent, Check No. 821, $975.

    4   Paid Leslie Company, a creditor, on account, Check No. 822, $372.45.

    7   Paid electricity bill, Check No. 823, $97.62.

   10   Paid Lujak Corporation, a creditor, on account, Check No. 824, $820 (merchandise) less 1 percent cash discount.

   14   Voided Check No. 825.

   16   Purchased merchandise for cash, Check No. 826, $420.

Feb. 18   Paid transportation charges on merchandise purchased on February 16, Check No. 827, $38.

21   Paid Crawford Company, a creditor, on account, Check No. 828, $1,560 ($1,500 merchandise, $60 transportation) less a 2 percent cash discount.

24   Paid for minor repair, Check No. 829, $35.

28   Paid Mumford Associates, a creditor, on account, Check No. 830, $219.05.

INSTRUCTIONS

1. For those students not using the working papers:
   a. This company uses a cash payments journal as shown on page 460.
   b. Number this journal page 62.

2. Record these transactions in the cash payments journal.

3. Total the amount columns in the journal.

4. Verify the equality of the debit and credit totals.

5. Rule the journal.

PROBLEM 13-3A
SPECIAL JOURNALS;
ACCOUNTS RECEIVABLE
LEDGER
(L.O.2, 4)

Pershing Enterprises, a new wholesale business, completed the following selected transactions during July 19XX:

July 1   Linda Pershing, the owner, invested $10,000 cash in the business.

2   Sold merchandise on account to Richard and Associates, Invoice No. 101, $650.

3   Received a cash refund on damaged merchandise returned to a supplier, $130. (No cash discount was involved in the original purchase.)

5   Sold merchandise for cash, Invoice No. 102, $215.

5   Sold merchandise on account to Leetle Corporation, Invoice No. 103, $1,475.

7   Sold merchandise for cash, Invoice No. 104, $84.50.

10   Received payment on account from Richard and Associates, Invoice No. 101, $650 (merchandise) less a 2 percent cash discount.

12   Issued Credit Memorandum No. 1 to Leetle Corporation for merchandise returned, $75.

July 15   Received payment on account from Leetle Corporation,
            Invoice No. 103, $1,475 (merchandise) less credit
            memo and 2 percent cash discount.

     16   Sold merchandise on account to Daughters Company, In-
            voice No. 105, $1,800.

     19   Sold merchandise on account to Harris Corporation, In-
            voice No. 106, $610.

     21   Issued Credit Memorandum No. 2 to Daughters Com-
            pany for merchandise returned, $50.

     23   Sold merchandise on account to Richard and Associates,
            Invoice No. 107, $895.

     26   Received payment on account from Daughters Company,
            Invoice No. 105, $1,800 (merchandise) less credit
            memo and 2 percent cash discount.

     28   Sold merchandise for cash, Invoice No. 108, $127.25.

     31   Received payment on account from Harris Corporation,
            Invoice No. 106, $610, no discount.

INSTRUCTIONS

1. For those students not using the working papers:
   a. This company uses a cash receipts journal (as shown on page 457 of
      this chapter), a sales journal (as shown on page 374 of Chapter 11),
      and a general journal.
   b. Number the cash receipts journal page 1, the sales journal page 1, and
      the general journal page 1.
   c. Open ledger accounts as follows:

GENERAL LEDGER

Account Title	Account No.
Cash	110
Accounts Receivable	111
Linda Pershing, Capital	310
Sales	410
Sales Discount	411
Sales Returns and Allowances	412
Purchases Returns and Allowances	502

ACCOUNTS RECEIVABLE LEDGER

Account Title
Daughters Company
Harris Corporation
Leetle Corporation
Richard and Associates

2. Record these transactions in the appropriate journals.
   a. Post to the accounts receivable ledger daily.
   b. Post the Sundry Accounts Credit column daily.
   c. Post the general journal daily.

3. At the end of the month:
   a. Total columns, verify equality of debits and credits, and rule the special journals.
   b. Post the Sales Journal column total.
   c. Post the Cash Receipts Journal column totals.

PROBLEM 13-4A
SPECIAL JOURNALS;
SUBSIDIARY LEDGERS
(L.O.2, 4, 5)

Comiskey Company, a new wholesale business, completed the following transactions during June 19XX:

June 1   Sandra Comiskey, the owner, invested $25,000 cash in the business.

  1   Paid monthly rent, Check No. 101, $985.

  2   Purchased merchandise on account from Chung Enterprises, Invoice No. 699, dated June 1, terms 2/10, n/30, $2,890.

  2   Purchased supplies on account from Ferris Products, Invoice No. 461, dated June 1, net 30, $397.50.

  3   Sold merchandise on account to Markum Company, Invoice No. 1001, $1,210.

  4   Sold merchandise for cash, Invoice No. 1002, $826.72.

  5   Purchased equipment for cash, Check No. 102, $3,265.

  8   Sold merchandise on account to Laramie Brothers, Invoice No. 1003, $872.50.

  9   Received payment on account from Markum Company, Invoice No. 1001, $1,210 (merchandise) less a 2 percent cash discount.

  10   Purchased merchandise on account from Jensen Products, Invoice No. 1829, dated June 9, terms 1/10, n/30, $3,675.

  11   Paid Chung Enterprises, a creditor, on account, Check No. 103, $2,890 (merchandise) less 2 percent cash discount.

  12   Paid Ferris Products, a creditor, on account, Check No. 104, $397.50.

  15   Sold merchandise on account to Acme Corporation, Invoice No. 1004, $765.

June 16   Issued Credit Memorandum No. 1 to Laramie Brothers for merchandise returned, $98.

17   Received Credit Memorandum No. 89 from Jensen Products, a supplier, for merchandise returned, $200.

18   Received payment on account from Laramie Brothers, Invoice No. 1003, $872.50 (merchandise) less credit memo and 2 percent cash discount.

19   Sold merchandise on account to Parra Company, Invoice No. 1005, $990.

19   Paid Jensen Products, a creditor, on account, Check No. 105, $3,675 (merchandise) less credit memo and 1 percent cash discount.

22   Purchased merchandise on account from Chung Enterprises, Invoice No. 746, dated June 20, terms 2/10, n/30, $1,250.

23   Received payment on account from Acme Corporation, Invoice No. 1004, $765 less 2 percent cash discount.

24   Sold merchandise on account to Laramie Brothers, Invoice No. 1006, $968.

25   Issued Credit Memorandum No. 2 to Parra Company for merchandise returned, $85.

26   Purchased merchandise on account from Aroya Company, Invoice No. 221, dated June 23, terms net 30, $1,997.

29   Received payment on account from Parra Company, Invoice No. 1005, $990 (merchandise) less credit memo and 2 percent cash discount.

30   Sold merchandise on account to Markum Company, Invoice No. 1007, $1,497.

30   Paid electricity bill, Check No. 106, $145.

INSTRUCTIONS

1. For those students not using the working papers:
    a. This company uses a sales journal (as shown on page 374 of Chapter 11), a purchases journal (as shown on page 409 of Chapter 12), a cash receipts journal (as shown on page 457 of this chapter), a cash payments journal (as shown on page 460 of this chapter), and a general journal.
    b. Number each journal page 1.
    c. Open ledger accounts as follows:

GENERAL LEDGER

Account Title	Account No.
Cash	110
Accounts Receivable	111
Supplies	112
Equipment	115
Accounts Payable	210
Sandra Comiskey, Capital	310
Sales	410
Sales Discount	411
Sales Returns and Allowances	412
Purchases	501
Purchases Discount	502
Purchases Returns and Allowances . . .	503
Rent Expense	510
Utilities Expense	515

ACCOUNTS RECEIVABLE LEDGER

Acme Corporation
Laramie Brothers
Markum Company
Parra Company

ACCOUNTS PAYABLE LEDGER

Aroya Company
Chung Enterprises
Ferris Products
Jensen Products

2. Record these transactions in the appropriate journals.
   a. Post to the accounts receivable ledger daily.
   b. Post to the accounts payable ledger daily.
   c. Post the sundry accounts columns daily.
   d. Post the general journal daily.

3. At the end of the month:
   a. Total columns, verify equality of debits and credits, and rule the special journals.
   b. Post the Sales Journal column total.
   c. Post the Purchases Journal column total.
   d. Post the Cash Receipts Journal column totals.
   e. Post the Cash Payments Journal column totals.

Problems—Set B

**PROBLEM
13-1B**

CASH RECEIPTS
JOURNAL
(L.O.3, 4

During November 19XX, Cardinal Boutique, a retail business, completed the selected transactions that follow. The state levies a 6 percent sales tax on retail sales.

<table>
<tr><td>Partial Chart of Accounts</td></tr>
<tr><td>Cash</td></tr>
<tr><td>Accounts Receivable</td></tr>
<tr><td>Sales Tax Payable</td></tr>
<tr><td>Hilary Cardinal, Capital</td></tr>
<tr><td>Sales</td></tr>
<tr><td>Purchases Returns and Allowances</td></tr>
<tr><td>Credit Card Expense</td></tr>
</table>

Nov. 1   Sold merchandise for cash, $850 plus sales tax.

2   Sold merchandise, $410 plus sales tax; customer used a bank credit card charging a fee equal to 5 percent of sales plus tax.

5   Received payment on account from Merle Salasnek, a charge customer, $365.12.

9   Hilary Cardinal, the owner, invested an additional $8,000 cash in the business.

13   Sold merchandise, $700 plus sales tax; customer used a bank credit card charging a fee equal to 4 percent of sales plus tax.

16   Received a check from Magic Charge, $2,090. This check covered nonbank credit card invoices totaling $2,200 less their $110 fee.

19   Sold merchandise for cash, $150 plus sales tax.

22   Received a cash refund on merchandise returned to a

supplier, $45.20. (No cash discount was involved in the original purchase.)

Nov. 26   Received payment on account from Rita LaPointe, a charge customer, $726.

30   Received a check from Easy Charge, $1,710. This check covered nonbank credit card invoices totaling $1,800 less their $90 fee.

INSTRUCTIONS

1. For those students not using the working papers:
   a. This company uses a cash receipts journal as shown on page 449.
   b. Number this journal page 46.

2. Record these transactions in the cash receipts journal.

3. Total the amount columns in the journal.

4. Verify the equality of the debit and credit totals.

5. Rule the journal.

**PROBLEM
13-2B**
CASH PAYMENTS
JOURNAL
(L.O.2, 5)

Canton Company, a retail business, completed the following selected transactions during March 19XX:

Partial Chart of Accounts

Cash
Accounts Payable
Purchases
Purchases Discount
Rent Expense
Repair Expense
Utilities Expense

Mar. 1   Paid monthly rent, Check No. 785, $895.

3   Paid Santee Company, a creditor, on account, Check No. 786, $412.50.

6   Paid electricity bill, Check No. 787, $74.86.

9   Paid Grant Corporation, a creditor, on account, Check No. 788, $750 (merchandise) less 1 percent cash discount.

13   Voided Check No. 789.

Mar. 17   Purchased merchandise for cash, Check No. 790, $515.

19   Paid transportation charges on merchandise purchased on March 17, Check No. 791, $32.

22   Paid Baronson Company, a creditor, on account, Check No. 792, $1,480 ($1,400 merchandise, $80 transportation) less a 2 percent cash discount.

26   Paid for minor repair, Check No. 793, $41.

31   Paid Fordham Associates, a creditor, on account, Check No. 794, $323.75.

INSTRUCTIONS

1. For those students not using the working papers:
   a. This company uses a cash payments journal as shown on page 460.
   b. Number this journal page 62.

2. Record these transactions in the cash payments journal.

3. Total the amount columns in the journal.

4. Verify the equality of the debit and credit totals.

5. Rule the journal.

PROBLEM 13-3B

SPECIAL JOURNALS; ACCOUNTS RECEIVABLE LEDGER
(L.O.2, 4)

Kerrigan Corporation, a new wholesale business, completed the following selected transactions during January 19XX:

Jan. 1   Ralph Kerrigan, the owner, invested $15,000 cash in the business.

2   Sold merchandise on account to Paladin Company, Invoice No. 101, $540.

4   Received a cash refund on damaged merchandise returned to a supplier, $117. (No cash discount was involved in the original purchase.)

5   Sold merchandise for cash, Invoice No. 102, $184.

5   Sold merchandise on account to Duncan Corporation, Invoice No. 103, $1,210.

7   Sold merchandise for cash, Invoice No. 104, $97.30.

11   Received payment on account from Paladin Company, Invoice No. 101, $540 (merchandise) less a 2 percent cash discount.

13   Issued Credit Memorandum No. 1 to Duncan Corporation for merchandise returned, $94.

Jan. 15   Received payment on account from Duncan Corporation, Invoice No. 103, $1,210 (merchandise) less credit memo and 2 percent cash discount.

16   Sold merchandise on account to Anastasia Company, Invoice No. 105, $2,100.

19   Sold merchandise on account to Center Corporation, Invoice No. 106, $820.

20   Issued Credit Memorandum No. 2 to Anastasia Company for merchandise returned, $45.

23   Sold merchandise on account to Paladin Company, Invoice No. 107, $630.

26   Received payment on account from Anastasia Company, Invoice No. 105, $2,100 (merchandise) less credit memo and 2 percent cash discount.

29   Sold merchandise for cash, Invoice No. 108, $349.75.

31   Received payment on account from Center Corporation, Invoice No. 106, $820, no discount.

INSTRUCTIONS

1. For those students not using the working papers:
   a. This company uses a cash receipts journal (as shown on page 457 of this chapter), a sales journal (as shown on page 374 of Chapter 11), and a general journal.
   b. Number the cash receipts journal page 1, the sales journal page 1, and the general journal page 1.
   c. Open ledger accounts as follows:

GENERAL LEDGER

Account Title	Account No.
Cash	110
Accounts Receivable	111
Ralph Kerrigan, Capital	310
Sales	410
Sales Discount	411
Sales Returns and Allowances	412
Purchases Returns and Allowances	502

ACCOUNTS RECEIVABLE LEDGER

Account Title
Anastasia Company
Center Corporation
Duncan Corporation
Paladin Company

2. Record these transactions in the appropriate journals.
   a. Post to the accounts receivable ledger daily.
   b. Post the Sundry Accounts Credit column daily.
   c. Post the general journal daily.

3. At the end of the month:
   a. Total columns, verify equality of debits and credits, and rule the special journals.
   b. Post the Sales Journal column total.
   c. Post the Cash Receipts Journal column totals.

PROBLEM 13-4B
SPECIAL JOURNALS; SUBSIDIARY LEDGERS (L.O.2, 4, 5)

Flanigan Company, a new wholesale business, completed the following transactions during July 19XX:

July 1   Robert Flanigan, the owner, invested $30,000 cash in the business.

1   Paid monthly rent, Check No. 101, $890.

2   Purchased merchandise on account from Frank Enterprises, Invoice No. 727, dated July 1, terms 2/10, n/30, $3,150.

3   Purchased supplies on account from Marlow Products, Invoice No. 592, dated July 1, net 30, $529.60.

4   Sold merchandise on account to Lasker Company, Invoice No. 1001, $1,550.

4   Sold merchandise for cash, Invoice No. 1002, $475.56.

5   Purchased equipment for cash, Check No. 102, $3,698.

8   Sold merchandise on account to Caltron Brothers, Invoice No. 1003, $937.50.

8   Received payment on account from Lasker Company, Invoice No. 1001, $1,550 (merchandise) less a 2 percent cash discount.

10   Purchased merchandise on account from Target Products, Invoice No. 2184, dated July 9, terms 1/10, n/30, $2,980.

11   Paid Frank Enterprises, a creditor, on account, Check No. 103, $3,150 (merchandise) less 2 percent cash discount.

12   Paid Marlow Products, a creditor, on account, Check No. 104, $529.60.

15   Sold merchandise on account to Barr Corporation, Invoice No. 1004, $985.

July 16   Issued Credit Memorandum No. 1 to Caltron Brothers for merchandise returned, $72.

17   Received Credit Memorandum No. 97 from Target Products, a supplier, for merchandise returned, $100.

18   Received payment on account from Caltron Brothers, Invoice No. 1003, $937.50 (merchandise) less credit memo and 2 percent cash discount.

19   Sold merchandise on account to Varga Company, Invoice No. 1005, $730.

19   Paid Target Products, a creditor, on account, Check No. 105, $2,980 (merchandise) less credit memo and 1 percent cash discount.

22   Purchased merchandise on account from Frank Enterprises, Invoice No. 759, dated July 20, terms 2/10, n/30, $1,460.

23   Received payment on account from Barr Corporation, Invoice No. 1004, $985 less 2 percent cash discount.

24   Sold merchandise on account to Caltron Brothers, Invoice No. 1006, $895.

25   Issued Credit Memorandum No. 2 to Varga Company for merchandise returned, $70.

26   Purchased merchandise on account from Brent Company, Invoice No. 315, dated July 23, terms net 30, $1,874.

29   Received payment on account from Varga Company, Invoice No. 1005, $730 (merchandise) less credit memo and 2 percent cash discount.

30   Sold merchandise on account to Lasker Company, Invoice No. 1007, $1,625.

30   Paid utility bill, Check No. 106, $179.

INSTRUCTIONS

1. For those students not using the working papers:
   a. This company uses a sales journal (as shown on page 374 of Chapter 11), a purchases journal (as shown on page 409 of Chapter 12), a cash receipts journal (as shown on page 457 of this chapter), a cash payments journal (as shown on page 460 of this chapter), and a general journal.
   b. Number each journal page 1.
   c. Open ledger accounts as follows:

GENERAL LEDGER

Account Title	Account No.
Cash	110
Accounts Receivable	111
Supplies	112
Equipment	115
Accounts Payable	210
Robert Flanigan, Capital	310
Sales	410
Sales Discount	411
Sales Returns and Allowances	412
Purchases	501
Purchases Discount	502
Purchases Returns and Allowances	503
Rent Expense	510
Utilities Expense	515

ACCOUNTS RECEIVABLE LEDGER

Barr Corporation
Caltron Brothers
Lasker Company
Varga Company

ACCOUNTS PAYABLE LEDGER

Brent Company
Frank Enterprises
Marlow Products
Target Products

2. Record these transactions in the appropriate journals.
   a. Post to the accounts receivable ledger daily.
   b. Post to the accounts payable ledger daily.
   c. Post the sundry accounts columns daily.
   d. Post the general journal daily.

3. At the end of the month:
   a. Total columns, verify equality of debits and credits, and rule the special journals.
   b. Post the Sales Journal column total.
   c. Post the Purchases Journal column total.
   d. Post the Cash Receipts Journal column totals.
   e. Post the Cash Payments Journal column totals.

Mini-Cases

Your friend Max is self-employed. He is shopping around for a good price on a file cabinet for his office. Showing you a wholesale catalog, Max says: "This list price seems high. I paid a lot less for the last one I purchased from this same company." How would you respond to Max's comment?

Sarah, your neighbor, has just started a new business. A potential supplier has offered credit terms of 2/10, n/30. Sarah's accountant has explained that they will be able to deduct a 2 percent cash discount if they pay this supplier within 10 days. Sarah, however, believes her accountant is wrong. She believes 2/10 means they will be able to deduct a 10 percent discount if they pay within two days. "After all," says Sarah, "who would ever bother if the discount was only 2 percent!" How would you respond?

Your client, owner of a small retail business, is thinking of allowing customers to use bank and nonbank credit cards to pay for their purchases. He asks your opinion of the pros and cons of such an arrangement.

CHAPTER 14

Merchandising Business: The Work Sheet

||||||||||||||||||
L E A R N I N G
O B J E C T I V E S

AFTER STUDYING THIS CHAPTER, YOU SHOULD BE ABLE TO:

1 Prepare a work sheet for a mechandising business.

2 Adjust the Merchandise Inventory account.

3 Adjust for unearned revenue.

4 Record adjustments for supplies, insurance, wages, and depreciation.

In the last three chapters, you learned how to journalize and post the day-to-day transactions of a merchandising business using special journals and subsidiary ledgers. In this chapter, you will continue with the accounting cycle for a merchandising business by studying the preparation of a work sheet.

As you will recall, the work sheet is a tool used by accountants to rough draft adjustments and financial statements. This process of rough drafting helps to organize information as well as to detect and correct errors before preparing formal financial statements and adjusting entries.

▋▋▋▋ PREPARING THE WORK SHEET

OBJECTIVE 1
PREPARE A WORK SHEET FOR A MERCHANDISING BUSINESS

In Chapter 5, you learned to prepare a work sheet for a service business. A work sheet for a merchandising business follows the same basic format.

To demonstrate, let's return to The Kitchen Taylor. Before preparing year-end financial statements, The Kitchen Taylor (now a merchandising business) will prepare a work sheet following the steps outlined in Chapter 5.

Step 1: Prepare a three-line heading containing the following:
   a. Company name.
   b. Work sheet.
   c. Date.

Step 2: Prepare the trial balance.

Step 3: Rough draft the adjustments.

As you know, adjusting entries are really updating entries. The need to update exists because a few internal transactions have occurred that have not yet been recorded. It is acceptable to allow these internal transactions to go unrecorded on a daily basis, but we cannot prepare financial statements with incorrect account balances. Therefore, before preparing financial statements, we must adjust the accounts.

Figure 14-1 shows The Kitchen Taylor's work sheet completed through Step 3. Let's study the adjustments, paying particular attention to those that are new—adjustments *(a), (b),* and *(c).*

THE ADJUSTMENT FOR MERCHANDISE INVENTORY

OBJECTIVE 2
ADJUST THE MERCHANDISE INVENTORY ACCOUNT

The Merchandise Inventory account is an asset account. Its balance should indicate the cost of unsold merchandise. As you learned in Chapters 11 and 12, the following entries are recorded when merchandise is purchased and sold.

FIGURE 14 - 1

THE KITCHEN TAYLOR
Work Sheet
For the Year Ended December 31, 19X3

Account Title	Trial Balance Debit	Trial Balance Credit	Adjustments Debit	Adjustments Credit
Cash	12,395 00			
Accounts Receivable	17,800 00			
Merchandise Inventory	24,500 00		(b) 26,000 00	(a) 24,500 00
Supplies	1,137 00			(d) 640 00
Prepaid Insurance	1,260 00			(e) 930 00
Truck	6,000 00			
Accumulated Depreciation—Truck		2,200 00		(g) 1,100 00
Building	85,000 00			
Accumulated Depreciation—Building		12,900 00		(h) 4,300 00
Land	10,000 00			
Accounts Payable		10,518 00		
Unearned Revenue		1,000 00	(c) 600 00	
Mortgage Payable		62,500 00		
Dennis Taylor, Capital		73,524 00		
Dennis Taylor, Drawing	29,239 00			
Sales		105,475 00		(c) 600 00
Sales Returns and Allowances	1,472 00			
Sales Discount	1,546 00			
Interest Income		1,850 00		
Purchases	51,000 00			
Purchases Returns and Allowances		693 00		
Purchases Discount		985 00		
Interest Expense	2,376 00			
Utilities Expense	3,130 00			
Wages Expense	24,790 00		(f) 300 00	
	271,645 00	271,645 00		
Income Summary			(a) 24,500 00	(b) 26,000 00
Supplies Expense			(d) 640 00	
Insurance Expense			(e) 930 00	
Wages Payable				(f) 300 00
Depreciation Expense—Truck			(g) 1,100 00	
Depreciation Expense—Building			(h) 4,300 00	
			58,370 00	58,370 00

(handwritten note in margin: Purchases is an Income Statement Balance)

To record a purchase:

    Dr. Purchases
           Cr. Accounts Payable or Cash

To record a sale:

    Dr. Accounts Receivable or Cash
           Cr. Sales

Although a purchase increases the inventory of merchandise and a sale decreases the inventory of merchandise, the Merchandise Inventory account is not touched in these entries. By the end of the fiscal year, the balance in this account is out of date. Before preparing financial statements, the Merchandise Inventory account is updated in two parts. These two parts are labeled adjustments *(a)* and *(b)* on The Kitchen Taylor's work sheet. Through these adjustments, the Merchandise Inventory account is updated as follows:

  a. The old or beginning balance ($24,500), as shown in the trial balance, is taken out of the Merchandise Inventory account with a credit. It is transferred to the Income Summary account with a debit.

Merchandise Inventory		Income Summary	
Dr.	Cr.	Dr.	Cr.
Bal. 24,500	Adj. *(a)* 24,500	Adj. *(a)* 24,500	

The balance in the Merchandise Inventory account is now zero.

  b. The up-to-date or ending balance ($26,000) is entered in the Merchandise Inventory account with a debit. The balancing credit goes to the Income Summary account.

Merchandise Inventory		Income Summary	
Dr.	Cr.	Dr.	Cr.
Bal. 24,500	Adj. 24,500	Adj. 24,500	Adj. *(b)* 26,000
Adj. *(b)* 26,000			

The balance in the Merchandise Inventory account is now $26,000.

|||||||||||||||||||||||

C O M M E N T   The up-to-date or ending balance is based on the results of a physical inventory taken at year-end. The **physical inventory** is an actual count of the units on hand at the end of the fiscal year. In the exercises and problems, you will be given this figure.

After adjustments *(a)* and *(b)*, the balance in the Merchandise Inventory account represents the cost of unsold merchandise. The cost of merchandise that has been sold is shown in the Income Summary account.

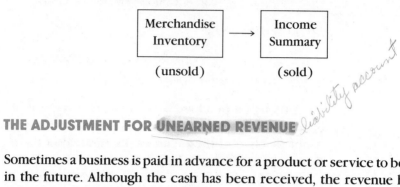

THE ADJUSTMENT FOR UNEARNED REVENUE *liability account*

OBJECTIVE 3
ADJUST FOR UNEARNED REVENUE

Sometimes a business is paid in advance for a product or service to be delivered in the future. Although the cash has been received, the revenue has not yet been earned. This creates a liability for the seller. The seller now owes the customer the product or service.

To demonstrate, let's assume The Kitchen Taylor received $1,000 from a customer as an advance payment for five cabinets ($200 each) that had to be special ordered. This transaction was recorded as follows:

Cash	1,000	
Unearned Revenue		1,000

|||||||||||||||||||||||
C O M M E N T

Unearned Revenue is a liability account. Although most liability accounts end with the word *payable,* accounts that begin with the word *unearned* are also liability accounts.

By December 31, the end of The Kitchen Taylor's fiscal year, three of the five cabinets have been delivered to the customer. The accounts must now be updated if the year-end financial statements are to be accurate. The updating is accomplished through the following adjustment. This adjustment is labeled *(c)* on The Kitchen Taylor's work sheet.

Unearned Revenue *liability*				**Sales** *revenue*		
Dr.		Cr.		Dr.		Cr.
Adj. *(c)* 600		Bal. 1,000				Adj. *(c)* 600

Computations:
  Earned revenue = 3 × $200 = $600
  Unearned revenue = 2 × $200 = $400

The revenue associated with the three cabinets that have been delivered to the customer has now been earned. Accordingly, $600 must be removed from the liability account, Unearned Revenue, and transferred to the revenue account, Sales. The $400 associated with the two cabinets that have not been delivered remains a liability until the cabinets are delivered to the customer.

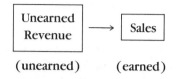

(unearned)   (earned)

Chapter 5 contains a detailed discussion of the remaining adjustments. The following will serve as a brief review.

THE ADJUSTMENT FOR SUPPLIES

OBJECTIVE 4
RECORD ADJUSTMENTS
FOR SUPPLIES,
INSURANCE, WAGES,
AND DEPRECIATION

The Kitchen Taylor has determined that $640 of supplies have been used. The cost of used supplies must be transferred from the Supplies account to the Supplies Expense account. This adjustment is labeled *(d)* on The Kitchen Taylor's work sheet.

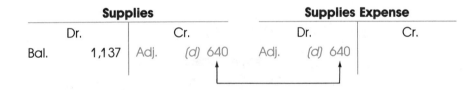

After adjustment *(d)*, the balance in the Supplies account represents the cost of unused supplies. The balance in the Supplies Expense account represents the cost of used supplies.

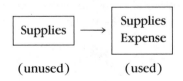

(unused)   (used)

THE ADJUSTMENT FOR INSURANCE

The Kitchen Taylor has determined that $930 of insurance has expired. The cost of the expired insurance must be transferred from the Prepaid Insurance account to the Insurance Expense account. This adjustment is labeled *(e)* on The Kitchen Taylor's work sheet.

	Prepaid Insurance				Insurance Expense	
	Dr.	Cr.			Dr.	Cr.
Bal.	1,260	Adj. *(e)* 930		Adj.	*(e)* 930	

After adjustment *(e),* the balance in the Prepaid Insurance account represents the cost of unexpired insurance. The balance in the Insurance Expense account represents the cost of expired insurance.

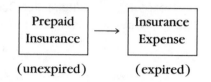

Prepaid Insurance	→	Insurance Expense
(unexpired)		(expired)

THE ADJUSTMENT FOR WAGES

As of December 31, $300 of wages expense has been incurred but not yet paid. Since this expense has been incurred, it must be recorded in the Wages Expense account even though it is not yet paid. The resulting liability to employees is recorded in the Wages Payable account. This adjustment is labeled *(f)* on The Kitchen Taylor's work sheet.

	Wages Expense				Wages Payable	
	Dr.	Cr.			Dr.	. Cr.
Bal.	24,790				Adj.	*(f)* 300
Adj.	*(f)* 300					

After adjustment *(f),* the balance in the Wages Expense account represents the total wages expense that has been incurred (paid or unpaid). The balance in the Wages Payable account represents wages that are owed to employees.

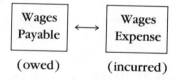

Wages Payable	↔	Wages Expense
(owed)		(incurred)

THE ADJUSTMENT FOR DEPRECIATION ON THE TRUCK

The annual depreciation on the truck amounts to $1,100. As you will recall, the purchase of a plant asset is recorded by increasing an asset account. As the asset is used up, the cost associated with the used-up portion is transferred to the depreciation expense account. However, the asset account is reduced indirectly through the accumulated depreciation account, a contra-asset account. This year, The Kitchen Taylor is transferring $1,100 of used-up cost associated with the truck to the Depreciation Expense—Truck account. This adjustment is labeled *(g)* on The Kitchen Taylor's work sheet.

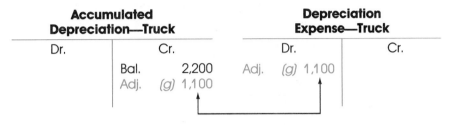

After adjustment *(g)*, the balance in the Truck account less the balance in the Accumulated Depreciation —Truck account represents the unused cost of the truck. The balance in the Depreciation Expense—Truck account represents the cost that has been used up this year.

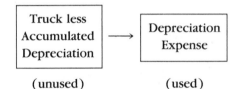

THE ADJUSTMENT FOR DEPRECIATION ON THE BUILDING

The annual depreciation on the building amounts to $4,300. This year, The Kitchen Taylor is transferring $4,300 of used-up cost associated with the building to the Depreciation Expense—Building account. This adjustment is labeled *(h)* on The Kitchen Taylor's work sheet.

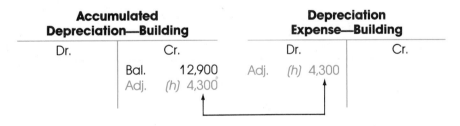

After adjustment *(h)*, the balance in the Building account less the balance in the Accumulated Depreciation—Building account represents the unused cost of the building. The balance in the Depreciation Expense—Building account represents the cost that has been used up this year.

FIGURE 14 - 2

THE KITCHEN TAYLOR
Work Sheet
For the Year Ended December 31, 19X3

Account Title	Trial Balance		Adjustments	
	Debit	Credit	Debit	Credit
Cash	12,395 00			
Accounts Receivable	17,800 00			
Merchandise Inventory	24,500 00		(b) 26,000 00	(a) 24,500 00
Supplies	1,137 00			(d) 640 00
Prepaid Insurance	1,260 00			(e) 930 00
Truck	6,000 00			
Accumulated Depreciation—Truck		2,200 00		(g) 1,100 00
Building	85,000 00			
Accumulated Depreciation—Building		12,900 00		(h) 4,300 00
Land	10,000 00			
Accounts Payable		10,518 00		
Unearned Revenue		1,000 00	(c) 600 00	
Mortgage Payable		62,500 00		
Dennis Taylor, Capital		73,524 00		
Dennis Taylor, Drawing	29,239 00			
Sales		105,475 00		(c) 600 00
Sales Returns and Allowances	1,472 00			
Sales Discount	1,546 00			
Interest Income		1,850 00		
Purchases	51,000 00			
Purchases Returns and Allowances		693 00		
Purchases Discount		985 00		
Interest Expense	2,376 00			
Utilities Expense	3,130 00			
Wages Expense	24,790 00		(f) 300 00	
	271,645 00	271,645 00		
Income Summary			(a) 24,500 00	(b) 26,000 00
Supplies Expense			(d) 640 00	
Insurance Expense			(e) 930 00	
Wages Payable				(f) 300 00
Depreciation Expense–Truck			(g) 1,100 00	
Depreciation Expense—Building			(h) 4,300 00	
			58,370 00	58,370 00
Net Income				

Adjusted Trial Balance		Income Statement		Balance Sheet	
Debit	Credit	Debit	Credit	Debit	Credit
12,395 00				12,395 00	
17,800 00				17,800 00	
26,000 00				26,000 00	
497 00				497 00	
330 00				330 00	
6,000 00				6,000 00	
	3,300 00				3,300 00
85,000 00				85,000 00	
	17,200 00				17,200 00
10,000 00				10,000 00	
	10,518 00				10,518 00
	400 00				400 00
	62,500 00				62,500 00
	73,524 00				73,524 00
29,239 00				29,239 00	
	106,075 00		106,075 00		
1,472 00		1,472 00			
1,546 00		1,546 00			
	1,850 00		1,850 00		
51,000 00		51,000 00			
	693 00		693 00		
	985 00		985 00		
2,376 00		2,376 00			
3,130 00		3,130 00			
25,090 00		25,090 00			
24,500 00	26,000 00	24,500 00	26,000 00		
640 00		640 00			
930 00		930 00			
	300 00				300 00
1,100 00		1,100 00			
4,300 00		4,300 00			
303,345 00	303,345 00	116,084 00	135,603 00	187,261 00	167,742 00
		19,519 00			19,519 00
		135,603 00	135,603 00	187,261 00	187,261 00

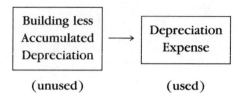

(unused)   (used)

COMPLETION OF THE WORK SHEET

Now that the adjustments are complete, the Adjustments columns should be totaled and checked for equality. The remainder of the work sheet is completed following the steps described in Chapter 5.

Step 4:   Prepare the adjusted trial balance.

Step 5:   Rough draft the income statement and balance sheet.

Step 6:   Total and balance the Income Statement columns.

Step 7:   Total and balance the Balance Sheet columns.

Figure 14-2 shows The Kitchen Taylor's completed work sheet.

||||||||||||||||||||||
COMMENT

Observe that both the debit and the credit in the Income Summary account are extended separately to the Adjusted Trial Balance and Income Statement columns of the work sheet. These two figures represent the beginning and ending Merchandise Inventory account balances. Since both are needed on the formal income statement, both are extended on the work sheet. This will be discussed in greater detail in Chapter 15.

In the next chapter, you will use The Kitchen Taylor's completed work sheet to prepare formal financial statements and to record the adjustments in the general journal.

Chapter Summary

A work sheet is a tool used by accountants to rough draft adjustments and financial statements. This process of rough drafting helps to organize information as well as to detect mathematical errors before preparing formal financial statements and journal entries.

In Chapter 5, you learned to prepare a work sheet for a service business. A work sheet for a merchandising business follows the same basic format.

Step 1: Prepare a three-line heading.

Step 2: Prepare the trial balance.

Step 3: Rough draft the adjustments. Two new adjustments were presented in this chapter.

- Merchandise Inventory. By year end, the balance in this account is out of date. We update the balance in two parts.
  a. The old or beginning balance is taken out of the Merchandise Inventory account with a credit. The Income Summary account is debited for the same amount.

Merchandise Inventory		Income Summary	
Dr.	Cr.	Dr.	Cr.
Bal. 24,500	Adj. *(a)* 24,500	Adj. *(a)* 24,500	

  b. The up-to-date or ending balance is entered in the Merchandise Inventory account with a debit. The Income Summary account is credited for the same amount.

Merchandise Inventory		Income Summary	
Dr.	Cr.	Dr.	Cr.
Bal. 24,500	Adj. 24,500	Adj. 24,500	Adj. *(b)* 26,000
Adj. *(b)* 26,000			

- Unearned Revenue. When a business is paid in advance for a product or service to be delivered in the future, Cash is debited and Unearned Revenue, a liability account, is credited.

Cash 1,000
      Unearned Revenue 1,000

At year-end, earned revenue must be removed from the liability account, Unearned Revenue, with a debit and transferred to the appropriate revenue account with a credit.

Unearned Revenue				Sales		
Dr.		**Cr.**		**Dr.**		**Cr.**
Adj.	*(c)* 600	Bal.	1,000		Adj.	*(c)* 600

Step 4:   Prepare the adjusted trial balance.

Step 5:   Rough draft the income statement and balance sheet.

Step 6:   Total and balance the Income Statement columns.

Step 7:   Total and balance the Balance Sheet columns.

In Chapter 15, you will complete the accounting cycle for a merchandising business with the preparation of financial statements, adjusting entries, closing entries, and a post-closing trial balance.

Glossary

PHYSICAL INVENTORY

An actual count of the units on hand at the end of the fiscal year.

UNEARNED REVENUE

The liability to the customer created when cash has been received for a product or service to be delivered in the future. The seller now owes the customer the product or service.

Questions for Discussion

1. How is the work sheet for a merchandising business different from the work sheet for a service business?

2. Why must the Merchandise Inventory account be adjusted?

3. The Merchandise Inventory account is adjusted in two parts. Describe each part.

4. *a.* What is a physical inventory?
   b. How does a physical inventory relate to the adjustment of the Merchandise Inventory account?

5. *a.* What is unearned revenue?
   b. Why is unearned revenue a liability to the seller?

6. Why must the Supplies account be adjusted?

7. Why must the Prepaid Insurance account be adjusted?

8. Why is an adjustment for wages necessary?

9. In recording annual depreciation:
   a. What account is debited? On what statement will it appear? What information does its balance convey?
   b. What account is credited? On what statement will it appear? What information does its balance convey?

10. After the adjustment of merchandise inventory, why are both the debit and the credit figures in the Income Summary account extended to the Income Statement columns of the work sheet?

Exercises

EXERCISE 14-1
ADJUSTMENT OF
MERCHANDISE
INVENTORY
(L.O.2)

Before adjustment on December 31, 19X1, the Merchandise Inventory account appears as follows:

Account	Merchandise Inventory					Account No.	113
						Balance	
Date	Item	Post. Ref.	Debit	Credit	Debit	Credit	
19X1 Jan. 1	Balance	√			64,350 00		

A physical inventory indicates an ending inventory of $69,675 on December 31, 19X1. In general journal form, record the entries necessary to adjust the Merchandise Inventory account at the end of the fiscal year.

EXERCISE 14-2
MERCHANDISE
INVENTORY
(L.O.2)

After the adjustment of merchandise inventory on December 31, 19X1, the Income Summary account appears as follows:

Account	Income Summary					Account No.	313
						Balance	
Date	Item	Post. Ref.	Debit	Credit	− Debit	+ Credit	
19X1 Dec. 31	Adjusting	J56	83,240 00		83,240 00		
31	Adjusting	J56		85,972 00		2,732 00	

Based on this information:

    a. What was the beginning merchandise inventory?

    b. What was the ending merchandise inventory?

EXERCISE 14-3
ADJUSTMENT FOR
UNEARNED REVENUE
(L.O.3)

On August 1, 19X1, RMP Enterprises received $6,000 in cash from a commercial tenant representing an advance payment of rent for the six-month period August 1, 19X1, through January 31, 19X2. This transaction was recorded with the following entry:

```
19X1
Aug.  1   Cash . . . . . . . . . . . . . . .   6,000
                Unearned Revenue   . . . . . .        6,000
```

    a. In general journal form, record the adjusting entry necessary on December 31, 19X1, the end of RMP's fiscal year. RMP has an account titled Rental Revenue in its general ledger.

    b. Relative to this situation, the December 31, 19X1, balance sheet will show what account and balance?

    c. Relative to this situation, the December 31, 19X1, income statement will show what account and balance?

EXERCISE 14-4
ADJUSTMENT FOR
SUPPLIES
(L.O.4)

The December 1, 19X1, balance in the Supplies account is $736. On December 31, 19X1, $495 worth of supplies are left unused in the storeroom.

    a. In general journal form, record the adjusting entry necessary on December 31.

    b. Relative to this situation, the December 31 balance sheet will show what account and balance?

    c. Relative to this situation, the December 31 income statement will show what account and balance?

EXERCISE 14-5
ADJUSTMENT FOR
PREPAID INSURANCE
(L.O.4)

On September 1, 19X1, an enterprise paid a $360 premium for one year of insurance coverage. This future coverage was recorded in the Prepaid Insurance account.

    a. In general journal form, record the adjusting entry necessary on December 31, 19X1.

    b. Relative to this situation, the December 31 balance sheet will show what account and balance?

c. Relative to this situation, the December 31 income statement will show what account and balance?

EXERCISE 14-6
ADJUSTMENT FOR WAGES
(L.O.4)

A business pays its employees a total of $1,500 for a five-day workweek (Monday through Friday). Payday is each Friday. December 31, 19X1, falls on Thursday.

a. In general journal form, record the adjusting entry necessary on December 31, 19X1.

b. Relative to this situation, the December 31 balance sheet will show what account and balance?

c. Relative to this situation, the December 31 income statement will show what account and balance?

EXERCISE 14-7
ADJUSTMENT FOR DEPRECIATION
(L.O.4)

On December 31, 19X1, Cub Products wishes to record $920 of depreciation on equipment purchased earlier in 19X1.

a. In general journal form, record the adjusting entry necessary on December 31, 19X1.

b. Relative to this situation, the December 31 balance sheet will show what account and balance?

c. Relative to this situation, the December 31 income statement will show what account and balance?

EXERCISE 14-8
ACCOUNT CLASSIFICATION; NORMAL BALANCE
(L.O.1)

Identify each of the accounts in the numbered list shown on page 504 as one of the following classes of accounts:

a. Asset.

b. Contra asset.

c. Liability.

d. Owner's equity.

e. Revenue.

f. Contra revenue.

g. Purchases.

h. Contra purchases.

i. Expense.

Also indicate each account's normal balance (debit or credit).

Account	Classification	Normal Balance
1. Sales		
2. Wages Payable		
3. Purchases Discount		
4. Depreciation Expense		
5. Merchandise Inventory		
6. Denise Jones, Capital		
7. Sales Returns and Allowances		
8. Accumulated Depreciation		
9. Purchases		
10. Unearned Revenue		
11. Sales Discount		
12. Prepaid Insurance		
13. Purchases Returns and Allowances		
14. Wages Expense		
15. Cash		

Problems—Set A

PROBLEM
14-1A
WORK SHEET
(L.O.1–4)

On December 31, 19X1, the end of the fiscal year, Sandberg Company's ledger shows the following accounts and balances before adjustment:

	Debit	Credit
Cash	4,600 00	
Accounts Receivable	8,750 00	
Merchandise Inventory	10,342 00	
Supplies	1,076 00	
Prepaid Insurance	420 00	
Equipment	12,000 00	
Accumulated Depreciation—Equipment		2,000 00
Accounts Payable		7,325 00
Unearned Revenue		1,020 00
Carol Sandberg, Capital		35,900 00
Carol Sandberg, Drawing	31,092 00	
Sales		65,500 00
Purchases	18,375 00	
Rent Expense	10,200 00	
Utilities Expense	2,340 00	
Wages Expense	12,550 00	

INSTRUCTIONS

Prepare a work sheet for the fiscal year ended December 31, 19X1, using the following adjustment data:

    a.–b. Ending merchandise inventory on December 31, $12,654.

       c. Unearned revenue of $720 has now been earned.

> *d.* Used supplies amount to $563.
>
> *e.* Insurance expired during the year, $305.
>
> *f.* Wages expense incurred but not yet paid as of December 31, $480.
>
> *g.* Annual depreciation on the equipment, $1,000.

PROBLEM 14-2A
WORK SHEET
(L.O.1–4)

On June 30, 19X1, the end of the fiscal year, LaPointe Company's ledger shows the following accounts and balances before adjustment:

	Debit	Credit
Cash	6,450 00	
Accounts Receivable	10,922 00	
Merchandise Inventory	15,218 00	
Supplies	946 00	
Prepaid Insurance	1,408 00	
Truck	12,500 00	
Accumulated Depreciation—Truck		2,250 00
Accounts Payable		11,826 00
Unearned Revenue		3,690 00
Rita LaPointe, Capital		33,200 00
Rita LaPointe, Drawing	20,400 00	
Sales		75,100 00
Sales Returns and Allowances	312 00	
Purchases	27,810 00	
Purchases Returns and Allowances		210 00
Rent Expense	9,600 00	
Utilities Expense	2,170 00	
Wages Expense	18,540 00	

INSTRUCTIONS
Prepare a work sheet for the fiscal year ended June 30, 19X1, using the following adjustment data:

> *a.–b.* Ending merchandise inventory on June 30, $14,104.
>
> *c.* Unearned revenue of $2,650 has now been earned.

> d. Used supplies amount to $610.
>
> e. Insurance expired during the year, $926.
>
> f. Wages expense incurred but not yet paid as of June 30, $840.
>
> g. Annual depreciation on the truck, $1,125.

**PROBLEM
14-3A**
WORK SHEET
(L.O.1–4)

On September 30, 19X1, the end of the fiscal year, Waubonsee Enterprises' ledger shows the following accounts and balances before adjustment:

	Debit	Credit
Cash	18,212 00	
Accounts Receivable	24,376 00	
Merchandise Inventory	35,420 00	
Supplies	1,790 00	
Prepaid Insurance	2,472 00	
Building	86,400 00	
Accumulated Depreciation—Building		6,930 00
Land	18,000 00	
Accounts Payable		25,698 00
Unearned Revenue		1,760 00
Mortgage Payable		62,500 00
Charles Woods, Capital		100,712 00
Charles Woods, Drawing	36,500 00	
Sales		165,900 00
Sales Returns and Allowances	1,904 00	
Sales Discount	2,310 00	
Purchases	105,986 00	
Purchases Returns and Allowances		612 00
Purchases Discount		1,594 00
Interest Expense	5,632 00	
Utilities Expense	2,978 00	
Wages Expense	23,726 00	

INSTRUCTIONS
Prepare a work sheet for the fiscal year ended September 30, 19X1, using the following adjustment data:

a.–b. Ending merchandise inventory on September 30, $39,610.

   c. Unearned revenue of $1,450 has now been earned.

   d. Supplies on hand on September 30, $814.

   e. Insurance expired during the year, $1,682.

   f. Wages expense incurred but not yet paid as of September 30, $1,946.

   g. Annual depreciation on the building, $2,472.

PROBLEM 14-4A
WORK SHEET
(L.O.1–4)

On December 31, 19X1, the end of the fiscal year, Superior Company's ledger shows the following accounts and balances before adjustment:

	Debit	Credit
Cash	9,270 00	
Accounts Receivable	13,468 00	
Merchandise Inventory	18,976 00	
Supplies	1,324 00	
Prepaid Insurance	2,182 00	
Equipment	25,336 00	
Accumulated Depreciation—Equipment		3,580 00
Building	99,500 00	
Accumulated Depreciation—Building		7,936 00
Land	25,000 00	
Accounts Payable		14,710 00
Unearned Revenue		2,406 00
Mortgage Payable		65,000 00
Ralph Schirmer, Capital		96,270 00
Ralph Schirmer, Drawing	31,500 00	
Sales		145,800 00
Sales Returns and Allowances	1,082 00	
Sales Discount	2,148 00	
Purchases	67,924 00	
Purchases Returns and Allowances		544 00
Purchases Discount		786 00
Interest Expense	7,250 00	
Utilities Expense	2,712 00	
Wages Expense	29,360 00	

INSTRUCTIONS

Prepare a work sheet for the fiscal year ended December 31, 19X1, using the following adjustment data:

a.–b. Ending merchandise inventory on December 31, $21,542.

c. Unearned revenue of $1,732 has now been earned.

d. Supplies on hand on December 31, $590.

e. Insurance expired during the year, $1,746.

f. Wages expense incurred but not yet paid as of December 31, $1,280.

g. Annual depreciation on the equipment, $1,050.

h. Annual depreciation on the building, $4,100.

Problems—Set B

PROBLEM
14-1B
WORK SHEET
(L.O.1–4)

On December 31, 19X1, the end of the fiscal year, Barberra Company's ledger shows the following accounts and balances before adjustment:

	Debit	Credit
Cash	9,200 00	
Accounts Receivable	17,500 00	
Merchandise Inventory	20,684 00	
Supplies	2,152 00	
Prepaid Insurance	840 00	
Equipment	24,000 00	
Accumulated Depreciation—Equipment		4,000 00
Accounts Payable		14,650 00
Unearned Revenue		2,040 00
John Barberra, Capital		71,800 00
John Barberra, Drawing	62,184 00	
Sales		131,000 00
Purchases	36,750 00	
Rent Expense	20,400 00	
Utilities Expense	4,680 00	
Wages Expense	25,100 00	

INSTRUCTIONS

Prepare a work sheet for the fiscal year ended December 31, 19X1, using the following adjustment data:

    a.–b. Ending merchandise inventory on December 31, $25,308.

        c. Unearned revenue of $1,440 has now been earned.

 d. Used supplies amount to $1,123.

 e. Insurance expired during the year, $610.

 f. Wages expense incurred but not yet paid as of December 31, $960.

 g. Annual depreciation on the equipment, $2,000.

PROBLEM 14-2B
WORK SHEET
(L.O.1–4)

On June 30, 19X1, the end of the fiscal year, Wargo Company's ledger shows the following accounts and balances before adjustment:

	Debit	Credit
Cash	12,900 00	
Accounts Receivable	21,844 00	
Merchandise Inventory	30,436 00	
Supplies	1,892 00	
Prepaid Insurance	2,816 00	
Truck	14,600 00	
Accumulated Depreciation—Truck		2,510 00
Accounts Payable		23,652 00
Unearned Revenue		7,380 00
Peter Wargo, Capital		57,990 00
Peter Wargo, Drawing	40,800 00	
Sales		150,200 00
Sales Returns and Allowances	624 00	
Purchases	55,620 00	
Purchases Returns and Allowances		420 00
Rent Expense	19,200 00	
Utilities Expense	4,340 00	
Wages Expense	37,080 00	

INSTRUCTIONS
Prepare a work sheet for the fiscal year ended June 30, 19X1, using the following adjustment data:

 a.–b. Ending merchandise inventory on June 30, $28,204.

 c. Unearned revenue of $5,300 has now been earned.

    d. Used supplies amount to $1,220.

    e. Insurance expired during the year, $1,852.

    f. Wages expense incurred but not yet paid as of June 30, $1,680.

    g. Annual depreciation on the truck, $1,255.

**PROBLEM
14-3B**
WORK SHEET
(L.O.1–4)

On September 30, 19X1, the end of the fiscal year, Moran Industries' ledger shows the following accounts and balances before adjustment:

	Debit	Credit
Cash	9,106 00	
Accounts Receivable	12,188 00	
Merchandise Inventory	17,710 00	
Supplies	895 00	
Prepaid Insurance	1,236 00	
Building	43,200 00	
Accumulated Depreciation—Building		3,465 00
Land	8,500 00	
Accounts Payable		12,849 00
Unearned Revenue		880 00
Mortgage Payable		31,250 00
Grace Moran, Capital		49,856 00
Grace Moran, Drawing	18,250 00	
Sales		82,950 00
Sales Returns and Allowances	952 00	
Sales Discount	1,155 00	
Purchases	52,993 00	
Purchases Returns and Allowances		306 00
Purchases Discount		797 00
Interest Expense	2,816 00	
Utilities Expense	1,489 00	
Wages Expense	11,863 00	

INSTRUCTIONS
Prepare a work sheet for the fiscal year ended September 30, 19X1, using the following adjustment data:

a.–b. Ending merchandise inventory on September 30, $19,805.

   c. Unearned revenue of $725 has now been earned.

   d. Supplies on hand on September 30, $407.

   e. Insurance expired during the year, $841.

   f. Wages expense incurred but not yet paid as of September 30, $973.

   g. Annual depreciation on the building, $1,236.

PROBLEM 14-4B
WORK SHEET (L.O.1–4)

On December 31, 19X1, the end of the fiscal year, Arrow Company's ledger shows the following accounts and balances before adjustment:

	Debit	Credit
Cash	4,635 00	
Accounts Receivable	6,734 00	
Merchandise Inventory	9,488 00	
Supplies	662 00	
Prepaid Insurance	1,091 00	
Equipment	12,668 00	
Accumulated Depreciation—Equipment		1,790 00
Building	49,750 00	
Accumulated Depreciation—Building		3,968 00
Land	10,000 00	
Accounts Payable		7,355 00
Unearned Revenue		1,203 00
Mortgage Payable		32,500 00
Alex Arnot, Capital		45,635 00
Alex Arnot, Drawing	15,750 00	
Sales		72,900 00
Sales Returns and Allowances	541 00	
Sales Discount	1,074 00	
Purchases	33,962 00	
Purchases Returns and Allowances		272 00
Purchases Discount		393 00
Interest Expense	3,625 00	
Utilities Expense	1,356 00	
Wages Expense	14,680 00	

INSTRUCTIONS

Prepare a work sheet for the fiscal year ended December 31, 19X1, using the following adjustment data:

a.–b. Ending merchandise inventory on December 31, $10,771.

c. Unearned revenue of $866 has now been earned.

d. Supplies on hand on December 31, $295.

e. Insurance expired during the year, $873.

f. Wages expense incurred but not yet paid as of December 31, $640.

g. Annual depreciation on the equipment, $525.

h. Annual depreciation on the building, $2,050.

Mini-Cases

CASE 14-1

John Lutke, owner of Lut-Scan Products, is your new employer. Although Mr. Lutke is a highly successful computer engineer, his background in accounting is weak. It is the end of the fiscal year, and Mr. Lutke has just given you a figure to be used in adjusting the Merchandise Inventory account. Since you know the physical inventory has not yet been taken, you inquire about the origin of this figure. "I simply converted the current balance in the Merchandise Inventory account from a cost figure to a selling price. Why? Is there something wrong with my figure?" replies Mr. Lutke. Respond.

CASE 14-2

Your friend, Annette, owns a clothing store. She has recently begun accepting orders for custom-made dresses and suits. In these situations, Annette requires the customer to pay for the merchandise in advance. Upon receiving the cash, she locks it in the safe and makes no entry until the order is delivered to the customer four to six weeks later. Her accountant wants her to deposit the cash and to show this prepayment as a liability until the order is delivered to the customer. She doesn't understand why this is necessary. Explain.

CASE 14-3

Your neighbor, Keith, is upset with his accountant. "Today he admitted that he doesn't keep the Supplies and Prepaid Insurance accounts up to date on a daily basis. Do you think I should fire him?" asks Keith. Respond.

Merchandising Business:
Year-End

||||||||||||||||||
L E A R N I N G
O B J E C T I V E S

AFTER STUDYING THIS CHAPTER, YOU SHOULD BE ABLE TO:

1 Prepare a multiple-step income statement for a
merchandising business.

2 Prepare a classified balance sheet.

3 Prepare adjusting entries for a merchandising business.

4 Prepare closing entries for a merchandising business.

5 Prepare reversing entries.

In Chapter 14, you learned how to prepare a work sheet for a merchandising business. In Chapter 15, you will use the work sheet in completing the accounting cycle for a merchandising business. Recall that the accounting cycle consists of the following steps:

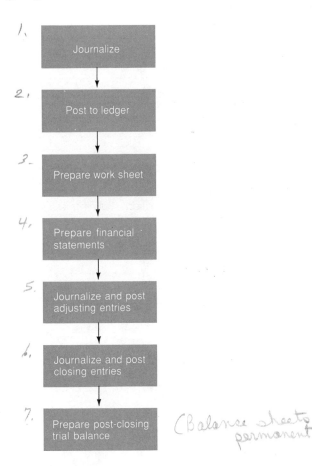

1. Journalize

2. Post to ledger

3. Prepare work sheet

4. Prepare financial statements

5. Journalize and post adjusting entries

6. Journalize and post closing entries

7. Prepare post-closing trial balance   (Balance sheets or permanent accounts)

In this chapter, you will learn to prepare financial statements, adjusting entries, closing entries, and a post-closing trial balance for a merchandising business. You will also study reversing entries, which are an optional part of the basic accounting cycle.

▌▌▌▌ PREPARING THE FINANCIAL STATEMENTS

Once the work sheet is complete, we are ready to prepare the formal financial statements. Since the statements have already been rough drafted on the work sheet, this is basically a matter of formatting. The information is taken directly from the work sheet and written up in the appropriate statement format.

To demonstrate the procedure for a merchandising business, let's return to The Kitchen Taylor. Figure 15-1 shows The Kitchen Taylor's work sheet as completed in Chapter 14.

FIGURE 15 - 1

THE KITCHEN TAYLOR
Work Sheet
For the Year Ended December 31, 19X3

Account Title	Trial Balance Debit	Trial Balance Credit	Adjustments Debit	Adjustments Credit
Cash	12,395 00			
Accounts Receivable	17,800 00			
Merchandise Inventory	24,500 00		(b) 26,000 00	(a) 24,500 00
Supplies	1,137 00			(d) 640 00
Prepaid Insurance	1,260 00			(e) 930 00
Truck	6,000 00			
Accumulated Depreciation—Truck		2,200 00		(g) 1,100 00
Building	85,000 00			
Accumulated Depreciation—Building		12,900 00		(h) 4,300 00
Land	10,000 00			
Accounts Payable		10,518 00		
Unearned Revenue		1,000 00	(c) 600 00	
Mortgage Payable		62,500 00		
Dennis Taylor, Capital		73,524 00		
Dennis Taylor, Drawing temporary account	29,239 00			
Sales		105,475 00		(c) 600 00
Sales Returns and Allowances	1,472 00			
Sales Discount	1,546 00			
Interest Income		1,850 00		
Purchases	51,000 00			
Purchases Returns and Allowances		693 00		
Purchases Discount		985 00		
Interest Expense	2,376 00			
Utilities Expense	3,130 00			
Wages Expense	24,790 00		(f) 300 00	
	271,645 00	271,645 00		
Income Summary			(a) 24,500 00	(b) 26,000 00
Supplies Expense			(d) 640 00	
Insurance Expense			(e) 930 00	
Wages Payable				(f) 300 00
Depreciation Expense—Truck			(g) 1,100 00	
Depreciation Expense—Building			(h) 4,300 00	
			58,370 00	58,370 00
Net income				

Adjusted Trial Balance		Income Statement		Balance Sheet	
Debit	Credit	Debit	Credit	Debit	Credit
12,395 00				12,395 00	
17,800 00				17,800 00	
26,000 00				26,000 00	
497 00				497 00	
330 00				330 00	
6,000 00				6,000 00	
	3,300 00				3,300 00
85,000 00				85,000 00	
	17,200 00				17,200 00
10,000 00				10,000 00	
	10,518 00				10,518 00
	400 00				400 00
	62,500 00				62,500 00
	73,524 00				73,524 00
29,239 00				29,239 00	
	106,075 00		106,075 00		
1,472 00		1,472 00			
1,546 00		1,546 00			
	1,850 00		1,850 00		
51,000 00		51,000 00			
	693 00		693 00		
	985 00		985 00		
2,376 00		2,376 00			
3,130 00		3,130 00			
25,090 00		25,090 00			
24,500 00	26,000 00	24,500 00	26,000 00		
640 00		640 00			
930 00		930 00			
	300 00				300 00
1,100 00		1,100 00			
4,300 00		4,300 00			
303,345 00	303,345 00	116,084 00	135,603 00	187,261 00	167,742 00
		19,519 00			19,519 00
		135,603 00	135,603 00	187,261 00	187,261 00

not on test

THE INCOME STATEMENT

OBJECTIVE 1
PREPARE A MULTIPLE-
STEP INCOME
STATEMENT FOR A
MERCHANDISING
BUSINESS

We will prepare a multiple-step income statement for The Kitchen Taylor. This is a slightly expanded version of the income statement prepared in earlier chapters. For the most part, this expansion is necessary to accommodate the additional needs of a merchandising business. However, the extra detail shown on the multiple-step income statement also makes it more informative to the user of the statement. In outline form, it appears as follows:

Net sales
− Cost of merchandise sold
Gross profit
− Operating expenses
Operating income (loss)
+ Other income
− Other expenses
Net income (loss)

Let's look at these steps in greater detail.

NET SALES   Sales figures are selling prices. They represent how much the customer was charged when the merchandise was sold. **Net sales** is equal to sales minus the contra-sales accounts.

Sales	
Less:	Sales returns and allowances
	Sales discount
Net sales	

The concept of net sales was previously discussed in Chapters 11 and 13.

COST OF MERCHANDISE SOLD   In this section, we will compute the cost associated with the merchandise that has been sold. In other words, we will determine how much the business paid (during this accounting period or an earlier period) to acquire the units that were actually sold during this accounting period. Let's study the basic computation for the **cost of merchandise sold.**

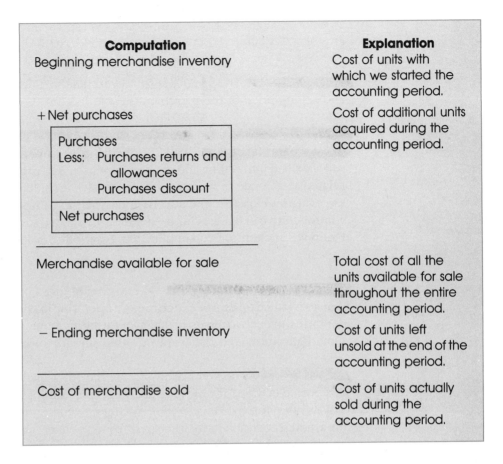

Computation	Explanation
Beginning merchandise inventory	Cost of units with which we started the accounting period.
+ Net purchases	Cost of additional units acquired during the accounting period.

Purchases	
Less: Purchases returns and allowances	
Purchases discount	
Net purchases	

Merchandise available for sale	Total cost of all the units available for sale throughout the entire accounting period.
− Ending merchandise inventory	Cost of units left unsold at the end of the accounting period.
Cost of merchandise sold	Cost of units actually sold during the accounting period.

For practice, let's compute the cost of merchandise sold for The Kitchen Taylor. The information for this computation comes from the Income Statement columns of the work sheet shown in Figure 15-1.

Merchandise inventory, January 1, 19X3		$24,500
Purchases	$51,000	
Less: Purchases returns and allowances	−693	
Purchases discount	−985	
Net purchases		+49,322
Merchandise available for sale		$73,822
Less merchandise inventory,		
December 31, 19X3		−26,000
Cost of merchandise sold		$47,822

||||||||||||||||||||||
COMMENT
The beginning and ending Merchandise Inventory account balances are taken from the income summary line shown in the Income Statement columns of the work sheet. As you will recall, these two figures are the result of the adjustment of merchandise inventory. The debit figure represents the beginning Merchandise

Inventory account balance. The credit figure represents the ending Merchandise Inventory account balance.

GROSS PROFIT   The **gross profit** represents the difference between the cost and selling price of the merchandise sold.

OPERATING EXPENSES   Expenses incurred in the normal day-to-day operation of the business are called **operating expenses.** They are frequently subclassified into selling and general expenses. **Selling expenses** are directly related to the sale of merchandise. Examples include store supplies expense, sales salaries expense, and advertising expense. **General expenses** are more administrative in nature and are not directly related to the sale of merchandise. Examples include office supplies expense, office salaries expense, and rent expense.

OPERATING INCOME (LOSS)   The excess of gross profit over operating expenses is called **operating income.** An operating loss would result if operating expenses exceeded gross profit. Operating income and net income are the same figure provided there are no other income or expense items.

OTHER INCOME   Revenue from any source other than the sale of merchandise is reported in the **other income** section of the multiple-step income statement. This is often referred to as *nonoperating revenue.* Some examples are interest on a note receivable, rent received from a tenant, and a gain on the sale of an old piece of equipment no longer needed or used. Other income is added to operating income in arriving at net income.

OTHER EXPENSES   Expenses incurred outside the normal scope of merchandising activities are reported in the **other expenses** section of the income statement. These expenses are also known as *nonoperating expenses.* Examples would include interest on a debt and a loss on the sale of an old piece of equipment. Other expenses are subtracted from operating income in arriving at net income.

NET INCOME (LOSS)   The excess of all revenue (both operating and nonoperating) over all expenses is called **net income.** An excess of expenses over revenue would result in a net loss. This figure is often referred to as *the bottom line.*

||||||||||||||||||||
C O M M E N T   Nonoperating items tend to be short term in nature, often one-time occurrences. Consequently, in evaluating a company's performance over a number of years, it is useful to separate these items from items of an ongoing nature.

Figure 15-2 shows The Kitchen Taylor's multiple-step income statement. Remember, the information needed to prepare this statement came from the

FIGURE 15 - 2

THE KITCHEN TAYLOR
Income Statement
For the Year Ended December 31, 19X3

Revenue from sales:								
Sales				$106,075	00			
Less: Sales returns and allowances	$ 1,472	00						
Sales discount	1,546	00		3,018	00			
Net Sales						$103,057	00	
Cost of merchandise sold:								
Merchandise inventory,								
January 1, 19X3				$ 24,500	00			
Purchases	$51,000	00						
Less: Purchases returns								
and allowances	$693.00							
Purchases discount	985.00	1,678	00					
Net purchases				49,322	00			
Merchandise available for sale				$ 73,822	00			
Less merchandise inventory,								
December 31, 19X3				26,000	00			
Cost of merchandise sold						47,822	00	
Gross profit						$ 55,235	00	
Operating expenses:								
Wages expense				$ 25,090	00			
Depreciation expense–building				4,300	00			
Utilities expense				3,130	00			
Depreciation expense—truck				1,100	00			
Insurance expense				930	00			
Supplies expense				640	00			
Total operating expenses						35,190	00	
Operating income						$ 20,045	00	
Other income:								
Interest income				$ 1,850	00			
Other expense:								
Interest expense				2,376	00		526	00
Net income							$ 19,519	00

Income Statement columns of the work sheet shown in Figure 15-1. From now on, this is the format you will use unless otherwise instructed. Some accountants refer to this format as a *classified income statement*.

||||||||||||||||||||
COMMENT

Amount columns on financial statements do not represent debits or credits. As statements become more complex, multiple columns are used to display figures in a format that is easy to read and understand. This is generally achieved by grouping figures used in a computation together in a column to the left and entering the result of the computation in a column to the right.

THE STATEMENT OF OWNER'S EQUITY — *What increases this?*

2 ways to knock down: 1. expenses & 2. owner's withdrawals   *1. Revenue 2. Capital*

The preparation of the statement of owner's equity is the same regardless of whether the business is a service or merchandising concern. The statement of owner's equity updates the owner's capital account, beginning with the capital account balance on the first day of the specified accounting period and ending with the capital account balance on the last day of the specified accounting period. In between the beginning and ending capital account balances, the items that created the change are displayed:

+ Net income
+ Investments by the owner
− Net loss
− Withdrawals by the owner

||||||||||||||||||||
COMMENT

As you will recall from Chapter 5, all information for the financial statements comes directly from the work sheet with one exception: an additional investment by the owner. We must check the owner's capital account in the general ledger to determine whether an additional investment has been made.

Figure 15-3 shows The Kitchen Taylor's statement of owner's equity. After the statement of owner's equity is completed, we have the up-to-date capital account balance needed to prepare the owner's equity section of the balance sheet.

THE BALANCE SHEET

OBJECTIVE 2
PREPARE A CLASSIFIED
BALANCE SHEET

We will now prepare a classified balance sheet for The Kitchen Taylor. Using this slightly expanded format, assets are separated into two classes: current assets and plant assets. Liabilities are also separated into two classes: current liabilities and long-term liabilities. The owner's equity section remains the same. Let's consider the expanded classes in greater detail.

FIGURE 15 - 3

THE KITCHEN TAYLOR
Statement of Owner's Equity
For the Year Ended December 31, 19X3

Dennis Taylor, capital, January 1, 19X3 *owners equity*	$73,524	00
Add: Net income for the year *get from work sheet*	19,519	00
Subtotal	$93,043	00
Less: Withdrawals by Dennis Taylor	29,239	00
Dennis Taylor, capital, December 31, 19X3 *owners equity at end of month*	$63,804	00

CURRENT ASSETS   **Current assets** consist of cash or other assets that will either be converted into cash or used up within one year. Examples include cash, accounts receivable, merchandise inventory, supplies, and prepaid insurance. On the balance sheet, these assets are listed in liquidity order. By **liquidity,** we mean closeness to cash. A liquid asset is cash or an asset that can be quickly converted into cash.

PLANT ASSETS   **Plant assets** are used by a business to generate revenue for a period greater than one year. They are often referred to as *long-lived assets* or *fixed assets.* Examples include equipment, vehicles, buildings, and land. With the exception of land, these are depreciable assets. On the balance sheet, plant assets are usually listed with their related accumulated depreciation accounts according to their useful life, going from the shortest to the longest. Since land never wears out, it is shown last.

CURRENT LIABILITIES   **Current liabilities** are debts that will become due within one year. They are normally paid out of current assets. Examples include accounts payable, mortgage payable (current portion), wages payable, and unearned revenue. On the balance sheet, current liabilities are usually listed in the order in which they will be paid.

|||||||||||||||||||||
C O M M E N T

Although a mortgage is primarily a long-term obligation, the portion due and payable within one year is considered to be a current liability.

LONG-TERM LIABILITIES   **Long-term liabilities** are debts that will become due and payable beyond one year. For the time being, the Mortgage Payable account is our only long-term liability.

Figure 15-4 shows The Kitchen Taylor's classified balance sheet. The information needed to prepare this statement came from the Balance Sheet

▌ **FIGURE 15 - 4**

THE KITCHEN TAYLOR
Balance Sheet
December 31, 19X3

Assets							
Current assets:							
Cash				$ 12,395	00		
Accounts receivable				17,800	00		
Merchandise inventory				26,000	00		
Supplies				497	00		
Prepaid insurance				330	00		
Total current assets						$ 57,022	00
Plant assets:							
Truck	$ 6,000	00					
Less accumulated depreciation	3,300	00	$ 2,700	00			
Building	$85,000	00					
Less accumulated depreciation	17,200	00	67,800	00			
Land			10,000	00			
Total plant assets						80,500	00
Total assets						$137,522	00
Liabilities							
Current liabilities:							
Accounts payable				$10,518	00		
Mortgage payable (current portion)				2,500	00		
Wages payable				300	00		
Unearned revenue				400	00		
Total current liabilities						$ 13,718	00
Long-term liabilities:							
Mortgage payable						60,000	00
Total liabilities						$ 73,718	00
Owner's Equity							
Dennis Taylor, capital						63,804	00
Total liabilities and owner's equity						$137,522	00

columns of the work sheet shown in Figure 15-1 with the exception of the capital account balance. The up-to-date capital account balance was taken from the statement of owner's equity. From now on, you will use the classified balance sheet format unless otherwise instructed.

▮▮▮▮ ADJUSTING ENTRIES

OBJECTIVE 3
PREPARE ADJUSTING
ENTRIES FOR A
MERCHANDISING
BUSINESS

The adjustments rough drafted on the work sheet shown in Figure 15-1 must be formally recorded in the journal. The adjustment information, taken directly from the Adjustments columns of the work sheet, is written up in general journal form. Figure 15-5 shows The Kitchen Taylor's journal after adjustments *(a)* through *(b)* have been recorded.

▮▮▮▮ CLOSING ENTRIES

OBJECTIVE 4
PREPARE CLOSING
ENTRIES FOR A
MERCHANDISING
BUSINESS

In Chapter 6, we studied the closing procedure for a service business. The same four-step procedure is used for a merchandising business.

At the end of every fiscal year, the temporary owner's equity accounts (**revenue, expense, drawing**) must be closed to the permanent owner's equity account (**capital**).

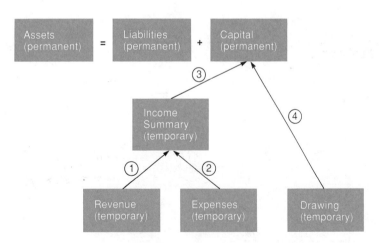

Since Chapter 6, we have studied several new temporary accounts: Sales Returns and Allowances, Sales Discount, Purchases, Purchases Returns and Allowances, and Purchases Discount. The closing of these new income statement accounts is integrated into Steps 1 and 2 of the usual four-step closing procedure. Let's review the four steps:

Step 1:   Close all revenue accounts and other credit-balance temporary accounts (such as Purchases Returns and Allowances and Purchases Discount) to the Income Summary account.

FIGURE 15 - 5

		GENERAL JOURNAL				Page 102	
Date		Description	Post. Ref.	Debit		Credit	
		Adjusting Entries					
19X3 Dec.	31	Income Summary		24,500	00		
		Merchandise Inventory				24,500	00
	31	Merchandise Inventory		26,000	00		
		Income Summary				26,000	00
	31	Unearned Revenue		600	00		
		Sales				600	00
	31	Supplies Expense		640	00		
		Supplies				640	00
	31	Insurance Expense		930	00		
		Prepaid Insurance				930	00
	31	Wages Expense		300	00		
		Wages Payable				300	00
	31	Depreciation Expense—Truck		1,100	00		
		Accumulated Depreciation—Truck				1,100	00
	31	Depreciation Expense—Building		4,300	00		
		Accumulated Depreciation—Building				4,300	00

Step 2: Close all expense accounts and other debit-balance temporary accounts (such as Sales Returns and Allowances, Sales Discount, and Purchases) to the Income Summary account.

Step 3: Close the Income Summary account to the owner's capital account.

Step 4:   Close the owner's drawing account to the owner's capital account.

To demonstrate, let's return to The Kitchen Taylor. The information necessary for closing entries can be obtained from the work sheet shown in Figure 15-1. The account balances needed for Steps 1 and 2 are clearly displayed in

FIGURE 15 - 6

		GENERAL JOURNAL						Page 103	
Date		Description	Post. Ref.	Debit			Credit		
		Closing Entries							
19X3 Dec.	31	Sales		106,075	00				
		Interest Income		1,850	00				
		Purchases Returns and Allowances		693	00				
		Purchases Discount		985	00				
		Income Summary					109,603	00	
	31	Income Summary		91,584	00				
		Sales Returns and Allowances					1,472	00	
		Sales Discount					1,546	00	
		Purchases					51,000	00	
		Interest Expense					2,376	00	
		Utilities Expense					3,130	00	
		Wages Expense					25,090	00	
		Supplies Expense					640	00	
		Insurance Expense					930	00	
		Depreciation Expense–Truck					1,100	00	
		Depreciation Expense–Building					4,300	00	
	31	Income Summary		19,519	00				
		Dennis Taylor, Capital					19,519	00	
	31	Dennis Taylor, Capital		29,239	00				
		Dennis Taylor, Drawing					29,239	00	

the Income Statement columns of the work sheet. The drawing account balance (Step 4) is shown in the Balance Sheet Debit column of the work sheet. Figure 15-6 shows The Kitchen Taylor's journal after the closing entries have been recorded.

|||||||||||||||||||||||
C O M M E N T

Recall that the Merchandise Inventory account is adjusted through the Income Summary account. Therefore, after the second closing entry, The Kitchen Taylor's Income Summary account appears as follows:

Account **Income Summary**   Account No. 313

Date		Item	Post. Ref.	Debit	Credit	Balance Debit	Balance Credit
19X3							
Dec.	31	Adjusting *(a)*	J102	24,500 00		24,500 00	
	31	Adjusting *(h)*	J102		26,000 00		1,500 00
	31	Closing (1)	J103		109,603 00		111,103 00
	31	Closing (2)	J103	91,584 00			19,519 00

The resulting $19,519 credit balance (net income) is closed to capital in the third closing entry.

▊▊▊▊ **THE POST-CLOSING TRIAL BALANCE**

After closing entries have been journalized and posted, a post-closing trial balance is prepared. The procedure for preparing the post-closing trial balance for a merchandising business is the same as that described in Chapter 6 for a service business. Figures should be taken directly from the ledger accounts since this represents a final check on the overall equality of debits and credits in the general ledger. Only permanent accounts appear on the post-closing trial balance because all temporary accounts have been closed. Figure 15-7 shows The Kitchen Taylor's post-closing trial balance. This completes the basic accounting cycle for a merchandising business.

▊▊▊▊ **REVERSING ENTRIES**

OBJECTIVE 5
PREPARE REVERSING
ENTRIES

Reversing entries reverse adjusting entries. They are an optional part of the accounting cycle. If a company chooses to make reversing entries, they are recorded the first day of the new fiscal year.

FIGURE 15 - 7

THE KITCHEN TAYLOR
Post-Closing Trial Balance
December 31, 19X3

	Debit		Credit	
Cash	12,395	00		
Accounts Receivable	17,800	00		
Merchandise Inventory	26,000	00		
Supplies	497	00		
Prepaid Insurance	330	00		
Truck	6,000	00		
Accumulated Depreciation—Truck			3,300	00
Building	85,000	00		
Accumulated Depreciation—Building			17,200	00
Land	10,000	00		
Accounts Payable			10,518	00
Wages Payable			300	00
Unearned Revenue			400	00
Mortgage Payable			62,500	00
Dennis Taylor, Capital			63,804	00
	158,022	00	158,022	00

Since reversing entries are optional, they must offer some advantage or no one would choose to use them. The advantage offered by reversing entries is that they make it possible to return to the normal accounting routine as soon as they have been recorded. Since departing from the normal routine increases the risk of error, accountants commonly choose to make reversing entries to avoid potential problems.

Let's demonstrate the advantage of reversing entries with an example. Assume The Kitchen Taylor pays its employees $500 every Friday for a five-day workweek—$100 per day, Monday through Friday. The routine entry to record each Friday's payroll would be as follows:

```
Wages Expense  . . . . . . . . . .  500
     Cash  . . . . . . . . . . . . . .              500
```

Let's further assume that December 31, 19X1, the end of the fiscal year, falls on Wednesday. Beginning with the December 31, 19X1, adjusting entry and

▮ **FIGURE 15 - 8**

WITH REVERSING ENTRY	WITHOUT REVERSING ENTRY
Adjusting Entry	**Adjusting Entry**
19X1	19X1
Dec. 31 Wages Expense . . 300	Dec. 31 Wages Expense . . 300
Wages Payable . . 300	Wages Payable . . 300
Closing Entry	**Closing Entry**
19X1	19X1
Dec. 31 Income Summary . . 25,090	Dec. 31 Income Summary . . 25,090
Wages Expense . . 25,090	Wages Expense . . 25,090
Reversing Entry	
19X2	
Jan. 1 Wages Payable . . . 300	No Entry
Wages Expense . . 300	
Payroll Entry	**Payroll Entry**
19X2	19X2
Jan. 2 Wages Expense . . . 500	Jan. 2 Wages Payable . . . 300
Cash 500	Wages Expense . . . 200
	Cash 500

ending with the January 2, 19X2, payroll entry, let's compare the payroll-related entries with and without the use of a reversing entry. Observe the difference in the January 2 payroll entries. With a reversing entry, the routine entry can be recorded. Without a reversing entry, the routine entry cannot be recorded—the previous year's adjusting entry must be taken into consideration.

The following partial ledgers show the Wages Payable and Wages Expense accounts after posting the entries recorded in Figure 15-8.

PARTIAL LEDGER WITH REVERSING ENTRIES			PARTIAL LEDGER WITHOUT REVERSING ENTRIES		
Wages Payable			**Wages Payable**		
19X2	19X1		19X2	19X1	
Jan. 1 Reversing 300	Dec. 31 Adjusting 300		Jan. 2 Payroll 300	Dec. 31 Adjusting 300	
Wages Expense			**Wages Expense**		
Balance 24,790			Balance 24,790		
19X1	19X1		19X1	19X1	
Dec. 31 Adjusting 300	Dec. 31 Closing 25,090		Dec. 31 Adjusting 300	Dec. 31 Closing 25,090	
19X2	19X2		19X2		
Jan. 2 Payroll 500	Jan. 1 Reversing 300		Jan. 2 Payroll 200		

Notice that after posting the January 2 payroll entry, the balances in Wages Payable (zero) and Wages Expense ($200 debit) are the same with or without a reversing entry.

||||||||||||||||||||||||| Observe the abnormal balance in the Wages Expense account ($300 credit)
C O M M E N T   created by the reversing entry. This abnormal balance is what allows us to return immediately to the normal routine. On Friday, January 2, when the routine payroll entry is recorded, this abnormal balance automatically "washes out" the wages expense incurred and recorded in the previous year.

If a company decides to use reversing entries, does that mean all adjusting entries should be reversed? NO! Use the following rule to determine which adjusting entries should be reversed:

Reverse any adjusting entry that creates a new asset or liability account. By new, we mean an asset or liability account that had no balance prior to adjustment.

Exceptions: Never reverse the adjustment of merchandise inventory or the recording of depreciation.

Let's use this rule to determine which of The Kitchen Taylor's 19X3 adjusting entries should be reversed. We will refer to the Trial Balance (unadjusted) columns of the work sheet to determine whether an asset or liability account had a balance prior to adjustment. This portion of the work sheet is shown in Figure 15-9.

Figure 15-10 shows The Kitchen Taylor's journal after the reversing entry has been recorded.

FIGURE 15 - 9

THE KITCHEN TAYLOR
Work Sheet
For the Year Ended December 31, 19X3

Account Title	Trial Balance Debit		Trial Balance Credit		Adjustments Debit		Adjustments Credit	
Cash	12,395	00						
Accounts Receivable	17,800	00						
Merchandise Inventory	24,500	00			(b) 26,000	00	(a) 24,500	00
Supplies	1,137	00					(d) 640	00
Prepaid Insurance	1,260	00					(e) 930	00
Truck	6,000	00						
Accumulated Depreciation—Truck			2,200	00			(g) 1,100	00
Building	85,000	00						
Accumulated Depreciation—Building			12,900	00			(h) 4,300	00
Land	10,000	00						
Accounts Payable			10,518	00				
Unearned Revenue			1,000	00	(c) 600	00		
Mortgage Payable			62,500	00				
Dennis Taylor, Capital			73,524	00				
Dennis Taylor, Drawing	29,239	00						
Sales			105,475	00			(c) 600	00
Sales Returns and Allowances	1,472	00						
Sales Discount	1,546	00						
Interest Income			1,850	00				
Purchases	51,000	00						
Purchases Returns and Allowances			693	00				
Purchases Discount			985	00				
Interest Expense	2,376	00						
Utilities Expense	3,130	00						
Wages Expense	24,790	00			(f) 300	00		
	271,645	00	271,645	00				
Income Summary					(a) 24,500	00	(b) 26,000	00
Supplies Expense					(d) 640	00		
Insurance Expense					(e) 930	00		
Wages Payable							(f) 300	00
Depreciation Expense—Truck					(g) 1,100	00		
Depreciation Expense—Building					(h) 4,300	00		
					58,370	00	58,370	00
Net income								

GENERAL JOURNAL							Page 102	Reverse—yes or no?
Date		Description	Post. Ref.	Debit		Credit		
		Adjusting Entries						
19X3 Dec.	31	Income Summary		24,500	00			
		Merchandise Inventory				24,500	00	Never
	31	Merchandise Inventory		26,000	00			
		Income Summary				26,000	00	Never
	31	Unearned Revenue		600	00			No (no new asset
		Sales				600	00	or liability)
	31	Supplies Expense		640	00			No (no new asset
		Supplies				640	00	or liability)
	31	Insurance Expense		930	00			No (no new asset
		Prepaid Insurance				930	00	or liability)
	31	Wages Expense		300	00			
		Wages Payable				300	00	Yes (new liability)
	31	Depreciation Expense—Truck		1,100	00			
		Accumulated Depreciation—Truck				1,100	00	Never
	31	Depreciation Expense—Building		4,300	00			
		Accumulated Depreciation—Building				4,300	00	Never

FIGURE 15 - 10

GENERAL JOURNAL							Page 104
Date		Description	Post. Ref.	Debit		Credit	
		Reversing Entry					
19X4 Jan.	1	Wages Payable		300	00		
		Wages Expense				300	00

Chapter Summary

Using the work sheet prepared in Chapter 14, we completed the basic accounting cycle for a merchandising business.

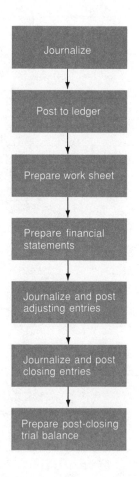

FINANCIAL STATEMENTS A multiple-step income statement in outline form appears as follows:

Net sales
− Cost of merchandise sold:
    Beginning merchandise inventory
    + Net purchases

    Merchandise available for sale
    − Ending merchandise inventory

    Cost of merchandise sold

Gross profit
− Operating expenses

Operating income (loss)
+ Other income
− Other expenses

Net income (loss)

The statement of owner's equity is the same for both a service and a merchandising business.

In preparing a classified balance sheet, the asset and liability sections are expanded as follows:

Assets
Current assets   (life—less than one year)
Plant assets   (life—more than one year)
Total assets

Liabilities
Current liabilities   (due—within one year)
Long-term liabilities   (due—beyond one year)
Total liabilities

ADJUSTING ENTRIES   The adjustments rough drafted on the work sheet must be formally recorded in the journal. The information for adjusting entries comes directly from the work sheet.

CLOSING ENTRIES   The same four-step closing procedure studied in Chapter 6 is used for a merchandising business.

Step 1:   Close all revenue and other credit-balance temporary accounts to Income Summary.

Step 2:   Close all expense and other debit-balance temporary accounts to Income Summary.

Step 3: Close Income Summary to capital.

Step 4: Close drawing to capital.

POST-CLOSING TRIAL BALANCE The procedure for preparing a post-closing trial balance for a merchandising business is the same as for a service business. Figures should be taken directly from the ledger accounts since this represents a final check on the overall equality of debits and credits in the general ledger.

REVERSING ENTRIES Reversing entries reverse adjusting entries. They are an optional part of the accounting cycle. If used, they are recorded the first day of the new fiscal year. Reversing entries make it possible to return to the normal accounting routine as soon as they have been recorded. The following rule is used to determine which adjusting entries should be reversed:

Reverse any adjusting entry that creates a new asset or liability account. By new, we mean an asset or liability account that had no balance prior to adjustment.

Exceptions: Never reverse the adjustment of merchandise inventory or the recording of depreciation.

Glossary

COST OF MERCHANDISE SOLD

A figure representing how much a business paid to acquire the units that have actually been sold during an accounting period.

CURRENT ASSET

Cash or an asset that will either be converted into cash or used up within one year.

CURRENT LIABILITY

A debt that will become due within one year; normally paid out of current assets.

GENERAL EXPENSES

Operating expenses of a general or administrative nature not directly related to the sale of merchandise.

GROSS PROFIT

Represents the difference between the cost and selling price of the merchandise sold: Net sales minus cost of merchandise sold equals gross profit.

LIQUIDITY

Closeness to cash. For example, accounts receivable are more liquid than land because they can be converted to cash more quickly.

LONG-TERM LIABILITY

A debt that will become due and payable beyond one year.

NET INCOME

The excess of all revenue over all expenses. Often referred to as *the bottom line*.

NET PURCHASES

Purchases minus contra-purchases accounts (such as Purchases Discount and Purchases Returns and Allowances).

NET SALES

Sales minus contra-sales accounts (such as Sales Discount and Sales Returns and Allowances).

OPERATING EXPENSES

Expenses incurred in the normal day-to-day operation of the business; frequently subdivided into selling and general expenses.

OPERATING INCOME

The excess of gross profit over operating expenses.

OTHER EXPENSES

Expenses incurred outside the normal scope of merchandising activities. Also known as nonoperating expenses.

OTHER INCOME

Revenue from any source other than the sale of merchandise. Also known as nonoperating revenue.

PLANT ASSET

An asset used to generate revenue for a period greater than a year.

REVERSING ENTRIES

Optional entries that reverse adjusting entries. They make it possible to return to the normal accounting routine as soon as they have been recorded. If used, they are recorded the first day of the new fiscal period.

SELLING EXPENSES

Operating expenses directly related to the sale of merchandise.

Questions for Discussion

1. Describe the differences between an income statement for a merchandising business and an income statement for a service business.

2. Explain the difference between operating income and net income.

3. Why is operating income sometimes a more useful figure than net income?

4. Explain the difference between current assets and plant assets.

5. Explain the difference between current liabilities and long-term liabilities.

6. Describe the four-step closing procedure for a merchandising business.

7. *a.* What do reversing entries reverse?
   b. When are they recorded?
   c. Since reversing entries are an optional part of the accounting cycle, why would a business choose to make reversing entries?

8. What is the rule used to determine which adjusting entries should be reversed? Exceptions?

Exercises

EXERCISE 15-1
DEFINITIONS
(L.O.1–5)

Match the following terms with the definitions shown below:

h – **1.** Cost of merchandise sold.   *j* – **7.** Operating expenses.

L – **2.** Current asset.   *b* – **8.** Operating income.

g – **3.** Current liability.   *e* – **9.** Other expenses.

K – **4.** Gross profit.   *i* – **10.** Other income.

C – **5.** Long-term liability.   *a* – **11.** Plant asset.

F – **6.** Net income.   *d* – **12.** Reversing entries.

Definitions:

11 – *a.* An asset that will generate revenue for a period greater than one year.

8 – *b.* The excess of gross profit over operating expenses.

5 – *c.* A debt that will become due and payable beyond one year.

12 – *d.* Optional entries that reverse adjusting entries. They make it possible to return to the normal accounting routine as soon as they have been recorded. If used, they are recorded the first day of the new fiscal period.

9 – *e.* Expenses incurred outside the normal scope of merchandising activities. Also known as nonoperating expenses.

6 – *f.* The excess of all revenue over all expenses. Often referred to as *the bottom line.*

3 – *g.* A debt that will become due within one year; normally paid out of current assets.

1 – *h.* A figure representing how much a business paid to acquire the units that have actually been sold during an accounting period.

10 – *i.* Revenue from any source other than the sale of merchandise. Also known as nonoperating revenue.

? —*j.* Expenses incurred in the normal day-to-day operation of the business; frequently subdivided into selling and general expenses.

4 —*k.* Represents the difference between the cost and selling price of the merchandise sold.

2 —*l.* Cash or an asset that will either be converted into cash or used up within one year.

EXERCISE 15-2
COST OF MERCHANDISE
SOLD
(L.O.1)

From the following information, prepare the cost of merchandise sold section of an income statement:

Purchases discount	$ 1,256
Merchandise inventory, January 1.	18,500
Purchases returns and allowances	1,884
Merchandise inventory, December 31	12,400
Purchases	62,800

EXERCISE 15-3
MULTIPLE-STEP INCOME
STATEMENT
(L.O.1)

From the following information, prepare a multiple-step income statement in outline form:

Operating expenses	$ 23,900
Other income	1,850
Net sales	135,000
Other expenses	720
Cost of merchandise sold . . .	89,200

EXERCISE 15-4
MISSING INCOME
STATEMENT DATA
(L.O.1)

Supply the missing information:

	Ace Company	Bell Company
Sales	$91,500	$56,000
Sales returns and allowances	1,830	(E)
Net sales	(A)	54,880
Beginning merchandise inventory	19,725	(F)
Purchases	(B)	41,280
Purchases returns and allowances	1,467	830
Net purchases	73,345	(G)
Merchandise available for sale	93,070	48,650
Ending merchandise inventory	(C)	9,150
Cost of merchandise sold	71,470	(H)
Gross profit	(D)	15,380

EXERCISE 15-5
ACCOUNT
CLASSIFICATIONS
(L.O.2)

Classify each of the accounts listed below as one of the following:

> CA—current asset
> PA—plant asset
> CL—current liability
> LT—long-term liability

1. Accounts Payable.	**7.** Wages Payable.
2. Equipment.	**8.** Merchandise Inventory.
3. Accounts Receivable.	**9.** Cash.
4. Unearned Revenue.	**10.** Mortgage Payable.
5. Prepaid Insurance.	**11.** Land.
6. Building.	**12.** Supplies.

EXERCISE 15-6
CLOSING PROCEDURE
(L.O.4)

Draw a flowchart that demonstrates the four-step closing procedure.

EXERCISE 15-7
CLOSING ENTRIES
(L.O.4)

From the following information, prepare closing entries:

Income Summary

Dr.		Cr.	
Adj.	12,500	Adj.	9,600

Sales

Dr.	Cr.
	74,900

Sales Returns and Allowances

Dr.	Cr.
1,450	

Purchases

Dr.	Cr.
49,000	

Sales Discount

Dr.	Cr.
1,375	

Purchases Returns and Allowances

Dr.	Cr.
	830

Purchases Discount		Wages Expense	
Dr.	Cr.	Dr.	Cr.
	980	21,800	

Insurance Expense		Ed Hammond, Drawing	
Dr.	Cr.	Dr.	Cr.
2,150		18,500	

Rent Expense		Ed Hammond, Capital	
Dr.	Cr.	Dr.	Cr.
11,700			45,200

Supplies Expense	
Dr.	Cr.
1,560	

EXERCISE 15-8
REVERSING ENTRIES
(L.O.3, 5)

Carver Company's unadjusted trial balance is shown on page 546.

CARVER COMPANY
Unadjusted Trial Balance
December 31, 19X1

	Debit	Credit
Cash	10,500 00	
Accounts Receivable	16,774 00	
Merchandise Inventory	21,600 00	
Supplies	1,180 00	
Prepaid Insurance	1,372 00	
Truck	8,500 00	
Accumulated Depreciation—Truck		3,200 00
Building	100,000 00	
Accumulated Depreciation—Building		15,400 00
Land	20,000 00	
Accounts Payable		9,760 00
Unearned Revenue		1,800 00
Mortgage Payable		71,000 00
Ed Carver, Capital		86,287 00
Ed Carver, Drawing	28,300 00	
Sales		108,300 00
Sales Returns and Allowances	1,572 00	
Sales Discount	2,100 00	
Purchases	54,250 00	
Purchases Returns and Allowances		1,085 00
Purchases Discount		990 00
Interest Expense	2,595 00	
Utilities Expense	3,259 00	
Wages Expense	25,820 00	
	297,822 00	297,822 00

Indicate whether each of the following adjusting entries should be reversed or not (yes or no):

		GENERAL JOURNAL						Page 102		Reverse— yes or no?
Date		Description	Post. Ref.	Debit		Credit				
		Adjusting Entries								
19X1 Dec.	31	Income Summary		21,600	00					
		Merchandise Inventory				21,600	00			_NEVER_ (1)
	31	Merchandise Inventory		18,300	00					
		Income Summary				18,300	00			_NEVER_ (2)
	31	Unearned Revenue		1,250	00					
		Sales				1,250	00			_No_ (3)
	31	Supplies Expense		420	00					
		Supplies				420	00			_NO_ (4)
	31	Insurance Expense		875	00					
		Prepaid Insurance				875	00			_NO_ (5)
	31	Wages Expense		940	00					
		Wages Payable				940	00			_YES_ (6)
	31	Depreciation Expense—Truck		1,200	00					
		Accumulated Depreciation— Truck				1,200	00			_NO_ (7)
	31	Depreciation Expense—Building		2,500	00					
		Accumulated Depreciation— Building				2,500	00			_NO_ (8)

Problems—Set A

**PROBLEM
15-1A**

FINANCIAL STATEMENTS
(L.O.1, 2)

As of December 31, 19X1, Burnet Ridge Company's completed work sheet appears as shown in Figure 15-11.

INSTRUCTIONS

1. Prepare an income statement.

2. Prepare a statement of owner's equity assuming the owner made no additional investment.

3. Prepare a balance sheet. (Note: Show the entire balance in the Mortgage Payable account as a long-term liability. Assume there is no current portion.)

**PROBLEM
15-2A**

ADJUSTING, CLOSING,
AND REVERSING ENTRIES
(L.O.3–5)

Refer to the work sheet presented in Figure 15-11.

INSTRUCTIONS

1. Journalize the adjusting entries.

2. Journalize the closing entries.

3. Journalize the reversing entry or entries.

FIGURE 15 - 11

BURNET RIDGE COMPANY
Work Sheet
For the Year Ended December 31, 19X1

Account Title	Trial Balance Debit	Trial Balance Credit	Adjustments Debit	Adjustments Credit
Cash	10,215 00			
Accounts Receivable	16,890 00			
Merchandise Inventory	26,814 00		(b) 23,150 00	(a) 26,814 00
Supplies	1,760 00			(d) 940 00
Prepaid Insurance	2,532 00			(e) 1,789 00
Equipment	14,900 00			
Accumulated Depreciation—Equipment		4,470 00		(g) 1,320 00
Building	98,000 00			
Accumulated Depreciation—Building		11,765 00		(h) 4,100 00
Land	25,000 00			
Accounts Payable		12,430 00		
Unearned Revenue		3,540 00	(c) 2,785 00	
Mortgage Payable		72,000 00		
Susan Harmon, Capital		89,550 00		
Susan Harmon, Drawing	41,600 00			
Sales		156,800 00		(c) 2,785 00
Sales Returns and Allowances	2,347 00			
Sales Discount	3,135 00			
Interest Income		2,900 00		
Purchases	64,250 00			
Purchases Returns and Allowances		963 00		
Purchases Discount		1,285 00		
Interest Expense	5,760 00			
Utilities Expense	3,100 00			
Wages Expense	39,400 00		(f) 1,698 00	
	355,703 00	355,703 00		
Income Summary			(a) 26,814 00	(b) 23,150 00
Supplies Expense			(d) 940 00	
Insurance Expense			(e) 1,789 00	
Wages Payable				(f) 1,698 00
Depreciation Expense—Equipment			(g) 1,320 00	
Depreciation Expense—Building			(h) 4,100 00	
			62,596 00	62,596 00
Net income				

Adjusted Trial Balance		Income Statement		Balance Sheet	
Debit	**Credit**	**Debit**	**Credit**	**Debit**	**Credit**
10,215 00				10,215 00	
16,890 00				16,890 00	
23,150 00				23,150 00	
820 00				820 00	
743 00				743 00	
14,900 00				14,900 00	
	5,790 00				5,790 00
98,000 00				98,000 00	
	15,865 00				15,865 00
25,000 00				25,000 00	
	12,430 00				12,430 00
	755 00				755 00
	72,000 00				72,000 00
	89,550 00				89,550 00
41,600 00				41,600 00	
	159,585 00		159,585 00		
2,347 00		2,347 00			
3,135 00		3,135 00			
	2,900 00		2,900 00		
64,250 00		64,250 00			
	963 00		963 00		
	1,285 00		1,285 00		
5,760 00		5,760 00			
3,100 00		3,100 00			
41,098 00		41,098 00			
26,814 00	23,150 00	26,814 00	23,150 00		
940 00		940 00			
1,789 00		1,789 00			
	1,698 00				1,698 00
1,320 00		1,320 00			
4,100 00		4,100 00			
385,971 00	385,971 00	154,653 00	187,883 00	231,318 00	198,088 00
		33,230 00			33,230 00
		187,883 00	187,883 00	231,318 00	231,318 00

PROBLEM 15-3A
FINANCIAL STATEMENTS; ADJUSTING, CLOSING, AND REVERSING ENTRIES (L.O.1–5)

Omit this problem if working papers are not being used.

As of June 30, 19X1, Pearl Enterprises' completed work sheet appears as shown in the working papers.

INSTRUCTIONS

1. Prepare an income statement.

2. Prepare a statement of owner's equity assuming the owner made no additional investment.

3. Prepare a balance sheet. (Note: Show the entire balance in the Mortgage Payable account as a long-term liability. Assume there is no current portion.)

4. Journalize the adjusting entries.

5. Journalize the closing entries.

6. Journalize the reversing entry or entries.

PROBLEM 15-4A
WORK SHEET; FINANCIAL STATEMENTS; ADJUSTING, CLOSING, AND REVERSING ENTRIES (L.O.1–5)

On September 30, 19X1, the end of the fiscal year, Rula Company's ledger shows the following accounts and balances before adjustment:

	Debit	Credit
Cash	$ 13,905.00	
Accounts Receivable	20,400.00	
Merchandise Inventory	28,564.00	
Supplies	1,986.00	
Prepaid Insurance	3,273.00	
Equipment	38,400.00	
Accumulated Depreciation—Equipment		$ 5,370.00
Building	149,250.00	
Accumulated Depreciation—Building		11,904.00
Land	35,000.00	
Accounts Payable		23,065.00
Unearned Revenue		3,690.00
Mortgage Payable		97,500.00
Gary Rula, Capital		135,450.00
Gary Rula, Drawing	47,250.00	
Sales		218,700.00
Sales Returns and Allowances	1,623.00	
Sales Discount	3,250.00	
Interest Income		4,900.00

	Debit	Credit
Purchases	102,800.00	
Purchases Returns and Allowances		816.00
Purchases Discount		1,179.00
Interest Expense	10,875.00	
Utilities Expense	4,068.00	
Wages Expense	41,930.00	

INSTRUCTIONS

1. Prepare a work sheet for the fiscal year ended September 30, 19X1, using the following adjustment data:

a.–b. Ending merchandise inventory on September 30, 19X1, $25,690.

c. Unearned revenue of $2,480 has now been earned.

d. Supplies on hand on September 30, 19X1, $723.

e. Expired insurance, $1,972.

f. Wages expense incurred but not yet paid as of September 30, 19X1, $3,150.

g. Annual depreciation on the equipment, $1,670.

h. Annual depreciation on the building, $3,968.

2. Prepare an income statement.

3. Prepare a statement of owner's equity assuming the owner made no additional investment.

4. Prepare a balance sheet. (Note: Show the entire balance in the Mortgage Payable account as a long-term liability. Assume there is no current portion.)

5. Journalize the adjusting entries.

6. Journalize the closing entries.

7. Journalize the reversing entry or entries.

Problems—Set B

PROBLEM 15-1B
FINANCIAL STATEMENTS
(L.O.1, 2)

As of December 31, 19X1, Columbia Products' completed work sheet appears as shown in Figure 15-12.

INSTRUCTIONS

1. Prepare an income statement.

2. Prepare a statement of owner's equity assuming the owner made no additional investment.

3. Prepare a balance sheet. (Note: Show the entire balance in the Mortgage Payable account as a long-term liability. Assume there is no current portion.)

PROBLEM 15-2B
ADJUSTING, CLOSING, AND REVERSING ENTRIES
(L.O.3–5)

Refer to the work sheet presented in Figure 15-12.

INSTRUCTIONS

1. Journalize the adjusting entries.

2. Journalize the closing entries.

3. Journalize the reversing entry or entries.

COLUMBIA PRODUCTS
Work Sheet
For the Year Ended December 31, 19X1

Account Title	Trial Balance Debit	Trial Balance Credit	Adjustments Debit	Adjustments Credit
Cash	20,430 00			
Accounts Receivable	33,780 00			
Merchandise Inventory	53,628 00		(b) 46,300 00	(a) 53,628 00
Supplies	3,520 00			(d) 1,880 00
Prepaid Insurance	5,064 00			(e) 3,578 00
Equipment	29,800 00			
Accumulated Depreciation—Equipment		8,940 00		(g) 2,640 00
Building	196,000 00			
Accumulated Depreciation—Building		23,530 00		(h) 8,200 00
Land	50,000 00			
Accounts Payable		24,860 00		
Unearned Revenue		7,080 00	(c) 5,570 00	
Mortgage Payable		144,000 00		
Ronald Smith, Capital		179,100 00		
Ronald Smith, Drawing	83,200 00			
Sales		313,600 00		(c) 5,570 00
Sales Returns and Allowances	4,694 00			
Sales Discount	6,270 00			
Interest Income		5,800 00		
Purchases	128,500 00			
Purchases Returns and Allowances		1,926 00		
Purchases Discount		2,570 00		
Interest Expense	11,520 00			
Utilities Expense	6,200 00			
Wages Expense	78,800 00		(f) 3,396 00	
	711,406 00	711,406 00		
Income Summary			(a) 53,628 00	(b) 46,300 00
Supplies Expense			(d) 1,880 00	
Insurance Expense			(e) 3,578 00	
Wages Payable				(f) 3,396 00
Depreciation Expense—Equipment			(g) 2,640 00	
Depreciation Expense—Building			(h) 8,200 00	
			125,192 00	125,192 00
Net income				

Adjusted Trial Balance				Income Statement				Balance Sheet			
Debit		Credit		Debit		Credit		Debit		Credit	
20,430	00							20,430	00		
33,780	00							33,780	00		
46,300	00							46,300	00		
1,640	00							1,640	00		
1,486	00							1,486	00		
29,800	00							29,800	00		
		11,580	00							11,580	00
196,000	00							196,000	00		
		31,730	00							31,730	00
50,000	00							50,000	00		
		24,860	00							24,860	00
		1,510	00							1,510	00
		144,000	00							144,000	00
		179,100	00							179,100	00
83,200	00							83,200	00		
		319,170	00			319,170	00				
4,694	00			4,694	00						
6,270	00			6,270	00						
		5,800	00			5,800	00				
128,500	00			128,500	00						
		1,926	00			1,926	00				
		2,570	00			2,570	00				
11,520	00			11,520	00						
6,200	00			6,200	00						
82,196	00			82,196	00						
53,628	00	46,300	00	53,628	00	46,300	00				
1,880	00			1,880	00						
3,578	00			3,578	00						
		3,396	00							3,396	00
2,640	00			2,640	00						
8,200	00			8,200	00						
771,942	00	771,942	00	309,306	00	375,766	00	462,636	00	396,176	00
				66,460	00					66,460	00
				375,766	00	375,766	00	462,636	00	462,636	00

PROBLEM 15-3B
FINANCIAL STATEMENTS; ADJUSTING, CLOSING, AND REVERSING ENTRIES (L.O.1–5)

Omit this problem if working papers are not being used.

As of June 30, 19X1, Wixom Company's completed work sheet appears as shown in the working papers.

INSTRUCTIONS

1. Prepare an income statement.

2. Prepare a statement of owner's equity assuming the owner made no additional investment.

3. Prepare a balance sheet. (Note: Show the entire balance in the Mortgage Payable account as a long-term liability. Assume there is no current portion.)

4. Journalize the adjusting entries.

5. Journalize the closing entries.

6. Journalize the reversing entry or entries.

PROBLEM 15-4B
WORK SHEET; FINANCIAL STATEMENTS; ADJUSTING, CLOSING, AND REVERSING ENTRIES (L.O.1–5)

On September 30, 19X1, the end of the fiscal year, Carrico Products' ledger shows the following accounts and balances before adjustment:

	Debit	Credit
Cash	$ 27,810.00	
Accounts Receivable	40,800.00	
Merchandise Inventory	57,128.00	
Supplies	3,972.00	
Prepaid Insurance	6,546.00	
Equipment	76,800.00	
Accumulated Depreciation—Equipment . .		$ 10,740.00
Building	198,500.00	
Accumulated Depreciation—Building . . .		23,808.00
Land	70,000.00	
Accounts Payable		36,095.00
Unearned Revenue		7,380.00
Mortgage Payable		141,200.00
Pat Carrico, Capital		227,558.00
Pat Carrico, Drawing	94,500.00	
Sales		437,400.00
Sales Returns and Allowances	3,246.00	
Sales Discount	6,500.00	
Interest Income		9,800.00
Purchases	205,600.00	
Purchases Returns and Allowances		1,632.00

	Debit	Credit
Purchases Discount		2,358.00
Interest Expense	14,573.00	
Utilities Expense	8,136.00	
Wages Expense	83,860.00	

INSTRUCTIONS

1. Prepare a work sheet for the fiscal year ended September 30, 19X1, using the following adjustment data:

   a.–b. Ending merchandise inventory on September 30, 19X1, $51,380.

   c. Unearned revenue of $4,960 has now been earned.

   d. Supplies on hand on September 30, 19X1, $1,546.

   e. Expired insurance, $3,940.

   f. Wages expense incurred but not yet paid as of September 30, 19X1, $6,300.

   g. Annual depreciation on the equipment, $3,240.

   h. Annual depreciation on the building, $7,836.

2. Prepare an income statement.

3. Prepare a statement of owner's equity assuming the owner made no additional investment.

4. Prepare a balance sheet. (Note: Show the entire balance in the Mortgage Payable account as a long-term liability. Assume there is no current portion.)

5. Journalize the adjusting entries.

6. Journalize the closing entries.

7. Journalize the reversing entry or entries.

Mini-Cases

CASE 15-1

Mr. Carlton, owner of Carlton Drugs, is a new client. Although a knowledgeable pharmacist, Mr. Carlton knows little about accounting. He doesn't understand why it is necessary to compute the cost of merchandise sold. "Why go to all that trouble? It would be a lot easier to simply subtract net purchases from net sales to get gross profit," says Mr. Carlton. Respond.

CASE 15-2

Your friend Cathy recently started her own business. Her accountant has suggested making reversing entries. "If they're optional, why bother?" asks Cathy. Respond.

CASE 15-3

Your neighbor Fred owns his own business. To cut costs, Fred has released his accountant and is attempting to keep the books himself. Fred has taken an introductory accounting course and understands the advantage of making reversing entries. However, Fred is having a difficult time deciding which adjusting entries should be reversed. Can you help Fred?

Comprehensive Review Problem 2
Covering Chapters 9–15

Dawson Products is a wholesale merchandising business that has been in operation for several years. The following information was taken from Dawson's records on December 1, 19X8:

GENERAL LEDGER

No.	Account Title	Debit	Credit
110	Cash	$ 6,802.75	
111	Accounts Receivable	3,959.50	
112	Merchandise Inventory	14,282.00	
113	Supplies	993.80	
114	Prepaid Insurance	1,636.50	
115	Equipment	7,000.00	
116	Accumulated Depreciation—Equipment		$ 4,200.00
117	Building	74,625.00	
118	Accumulated Depreciation—Building		5,952.00
119	Land	17,500.00	
210	Accounts Payable		3,208.00
211	Wages Payable		–0–
212	Federal Income Tax Payable		895.36
213	FICA Tax Payable		866.80
214	Federal Unemployment Tax Payable		18.12
215	State Unemployment Tax Payable		122.36
216	Unearned Revenue		1,845.00
217	Mortgage Payable		48,750.00
310	Angela Dawson, Capital (Jan. 1, 19X8, bal.)		60,171.31
311	Angela Dawson, Drawing	23,625.00	
312	Income Summary	–0–	–0–
410	Sales		109,350.95
411	Sales Returns and Allowances	811.50	
412	Sales Discount	1,625.00	
413	Interest Income		2,450.00
501	Purchases	51,400.10	
502	Purchases Returns and Allowances		408.00

GENERAL LEDGER (concluded)

No.	Account Title	Balance Debit	Credit
503	Purchases Discount		589.50
510	Advertising Expense	1,274.00	
511	Depreciation Expense—Equipment	–0–	
512	Depreciation Expense—Building	–0–	
513	Insurance Expense	–0–	
514	Interest Expense	5,437.40	
515	Payroll Tax Expense	2,872.23	
516	Supplies Expense	–0–	
517	Telephone Expense	1,982.68	
518	Utilities Expense	2,034.79	
519	Wages Expense	20,965.15	

ACCOUNTS RECEIVABLE LEDGER

Capella Products	$ –0–	
Farbman Associates	2,695.00	
Majeski Brothers	728.50	
Washington Corporation	536.00	

ACCOUNTS PAYABLE LEDGER

Arrow Company	$1,948.00
Frankel Enterprises	365.00
Hernandez Corporation	–0–
Williams Products	895.00

Dawson Products completed the following transactions during December 19X8:

Dec. 1   Received payment on account from Farbman Associates, Invoice No. 7335, $2,695 (merchandise) less 2 percent cash discount.

1   Paid bill for advertisement in local newspaper, Check No. 3862, $95.

2   Received payment on account from Majeski Brothers, Invoice No. 7319, $728.50 (no discount).

2   Sold merchandise for cash, Invoice No. 7340, $1,236.95.

3   Paid Arrow Company, a creditor, on account, Check No. 3863, $1,948 (merchandise) less 2 percent cash discount.

3   Sold merchandise on account to Capella Products, Invoice No. 7341, $1,810.

4   Purchased supplies for cash, Check No. 3864, $56.90.

Dec. 5   Paid Frankel Enterprises, a creditor, on account, Check No. 3865, $365 (merchandise) less 1 percent cash discount.

     5   Purchased merchandise on account from Williams Products, Invoice No. 604, dated December 4, terms 2/10, n/30, $1,480.

     8   Sold merchandise for cash, Invoice No. 7342, $2,347.59.

     8   Issued Credit Memorandum No. 1529 to Washington Corporation for merchandise returned, $136.

     9   Paid Williams Products, a creditor, on account, Check No. 3866, $895 (merchandise) less 2 percent cash discount.

     9   Sold merchandise on account to Farbman Associates, Invoice No.7343, $2,394.50.

    10   Paid electricity bill, Check No. 3867, $147.82.

    11   Received payment on account from Capella Products, Invoice No. 7341, $1,810 (merchandise) less 2 percent cash discount.

    12   Recorded the payroll based on the following information from the payroll register: total earnings, $1,266; federal income tax withheld, $196.05; FICA tax withheld, $94.95; and net pay, $975.

    12   Recorded the employer's payroll taxes: FICA tax, $94.95; federal unemployment tax, $5.06; and state unemployment tax, $34.18.

    12   Paid employees' wages, Check No. 3868, $975.

    12   Paid Williams Products, a creditor, on account, Check No. 3869, $1,480 (merchandise) less 2 percent cash discount.

    15   Received payment on account from Washington Corporation, Invoice No. 7329, $400 (no discount).

    16   Purchased merchandise on account from Hernandez Corporation, Invoice No. 5681, dated December 15, terms 1/10, n/30, $1,754.

    16   Sold merchandise on account to Capella Products, Invoice No. 7344, $2,868.

    17   Purchased equipment for cash, Check No. 3870, $3,500.

    18   Paid telephone bill, Check No. 3871. $198.35.

Dec. 19   Received payment on account from Farbman Associates, Invoice No. 7343, $2,394.50 (merchandise) less 2 percent cash discount.

19   The owner, Angela Dawson, withdrew cash for personal use, Check No. 3872, $500.

22   Received Credit Memorandum No. 97 from Hernandez Corporation, a supplier, for merchandise returned, $254.

23   Sold merchandise on account to Majeski Brothers, Invoice No. 7345, $921.85.

23   Purchased merchandise on account from Arrow Company, Invoice No. 1202, dated December 22, terms 2/10, n/30, $2,167.20.

24   Paid Hernandez Corporation, a creditor, on account, Check No. 3873, $1,754 less credit memo and 1 percent cash discount.

26   Recorded the payroll based on the following information from the payroll register: total earnings, $1,623.38; federal income tax withheld, $251.63; FICA tax withheld, $121.75; and net pay, $1,250.

26   Recorded the employer's payroll taxes: FICA tax, $121.75; federal unemployment tax, $4; and state unemployment tax, $27.

26   Paid employees' wages, Check No. 3874, $1,250.

26   Purchased merchandise on account from Frankel Enterprises, Invoice No. 9871, dated December 24, terms 1/10, n/30, $455.

29   Sold merchandise on account to Washington Corporation, Invoice No. 7346, $1,247.50.

30   Purchased merchandise on account from Williams Products, Invoice No. 649, dated December 29, terms 2/10, n/30, $1,175.40.

30   Issued Credit Memorandum No. 1530 to Majeski Brothers for merchandise returned, $54.

31   Sold merchandise on account to Farbman Associates, Invoice No. 7347, $1,647.80.

INSTRUCTIONS

1. For those students not using working papers:
   a. Dawson Products uses the following journals:

Sales journal (as shown on page 374 in Chapter 11—begin numbering pages at page 92).

Purchases journal (as shown on page 409 in Chapter 12—begin numbering pages at page 87).

Cash receipts journal (as shown on page 457 in Chapter 13—begin numbering pages at page 89).

Cash payments journal (as shown on page 460 in Chapter 13—begin numbering pages at page 85).

General journal (begin numbering pages at page 73).

    b. Open general ledger, accounts receivable ledger, and accounts payable ledger accounts as indicated by the listing of December 1, 19X8, balances given at the beginning of this problem.

2. Record the December transactions in the appropriate journals.

    a. Post to the accounts receivable ledger daily.

    b. Post to the accounts payable ledger daily.

    c. Post the sundry columns daily.

    d. Post the general journal daily.

3. At the end of December:

    a. Total columns, verify equality of debits and credits, and rule the special journals.

    b. Post the Sales Journal column total.

    c. Post the Purchases Journal column totals.

    d. Post the Cash Receipts Journal column totals.

    e. Post the Cash Payment Journal column totals.

4. Prepare a work sheet for fiscal year ended December 31, 19X8, using the following adjustment data:

    a.–b. Ending merchandise inventory on December 31, 19X8, $13,250.

    c. Unearned revenue of $1,260 has now been earned.

    d. Supplies on hand on December 31, 19X8, $215.

    e. Expired insurance, $1,384.

    f. Wages expense incurred but not yet paid as of December 31, 19X8, $690.

    g. Annual depreciation on the equipment, $1,400.

    h. Annual depreciation on the building, $2,500.

5. Prepare a schedule of accounts receivable.

6. Prepare a schedule of accounts payable.

7. Prepare an income statement.

8. Prepare a statement of owner's equity assuming the owner made no additional investment.

9. Prepare a balance sheet. (Note: Show the entire balance in the Mortgage Payable account as a long-term liability.)

10. Journalize the adjusting entries.

11. Post the adjusting entries.

12. Journalize the closing entries.

13. Post the closing entries.

14. Prepare a post-closing trial balance.

15. Journalize the reversing entry or entries.

16. Post the reversing entry or entries.

ACCOUNT

A record used to record increases and decreases within each component of the accounting equation. (2)

ACCOUNTING

The process of analyzing, classifying, recording, summarizing, and interpreting economic events. (1)

ACCOUNTING CYCLE

The accounting process completed during each fiscal year: journalizing, posting to the ledger, preparing a work sheet, financial statements, adjusting entries, closing entries, and a post-closing trial balance. (6)

ACCOUNTING EQUATION

Assets = Liabilities + Owner's Equity
The framework in which all business transactions are analyzed. (2)

ACCOUNTS PAYABLE LEDGER

A subsidiary ledger containing a separate account for each creditor. This ledger supports or explains one general ledger account—the Accounts Payable (control) account. (12)

ACCOUNTS RECEIVABLE LEDGER

A subsidiary ledger containing a separate account for each charge customer. This ledger supports or explains one general ledger account—the Accounts Receivable (control) account. (11)

ACCRUAL-BASIS ACCOUNTING

A system of recording financial information that requires revenues be recorded when they are earned and expenses be recorded when they are incurred regardless of whether cash has been received or paid. (1, 2, 7)

ADJUSTING ENTRIES

Entries that update for internal transactions that have occurred but have not yet been recorded (journalized). (5)

AMERICAN BANKING ASSOCIATION (ABA) NUMBER

The number that is printed in the upper right corner of each check in the form of a fraction. The numerator indicates the city or state and the specific bank; the denominator indicates the Federal Reserve District and the routing number. (8)

ASSETS

Things of value owned by a business. (2)

BALANCE—ACCOUNT

The difference between total debits and total credits. Written on side with larger total. (3)

BALANCE—ACCOUNTING EQUATION

Total debits equal total credits. (3)

BALANCE—BOUGHT FORWARD

A balance copied from the bottom of one page to the top of a new page. (6)

BALANCE—JOURNAL ENTRY

Debits equal credits. (4)

BANK CREDIT CARD

A credit card used by retail customers to pay for merchandise. The retailer collects cash from the bank rather than individual customers. The bank deducts a fee for this service. Visa and MasterCard are common examples. (13)

BANK RECONCILIATION

The process of bringing the bank statement balance and the Cash account balance into agreement. The resulting balance is known as the *adjusted* or *true balance* as of a given date. (8)

BANK STATEMENT
A statement prepared by the bank showing account activity for a specified period of time. (8)

BOOK VALUE
Cost minus accumulated depreciation equals book value. (5)

BUSINESS ENTITY CONCEPT
An accounting rule requiring that a business entity be treated as an economic unit that is separate from its owner(s) and other businesses; it requires a separation of personal and business transactions. (1)

BUSINESS TRANSACTION
An economic event that can be measured in dollars and affects the financial condition of a business. (1, 2)

CALENDAR YEAR
A year consisting of 12 consecutive months always beginning in January and ending in December. (6)

CANCELED CHECKS
Checks that have been presented to the bank for payment. They are usually returned to the depositor along with the bank statement. (8)

CASH
An asset; includes coin, currency, and checks. (2)

CASH-BASIS ACCOUNTING
A system of recording financial information that requires revenues to be recorded only when cash is received and expenses to be recorded when the cash is paid out. No adjusting entries are required. (1, 7)

CASH DISCOUNT
A discount offered by the seller to encourage charge customers to pay promptly. (13)

CASH PAYMENTS JOURNAL
A special journal used to record all outflows of cash. (11, 13)

CASH RECEIPTS JOURNAL
A special journal used to record all inflows of cash. (11, 13)

CERTIFIED MANAGEMENT ACCOUNTANTS (CMAs)
A title given to management accountants who pass a rigorous examination. (1)

CERTIFIED PUBLIC ACCOUNTANTS (CPAs)
A title given to public accountants who pass an examination prepared and graded by the American Institute of Certified Public Accountants (AICPA) and also fulfill other educational and work experience requirements. (1)

CHANGE FUND
A fixed amount of cash kept in the cash drawer on a permanent basis for the purpose of making change. (8)

CHART OF ACCOUNTS
A list showing the arrangement of the accounts within the ledger, as well as the official account titles and account numbers. (4)

CHECK
A document signed by the depositor ordering the bank to pay a certain amount of money to a certain party. (8)

CIRCULAR E
Employer's Tax Guide published by the Internal Revenue Service. It discusses the tax rates, forms, due dates, payments, etc. It also contains withholding tables for federal income tax and FICA. (10)

CLOSED ACCOUNT
An account with a zero balance. (6)

CLOSING ENTRIES
Four entries prepared at the end of the fiscal year to close the temporary owner's equity accounts (revenue, expense, and drawing) to the permanent owner's equity account (capital). (6)

COMBINATION JOURNAL
A journal with special columns as well as General Debit and Credit columns. It is commonly used by service businesses in place of a general journal be-

cause of its greater efficiency in journalizing and posting. (7)

COMPOUND JOURNAL ENTRY

A journal entry requiring debits and/or credits to more than one account. (4)

CONTRA-ASSET ACCOUNT

An account that is contrary to assets. It is a subtraction from assets. (5)

CONTRA-PURCHASES ACCOUNT

A credit-balance account that appears on the income statement as a subtraction from purchases in arriving at net purchases. (12)

CONTRA-SALES ACCOUNT

A debit-balance account that appears on the income statement as a subtraction from sales. Also referred to as a *contra-revenue account.* (11)

CONTROLLING ACCOUNT

A general ledger account containing summary information, which is supported by a subsidiary ledger. (11)

CORPORATION

A business owned by many individuals whose participation in the business is often limited; ownership is evidenced by shares of stock. (1)

COST OF MERCHANDISE SOLD

A figure representing how much a business paid to acquire the units that have actually been sold during an accounting period. (15)

CREDIT

Used to increase liability, owner's equity, and revenue accounts. Used to decrease asset, expense, and drawing accounts. Abbreviation: cr. (3)

CREDIT MEMORANDUM

A business document prepared by the seller containing information relevant to a sales return or allowance. The word *credit* refers to the credit that will reduce the customer's account receivable. (11)

CREDIT PERIOD

The time between the invoice date and the date full payment is due. (13)

CREDIT TERMS

Terms of payment determined by the seller. (13)

CREDITOR

A person or company to whom a debt is owed. (2)

CROSSFOOTING

The process of proving the equality of debit and credit column totals. (13)

CURRENT ASSET

Cash or an asset that will either be converted into cash or used up within one year. (5, 15)

CURRENT LIABILITY

A debt that will become due within one year; normally paid out of current assets. (15)

DEBIT

Used to increase asset, expense, and drawing accounts. Used to decrease liability, owner's equity, and revenue accounts. Abbreviation: dr. (3)

DEPOSIT IN TRANSIT

A deposit made before the end of the month but not processed by the bank in time to appear on the bank statement. (8)

DEPOSIT TICKET

A form supplied by the bank but prepared by the depositor that must accompany each deposit. Currency, coins, and checks being deposited are listed separately. (8)

DEPRECIATION

The process of spreading the cost of a plant asset over its useful life of more than one year. (5)

DISCOUNT PERIOD

A specified time during which a cash discount may be taken. (13)

DOUBLE-ENTRY ACCOUNTING

A system requiring a minimum of two accounts in each journal entry: the account being debited and the account being credited. This is necessary to keep the accounting equation in balance. (4)

EMPLOYEE

A person who works under the control and direction of an employer. (9)

EMPLOYEE EARNINGS RECORD

A form containing payroll data for an individual employee. (9)

EMPLOYER IDENTIFICATION NUMBER

A number assigned by the Internal Revenue Service that must be included on all employer reports, forms, or correspondence submitted to the IRS. (10)

ENDORSEMENT

A signature or stamp on the back of a check transferring ownership and guaranteeing payment of the check. (8)

EXPENSES

Costs incurred in the process of earning revenue. (1, 2)

EXTERNAL USERS

External users of accounting information are individuals and groups outside the business who have either a direct or indirect financial interest in the business. (1)

FEDERAL UNEMPLOYMENT TAX

Funds raised by this tax are used to cover the cost of administering the various state unemployment programs. This tax is paid by the employer only. (10)

FICA TAX

This tax supports a variety of programs that include pension, disability, survivor's benefits, and health care for retired persons. It is paid by both the employee and the employer. (10)

FINANCIAL ACCOUNTING STANDARDS BOARD (FASB)

A group consisting of seven, independent, full-time members that is influential in the development of GAAP. (1)

FISCAL YEAR

A financial year consisting of 12 consecutive months. The most popular fiscal year is the calendar year (January through December), but it could be any grouping of 12 consecutive months—for example, July 1 through the following June 30. (6)

FOB DESTINATION

The goods are shipped free on board (FOB) to the purchaser's place of business (destination). The seller pays the transportation charges. (12)

FOB SHIPPING POINT

The purchaser pays to transport goods from the seller's place of business (shipping point). (12)

FOOTING

A total placed in small pencil figures at the bottom of a column of figures. (3)

FORM 940

An annual form, filed by the employer, summarizing the federal unemployment tax liability incurred, payments already deposited, and any balance due or overpayment. (10)

FORM 941

A quarterly form, filed by the employer, showing federal income tax (employee) and FICA tax (employee and employer) liabilities, payments, and any resulting balance due or overpayment. (10)

FORM 8109

A deposit form, supplied by the IRS, used to deposit all federal tax payments (federal income tax, FICA, federal unemployment tax) at a Federal Reserve Bank or other authorized bank. (10)

FORM W-2

An annual wage and tax statement, prepared by the employer, which must be furnished to each employee by January 31. This form shows wages paid, federal income tax withheld, and FICA tax withheld during the preceding calendar year. (10)

GENERAL EXPENSES

Operating expenses of a general or administrative nature not directly related to the sale of merchandise. (15)

GENERAL JOURNAL
A two-column journal, one Debit column and one Credit column. (4)

GENERALLY ACCEPTED ACCOUNTING PRINCIPLES (GAAP)
The official concepts, rules, procedures, and guidelines followed by accountants. (1)

GROSS PROFIT
Represents the difference between the cost and selling price of the merchandise sold: Net sales minus cost of merchandise sold equals gross profit. (15)

HISTORICAL COST PRINCIPLE
A principle of accounting that requires accountants to record items at their original cost. The cost figure is not changed as the current value of the item changes. (1)

INDEPENDENT CONTRACTOR
A person hired by a company to do a specific job, but who does not work under the control or direction of the company. (9)

INTERIM PERIOD
A period of time shorter than one fiscal year. (6)

INTERIM STATEMENT
A statement prepared for a period less than one fiscal year. (6)

INTERNAL ACCOUNTING CONTROLS
Procedures primarily concerned with protecting assets and ensuring the accuracy of accounting data. (8)

INTERNAL ADMINISTRATIVE CONTROLS
Procedures primarily concerned with promoting efficiency and encouraging employee compliance with company policies. (8)

INTERNAL CONTROL
The procedures used by management to control business operations. These can be divided into internal administrative controls and internal accounting controls. (8)

INTERNAL TRANSACTION
A transaction occurring within a business that does not involve anyone outside the business. (5)

INTERNAL USERS
The internal users of accounting information are business managers who need a steady flow of reliable information in order to function as decision makers. (1)

INVOICE
A business document prepared by the seller containing all the relevant information about a sale. To the seller it is a sales invoice. To the purchaser it is a purchase invoice. (11, 12)

JOURNAL
A book in which journal entries are recorded. Frequently referred to as the book of original entry, since this is where the formal recording process begins. (4)

JOURNAL ENTRY
Formally records a transaction in the financial records of a business. Must include a debit part and a credit part. Debits must equal credits. (4)

JOURNALIZING
The process of recording journal entries. (4)

LEDGER
A group of accounts. (4)

LIABILITIES
Amounts owed to creditors; debts. (2)

LIQUIDITY
Closeness to cash. For example, accounts receivable are more liquid than land because they can be converted to cash more quickly. (2, 15)

LIST PRICE
A fixed price that is listed in a catalog. The list price minus a trade discount equals the selling price. (13)

LONG-TERM LIABILITY
A debt that will become due and payable beyond one year. (15)

MANAGEMENT ACCOUNTING
A field of accounting that provides accounting, tax, budget, and cost accounting services for a single employer. (1)

MANUFACTURING BUSINESS
A business that buys various components and makes a product that it sells. (1)

MARKET VALUE
The current price of an asset if it were bought or sold today. (5)

MATCHING PRINCIPLE
A principle that requires revenues and expenses to be recorded in the same time period they occur. (1)

MERCHANDISE
Units purchased by a merchandising business for resale to its customers. (11)

MERCHANDISING BUSINESS
A business that purchases a ready-made product from a supplier and resells it to its own customers. (1, 11)

MODIFIED-CASH-BASIS ACCOUNTING
A system of recording financial information which requires that revenues be recorded when the cash is received and expenses be recorded when the cash is paid. However, adjustments are recorded for depreciation and certain prepaid items such as supplies and insurance. (7)

NET INCOME
The excess of all revenues over all expenses. Often referred to as *the bottom line.* (2, 15)

NET LOSS
The excess of expenses over revenues. (2)

NET PAY
Total earnings minus total deductions equal net pay; also known as *take-home pay.* (9)

NET PURCHASES
Purchases minus contra-purchases accounts (such as Purchases Discount and Purchases Returns and Allowances). (12, 13, 15)

NET SALES
Sales minus contra-sales accounts (such as Sales Discount and Sales Returns and Allowances). (11, 13, 15)

NONBANK CREDIT CARD
A credit card used by retail customers to pay for merchandise. The retailer collects cash from the credit card company rather than individual customers. The credit card company deducts a fee for this service. American Express and Diners Club are common examples. (13)

NORMAL BALANCE
The increase side of an account. (3)

NSF (NONSUFFICIENT FUNDS) CHECK
A previously deposited check that has been returned to the depositor because the drawer's account did not contain enough cash. (8)

OPERATING EXPENSES
Expenses incurred in the normal day-to-day operation of the business; frequently subdivided into selling and general expenses. (15)

OPERATING INCOME
The excess of gross profit over operating expenses. (15)

OTHER EXPENSES
Expenses incurred outside the normal scope of merchandising activities. Also known as nonoperating expenses. (15)

OTHER INCOME
Revenue from any source other than the sale of merchandise. Also known as nonoperating revenue. (15)

OUTSTANDING CHECK
A check that has been written but not yet presented to the bank for payment. (8)

OVERTIME EARNINGS
Earnings for hours worked in excess of 40 in one workweek. The overtime rate per hour is usually one and a half times the regular hourly rate. (9)

OWNER'S EQUITY
The net worth of a business (assets minus liabilities); defines the owner's rights to business assets. (2)

PAID
Indicates an outflow of cash. (2)

PARTNERSHIP
A business owned by two or more persons; it is a multiple proprietorship. (1)

PAYMENT ON ACCOUNT
Paying for something previously purchased with a promise to pay in the future. (2)

PAYROLL REGISTER
A multicolumn form that aids in organizing, computing, and summarizing payroll data. (9)

PERMANENT ACCOUNTS
Asset, liability, and capital accounts are permanent in the sense that their year-end balances carry over and become beginning balances in the new fiscal year. (6)

PETTY CASH FUND
A cash fund used to pay small bills. (8)

PETTY CASH RECORD
A columnar form that summarizes all petty cash voucher information on a single sheet. (8)

PETTY CASH VOUCHER
A form prepared for each payment from a petty cash fund. The form contains the amount, date, and purpose of each payment, as well as signatures acknowledging approval and receipt. (8)

PHYSICAL INVENTORY
An actual count of the units on hand at the end of the fiscal year. (14)

PLANT ASSET
An asset used to generate revenue for a period greater than one year. (5, 15)

POSTING
The process of transferring information from the journal to the ledger. (4)

POSTING REFERENCE
A cross reference between the journal and the ledger. (4)

PUBLIC ACCOUNTING
A field of accounting that provides auditing, tax, and consulting services to many different individuals, businesses, and organizations for a fee. (1)

PURCHASE ALLOWANCE
A reduction in the price of previously purchased merchandise. The seller "allows" for defective merchandise by reducing the price to the purchaser. (12)

PURCHASE ON ACCOUNT
Buying something with a promise to pay in the future. (2)

PURCHASE ORDER
An offer to purchase goods from a supplier. (12)

PURCHASE REQUISITION
A form used by departments to request the purchase of necessary items. It is sent to the purchasing department. (12)

PURCHASE RETURN
The return of previously purchased merchandise to the supplier. (12)

PURCHASES DISCOUNT
The term used to describe a cash discount from the purchaser's point of view. (13)

PURCHASES JOURNAL
A special journal used to record the purchase of merchandise on account. (11, 12)

QUARTER
A time period consisting of three months. Calendar quarters end March 31, June 30, September 30, and December 31. (10)

REGULAR EARNINGS
Earnings for 40 or less hours per workweek. (9)

RESTRICTIVE ENDORSEMENT
Protects against theft by restricting further circulation of a check. (8)

RETAIL BUSINESS
A business that sells merchandise to the end user (final consumer). (11)

REVENUE
The amount that a business charges a customer for a service performed or a product provided. (1, 2)

REVERSING ENTRIES
Optional entries that reverse adjusting entries. They make it possible to return to the normal accounting routine as soon as they have been recorded. If used, they are recorded the first day of the new fiscal period. (15)

SALARY
A fixed amount per week, month, or year paid to managerial, administrative, and professional employees. (9)

SALE ON ACCOUNT
Providing a customer with a product or service in exchange for the customer's promise to pay in the future. (2)

SALES ALLOWANCE
A reduction in the price of previously sold merchandise. The seller "allows" for defective merchandise by reducing the price. (11)

SALES DISCOUNT
The term used to describe a cash discount from the seller's point of view. (13)

SALES JOURNAL
A special journal used to record sales of merchandise on account. (11)

SALES RETURN
The return of previously sold merchandise to the seller. (11)

SALES TAX
A tax on retail sales levied by a state or local municipality. It is paid by the retail customer but collected by the retail seller for the taxing authority. (11)

SERVICE BUSINESS
A business that sells a skill or technique that has no physical existence. (1)

SERVICE CHARGE
A fee charged by the bank for the routine processing of checks and deposits as well as for other special services. (8)

SIGNATURE CARD
A card that must be signed by each person authorized to sign checks drawn on a particular checking account. The bank uses the card to verify signatures on checks. (8)

SLIDE
An error occurring when a decimal point is inserted in the wrong place. (4)

SOLE PROPRIETORSHIP
A business owned by one person and usually managed by the same person. (1)

SPECIAL JOURNAL
A journal designed to facilitate the recording and posting of repetitive transactions. The repetitious portion of an entry is made a permanent part of the journal through the use of column headings. (11)

STATE UNEMPLOYMENT TAX
The funds raised by this tax are used to pay state unemployment benefits. In most states, this tax is paid by the employer only. (10)

SUBSIDIARY LEDGER
A group of accounts that supports or explains one general ledger account (controlling account). (11)

T-ACCOUNT
A simple T-shaped account form with debits on the left and credits on the right. (3)

TEMPORARY OWNER'S EQUITY ACCOUNTS
Accounts that accumulate data for only one fiscal year (revenue, expense, and drawing). At the end of each fiscal year, they are closed to capital. They

are temporary in the sense that there is no carryover of their balances from one year to the next. They begin every new year with a zero balance. (6)

TOTAL EARNINGS

Regular earnings plus overtime earnings equal total earnings; often referred to as *gross pay.* (9)

TRADE DISCOUNT

A discount used by sellers to change the selling price of a product without having to reprint an entire catalog. The list price minus the trade discount equals the selling price. (13)

TRANSPOSITION

An error involving the rearrangement of the digits within a number. (4)

TRIAL BALANCE

A list of accounts and balances to test the overall equality, or balance, of debits and credits in the ledger. (4)

UNEARNED REVENUE

The liability to the customer created when cash has been received for a product or service to be delivered in the future. The seller now owes the customer the product or service. (14)

USEFUL LIFE

Period of time over which an asset will help generate revenue. (5)

WAGES

The earnings of an employee who is paid on an hourly basis. (9)

WHOLESALE BUSINESS

A business that sells merchandise to another business. (11)

WITHHOLDING ALLOWANCE

Exempts a portion of an employee's earnings from federal income tax. (9)

WORKERS' COMPENSATION INSURANCE

Most states require employers to carry this insurance which protects workers in case of job-related illness or accident. The employer pays the cost of this coverage. (10)

WORK SHEET

A tool used by accountants to rough draft adjustments and financial statements and also to check for mathematical accuracy. (5)